June 1–3, 2011
Vancouver, BC, Canada

I0032194

**Association for
Computing Machinery**

Advancing Computing as a Science & Profession

NOSSDAV 2011

Proceedings of the 21st International Workshop on

Network and Operating Systems Support for Digital Audio & Video

Sponsored by:
ACM SIGMULTIMEDIA

In Cooperation with:
ACM SIGCOMM

Association for Computing Machinery

Advancing Computing as a Science & Profession

The Association for Computing Machinery
2 Penn Plaza, Suite 701
New York, New York 10121-0701

ISBN: 978-1-4503-0752-9

Additional copies may be ordered prepaid from:

ACM Order Department
PO Box 30777
New York, NY 10087-0777, USA

Phone: 1-800-342-6626 (USA and Canada)
+1-212-626-0500 (Global)
Fax: +1-212-944-1318
E-mail: acmhelp@acm.org
Hours of Operation: 8:30 am – 4:30 pm ET

ACM Order Number 477118

Printed in the USA

Preface

Welcome to NOSSDAV 2011, the 21st International Workshop on Network and Operating Systems Support for Digital Audio and Video. The workshop is sponsored by ACM SIGMM and in cooperation with SIGOPS and SIGCOMM. We are delighted to have you join us at the campus of University of British Columbia (UBC) in Vancouver.

NOSSDAV 2011 features a 2-day technical program featuring 21 technical papers. The technical papers cover traditional systems challenges of multimedia, such as streaming and media adaptation, as well as emerging fields such as mobile and social media. We hope that you will find this rich and varied program inspiring.

NOSSDAV 2011 received 61 submissions from the globe. This year's review process includes two stages. At the first stage, every submitted the paper received three reviews. The second stage includes discussions among the reviewers moderated by the TPC chairs. Based on the reviews and the discussion result from the reviewers, we accepted 21 for publication and presentation in the final NOSSDAV 2011 program. We are grateful for all the hard work of the NOSSDAV 2011 technical program committee. We like to thank the whole technical program committee as well as all the authors who provided the content to this workshop.

We are honored to have Jim Bankoski of Google join us as our keynote speaker to talk about WebM and VP8. Jim was Chief Technology Officer at On2 Technologies from 1998 until 2010, when Jim joined Google as part of their acquisition of On2. He co-invented and developed video technology used by over 1 billion people (through Adobe Flash, Skype, and Aim Triton). This includes On2's full line of codecs including TM2X / Wavelet Codec, VP3 to VP7 since 1998. Jim currently leads Google's efforts on the WebM project, which is dedicated to developing a high-quality, open video format for the web that is freely available to everyone.

We also like to thank a number of people for their help organizing the workshop. Ketan Mayer-Patel helped us with many conference setup details and our bridge with ACM organization. Wu-Chi Feng provided excellent advice and detail comments to the review system. Kuan-Ta Chen and Yong Liu did a great job publicizing the call for papers and participation of NOSSDAV. Aiman Erbad managed all the local arrangements and maintained the NOSSDAV 2011 web site.

We hope that you will find this program interesting and thought-provoking and that the symposium will provide you with a valuable opportunity to share ideas with other researchers and practitioners from institutions around the world.

Sincerely,
Charles 'Buck' Krasic and Kang Li
NOSSDAV 2011 co-Chairs

Table of Contents

Session 5: Systems

Session 6: Media Adaptation

Session 7: Foundation of Media Communication

NOSSDAV 2011 Organizing Committee

Program Co-Chairs: Charles 'Buck' Krasic, *Google Inc. (USA)*
Kang Li, *University of Georgia (USA)*

Publicity Chairs: Kuan-Ta Chen, *Academia Sinica (Taiwan)*
Yong Liu, *Polytechnic Institute of NYU (USA)*

Local Arrangements Chair: Aiman Erbad, *University of British Columbia (Canada)*

Technical Program Committee: Kevin Almeroth, *University of California, Santa Barbara (USA)*
Grenville Armitage, *Swinburne University of Technology (Australia)*
Ali C. Begen, *Cisco (Canada)*
Ernst Biersack, *Institute Eurecom (France)*
Surendar Chandra, *FXPAL (USA)*
Kuan-Ta Chen, *Academia Sinica (Taiwan)*
Songqing Chen, *George Mason University (USA)*
Mark Claypool, *Worcester Polytechnic Institute (USA)*
Wu-chang Feng, *Portland State University (USA)*
Wu-chi Feng, *Portland State University (USA)*
Carsten Griwodz, *University of Oslo (Norway)*
Yang Guo, *Bell Labs (USA)*
Pal Halvorsen, *University of Oslo (Norway)*
Mohamed Hefeeda, *Simon Fraser University (Canada)*
Cheng-Hsin Hsu, *Deutsche Telekom Lab (USA)*
JongWon Kim, *Gwangju Institute of Science and Technology (Korea)*
Andre Koenig, *Technische Universitat Darmstadt (Germany)*
Baochun Li, *University of Toronto (Canada)*
Jiangchuan Liu, *Simon Fraser University (Canada)*
Yong Liu, *Polytechnic University (USA)*
Andreas Mauthe, *Lancaster University (UK)*
Ketan Mayer-Patel, *University of North Carolina at Chapel Hill (USA)*
Klara Nahrstedt, *University of Illinois at Urbana-Champaign (USA)*
Wei Tsang Ooi, *National University of Singapore (Singapore)*
Sanjay Rao, *Purdue University (USA)*
Reza Rejaie, *University of Oregon (USA)*
Nabil Sarhan, *Wayne State University (USA)*
Karsten Schwan, *Georgia Institute of Technology (USA)*
Prashant Shenoy, *University of Massachusetts, Amherst (USA)*
Shervin Shirmohammadi, *University of Ottawa (Canada)*
Zhenyu Yang, *Florida International University (USA)*
Roger Zimmermann, *National University of Singapore (Singapore)*
Michael Zink, *University of Massachusetts, Amherst (USA)*

Sponsor: **acm sigmm**
SPECIAL INTEREST GROUP   MULTIMEDIA

In-cooperation with: **acm sigcomm**

Keynote Talk

Intro to WebM

Jim Bankoski
Google Inc.
Mountain View, CA

Abstract

Last year at Google IO, we launched the WebM Project (webmproject.org) a project that aims to develop a high-quality, open video format for the web that is freely available to everyone. In this session, we'll explore the history of the project and discuss the long term goals we have for WebM. We'll also deep dive in all the pieces that make up the WebM format, review related projects and present the technical features that make WebM work especially well for web video. Finally, we'll compare the performance of WebM to other formats used on the Internet and open up the floor for discussion.

Categories & Subject Descriptors: H.5.1 Multimedia Information Systems

General Terms: Algorithms, Measurement, Performance, Design, Standardization.

Bio

The speaker was Chief Technology Officer at On2 Technologies from 1998 until 2010, when Jim joined Google as part of their acquisition of On2. He co-Invented and developed video technology used by over 1 Billion people (through Adobe Flash, Skype, and Aim Triton). This includes On2's full line of codecs including TM2X / Wavelet Codec, VP3, VP4, VP5, VP6 and VP7 since 1998. Jim currently leads Google's efforts on the WebM project, which is dedicated to developing a high-quality, open video format for the web that is freely available to everyone.

NOSSDAV'11, June 1–3, 2011, Vancouver, British Columbia, Canada.
ACM 978-1-4503-0752-9/11/06.

LAN-Awareness: Improved P2P Live Streaming

Zhijie Shen
School of Computing
National University of Singapore
Singapore 117417
z-shen@comp.nus.edu.sg

Roger Zimmermann
School of Computing
National University of Singapore
Singapore 117417
rogerz@comp.nus.edu.sg

ABSTRACT

The popularity of P2P streaming systems has rapidly created extensive, far-reaching Internet traffic. Recent studies have demonstrated that localizing cross-ISP (Internet service provider) traffic can mitigate this challenge. Another trend shows that households own an increasing number of devices, which are sharing a LAN of 2 or more peers. To this date, however, no study has investigated the potential of localizing traffic within LANs. In our presented work, we propose the concept of *LAN-awareness* and introduce its threefold benefits: 1) reducing Internet streaming traffic, 2) lowering stream server workload, and 3) improving streaming quality. First we conduct a large-scale measurement on PPLive, confirming that a considerable number of peers (up to 21%) are connected to the LANs having 2 or more peers. Recognizing the opportunity of localizing traffic within LANs, we discuss the principles to construct a LAN-aware overlay and propose a heuristic. The results of our trace-driven simulations confirm the benefits outlined above.

Categories and Subject Descriptors

C.2.4 [**Computer-Communication Networks**]: Distributed Systems; C.2.5 [**Computer-Communication Networks**]: Local and Wide-Area Networks

General Terms

Measurement, Design, Performance

Keywords

P2P, streaming, LAN-aware, traffic locality

1. INTRODUCTION

A number of P2P live streaming systems, such as PPLive, PPStream and UUSee, have attracted large user communities in recent years. Such marvelous popularity has already resulted in heavy workload for both Internet service providers (ISPs) and content providers. Moreover, some forecasts predict that by 2014 Internet video will account for 57% of all consumer IP traffic [2]. Meanwhile, households possess increasingly more devices on which they

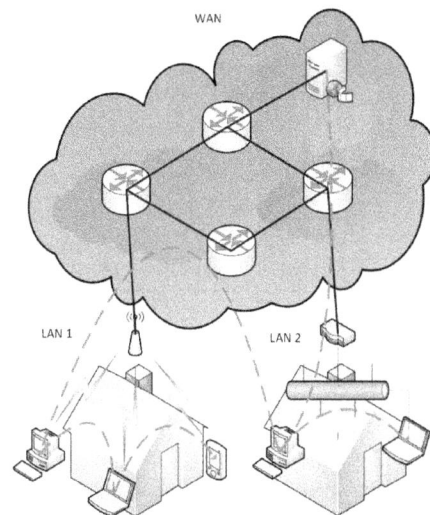

Figure 1: Exhibition of a LAN-aware overlay.

consume entertainment content: desktops, laptops, tablets (*e.g.*, Apple iPad), *etc.* These devices are connected through a wired or wireless router, form a home area network (HAN) and reach the Internet through a shared link. This link tends to be the bottleneck when multiple devices are accessing the Internet simultaneously.

Recently we conducted a comprehensive measurement study on PPLive, and one of the interesting observations was that a significant number of local area networks (LANs) accommodated multiple peers watching the same live channel. Surprisingly, up to 21% peers belonged to such LANs where they had local neighbors. This phenomenon is likely to be more prominent in the future, since the population of Internet subscribers is expected to dramatically increase [8]. Video streaming systems are bandwidth-intensive applications. Multiple peers further raise the bandwidth consumption on the link connected to the Internet (last-hop link), affecting other network-based applications or even disturbing the streaming quality of each other. Fortunately, the use of P2P architectures opens the opportunity for solving this problem. Here we define a new concept, *LAN-awareness*, indicating that *the overlay construction is optimized to exploit local peer resources within a LAN*. Fig. 1 exhibits a sample LAN-aware overlay, where only one peer in each LAN (or HAN) receives a stream from outside and then forwards it to its local neighbors. The benefits of LAN-awareness are threefold.

- Video delivery has become one of the most problematic traffic generators, heavily stressing ISPs. Prior studies [7, 9, 10, 12] have proposed to restrict traffic within autonomous systems (ASes) to lower ISPs' operating costs. LAN-awareness restricts the traffic entering the wide area network (WAN), thus reducing both intra-AS and inter-AS traffic.

- Recent measurement studies show that the bandwidth contribution of peers is limited [3, 5]. A stream server has to compensate for the upload deficit. In contrast, the intra-LAN bandwidth capacity is usually abundant. Hence if some peers can satisfy their video demand within the LAN, content providers need to purchase less bandwidth.

- For most Internet subscribers, their download bandwidth is still not enough to allow several concurrent streaming sessions while the trend in video rates is growing higher (more videos encoded at 700 Kbps and 2 Mbps are available on PPLive). LAN-awareness avoids the last-hop bandwidth competition, thus preventing a possible streaming quality decline. Even if the bandwidth is not the bottleneck, LAN-awareness is still helpful to leave more spare bandwidth for other applications.

Current P2P live streaming systems are not LAN-aware and often use random partner selection. This seldom results in peers connecting to neighbors in the same LAN. To exploit the potential benefits from LAN-awareness, we investigate the principles of designing a LAN-aware overlay, propose a lightweight solution and evaluate it with trace-driven simulations. Overall our work provides the following contributions.

- To the best of our knowledge, this is the first study that proposes the concept of LAN-awareness and discusses its benefits of reducing Internet streaming traffic, lowering stream server workload and improving streaming quality.

- We have performed large-scale measurements with PPLive. Our analysis of the collected data demonstrates that there exist a considerable number of LANs containing multiple peers when a channel is popular. This opens a significant opportunity to exploit LAN-awareness.

- We introduce the principles of designing a LAN-aware overlay and propose a lightweight solution. The results of our trace-driven simulations show that the LAN-aware solution can achieve the three benefits outlined earlier.

The rest of the paper are organized as follows. Section 2 surveys the related work. We explain our measurements and analyze the collected traces in Section 3. The LAN-aware solution is introduced in Section 4 and evaluated in Section 5. Concluding remarks are presented in Section 6.

2. RELATED WORK

There exist several recent studies that focus on a closely related topic, *i.e.*, AS-aware P2P streaming. One measurement study [6] has shown that PPLive naturally exhibits a certain traffic locality caused by the skewed ISP-size distribution. With some proactive solutions, the locality can be further improved. Picconi *et al.* [9] propose an ISP-friendly scheduling strategy where each peer requests most data from its topologically-close partners and only resorts to distant peers when data is not available locally. Similarly, a two-tier scheduling scheme is proposed by Magharei *et al.* [7].

Tomozei *et al.* [12] present an intriguing, fully decentralized algorithm based on flow control. The merit of decentralization is unfortunately offset by a slow adaptation to any load dynamics. Our previous work [10] proposes a self-adapting, QoS-protected peer selection algorithm.

There are only two other studies that are similar to our work. Tan *et al.* [11] propose to deploy caching agents at the access points (APs) of wireless networks to avoid duplicate traffic traversing the APs. Meanwhile, Lai *et al.* [4] also suggest to add agents at the APs, in order to leverage the broadcast protocol of WLAN to optimize the bandwidth usage of the APs. However, these studies have not provided detailed insights of whether multiple users are connected to the same AP, so that the potential improvement for real systems is not clear. Moreover, the infrastructure-based solutions will meet the same obstacle as IP multicast did when they are put into practice. Here we conducted a comprehensive measurement study on a real system, confirming the existence of multiple peers within the same LAN. Furthermore, we propose an LAN-aware solution that restricts the modification efforts to just the application layer. Thus, it can be easily deployed.

3. MEASUREMENT OF REAL-WORLD SYSTEM

The potential benefits of LAN-awareness naturally depends on the number of peers inside each LAN, *i.e.*, the peer density of a LAN. If there were just one peer in each LAN, it would be useless to design a LAN-aware solution. Therefore, as a first step, we require a better understanding of how peers are distributed among LANs in real-world systems. However, there is no such information available from prior related work [4,11] or recent measurement studies [3,5]. Thus, we conducted our own measurements and analysis.

3.1 Overview of PPLive Partnership Protocol

Our measurements target PPLive. We start by briefly introducing the partnership protocol of the live streaming functionality. Once a PPLive client (or peer) joins the system, it contacts the bootstrap server to retrieve the list of active channels. After the client chooses a program to watch, it informs the tracker server of its participation in the corresponding channel and obtains a list of active clients in this channel as the initial partners. Then, the client expands its partner list by querying the partners' neighborhoods. During the session, the client keeps updating the partnership information at regular intervals. Notably, PPLive constructs the overlay on a per-channel basis, containing the peers that are watching the channel.

Currently PPLive adopts UDP as the transport protocol by default. A client randomly chooses a unique port, through which all the IP packets related to PPLive are transmitted. Therefore, a UDP socket ⟨IP, port⟩ can exclusively represent a client. In our measurements, we observed a considerable number of sockets that share some common IPs. Since their ports were different, these sockets represented different clients. This phenomenon occurs because of network address translation (NAT), which is usually deployed at the gateway between WAN and LAN and translates private IPs of multiple clients within the same LAN into the same public IP.

3.2 Measurement Methodology

In our measurements, we are interested in the topology-related information. To acquire this information, we need to know all the concurrent peers in a channel, *i.e.*, obtain an *active peer population snapshot*. Thus, we implemented a PPLive crawler in Python, inspired by the method of Vu *et al.* [13]. The crawler imitates the

Name	Type	Event	Rate (Kbps)	Population (daily basis)
Hunan Satellite TV	Comprehensive	N/A	400	$481 - 17,949$
SiTV-Sports	Sports	3rd match of NBA Final	400	$47 - 11,160$
CCTV-5	Sports	4th match of NBA Final & 1st match of World Cup	700	$789 - 183,109$

Table 1: Summary of the studied channels. The one-day traces of these three channels were respectively collected on May 19th, June 9th and June 11th, 2010. The time zone is GTM+8.

behavior of a PPLive client to probe peers in the channel from both the tracker server and the clients. Probing peers from the tracker server is straightforward. The crawler repeatedly requests peers from the tracker server until it can no longer get any new peers. In contrast, probing peers from the clients is complex. Whenever the crawler acquires a new peer, it will query this peer for the peers in its local view. This operation is repeated until no new peer is discovered by the crawler. When both operations are complete, we have obtained the snapshot. Formally, let $\mathcal{S}$ denote the set of the captured peers and $\mathcal{T}$ denote the set of the peers returned by the tracker server. $Neighbor(p)$ represents the peers in the local view of peer p and $Neighbor(\mathcal{S}) = \bigcup_{p \in \mathcal{S}} Neighbor(p)$. Then, $\mathcal{S}$ can be defined as

$$\mathcal{S} = \{p | p \in \mathcal{T} \vee p \in Neighbor(\mathcal{S})\}. \qquad (1)$$

Actually, the crawler cannot probe all the concurrent peers at the same time due to the recursive nature of Eq. 1. $\mathcal{S}$ is an approximation of the snapshot and converges to it as the execution time decreases. Thus, we parallelized the independent probes so that the crawler could complete its work in just a few minutes. Additionally, to enable the communication with the tracker server and the clients, we have collected a considerable amount of PPLive traffic with Wireshark to recognize the packet format of the partnership protocol.

To avoid that the captured peers might be biased to the crawler's location, we deployed the copies on 44 PlanetLab nodes spread over 15 countries and regions and executed them simultaneously at the regular interval of 15 minutes. Our selection of the PlanetLab node number and execution interval is moderate to restrict the overhead brought to PPLive. The snapshot collection lasted from May 17th to June 13th, 2010 and we obtained more than 70 GB of raw log data. Afterwards, we merged the concurrent snapshots from different PlanetLab nodes to construct a complete snapshot. Furthermore, we utilized the Team Cymru service (whois.cymru.com) to retrieve the AS ID and the country information of each peer. While the data can be leveraged to infer many overlay properties such as churn behavior and AS-level peer distribution, in this paper, we concentrate on the peer distribution among LANs and analyze the data of three representative PPLive channels, which are summarized in Table 1.

3.3 Trace Analysis

From the data, we analyze the peer distribution among LANs. Here we assume that the recorded peers sharing the same IP are connected to the same LAN. This assumption may cause underestimation to some extent, because peers from some large LANs, such as a campus network, connect into the WAN through multiple gateways so that the peers are recorded with different IPs. However, even with this underestimation, we still observed abundant LANs hosting multiple peers.

Figs. 2(a) – (c) show the one-day evolutions of the channel population, the percentage of the IPs supplying at least 2 peers and the percentage of the peers within these IPs. While the evolution of Hunan Satellite TV (HunanTV) follows a diurnal pattern, those of the other two sports channels are event-related (peaks occur in the

morning of the NBA Final and at the night of the World Cup). At peak times, 2% to 7% of IPs supply at least 2 peers, and 5% to 21% of the total number of peers are associated with these IPs. Specifically, 21% of the population of CCTV-5 represents about 39,000 peers, the number of which is much more than the population of a whole channel at regular times. As we know, most ISPs charge content providers with the 95th percentile rule, implying that the monetary cost is determined by the peak bandwidth usage. Thus, both the percentage and the number illustrate a significant prospect for lowering the monetary cost for content providers if traffic is localized within LANs.

One important observation from the evolutions is that the incidence rate of multiple peers within a LAN is correlated with the channel population. Figs. 2(d) and 2(e) present a clearer picture. Let $\mathcal{X}(i)$ denote the number of IPs who supply at least i peers and $\mathcal{N}(i)$ denote the total number of peers within these IPs. For simplicity, the two terminologies are respectively reduced to $\mathcal{X}$ and $\mathcal{N}$ when $i = 1$. According to the traces, the correlations approximate

$$\mathcal{X}(2) \propto \mathcal{N} \log \mathcal{N}, \qquad (2)$$

$$\mathcal{N}(2) \propto \mathcal{N} \log \mathcal{N}. \qquad (3)$$

Eqs. 2 and 3 imply that the incidence rate of multiple peers within the same LAN increases $\log \mathcal{N}$ times faster than the channel population. Originally, Fig. 2(d) infers $\mathcal{X}(2) \propto \mathcal{X} \log \mathcal{N}$. However, we derive Eq. 2 as we find a linear dependence between $\mathcal{X}$ and $\mathcal{N}$ as well as between $\mathcal{X}(2)$ and $\mathcal{N}(2)$, shown in Figs. 2(h) and 2(i). Here we conducted curve fitting and obtained

$$\mathcal{N} = 1.16\mathcal{X} - 543, \qquad (4)$$

$$\mathcal{N}(2) = 3.4\mathcal{X}(2) - 112. \qquad (5)$$

Then, let $\Delta = \mathcal{N} - \mathcal{X} = \mathcal{N}(2) - \mathcal{X}(2)$, which indicates the number of peers that can satisfy their streaming demand within LANs if one peer in each LAN imports a stream from outside. As $\mathcal{N}$ is very large, Δ approximates $0.16\mathcal{X}$ and $0.14\mathcal{N}$. Therefore, if a LAN-aware solution is provided, about 14% of the traffic can be eliminated from the WAN.

Next, we would like to understand the peer distribution among the LANs accommodating multiple peers. Fig. 2(g) shows that the number of peers associated with one IP versus the IP's rank follows a *Zipf-like* distribution. Only a small fraction of IPs host tens of or even more peers. These IPs may be from some campuses or companies, where there are numerous users. In contrast, the remaining fraction of IPs come from households, where the members are few. Furthermore, an additional question is how crowded a LAN will be. In our traces, the most crowded IP supplied 214 peers. Fig. 2(f) shows the correlation between the number of peers in the top ranking IPs and the channel population, which can be approximately represented by

$$\mathcal{N}(i_{top}) \propto \mathcal{N} \qquad (6)$$

where i_{top} satisfies $\mathcal{X}(i_{top}) > 0$ and $\mathcal{X}(i_{top} + 1) = 0$.

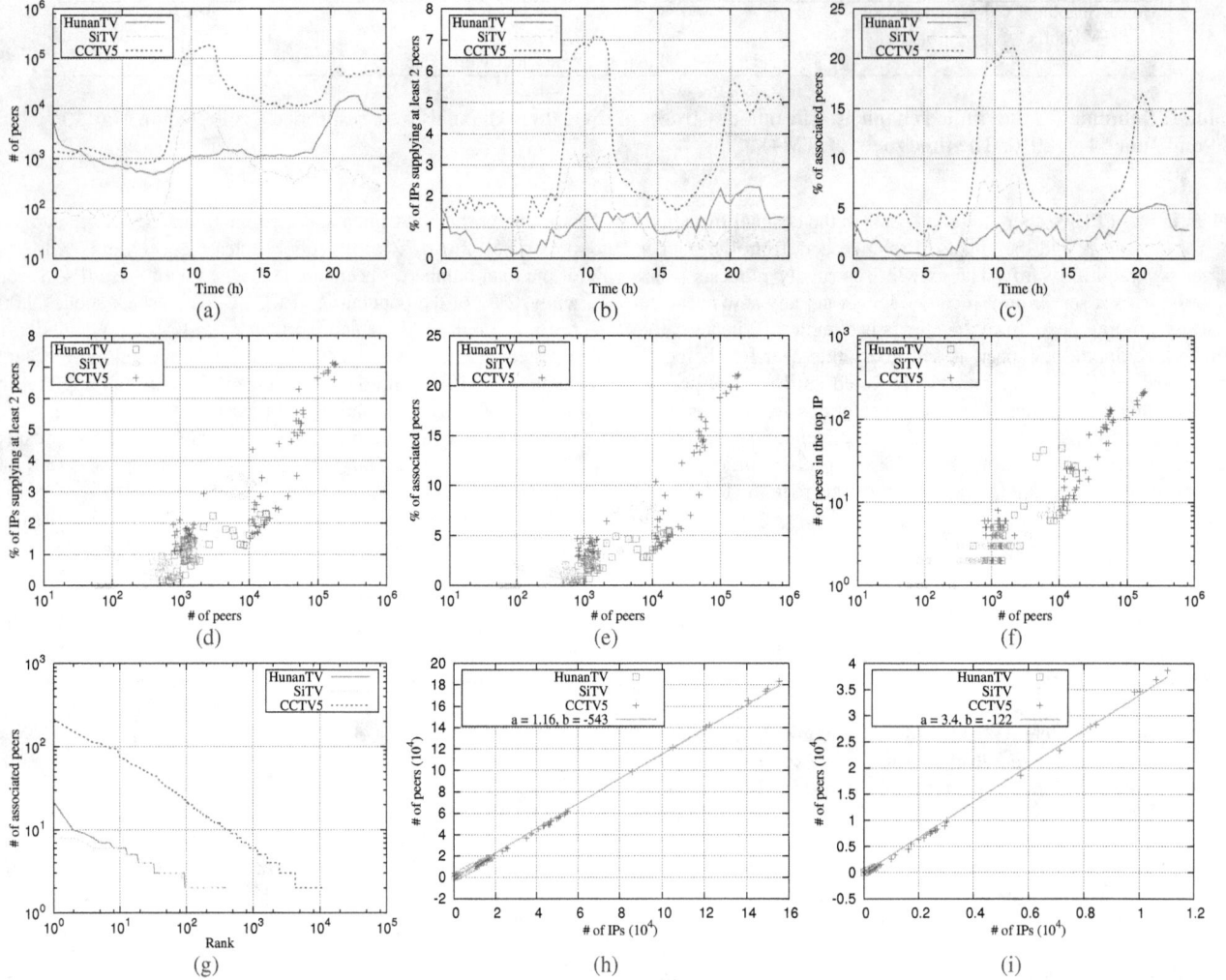

Figure 2: One-day evolutions of (a) the channel population, (b) the percentage of the IPs that supply at least 2 peers and (c) the percentage of the peers from the IPs that supply at least 2 peers; correlations between the channel population and (d) the percentage of the IPs that supply at least 2 peers, and (e) the percentage of the peers from the IPs that supply at least 2 peers, and (f) the number of peers in the top ranked IP, respectively; (g) peer distribution in the IPs that supply at least 2 peers at peak; (h) correlation between the number of IPs and the channel population; and (i) correlation between the number of the IPs that supply at least 2 peers and the number of the peers from them. The time zone is GTM+8.

4. CONSTRUCTING A LAN-AWARE OVERLAY TOPOLOGY

The prior section affirmed the existence of multiple peers in the same LAN, establishing the basis for our LAN-aware solution. Because of limited space, we concisely discuss the principles of designing such a solution and propose a heuristic. LAN-awareness aims to exploit local peer resources, thus minimizing the ingress traffic but still preserving streaming quality. There are two challenges that must be addressed to achieve LAN-awareness: 1) importing a complete, uninterrupted stream into a LAN with the least redundancy, and 2) disseminating the stream to all the peers in this LAN.

4.1 Maximizing Stream Integrity with Minimal Bandwidth

We first analyze the former challenge. The whole video stream is quantized as several sub-streams of equal rate, $s_1, s_2, \ldots, s_n$. They are equivalent to the sliding window containing n active chunks of equal size in a mesh-based pull scheme. k peers are assumed to simultaneously stay in a LAN. To assign the tasks of importing a complete stream from the WAN for these peers, we leverage a scoreboard

$$
\begin{matrix}
 & \begin{matrix} s_1 & s_2 & \ldots & s_n \end{matrix} \\
\begin{matrix} p_1 \\ p_2 \\ \vdots \\ p_k \end{matrix} &
\begin{bmatrix}
\clubsuit & \clubsuit & \ldots & \clubsuit \\
\clubsuit & \clubsuit & \ldots & \clubsuit \\
\vdots & \vdots & \ddots & \vdots \\
\clubsuit & \clubsuit & \ldots & \clubsuit
\end{bmatrix}
\end{matrix}
\qquad (7)
$$

where $\clubsuit$ can be replaced with 0 or 1. If p_i is designated to download s_j, $\langle p_i, s_j \rangle = 1$. Otherwise, $\langle p_i, s_j \rangle = 0$. In addition, we define the function

$$
sch(\vec{s_j}) = \begin{cases} 1, & \sum_{i=1}^{k} \langle p_i, s_j \rangle \geq 1 \\ 0, & \text{otherwise} \end{cases}
\qquad (8)
$$

Link type	Latency (ms)
Inter-AS	normal(50, 150)
Intra-AS	normal(10, 20)
Intra-LAN	normal(1, 2)

Table 2: Latency configuration.

Type	$\left(\dfrac{\text{download bandwidth}}{\text{upload bandwidth}}\right)$ combination (Kbps)
Homog.	$\binom{1,500}{384} \times 100\%$
Heterog.	$\binom{768}{128} \times 30\% + \binom{1,500}{384} \times 60\% + \binom{3,000}{768} \times 10\%$

Table 3: Bandwidth configuration.

$sch(\vec{s_j}) = 1$ means that the jth sub-stream is scheduled by at least one peer. Hence, the larger $\sum_{j=1}^{n} sch(\vec{s_j})$ is, the more of a complete video stream is imported. Conversely, it is better if $\sum_{i=1}^{k} \sum_{j=1}^{n} \langle p_i, s_j \rangle$ can be kept small, saving last-hop download bandwidth. Furthermore, this download bandwidth is always limited. For simplicity, we also quantize the bandwidth as the number of sub-streams that can be downloaded simultaneously, denoted by $\mathcal{C}$. Thus, the whole problem can be formulated as finding the optimal solution for the following linear program

$$\begin{aligned}
\textbf{min} \quad & \alpha \sum_{h=1}^{n} sch(\vec{s_h}) + \beta \sum_{i=1}^{k} \sum_{j=1}^{n} \langle p_i, s_j \rangle \\
\textbf{s.t.} \quad & \sum_{i=1}^{k} \sum_{j=1}^{n} \langle p_i, s_j \rangle \leq \mathcal{C}.
\end{aligned} \quad (9)$$

where α and β are weight variables ($\alpha < 0$, $\beta > 0$). This linear program has two goals. We prioritize streaming quality over bandwidth usage so that $|\alpha| \gg |\beta|$.

A heuristic is to nominate a peer as the agent of the LAN having multiple peers. The agent is the only peer that can receive stream data from outside. The video consumption requirement obligates it to bring a complete copy of the video into the LAN. As the network resources of the peers from the same LAN are usually similar, the agent nomination prefers the earliest-arriving peer, which is likely to provide long-term stability. The nomination algorithm can be implemented on the tracker. Assuming n peers participate in the channel in succession, the algorithm is only invoked less than n times when an agent leaves, causing little overhead. Certainly, the nomination could be improved by considering device heterogeneity and using a distributed protocol.

This heuristic is a special solution of the presented linear program, where $\vec{p_i}^\top = \vec{1}$ and $\forall j \neq i, \vec{p_j}^\top = \vec{0}$ as p_i is the agent. It may not be advisable to rely on the single peer to import a stream. Nevertheless, in this paper, we focus on demonstrating the feasibility and the potential benefits of such a solution. For the future work, we are interested in solving this linear program in a distributed and autonomic way since some other scenarios share a similar problem statement.

4.2 Intra-LAN Stream Dissemination

The other challenge that needs to be addressed is the intra-LAN stream dissemination. The first design choice is whether to utilize IP multicast or application-layer multicast. Usually, LANs are based on Ethernet or WiFi, which supports broadcast functionality. However, we still choose application-layer multicast to provide the broadcast compatibility. For example, some LAN administrators disable the broadcast function for security reasons, and some big LANs are divided into several subnets. Therefore, IP multicast may not always be available.

With application-layer multicast specified, there is another de-

sign choice: using a tree-based push scheme or a mesh-based pull scheme. The decision is made based on the network conditions. Intra-LAN bandwidth capacity is usually high, enough to support several peers. Therefore, the tree-based push scheme will not suffer the problem often encountered in the access links of WANs, *i.e.*, the wasting of insufficient upload bandwidth that is not enough to deliver a stream. Moreover, both latency and loss rate are quite low in LAN environments so that intra-LAN connections are relatively more reliable. Additionally, a tree-based overlay is controllable as the intra-LAN population is usually small. Therefore, the tree-based push scheme which introduces less signaling overhead is considered as a better choice. In our heuristic, we build an overlay similar to *ESM* [1] for intra-LAN connections. Since the number of peers in most LANs is small (less than 10), the tree depth is usually just 2. Nevertheless, existing systems, such as PPLive, can keep using a mesh-based pull scheme to minimize the system changes.

5. EVALUATION OF BENEFITS FROM LAN-AWARENESS

Now we evaluate the benefits of our LAN-aware solution through trace-driven simulations.

5.1 Simulation Setup

We built a mesh-based prototype on OMNeT++. The prototype incorporates a heuristic chunk scheduler similar to that of a real system [3]. The scheduler gives priority to the rarest chunks in the partners and to the recently played-back chunks. A stream server supplies peers with the chunks that are played back immediately but are inaccessible from their partners.

The overall simulation settings are as follows. The length of the simulation time is set to 2 hours. The number of concurrent peers is kept to around 10,000. We assume two levels of peer density in the LAN: 1) a low level (L) of about 2,400 peers staying in 1,100 LANs containing more than 1 peer, and 2) a high level (H) of about 4,200 peers in 1,300 such LANs. Next, the underlay topology is assumed to consist of 10 ASes, and peers non-uniformly spread among these ASes (our measurement reflects that 90% of peers gather in the top 10 ASes). The latency setting of different links is shown in Table 2. As to churn, we let the length of peer life follow a log-normal distribution (Log-$\mathcal{N}(3.5, 0.85)$ min). Furthermore, we consider both homogeneous (Hm) and heterogeneous (Htr) bandwidth settings of the last-hop link to the Internet, as Table 3 shows. Meanwhile, the intranet bandwidth is symmetrically set to 10 Mbps, and the video rate is set to 400 Kbps. Finally, an evaluation scenario can be represented by a triple $\langle$LAN-aware (A) or LAN-unaware (U), peer density level, bandwidth type$\rangle$.

5.2 Experimental Results

Generally, the experimental results, shown in Figs. 3(a) – (d), demonstrate the improvement of traffic efficiency with our LAN-aware solution, benefiting ISPs, content providers and users. Moreover, we observe the trend that the improvement is more prominent if the peer density in LANs is higher.

5.2.1 Reducing Internet Streaming Traffic

One obvious benefit is that less streaming traffic will enter the Internet if the LAN-aware solution is applied, shown in Fig. 3(a), because part of the peers ($\mathcal{N} - \mathcal{X}$) satisfy their streaming demand within the LAN. Specifically, there is always a certain fraction of traffic traversing through ASes due to the AS-level peer distribution. Thus, the problematic inter-AS traffic also decreases, indicating that our solution is ISP-friendly as well.

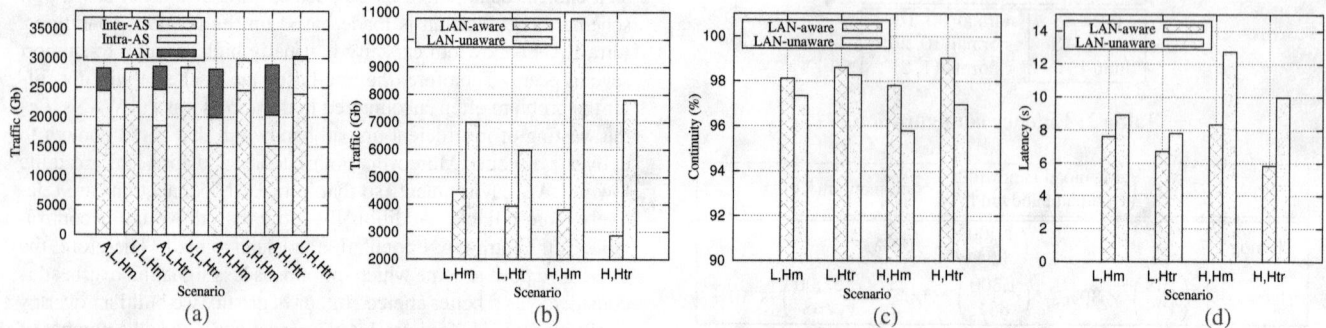

Figure 3: (a) Accumulated traffic of different types during 2-hour simulation time; **(b)** accumulated traffic delivered by the stream server; **(c)** playback continuity of the peers (inferring streaming quality); and **(d)** average latency of receiving the stream.

5.2.2 Lowering Stream Server Workload

Another benefit is for content providers. Usually, the last-hop upload bandwidth is not enough to make the system self-scaling. In particular, multiple peers sharing a single last-hop link intensifies the deficit in peers' contributions. To make up for the deficit, the stream server is required. The amount of compensation is proportional to the population. However, the LAN-aware solution addresses part of peers' streaming demand without any traffic coming from the Internet, equivalent to reducing the population of peers requesting the stream server's help. Hence, as is shown in Fig. 3(b), the amount of the stream server's upload traffic decreases with the LAN-aware solution.

5.2.3 Improving Streaming Quality

We are also interested in the impact on streaming quality. Fig. 3(c) presents the average playback continuity of the peers. The playback continuity equals the percentage of requested chunks that are received by the peers before their playback deadlines. With the LAN-aware solution, the concurrent peers are prevented from competing for the limited last-hop download bandwidth. The single agent can monopolize abundant bandwidth to make up for the suboptimal chunk scheduling. Meanwhile, the stream dissemination to other local peers is lossless. Therefore, the LAN-aware solution improves the playback continuity. Moreover, the good continuity achieved by our solution also implies a high chunk availability on peers, amplifying the benefits of lowering the stream server's workload.

Next, Fig. 3(d) shows that the latency drops when the LAN-aware solution is applied. The latency is proportional to the diameter of the mesh overlay. With the LAN-aware solution, a fraction of peers are removed from this overlay and participate in their intra-LAN overlays, thus decreasing the diameter and the latency over WAN as a consequence. In contrast, a LAN is so fast that the stream dissemination latency within a LAN is negligible against the latency over WAN. From another point of view, the LAN-aware solution effectively achieves that part of the distant links are replaced with short ones.

6. CONCLUSION

We presented the concept and the benefits of LAN-awareness. To confirm the potential of LAN-aware solutions, we conducted a large-scale measurement on PPLive. We then discussed the principles to construct a LAN-aware overlay and proposed a heuristic. The trace-driven simulations show that LAN-awareness helps to reduce Internet streaming traffic, lower stream server workload and improve streaming quality.

Acknowledgments

This research has been funded in part by A*Star grant 082 101 0028.

7. REFERENCES

[1] Y.-h. Chu, S. G. Rao, S. Seshan, and H. Zhang. A case for end system multicast. *IEEE Journal on Selected Areas in Communications*, 2002.

[2] Cisco Systems, Inc. Cisco Visual Networking Index: Forecast and Methodology, 2009-2014. White Paper, 2010.

[3] X. Hei, C. Liang, J. Liang, Y. Liu, and K. W. Ross. A Measurement Study of a Large-Scale P2P IPTV System. *IEEE Transactions on Multimedia*, 2007.

[4] C.-Y. Lai, C.-S. Hsu, and T.-J. Shang. Improved P2P Streaming in Wireless Networks Utilizing Access Point P2P Agents. In *IEEE International Symposium on Multimedia Workshops*, 2007.

[5] B. Li, S. Xie, Y. Qu, G. Y. Keung, C. Lin, J. Liu, and X. Zhang. Inside the New Coolstreaming: Principles, Measurements and Performance Implications. In *INFOCOM*, 2008.

[6] Y. Liu, L. Guo, F. Li, and S. Chen. A Case Study of Traffic Locality in Internet P2P Live Streaming Systems. In *ICDCS*, 2009.

[7] N. Magharei, R. Rejaie, V. Hilt, I. Rimac, and M. Hofmann. ISP-Friendly Live P2P Streaming. Technical report, University of Oregon, 2009.

[8] Miniwatts Marketing Group. Internet Growth Statistics. http://www.internetworldstats.com/emarketing.htm, 2010.

[9] F. Picconi and L. Massoulie. ISP Friend or Foe? Making P2P Live Streaming ISP-Aware. In *ICDCS*, 2009.

[10] Z. Shen and R. Zimmermann. ISP-friendly peer selection in P2P networks. In *ACM Multimedia*, 2009.

[11] E. Tan, L. Guo, S. Chen, and X. Zhang. SCAP: Smart Caching in Wireless Access Points to Improve P2P Streaming. In *ICDCS*, 2007.

[12] D.-C. Tomozei and L. Massoulie. Flow Control for Cost-Efficient Peer-to-Peer Streaming. In *INFOCOM*, 2010.

[13] L. Vu, I. Gupta, J. Liang, and K. Nahrstedt. Measurement of a large-scale overlay for multimedia streaming. In *International Symposium on High Performance Distributed Computing*, 2007.

In-Network Adaptation of H.264/SVC for HD Video Streaming over 802.11g Networks

Ingo Kofler, Robert Kuschnig, Hermann Hellwagner
Institute of Information Technology (ITEC)
Alpen-Adria-Universität Klagenfurt
Austria
firstname.lastname@itec.uni-klu.ac.at

ABSTRACT

In this paper, we present an approach for in-network adaptation of H.264/SVC in the context of 802.11 wireless networks. It builds upon our previous work on an adaptive RTSP/RTP proxy which allows to adapt video streams on Linux-based home router platforms. The proposed approach tackles the throughput variations that occur as a consequence of the physical rate adaptation in 802.11 equipment caused by the mobility of clients. By combining monitoring information available exclusively on the wireless router with the ability to adapt scalable video streams on-the-fly, the proposed in-network adaptation approach allows to quickly adjust the video bit rate to the current link conditions. Instead of reacting on packet loss, our approach uses an increase in queueing delay at the router to detect phases of throughput degradation. This allows a higher responsiveness compared to traditional end-to-end approaches that rely solely on RTCP feedback. The behavior of our novel approach was evaluated in several mobility scenarios in an experimental test bed. The results obtained by streaming and adapting high-definition content clearly demonstrate the feasibility and benefits of this approach.

Categories and Subject Descriptors

C.2.6 [[**Computer Communication Networks**]: Internetworking; H.4.3 [**Information System Applications**]: Communications Applications

General Terms

Design, Performance, Experimentation

Keywords

H.264/SVC, Video Streaming, In-network Adaptation

1. MOTIVATION

The advent of the scalable video coding (SVC) extension of H.264/AVC introduced new possibilities in multimedia

communication. In contrast to prior approaches, H.264/SVC offers scalability along different adaptation dimensions (temporal, spatial, SNR) at a comparatively low bit rate overhead. In our previous work [5], we proposed a light-weight adaptation mechanism for performing in-network adaptation of H.264/SVC on an off-the-shelf router platform. The approach that utilizes the layered encoding of the scalable video bit stream is based on an RTSP/RTP proxy running on the Linux-based home router. It allows for stateful and signaling-aware adaptation of H.264/SVC streams and therefore meets the requirements of a media-aware network element (MANE) [8]. Our initial evaluations based on a rather modest Linksys WRT54GL router in [5] showed that the adaptation of up to four parallel standard-definition video streams is feasible on such home router platforms. Latest results obtained using more recent router platforms (TP-Link TL-WR1043ND, UBNT Router Station Pro) demonstrated that even the handling of parallel high-definition streams with a cumulative bit rate up to 40 Mbps is possible. While our previous work was rather focused on the adaptation mechanism and protocol details, this paper proposes the application of in-network adaptation to wireless streaming in an 802.11g network. In these networks, streaming high-definition content still imposes challenges in case of sub-optimal wireless link conditions.

Significant research efforts have been made during the last decade in the context of 802.11 networks and video streaming. One of the core problems, however, is the medium access scheme of 802.11 that is used almost exclusively: the Distributed Coordination Function (DCF), which is tailored for best-effort services rather than providing guarantees for real-time applications. The access to the shared medium, the lack of a central point of coordination and the unreliable wireless communication cause a multitude of different research challenges. A lot of work either based on theoretical analysis, simulation or experimental evaluation can be found in the literature that tackles single issues like throughput limitations, contention-based loss, airtime-fairness, service differentiation, etc. But still there is no means for solving all the challenges with 802.11 networking. Following this observation, our work does not claim to do so but rather provides a solution for dealing with the varying throughput in 802.11g networks caused by a single mobile client. Compared to earlier work in this field [3] we make use of H.264/SVC-based in-network adaptation performed on real home router platforms instead of MPEG-2 combined with a PC-based solution. Using H.264/SVC in the context of

802.11 was already proposed in [2], where different layers were mapped to 802.11e access categories. However, the authors of [2] proposed a non-signaling aware approach which uses a fixed mapping and relies on packet dropping by the MAC layer. This is however, not aligned with the general concept of a MANE. Our approach of performing in-network adaptation directly on the router offers two major advantages. First, it is possible to access monitoring information that is only available locally. Second, the availability of this information allows to react much faster to link degradations instead of relying on traditional end-to-end feedback like RTCP reports.

2. LINK RATE ADAPTATION IN 802.11

In wireless networks the mobility of a station typically has a major impact on the wireless connectivity because of fading effects. A specific feature of the 802.11 standard is that it allows to switch the modulation and coding parameters to adapt the robustness of the transmission on a per-frame basis. As the selection of these parameters also influences the achievable transmission rate, this adaptive behavior also dictates the maximum achievable throughput to a single station. The variation in throughput can be very significant since the 802.11g standard offers physical rates between 1 Mbps and 54 Mbps. Furthermore, the overhead of the medium access scheme used by 802.11 devices limit the achievable throughput to values far below these nominal physical rates [4]. The adaptation of the physical rate according to the link conditions is controlled by the rate adaptation algorithm. No particular algorithm is specified in the standard which leaves the implementation up to vendors and researchers. Consequently, a variety of different algorithms [1] were proposed in the last decade. The algorithms typically use heuristics and transmissions statistics like packet loss and signal strength measurements [9] to decide which PHY rate to use for transmitting the next frame.

In the context of Linux-based devices, the *minstrel* algorithm turned out to perform very well under various conditions as investigated in recent work [10]. It uses packet loss as an indicator and maintains throughput and reliability statistics for all available physical rates. Additionally, it frequently uses probing frames to determine if it is possible to use a higher physical rate than currently in use. The minstrel algorithm is used as the default rate control algorithm on our Linux-based router platforms. In the Linux kernel, these algorithms are however separated from the actual drivers of the wireless devices. This allows to experiment with different algorithms or to implement another algorithm by providing an own kernel module. This modular concept was also utilized for our evaluation as discussed later.

One can conclude that in current 802.11 networks there is no way to guarantee a certain bandwidth to a mobile station for video streaming or other real-time services. Apart from 802.11e, which allows a basic service differentiation, the 802.11 standard lacks real QoS mechanisms for such services. This situation requires adaptive solutions on the application layer which can cope with varying link throughput. In the following, we propose an adaptive approach which adapts a scalable video stream according to the changing networking conditions caused by the mobility of a single client. We assume that the bottleneck is the wireless network and not the wired networks (Ethernet, VDSL) involved in the content delivery chain. In these wired networks the required bandwidth for high-definition content can be typically provisioned as it is already the case for VoD services in current IPTV deployments.

3. H.264/SVC IN-NETWORK ADAPTATION

In order to support the adaptation of the video stream according to the varying throughput of the 802.11 link, we extended the architecture of the RTSP/RTP proxy in [5] by an Adaptation Decision Taking and Monitoring component. Its task is to control the adaptation of the scalable video content based on the current wireless link conditions. For that purpose it makes use of the scalability information exchanged during the RTSP session setup to learn which layers (and resulting video bit rates) are contained in the video bit stream. In this work, we put the focus on spatial adaptation only. However, the concept can be easily applied to temporal or quality scalability as well.

Monitoring is based on the Linux monitoring interface offered by the *mac80211* wireless stack used by many wireless network drivers. It allows to obtain information of all packets that are transmitted or received via the wireless interface by the router. The information includes the packet's payload as well as details about the physical rate, the number of retransmissions used, etc. Obviously, this information can only be provided after the packet was successfully transmitted and acknowledged by the client. Consequently, this monitoring interface can be used to make acknowledgements at the link layer visible to the application layer. In our approach, the proxy uses this feedback to estimate how long the packet was queued in the networking stack at the router. This estimation is accomplished by keeping track of the timestamps of when a packet was sent via the socket API and when its acknowledgement was notified via the monitoring interface. The differences between both timestamps obviously also contain the serialization and propagation delays of the wireless transmission. However, it turned out that the monitored delay can be on the order of several hundred milliseconds which renders these two components rather negligible. The difference of the timestamps is therefore considered as an estimation of the queueing delay and is monitored on a per-packet basis. The obtained values are smoothed by the proxy using an exponential weighted moving average (EWMA).

The averaged queueing delay is subsequently used for controlling the in-network adaptation of the video bit stream. In contrast to traditional adaptation approaches that rely on packet loss as feedback to trigger adaptation, using the queueing delay allows to react much faster to varying throughput. Considering the queuing delay to control video adaptation is proposed among others in [7]. The proxy can detect a throughput degradation by a sharp increase of the queueing delay and decrease the video bit rate immediately. This prevents or at least reduces packet loss *a priori*, in contrast to relying on packet loss to trigger the adaptation *a posteriori*. The Adaptation Decision Taking and Monitoring component follows a rather simple but effective control mechanism to vary the video bit rate depending on the encountered queueing delay. If the queueing delay exceeds a certain threshold, the proxy determines the link's throughput during the last 200 ms. This comparatively short interval was chosen based on the observations in [9] which indicate that it does not make sense to incorporate packet history older than 150 ms to 250 ms due to the fast changing wireless conditions. Based on this current throughput, the proxy decides which spatial layers depending on its video bit rate requirements can be currently served. This decision also considers overhead introduced by the packetization and transport as well as a share of remaining bandwidth to drain the queue at the router again. The rationale is to immediately reduce the video bit rate to prevent packet loss.

If, on the other hand, the proxy encounters a very low queueing delay during a configurable interval, this is considered as an indicator for low link utilization. In this case, the current capacity of the wireless link might allow to stream the content in a higher spatial resolution. The proxy however, does not immediately switch to a higher layer but first performs a capacity estimation. As proposed in a recent paper [6], a packet pair technique can be used to estimate the capacity of the wireless link. In contrast to the approach in [6], our approach does not need to transmit explicit probing packet pairs. Instead, it uses the collected timestamps of the packets transmitted during the last second. In our experiments, it turned out that in the case of HD content many packets are sent back-to-back by the proxy and can be used for a packet pair approach. Even in the case of non HD content, the proxy could simply generate packet pairs by transmitting the same RTP packet twice without influencing the video streaming itself. Another advantage of our approach is that the packet dispersion must not be measured by the client. Since the proxy is aware of the link layer acknowledgements, it can easily calculate the packet dispersion on the router. Consequently, our approach does not need any additional interaction or support by the client. Based on the capacity estimation, the proxy decides to switch up to a higher spatial layer, depending on whether the estimated capacity is sufficient for the increased video bit rate or not.

In steady-state operation, the proxy typically encounters an average queueing delay between two thresholds and remains in serving the current spatial layer. At the beginning of the streaming session, the proxy follows a rather conservative approach and starts with serving the base layer only. For our evaluations, the thresholds were determined empirically from results of previous experiments. The threshold to switch down was set to 150 ms, while the capacity estimation and possible switch up was triggered after the queueing delay was permanently below 50 ms for a whole second. In the following, we provide an experimental evaluation of our proposed approach for in-network adaptation. Again, in this evaluation we focus on the adaptive wireless streaming to a single mobile client without considering any cross traffic on the network.

4. EVALUATION METHODOLOGY

Evaluating the performance of wireless systems under mobility aspects is a difficult task. In order to obtain reproducible results, we chose the following novel approach consisting of two distinct steps.

First, we collected traces of the wireless transmission conditions for four representative mobility scenarios. The traces were obtained in an office environment at the university. The floor plan is shown in Figure 1. The position and movement of the mobile client is represented by the numbers 1 – 4 in the plan. The wireless router, denoted as access point (AP),

was positioned at the corridor, while the mobile receiver was positioned at, and moved to, different places. The first two scenarios do not include movement, but represent the best and worst case where the receiver is located near (scenario 1) and very far (scenario 2) from the access point. The other two scenarios (scenarios 3 and 4) cover the movement at pedestrian speed away from the access point into two different directions as indicated by the arrows. The traces were obtained by transmitting UDP packets at a constant rate of 20 Mbps to the receiver and measuring per packet the signal strength and physical rate at the receiver, among other parameters. All of the traces consist of data collected over a time of 50 seconds and represent the behavior of the minstrel algorithm used by the router platform. Figures 2 and 3 show the traces for scenarios 2 and 3, respectively. Although evaluated, scenario 1 and 4 are not explicitly shown in this paper due to space constraints. However, scenario 1 can be summarized as a best-case scenario characterized by perfect reception conditions and the usage of the highest physical rate of 54 Mbps for more than 99 percent of the packets. In scenario 2, the receiver encounters a quite low signal strength of approx. -80 dBm, resulting in the selection of a modest physical rate of 11 Mbps for a vast majority of the packets. After 40 seconds a further degradation of the signal strength can be observed, which causes the minstrel algorithm to use even lower physical rates for some seconds. Scenario 3 consists of a movement away from the access point within the first 30 seconds while remaining at the end position for further 20 seconds until the end of the experiment. The signal strength measured for each frame shows a steady degradation during the actual movement of the receiver. However, the impact on the physical rate used by the minstrel algorithm does not show such steady degradation. Instead, the majority of frames is transmitted at the highest rate (54 Mbps) until second 25, followed by a transition phase of less than 5 seconds where the physical rate drops to 11 Mbps and even lower. After that, the physical rate settles at 11 Mbps although the minstrel algorithm continuously probes higher rates. The trace obtained in scenario 4 (not shown here) indicates a consistent behavior characterized by a smooth degradation of the signal strength and a sudden drop of the physical rate.

In the second step, the distribution of the physical rates used within a given time interval was determined based on the traces. The obtained distributions were integrated into our Linux kernel module *phyrateemu* that implements the interface for rate control algorithms. The wireless driver was configured to use the *phyrateemu* module instead of the minstrel algorithm. This means that instead of choosing the physical rates based on the current conditions, the physical rates were selected according to the obtained traces. Consequently, this allowed us to replay the mobility patterns

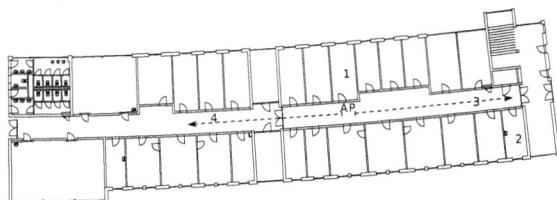

Figure 1: Floor plan showing the different scenarios

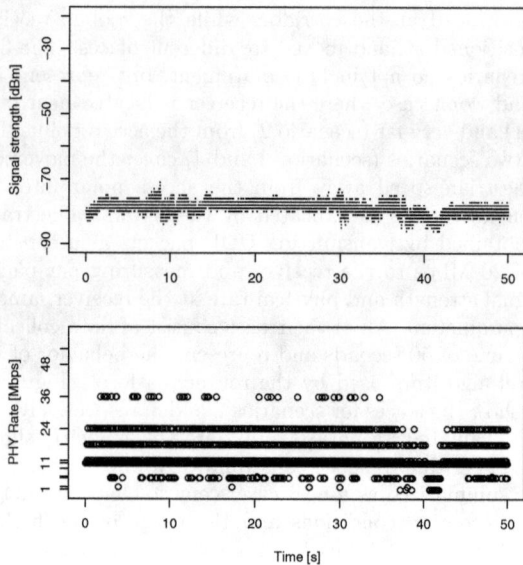

Figure 2: Signal strength and PHY rate in scenario 2

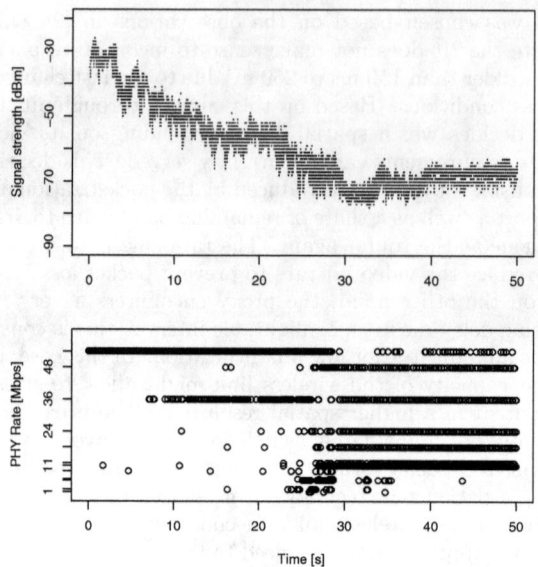

Figure 3: Signal strength and PHY rate in scenario 3

for the actual evaluations and to investigate the impact of adaptation in a reproducible manner.

The experimental setup for the evaluation consisted of a desktop PC acting as the streaming server, the home router running the proxy application and a laptop PC representing the client. The desktop PC was connected to the router via Gigabit Ethernet, while the client was connected using 802.11g. The client requested the scalable video stream using the openRTSP command line tool of the live555 library[1]. At the server side, the scalable video content was streamed using Apple's Darwin Streaming Server (DSS)[2]. The TP-Link TL-WR1043ND router platform was used for this particular evaluation.

The evaluation was performed using different high-definition video sequences. Again, only the results for a single sequence (tractor) can be discussed below due to space constraints. The sequence was encoded using JSVM reference software version 9.19.8. The base layer represents the content in 1024x576 resolution at 50 fps. The two spatial enhancement layers provide the possibility to increase the resolution to 1280x720 and 1920x1080, respectively. The sequences were encoded to achieve a constant bit rate for all of the three possible resolutions. In the case of the tractor sequence, the base layer results in a bit rate of 5 Mbps, while the additional spatial layers lead to a total bit rate of 9.8 (720p) and 15 Mbps (1080p). The media content was served in an infinite loop until the client explicitly closed the streaming session at the end of the experiment. The experiments were repeated at least three times to ensure consistent results.

5. EVALUATION RESULTS

In the following, the results of our experimental evaluation are presented. The metrics used for the evaluation are the throughput and the packet loss monitored at the client. Ad-

[1]http://www.live555.com/liveMedia
[2]http://dss.macosforge.org

ditionally, the average queueing delay at the router was measured during the experiment. We refrained from using video quality metrics like PSNR as they are not really representative when performing spatial or even temporal adaptation. Additionally, this metric is also influenced by the encoding settings as well as by the error concealment mechanisms employed at the decoder, e.g., in case of lost frames. Therefore, we rather focused on the networking point of view and argue that the video consumption at the client should not be negatively influenced by high packet loss and/or packets arriving too late at the client.

Again, the results of scenario 1 and 4 are not explicitly shown due to lack of space but are briefly discussed in the text. In scenario 1, the mobile client is located near the access point and enjoys good wireless connectivity, which means that the vast majority of packets are transmitted at the highest PHY rate of 54 Mbps. Consequently, the video stream can be served in the highest resolution (1080p) since the capacity of the link is sufficient to cope with the video bit rate of 15 Mbps. In fact, no adaptation would be necessary. However, because of the conservative strategy followed by the proxy only the base layer of the video stream is served at the beginning of the session. Since the encountered queueing delay is below the threshold during the first second of streaming, the proxy immediately performs the capacity estimation and ultimately switches to the highest resolution (and bit rate) after the first second of streaming. As a consequence of the high link capacity, the queueing delay remains at a low level which causes the proxy to maintain its steady-state operation and continues serving the highest resolution.

Scenario 2 can be characterized by bad wireless connectivity, which causes a majority of the packets to be transmitted at a PHY rate of 11 Mbps. Figure 4 illustrates the impact of these conditions on the video streaming if no adaptation would be performed and the video would be transmitted at the highest spatial resolution. The achieved throughput is around 6 Mbps, which is approximately the throughput that

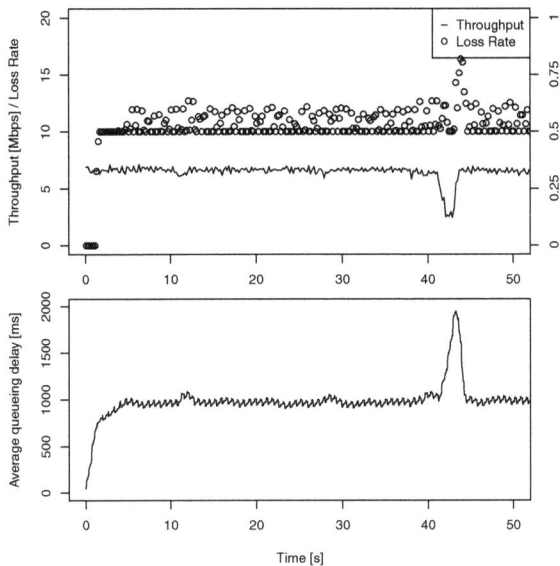

Figure 4: Scenario 2 without adaptation

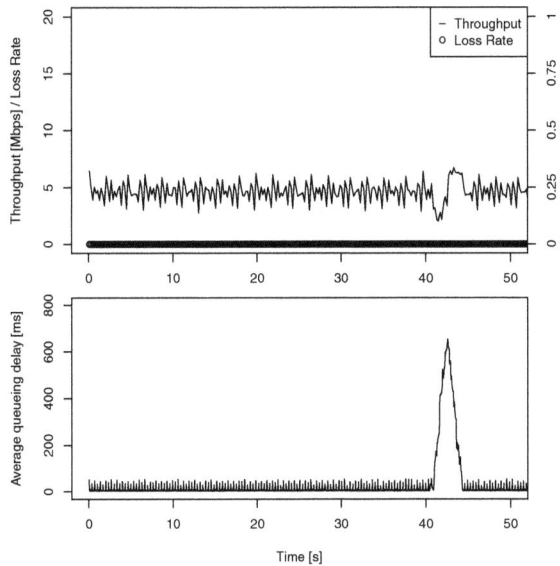

Figure 5: Scenario 2 with adaptation

can be achieved in an 802.11g network when using a physical rate of 11 Mbps and packet sizes of around 1500 bytes. As the video stream at the highest resolution requires 15 Mbps, the queue at the router quickly builds up and consequently the average queueing delay at the router quickly increases up to 1 second. If the maximum size of the queue is exceeded, the RTP packets are getting dropped at the router. This can be observed by the client as a loss rate of more than 50 percent. During the short interval around second 40 where the throughput is even lower, the queueing delay as well as the packet loss further increases.

The impact of our proposed adaptation mechanism in scenario 2 is illustrated in Figure 5. Again, the proxy starts to serve the base layer of the video (approx. 5 Mbps) at the beginning of the streaming session which can obviously be served under these link conditions. Although the average queueing delay is at a comparatively low level, the proxy does not switch to a higher resolution since the capacity estimation indicates that the capacity is insufficient to serve a higher layer. Therefore, the proxy continues to transmit only the base layer in standard-definition (576p) to the client. As it already serves the base layer only, there is also no room for further adapting the video during the short decrease of throughput around second 40. Instead, the throughput shortly degrades and an increase of the average queueing delay can be observed. However, as this degradation only takes place over a short period, the queue at the router can handle this fluctuation and no packet loss occurs. The average queueing delay, however, exceeds 600 ms during that time. Obviously, the encoding parameters of the video dictate a lower bound on the bit rate and therefore limit the operating range of approaches that rely on these scalability features.

From an adaptation point of view, the scenarios 3 and 4 are the most interesting ones. In both scenarios, the sudden drop of the physical rate also leads to a quick degradation of the video throughput, as shown in Figure 6 representing scenario 3. If no adaptation is performed, a significant increase of queueing delay takes place within a few seconds,

followed by a sudden increase of the packet loss. It should be noted that the observed increase in the average queueing delay precedes the packet loss by less than 2 seconds. This finding also confirms the decision to use the queueing delay rather than the encountered packet loss as the triggering event for adaptation decision-taking.

The impact of applying our approach to scenario 3 is illustrated in Figure 7. Again, the streaming starts with the delivery of the base layer and a switch to the highest spatial layer after 1 second due to sufficient capacity. During the short transition phase in which the physical rate rapidly decreases, the queueing delay exceeds the threshold of 150 ms and triggers decreasing the video bit rate. As the new adaptation parameters are applied immediately, the switch to a lower layer happens instantly. As a consequence of this quick response by the proxy, the average queueing delay can be kept below 400 ms. After the link conditions have stabilized and the majority of packets are sent at a physical rate of 11 Mbps, the proxy remains at serving the base layer with a bit rate of approximately 5 Mbps. Consistent results were obtained for scenario 4 where the physical rate degrades in a similar way due to the mobility of the client.

In summary, the proposed control mechanism to adjust the video bit rate according to the available monitoring data works very satisfactory. In all of the four evaluated scenarios, it succeeds in delivering the appropriate quality that is feasible with the current network conditions. The different evaluation runs for scenarios 3 and 4 have shown that no or only a few (not shown in this figure) packets are lost during this period. This enables a smooth playback of the received video at the mobile client without encountering severe service disruption for longer periods.

6. CONCLUSIONS

In this paper, we present an application of our previous work on in-network adaptation of H.264/SVC to wireless networks. Compared to traditional video coding, H.264/SVC allows for computationally cheap video adaptation compared

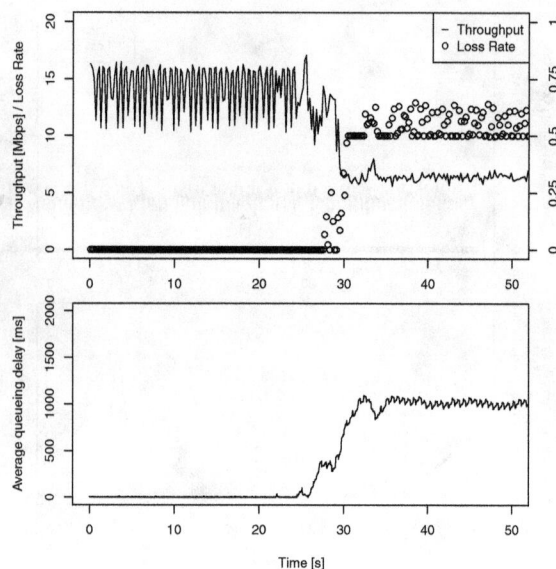

Figure 6: Scenario 3 without adaptation

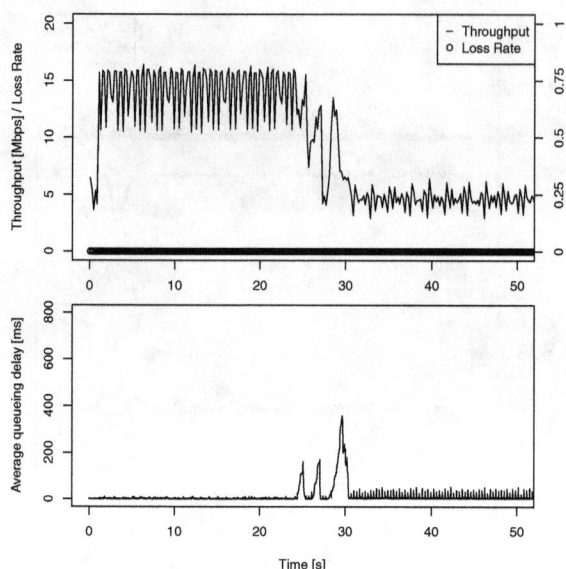

Figure 7: Scenario 3 with adaptation

to traditional video coding. This makes the in-network adaptation of high-definition streams on router platforms possible at all. Our proposed approach uses monitoring information that is available locally on the router to adjust the video bit rate according to the varying link throughput. In our work we focus on throughput changes caused by the mobility of a single client in combination with the multi-rate operation of 802.11. The adaptation is performed by an application-layer proxy-based approach which can be characterized as stateful and signaling-aware. The advantage of our approach is to use monitoring information, more particularly the queueing delay, on the router to control the adaptation. In contrast to control mechanisms that use packet loss as feedback, our approach detects changing link throughputs earlier and prevents or at least reduces packet loss. This information is obtained via a monitoring interface that allows applications to be notified of link layer acknowledgements. The same mechanism is used further to estimate the link capacity using a packet pair approach without requiring any support by the client. The proposed approach was successfully evaluated in the context of adapting different high-definition video streams in different mobility scenarios. Although the evaluation in this paper was based on spatial adaptation only, our concept can be easily applied to temporal or quality scalability as well. The main advantages of in-network adaptation compared to traditional end-to-end approaches are the monitoring information and its responsiveness. This means that it can make use of monitoring information that is only available locally, like the actual queueing delay, and react much faster as compared to end-to-end approaches that might use RTCP only. In the case of 802.11 networks where the physical rate changes quite fast, the typical RTCP feedback provided in intervals on the order of 5 seconds is obviously far too slow.

7. REFERENCES

[1] S. Biaz and S. Wu. Rate Adaptation Algorithms for IEEE 802.11 Networks: A Survey and Comparison. In *Proceedings of the ISCC'08*, pages 130–136, July 2008.

[2] H.-L. Chen, P.-C. Lee, and S.-H. Hu. Improving Scalable Video Transmission over IEEE 802.11e through a Cross-Layer Architecture. In *Proceedings of the IWCMC'08*, pages 241–246, Aug. 2008.

[3] I. Djama and T. Ahmed. A Cross-Layer Interworking of DVB-T and WLAN for Mobile IPTV Service Delivery. *IEEE Transactions on Broadcasting*, 53(1):382–390, Mar. 2007.

[4] J. Jun, P. Peddabachagari, and M. Sichitiu. Theoretical Maximum Throughput of IEEE 802.11 and its Applications. In *Proceedings of the NCA'03*, pages 249–256, May 2003.

[5] I. Kofler, M. Prangl, R. Kuschnig, and H. Hellwagner. An H.264/SVC-based Adaptation Proxy on a WiFi Router. In *Proceedings of the NOSSDAV'08*, pages 63–68. ACM, May 2008.

[6] M. Li, M. Claypool, and R. Kinicki. WBest: A bandwidth estimation tool for IEEE 802.11 wireless networks. In *Proceedings of the LCN'08*, pages 374–381, Oct. 2008.

[7] P. van Beek and M. U. Demircin. Delay-Constrained Rate Adaptation for Robust Video Transmission over Home Networks. In *Proceedings of the ICIP'05*, Sept. 2005.

[8] Y.-K. Wang, M. M. Hannuksela, S. Pateux, A. Eleftheriadis, and S. Wenger. System and Transport Interface of SVC. *IEEE Transactions on Circuits and Systems for Video Technology*, 17(9):1149–1163, Sept. 2007.

[9] S. H. Y. Wong, H. Yang, S. Lu, and V. Bharghavan. Robust Rate Adaptation for 802.11 Wireless Networks. In *Proceedings of the MobiCom'06*, pages 146–157, Sept. 2006.

[10] W. Yin, K. Bialkowski, J. Indulska, and P. Hu. Evaluations of MadWifi MAC layer rate control mechanisms. In *Proceedings of the IWQoS'10*, June 2010.

Media-aware Networking for SVC-based P2P Streaming

Osama Abboud*, Konstantin Pussep, Dominik Stingl, and Ralf Steinmetz

Multimedia Communications Lab, Technische Universität Darmstadt, Germany

{abboud, pussep, stingl, steinmetz}@kom.tu-darmstadt.de

ABSTRACT

There are currently two concurrent trends in the Internet. First, the number of Internet users and their connection speeds are increasing rapidly. Second, Internet-based applications are dominating how people receive information, communicate, and entertain themselves. Therefore, we are witnessing an enormous increase in IP-based multimedia traffic, which is putting an enormous strain on the network. Additionally, router and network virtualization are gaining importance, enabling more intelligent networks. Therefore, we argue that networks should not be merely bystanders to this multimedia revolution. In this paper we present a media-aware network solution based on router virtualization that aims at striking a balance between intelligence and adaptation at the edge and in the core of the network. Using an extensive simulative study, we demonstrate that our media-aware network not only helps in enhancing streaming performance during bottlenecks, but also minimizes the side effects of congestions on user perceived quality, making it a need for future Internet multimedia applications.

Categories and Subject Descriptors

C.2 [**Computer-Communication Networks**]: Distributed Systems

General Terms

Algorithms, Design, Performance

Keywords

Media Awareness, Router Virtualization, Scalable Video Coding, Peer-to-Peer, Multimedia Distribution, Streaming.

*This work has been supported in parts by the IT R&D program of MKE/KEIT of South Korea (10035587, Development of Social TV Service Enabler based on Next Generation IPTV Infrastructure) and by the Federal Ministry of Education and Research of the Federal Republic of Germany (support code 01BK0920, G-Lab VirtuRAMA).

1. INTRODUCTION

The increasing number of Internet users and their connection speeds along with the domination of Internet-based applications have created an enormous increase in IP-based multimedia applications and traffic. The challenge of transmitting multimedia data is due to its strict requirements on bandwidth, where more strain is put on the network. To aggravate this, video content is constantly gaining more quality and posing higher requirements on the required bandwidth. We have seen the rise of high definition content that requires more than 2 Mbps throughput, and, with the introduction of 3D and multi-view video, bit-rates are expected to explode.

Client/Server systems alone cannot cope with this steep increase in required bit-rates. Therefore, peer-assisted video streaming systems are becoming more attractive [8, 11]. In such systems, peers that have downloaded some content can assist servers in re-distributing it. This paradigm, therefore, allows streaming an increasing amount of multimedia content (with high bit-rates) to an increasing number of users. This shift in paradigm, however, inflicts a shift in the distribution bottleneck from the server side to the network core [3], since peers with high speed access act as micro video servers. This raises many questions: *are classical routing elements enough to cope with this shift? how can we implement efficient yet simple media-aware solutions?*

We argue that next generation multimedia applications must take this pressure on the network core into consideration. Since rolling out new high capacity links would inflict high costs for network providers, intelligent network elements become necessary to manage the enormous multimedia traffic. While the growth of multimedia traffic increases the load on the network, media awareness would help in alleviating its effects especially during congestions. Although streaming applications can use intelligent techniques at the *edge* of the network, they have no control in the core.

In this paper we present a media-aware network solution, which can be gradually introduced into the core network. Our solution helps to increase the perceived Quality of Service (QoS)[1] during congestions that arise in high quality P2P streaming systems. We make use of router virtualization to enable application-layer congestion control that can be activated on-demand. Additionally, the content provider can define how the virtual routers should handle the P2P streaming traffic upon a congestion. Therefore, we propose

[1]Perceived QoS constitutes a set of measurable metrics that reflect the user experience. These, as presented later, include session and video quality. QoS and perceived QoS will be used interchangeably throughout this paper.

that content providers use media-aware solutions that are specific to their applications.

In this paper, we design and evaluate a media-aware network solution for P2P streaming systems that are based on Scalable Video Coding (SVC). We show that media awareness can improve QoS and that even a basic intelligence inflicts substantial performance benefits.

The contributions of this paper are as follows: (1) we present a simple yet effective approach to implement media awareness using router virtualization techniques, (2) we analyze the impact of media awareness on various metrics that reflect the perceived video quality, (3) we show that even with minimal intelligence in the core, performance of SVC-based P2P streaming systems can be enhanced.

This paper is organized as follows. In Section 2, we give an overview on background and related work. The media-aware network solution is presented in Section 3. We present our evaluation methodology and results in Section 4 and finally conclude the paper in Section 5.

2. BACKGROUND AND RELATED WORK

Research on media awareness has been an active topic in the research community for some time [7, 6]. The aim is to find efficient methods to achieve a smooth and high quality playback. Approaches related to ours can be broadly summarized as solutions that utilize information on the importance of different media parts to either enhance the quality or limit video distortion. This utilization can either be done at the edge [9, 7] or the core of the network [6]. Solutions at the edge, on one hand, usually implement media awareness through overlay routing and media-aware scheduling. Further, there exist many solutions that fall into the distortion-aware media drop category [7, 12]. Upon congestions, such methods would drop media packets according to the distortion that would be inflicted on the video quality.

Solutions in the core, on the other hand, try to utilize QoS management capabilities available at network routing elements. In [6], Fidler shows how Differentiated Services [10] can be used to improve system performance when using layered video coding. Our solution differs since we systematically assess the priority of SVC streams and show that this priority consists of temporal and quality aspects. We further take a new approach, namely using router virtualization, to implement media awareness. We show that a simple media-aware network solution for SVC-based streaming systems can greatly enhance the perceived QoS.

SVC is the extension of the H.264 Advanced Video Coding (AVC) standard that offers encoding a video file with three dimensions of scalability. While the video has to be encoded only once, receivers can retrieve and play only certain subparts of the global stream. Therefore, different receivers can play-out the video stream with different resolutions (spatial scalability), frame-rates (temporal scalability), and picture quantization levels (quality scalability). SVC video streams are composed of two classes of video blocks, a base layer and further enhancement layers. The base layer is always needed for decoding the video file. With more enhancement layers available, a better quality can be achieved. However, when the base layer is missing, playback is not possible. This is known as stalling or playback freeze. SVC enables the support for heterogenous devices and quality adaptation. For example, a mobile device and a desktop machine can both receive the same video stream but with different resolutions.

Much research has been done on building P2P streaming systems that use SVC [1, 5, 2]. SVC is used in those solutions to adapt the streamed quality according to various resources available at the end devices. Therefore, we believe that such a video coding standard will become very important in the future. Thereby, it is essential that the networks are aware how such videos are structured to better manage and allocate resources.

3. MEDIA-AWARE NETWORK SOLUTION

Future Internet networks should be able to better react to congestion of multimedia traffic by taking into account the importance of different video packets. For streaming applications in general, it is very important to have prioritized traffic management to achieve QoS. When classical routers get congested, they usually drop packets that might be more important than others, i.e. in a media-agnostic fashion. But the question remains, how can we add more intelligence to routers for better congestion control?

Our approach is based on harnessing the power of router virtualization to enable advanced traffic management along with application layer control. Router virtualization is based on the idea of running multiple software routers on a single hardware router. The different software routers can have different roles and be activated and even migrated on demand. Recently, efficient implementations for router virtualization have been proposed where full network speeds can be achieved by combining a fast forwarding plane (e.g. OpenFlow[2]) with software routers [4].

Our network model and scenario are shown in Figure 1. There, routers connect different subnets and forward data from and to several end users. In a P2P streaming system, edge routers' upload utilization will generally become higher, since data would be flowing from end users to the core network [3]. This issue becomes especially evident when streaming video content with high quality.

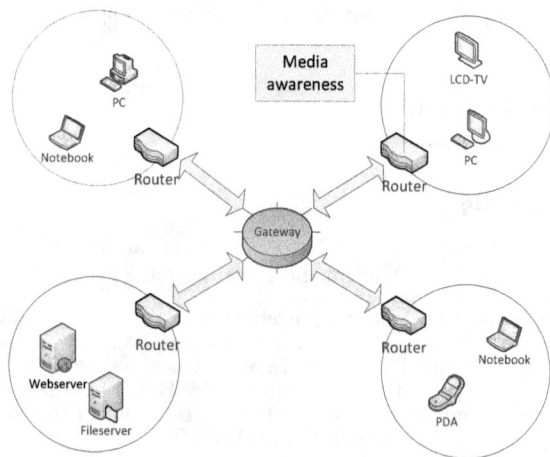

Figure 1: Media-aware network scenario

3.1 Router Virtualization Versus Classical QoS

Before detailing our architecture, we first stress the need for including router virtualization rather than classical QoS

---

[2]http://www.openflow.org

techniques. Using router virtualization, it is possible to have QoS at the application layer, therefore, enabling optimization in the direction of perceived QoS. Additionally, efficient and custom-made QoS solutions can be developed and used as needed. For example, different virtual routers can be deployed for live and on-demand streaming, since both use different techniques for media awareness.

Another advantage of router virtualization is that it enables the gradual development of media-aware solutions and protocols, which is not possible with classical approaches. Additionally, a virtualized router does not have to be running all the time as it can be executed only on-demand when bottlenecks occur, exactly at the point when performance and perceived quality would degrade. Nonetheless, one can still argue that prominent QoS management techniques such as Differentiated Services [10] can achieve similar goals. But the main issue there is that using the Type-of-Service bits, only limited priority information can be communicated with the router. Additionally, QoS can only be controlled by the network provider and not the content provider. Since the latter has a better idea about its users' access patterns, content popularity, and the scheduling of its own traffic, a router virtualization solution enables the implementation of more sophisticated management algorithms. Therefore, a solution similar to the one presented in this paper allows for homogenous QoS handling of multimedia traffic across different networks. Additionally, the content provider, based on some business model with the network operator, can deploy its own policies and algorithms to implement custom-made media-aware solutions.

3.2 P2P Streaming System

The media-aware solution presented in this paper is designed for a quality-adaptive P2P video streaming system that uses Scalable Video Coding (SVC) [1]. Here we give an overview on the core mechanisms of the system required to understand the contribution of this paper.

In this system, the content provider is interested in using P2P techniques to reduce its costs, but still has to deploy servers that would sustain QoS for the users. Such hybrid scenarios have shown to have highest potential in realistic scenarios [8, 11]. A tracker is used to coordinate all peers within the system and keeps track for each peer, its online status, selected video stream, and streamed layer. To enable multi-source download, the global SVC stream is divided into multiple parts called *pieces*. A piece constitutes a playback unit, usually ranging between 0.5 and 2 seconds. Each piece in turn is divided into multiple SVC blocks. Receiving more SVC blocks in the different SVC dimensions, leads to higher quality in the respective dimension.

During runtime, each peer performs local *quality adaptation* of the requested video quality according to various parameters of the device and the network. Therefore, the received quality can be adjusted according to static peer resources, as well as to the dynamic network status. When a streaming session is initiated, an assessment of static local resources has to be performed. This, as presented in [1], is called Initial Quality Adaptation (IQA). The IQA mechanism helps in matching requested video quality to local resources already from the beginning by taking into account the static peer resources: screen resolution, available bandwidth, and processing power. After streaming has started, a control loop has to make sure that playback remains smooth.

The module responsible for this is called *Progressive Quality Adaptation* (PQA). In addition to taking into account the static resources as for the IQA, the PQA additionally adapts to the dynamics of the system reflected through the active throughput and SVC layer availability. The PQA has to be performed periodically, and, therefore, defines the speed of adaptation. As presented in [1], having a smaller adaptation interval helps in quickly reacting to network changes and, therefore, playback is more smooth. Nonetheless, this comes at the expense of settling for lower SVC video quality.

3.3 Calculating Priority of SVC Streams

Every SVC video block has a certain temporal and quality priority, denoted by P_T and P_Q respectively. The temporal priority generally expresses how soon a certain video block is needed. Video blocks, which are closer to the current playback position, have a higher temporal priority than others. Suppose a certain receiver peer p_r with playback position B_{play} is requesting a block with index B_i from a sender peer p_s. The temporal priority of the block, as reported by p_s, is $-(B_i - B_{play})$. This priority is, therefore, higher when the requested block is closer to the playback position. We normalize this priority by the buffer size S to get:

$$P_T = -(B_i - B_{play})/S. \qquad (1)$$

The quality priority, on the other hand, reflects the important of the SVC enhancement layers. Using it, lower layers for the video stream are given higher priority. For example, without the base layer, the video cannot be decoded. Therefore, the base layer is given the highest priority. The quality priority is calculated as:

$$P_Q = -(W_d\, d + W_t t + W_q q), \qquad (2)$$

where d, t, and q denote the spatial, temporal and quality layers respectively (see Section 4.1). W_d, W_t, and W_q are used to weight the different scalability dimensions. This equation gives the base layer with $(d, t, q) = (0, 0, 0)$ the highest priority (0), while higher layers get a lower priority.

The temporal and quality priorities are included with every request. When a peer decides to serve a certain requested block, the respective priorities are reported along with the actual transmission.

3.4 Media-aware Virtual Router

We now present our approach for achieving media awareness in an SVC-based P2P streaming system. The goal here is not to present a complex prioritization algorithm, but rather to demonstrate how media awareness can be introduced into an SVC-based P2P streaming system. During bottlenecks, the virtual router prioritizes and controls block transfers based on priority information that reflect the perceived QoS or even policies that would depend on other network parameters as required by the content provider, for example content popularity. The main task of the virtual router is to prioritize block transfers. A video block is a video part as defined by our SVC-based P2P streaming protocol. The size of a block usually ranges from 16KB up to 2MB. The virtual router can retrieve the priority information for each block either using a separate communication channel or using deep packet inspection. To minimize processing overhead, only a single decision has to be made for all packets belonging to the same block. This greatly enhances scalability of the application layer processing algorithms.

The virtual router keeps a list of active transfers or connections that represent the blocks currently being uploaded along with their priorities. When there is a new incoming block, the router first retrieves the temporal (P_T) and quality (P_Q) priorities as defined above and adds this block to the list of outgoing transfers. When the virtual router is getting overloaded, congestion control is performed by using the priority algorithm to decide whether to forward, slow down or even drop some of the outgoing transfers. For actual priority calculation, we use exponential compensation to exaggerate the importance of blocks very close to the playback position or base layers. Therefore, the virtual router calculates a single priority for each block transfer by combining the temporal and quality aspects. This priority P is defined as:

$$P = T\,e^{P_T} + Q\,e^{P_Q} = Te^{-\frac{B_i-B_{play}}{S}} + Q\,e^{-(W_d d + W_t t + W_q q)}$$
(3)

where T and Q denote the weights for the temporal and quality aspects respectively, with $T + Q = 1$. Therefore, the priority as calculated above ranges between 1 (highest) to 0 (lowest). As next we evaluate the media-aware solution with different temporal and quality weighting factors.

4. EVALUATION

The described streaming system and the media-aware network were implemented in an event-based simulator. The reference approaches are a media agnostic network and a network that uses DiffServ. The media agnostic network applies classical congestion control and random packet drop. As for the DiffServ network, all packets of urgent blocks (within 7 seconds after playback position) are given a high priority service class. The DiffServ router prioritizes those blocks based on a first come first served policy.

4.1 Setup

We consider a typical Video-on-Demand (VoD) scenario with 90 peers actively participating in the streaming overlay. The peers are distributed over 4 subnets as depicted in Figure 1. All traffic leaving a subnet go through the router that performs media awareness upon congestions.

To ensure a minimum level of QoS, the content provider deploys servers that act as content seeds. We assume having 2 of these servers per subnet[3], with an upload bandwidth of 3 Mbps each. Peer resources are configured in a way to reflect heterogeneity. Therefore, peers are divided into 3 sets with different screen resolutions, namely: 176x144, 352x288, and 704x576. The bandwidth of the three sets is distributed as follows (upload/download): 128/256, 320/560, and 800/1200 Kbps, similar to [8]. Peers of the three sets are equally distributed over the four subnets of our network model.

We consider a 5 minute SVC video file with a total of 12 layers and a full bit rate of 1 Mbps. There are 3 resolutions (176x144, 352x288, and 704x576) and 4 frame-rate values (3.75, 7.5, 15 and 30 fps), resulting in $4 \cdot 3 = 12$ layers. For calculating the priority according to Equation 3 we choose an un-biased weighting: $W_d = W_t = W_q = 0.33\overline{3}$.

To assess the impact of media awareness as well as find the best router configuration we consider the following scenario: after streaming starts and peers start joining, we leave the system for 10 minutes to warm up. Then, we invoke an

---

[3]We tested the system with different number of servers and achieved consistent results.

upload bottleneck of 3 Mbps for 10 minutes. This means that, during the 10 minutes, the router can only upload at 3 Mbps. Such a bottleneck can be due to limited resources allocated for this specific video stream or due to cross traffic. For comparison, we run the system with media agnostic and DiffServ routers as explained above.

4.2 Metrics

We divide the metrics in use into two categories: *session quality* reflecting playback smoothness and *video quality* quantifying the achieved video quality as described below.

4.2.1 Session Quality Metrics

Session quality metrics are:

- *Average number of stalls*: that represents the number of stalling events during playback. Stalling is an event, where playback stops due to missing required video blocks.
- *Average duration of stalls*: that represents the time till the playback continues after a stall event has occurred.
- *Average total playback delay*: that combines the two metrics above by representing the total stalling time per peer.

In general, the fewer and shorter the stalling events and delay, the smoother playback becomes, and the better is the session quality of our system.

4.2.2 Video Quality Metrics

Video quality metrics are:

- *Average number of layer changes*. A high number of layer changes means that the received video quality has to be adapted to the current status very often. For example, the layer is changed when stalling events occur, or when the needed quality is not available at the other peers. The lower the value of this metric, the better is the video quality. This is due to the fact that users can get quite disgruntled by too frequent layer changes [13].
- *Average relative received layer*. Each video piece is received in a specific video quality. The maximal possible quality, as calculated by the IQA, depends on the static peer resources. Therefore we calculate the average received layer throughout the streaming session and normalize it with the initial layer selected by the IQA. This metric represents how well the peer was able to sustain the maximal quality it can support.

4.3 Experiment 1: Impact of Media-awareness

In this experiment we want to assess the impact of our media-aware network as well as find the best configurations. We test the virtual router for a bottleneck of 3 Mbps and with different T and Q values, namely: T100, T70/Q30, T50/Q50, T30/Q70, Q100. For this experiment, the PQA interval was fixed at 10 seconds, which represents a moderate value [1]. We focus on the performance during the bottleneck as then performance degradation takes place.

Session Quality. We first present in Figure 2 the session quality during the 10 minute bottleneck period. There we see the average number of stalls, average stall duration, and the total stalling duration, all calculated per peer.

Starting with Figure 2(a) and comparing the media agnostic with our media-aware system, we can see that the average number of stalling events per peer is reduced from 1.15

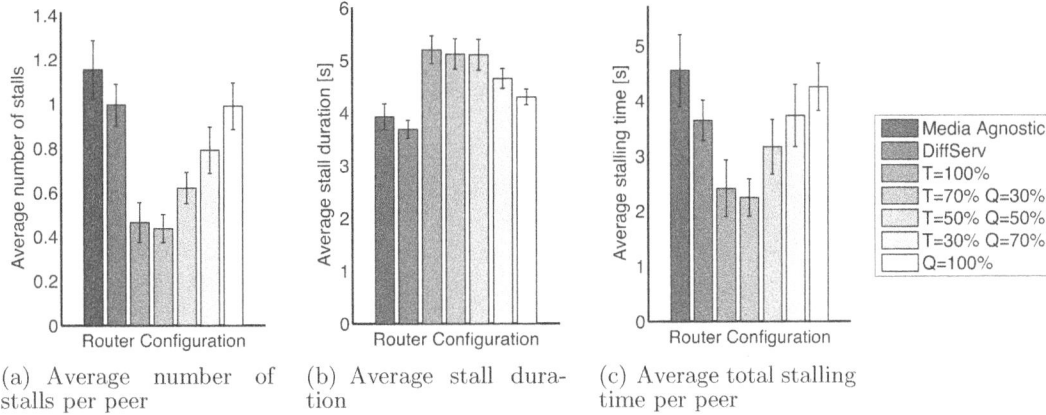

(a) Average number of stalls per peer

(b) Average stall duration

(c) Average total stalling time per peer

Figure 2: Session quality during bottleneck

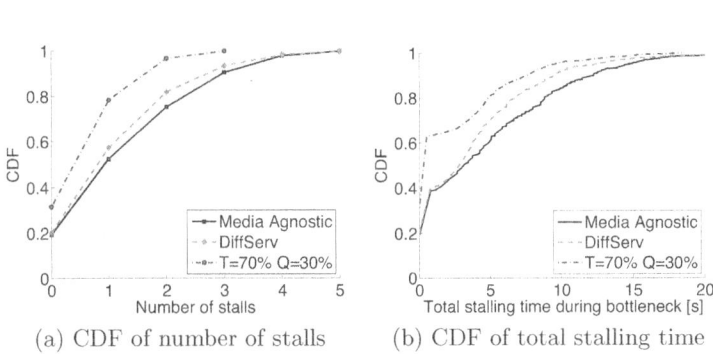

(a) CDF of number of stalls

(b) CDF of total stalling time

Figure 3: CDF of session quality during bottleneck

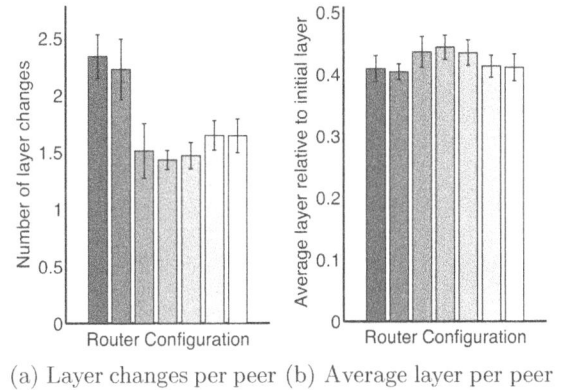

(a) Layer changes per peer   (b) Average layer per peer

Figure 4: Video quality during bottleneck

down to 0.44. Although media awareness slightly increased the duration of stalling events (Figure 2(b)), it reduced the total stalling duration during the bottleneck as depicted in Figure 2(c). That is, the total stalling duration is reduced from 4.6 down to 2.2 seconds per peer, resulting in 52% less stalling. Although DiffServ performed better than a media-agnostic network, it was still not able to compete with a full-pfledged media-aware solution.

Examining the different configurations of the virtual router, we can see that the best results were achieved with T70/Q30, where we just have 2.2 seconds of total stalling during the bottleneck. This can be explained by the fact that a larger T means that sooner needed video blocks, especially in the buffer zone, are sent faster. It was still nevertheless important to include the SVC quality dimension with $Q = 0.3$ to make sure that peers do not have to wait long for SVC layers they have already requested. Figures 3(a) and 3(b) present the results as a CDF. These graphs show the ratio of peers that had a specific number of stalls or stalling time. For T70/Q30 the highest number of stalls for any peer is 3. Furthermore, about 80% of the peers had less then 1 stall with T70/Q30, whereas for the media agnostic and DiffServ routers, those peers had around 2 stalling events.

Video Quality. Now we take a look at the video quality during the bottleneck. The results are presented in Figure 4. We see that the number of layer changes during the bottleneck is affected by media awareness (Figure 4(a)), while the average relative quality is minimally affected (Figure 4(b)).

Peers had the most layer changes with the media agnostic and DiffServ routers. This is due to the fact that those approaches have inflicted a larger number of stalls, which in turn caused the peers to adapt and reduce the requested layer, therefore, performing more layer changes. We can conclude that having media awareness leads to less quality changes because the peers are able to receive the requested quality. Again, the media-aware router with T70/Q30 yielded the best performance.

Concluding this experiment, we can say that media awareness based on a more weighted temporal priority (T70/Q30) has shown that video stalls and quality switches occur less often. Based on user studies [14, 13], our approach, therefore, helps in enhancing the perceived video quality since the video playback is smoother and has less quality switches.

4.4 Experiment 2: Variable PQA Interval

The second experiment deals with assessing the interdependencies between the PQA or adaptation interval and media awareness during a bottleneck. We want to check whether the adaptation interval depends on or affects our media-aware solution. Thus, we vary the adaptation interval choosing the values: 5, 10, 20, 30, and 45 seconds. We restrict our evaluation to the DiffServ and media-aware routers with T70/Q30.

Session Quality. Session quality with different adaptation intervals during the bottleneck and for the whole simulation are presented in Figure 5. We can see that our media-

19

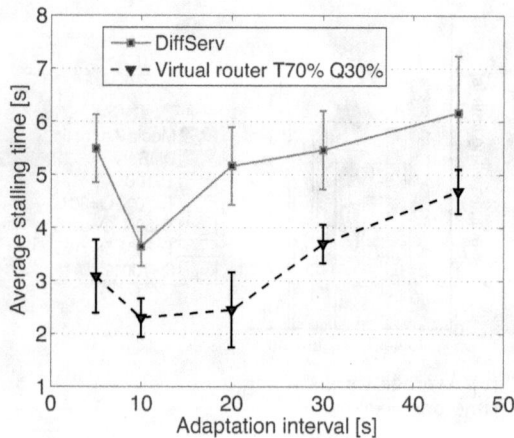

(a) Average stalling time per peer during bottleneck   (b) Average total delay per peer during simulation

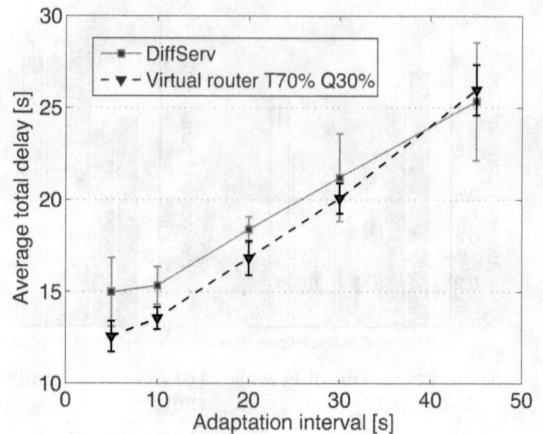

Figure 5: Session quality in Experiment 2

aware approach outperforms DiffServ. During the bottleneck, the average stalling time could be drastically reduced for the different adaptation intervals. Additionally, we see that for the DiffServ approach during bottleneck (Figure 5(a)), the relation between average stalling time and adaptation interval is not predictable, which is the case once the media awareness solution is in place. Therefore, media awareness is quite crucial especially in applications where the system provider would change the adaptation interval during runtime, which requires a more predictable relation.

Although the results for the total delay during the whole simulation (Figure 5(b)) do not show a huge performance gain over the whole simulation, it is the performance during the bottleneck that has the highest impact on the effective performance of the system, and therefore is more relevant.

Video Quality. Video quality in Experiment 2 did not show dependance on the PQA, so the graphs are excluded.

5. CONCLUSION

In this paper, we have presented a simple yet efficient media-aware network approach that achieves better perceived QoS without any additional traffic costs. This architecture, which is based on virtualized routers, enables building next generation multimedia applications.

We demonstrated that, during bottlenecks, our media-aware network improves both the session quality (regarding the total stalling delay) and video quality (regarding the need to switch the layer). Additionally, we saw that prioritizing video transmissions with more weight on the temporal aspect of video blocks brought the best performance and outperformed a DiffServ-based solution. More specifically, having a media-aware network helped in achieving 52% less stalling delay and 34% less SVC quality switches during bottlenecks. Regarding the interdependencies between the adaptation interval and media awareness, we saw that having more intelligence in the network makes the impact of the adaptation interval more predictable. This is especially important if this interval would be assigned dynamically depending on the device and network characteristics.

As future work, we plan to integrate the algorithms presented in this paper into a real virtual router and to perform prototype evaluation. To address more practical issues, we will study suitable control and management algorithms.

6. REFERENCES

[1] Abboud, O., Zinner, T., Pussep, K., Steinmetz, R.: On the Impact of Quality Adaptation in SVC-based P2P Video-on-Demand. In: ACM MMSys (2011)

[2] Baccichet, P., Schierl, T., Wiegand, T., Girod, B.: Low-delay Peer-to-peer Streaming Using Scalable Video Coding. In: Packet Video (2007)

[3] Bieberich, M.: Ip core network intelligence: Essential components and drivers. Cisco, Yankee Groug (2007)

[4] Bozakov, Z.: An open router virtualization framework using a programmable forwarding plane. In: SIGCOMM (2010)

[5] Cui, Y., Nahrstedt, K.: Layered peer-to-peer streaming. In: NOSSDAV (2003)

[6] Fidler, M.: Differentiated services based priority dropping and its application to layered video streams. In: IFIP Networking (2002)

[7] Guedes, B., Pereira, R., Vazao, T., Varela, A.: Simple media-aware packet discard algorithms. International Conference on Information Networking (Jan 2009)

[8] Huang, C., Li, J., Ross, K.W.: Can internet video-on-demand be profitable? In: SIGCOMM (2007)

[9] Jurca, D., Petrovic, S., Frossard, P.: Media aware routing in large scale networks with overlay. in Proc. IEEE ICME (2005)

[10] Nichols, K., Blake, S., Baker, F., Black, D.: Definition of the differentiated services field (ds field) in the ipv4 and ipv6 headers (1998)

[11] Yin, H., Liu, X., Zhan, T., Sekar, V., Qiu, F., Lin, C., Zhang, H., Li, B.: Design and deployment of a hybrid cdn-p2p system for live video streaming: experiences with livesky. In: ACM Multimedia (2009)

[12] Zhu, X., Agrawal, P., Singh, J., Alpcan, T., Girod, B.: Distributed rate allocation policies for multihomed video streaming over heterogeneous access networks. IEEE Transactions on Media (2009)

[13] Zink, M., Kuenzel, O., Schmitt, J., Steinmetz, R.: Subjective impression of variations in layer encoded videos. In: International Workshop on QoS (2003)

[14] Zinner, T., Hohlfeld, O., Abboud, O., Hoßfeld, T.: Impact of Frame Rate and Resolution on Objective QoE Metrics. In: QoMEX (2010)

Mobile Video Streaming Using Location-Based Network Prediction and Transparent Handover

Kristian Evensen[1], Andreas Petlund[1,2], Haakon Riiser[3], Paul Vigmostad[3],
Dominik Kaspar[1], Carsten Griwodz[1,2], Pål Halvorsen[1,2]

[1]Simula Research Laboratory, Norway
[2]Department of Informatics, University of Oslo, Norway
[3]Netview Technology AS, Norway

ABSTRACT

A well known challenge with mobile video streaming is fluctuating bandwidth. As the client devices move in and out of network coverage areas, the users may experience varying signal strengths, competition for the available resources and periods of network outage. These conditions have a significant effect on video quality.

In this paper, we present a video streaming solution for roaming clients that is able to compensate for the effects of oscillating bandwidth through bandwidth prediction and video quality scheduling. We combine our existing adaptive segmented HTTP streaming system with 1) an application layer framework for creating transparent multi-link applications, and 2) a location-based QoS information system containing GPS coordinates and accompanying bandwidth measurements, populated through crowd-sourcing. Additionally, we use real-time traffic information to improve the prediction by, for example, estimating the length of a commute route. To evaluate our prototype, we performed real-world experiments using a popular tram route in Oslo, Norway. The client connected to multiple networks, and the results show that our solution increases the perceived video quality significantly. Also, we used simulations to evaluate the potential of aggregating bandwidth along the route.

Categories and Subject Descriptors

C.2.4 [**Computer-Communication Networks**]: Distributed Systems; H.5.1 [**Information Interfaces and Presentation**]: Multimedia Information Systems

General Terms

Performance, Reliability

Keywords

Performance, Multilink, Streaming, Location-based, Mobile devices, Roaming, Bandwidth prediction

1. INTRODUCTION

A large portion of the traffic on the Internet today is streamed multimedia content from services such as YouTube, Fancast, Hulu, Joost, Spotify and Last.fm, or from one of the many providers of live video and audio feeds like BBC, TV2 and NRK. To adapt to varying resource availability, media adaptation is frequently used, and in the case of video delivery, adaptive HTTP streaming (e.g., [13,15,22]) is currently the dominating technology. In the case of streaming to mobile clients, a well known problem is fluctuating bandwidth [18]. The current HTTP solutions enable the video quality to adapt and follow the bandwidth fluctuations in the network. However, challenges still include handling of network outages, moving into and out of networks and determining which video quality to use. The video quality should preferably not change too often, nor should it change by too many levels in a single jump as it negatively affects the user's perceived quality [14,23].

In this paper, we address the fluctuating bandwidth challenge in mobile streaming scenarios. The solution is based on our bandwidth prediction service [17] for commuters, which uses a lookup service to predict 3G (HSDPA) bandwidth availability based on the geographical location of a device. We extend this by combining it with a technique for transparent network roaming and connection handover, without requiring operating system (OS) modifications or introducing new network protocols. Multi-homed devices can jump between available networks, without changing applications running on top, and, for example, concurrently use several interfaces to achieve bandwidth aggregation [5].

The network and bandwidth lookup service relies on a database of monitored networks. The database is populated through crowd-sourcing and contains bandwidth measurements made at different geographical locations along different commuter routes. Streaming clients query the lookup service to predict and plan which networks to use when, and the amount of data that can be downloaded or streamed at different locations. Such a solution enables buffering to fill gaps that result from periods of no connectivity or handover delays, smooth out quality-reducing bandwidth fluctuations, and increasing the video quality if higher quality networks are available along the path.

Our HTTP-based streaming video system [8] was used to evaluate the performance of the solution described in this paper. The system divides videos into two second segments, and then encodes these segments at different bitrates. We present experimental results from a tram commute route in Oslo (Norway), where the multi-link framework seamlessly switched between WLAN and 3G networks, Oslo's real-time traffic information system (Trafikanten) provided hints about tram arrivals and the lookup service provided resource availability information along the path to plan for the best possible video quality. The experiments demonstrate significant improvements in perceived video quality.

The rest of the paper is structured as follows. Section 2 introduces examples of related work, while section 3 describes the location-based transparent handover solution. The results from our experiments are presented and discussed in section 4, and we conclude our work in section 5.

2. RELATED WORK

System support for mobile video streaming has for some time been a hot research topic, and many video services are available for mobile devices. A remaining challenge is to adapt streaming to the unpredictable behavior of wireless networks like General Packet Radio Service (GPRS) and High-Speed Downlink Packet Access (HSDPA). With mobile receivers in such networks, fluctuating network bandwidths strongly influence the video streaming service performance [4, 18], raising a need for bitrate adaptation to cope with temporary connection loss, appearance of new networks, high error rates, insufficient channel capacity, etc.

In the area of *video streaming to mobile devices*, there are several existing systems, and, as in the wired network scenario, adaptive HTTP streaming solutions are frequently used. For example, Apple's HTTP Live Streaming [15] is used with Quicktime and the Darwin Streaming server to stream to the iPhone, and Windows-based phones can use Microsoft's Smooth Streaming [22], i.e., both monitor the download speed of video segments and dynamically adapt to resource availability changes by switching between video segments coded in different qualities and bitrates. To deal with fluctuations and connection loss, most systems today (HTTP streaming included) perform pre-buffering.

All major operating systems (OS) support *multi-homing*, i.e., a client can be connected to multiple networks simultaneously. However, the default behavior is to only use one link at a time. Different ways of enabling multiple links have been suggested for every layer of the network stack, but all of the approaches are tuned to a specific application, scenario, require modifications to either end system or are based on invalid assumptions. For example, [11] makes significant changes to both the client and server, while [6] is based on assumptions that are not valid in real world networks (it requires changes in all WLAN-access points). An example of an application-specific multi-link solution is presented in [5]. We used multiple links simultaneously to improve an adaptive HTTP-based streaming solution.

Roaming clients has been a popular research topic for many years. In addition to the IETF-standardized Mobile IP [9,16], different solutions have been proposed. For example, the work done in [2] concludes in a semi-transparent handover solutions. No changes have to be made to the actual applications, however, the solution requires knowledge of the applications running on top (the port numbers). Also, it relies on active probing to determine if links are available and user interaction to switch between links. Another example is Wiffler [1], where the main idea is to delay transfers in order to save money. Applications that send data specify their delay threshold, and the solution makes use of a proxy, switches between 3G and WLAN and tries to predict

WLAN-availability. However, unlike our work, the WLAN-availability is calculated on the fly and network switching only works for upstream traffic, among others.

Lookup services for QoS information and prediction have been suggested before. For example, Horsmanheimo et al. [7] investigated the usefulness of location-aided planning and adaptive coverage systems for network planning and resource management of mobile networks, and Sun et al. [19] presented an idea of using network resource awareness on the application level. Moreover, Wac et al. [20] described a general QoS-prediction service containing real-world performance data, and the feasibility of using such predictions based on geographical location, time and historical data was proven for a mobile health monitoring application [21]. Liva et al. [12] predicted network outage gaps using a wave-guide theory model and calculated the signal behavior, and, recently, a geo-predictive media delivery system [3] has been presented that predicts network outages and pre-buffers video.

In summary, a lot of work describing useful components in order to build our target solution exists – either as envisioned ideas, simulations or different application scenarios. However, to the best of our knowledge, no other system integrates everything into one solution and presents a running prototype with real-world experiments, i.e., they do not experience all the possible real-world complications [10, 17]. Our solution predicts the availability of several networks and their bandwidths at the different locations along the path, and then it plans and adapts video quality to available bandwidth for a mobile device.

3. SYSTEM ARCHITECTURE

This section describes our individual components and how they are integrated to meet the challenges of mobile video streaming. First, we introduce the core concepts of our multi-link framework, called MULTI. Then, we describe the lookup service, before showing how we use these components for bitrate prediction and video quality scheduling.

3.1 MULTI

To the best of our knowledge, generic, transparent ways of enabling multiple links simultaneously does not exist. To allow for the development of transparent multi-link solutions, we have created our own framework, MULTI. MULTI monitors the network subsystem of a client device, configures the interfaces and routing subsystem, and enables multiple links simultaneously. The applications that implement MULTI have access to a continuously updated list of available network interfaces. In this section, we first introduce the framework, before describing how we used it to implement transparent connection handover.

3.1.1 Enabling multiple links

How MULTI was used to implement transparent roaming is summarized in figure 1. MULTI consists of several modules and a globally reachable proxy is its central element that allows for the creation of transparent multi-link solutions. Without it, the remote application (for example a web-server) would have to be changed in order to support multiple connections. This is often not possible or desirable.

When MULTI detects a change in link state on a multi-homed client (for example using Linux' RTNetlink library), the link module either requests an IP address using DHCP or reads it from a pre-loaded configuration. Once the required

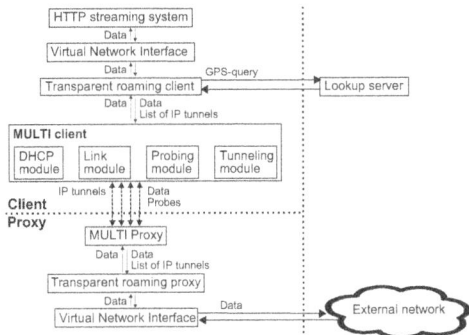

Figure 1: Roaming client architecture

information has been received or found, the link module configures the network interface (binds the IP address) and the routing tables. The routing tables must be updated, otherwise, the OS kernel does not know how to route packets to and from the different networks.

After the link has successfully been assigned an IP address, the link module notifies the probing module. The probing module is responsible for maintaining MULTI's multi-link overlay network between the client and the proxy. When notified of a change in link state, an IP tunnel is either added to or removed from the overlay network. Using IP tunnels allows MULTI to support most network and transport layer protocols. We use UDP as the tunneling transport protocol, and the probing module performs NAT hole punching by sending probes to the proxy with a configurable interval. The proxy replies to these probes, forcing the NAT to keep a state for each "connection". Finally, when a tunnel is added or has been removed, the application implementing MULTI is notified. The application is also informed of the different MTU sizes, allowing developers to, for example, discard packets that do not fit inside one or all of the tunnels.

The proxy-part of MULTI consists only of the probing module. Each tunnel is given a unique ID at the client, and each client a unique ID by the proxy. For each new tunnel, the proxy stores the "connection" information, and a list of all available tunnels is exposed to the proxy application. The probe packets contain also a list of all available tunnels. The probing module uses this information, in combination with timers, to determine when a tunnel has been removed and a link is no longer available.

3.1.2 Roaming and transparent handover

In order to support transparent connection handover, the transparent roaming client and proxy (the applications implementing MULTI) create virtual interfaces. Desired routes are configured to go through the virtual network, and applications cannot distinguish a virtual from an actual network interface. A virtual interface, however, is controlled by a user space application. All data sent to this interface is received by the application, and it is up to this application to send the data to the network.

To perform transparent handover, the roaming client at given intervals, or when changes in link state occurs, queries the lookup service described in the next section, using its GPS-coordinates. This service returns the capacity of the networks in the area, and the client selects the available link (tunnel) with the most capacity to use for upstream traffic. The ID of the selected tunnel is relayed to the roaming proxy, and the handover is completed when the proxy updates which tunnel it uses for downstream traffic. A han-

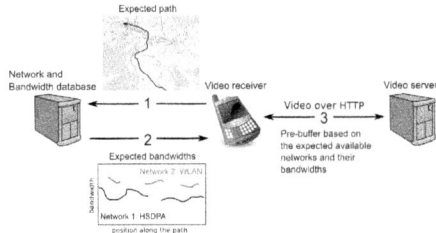

Figure 2: Streaming architecture

dover is also performed if a tunnel is removed. Because the "normal" applications on the multi-homed client are bound to the virtual interface, they will not be affected by the handover and will proceed as normal. Thus, they do not need to be modified to support handover.

The roaming proxy uses source NAT to enable the client requesting data outside of the overlay network. Source NAT rewrites the source IP of packets to be that of the proxy. The remote server believes it is connected to the proxy, and all packets destined for the client is routed through the proxy.

3.2 GPS-based lookup service

In [17], we introduced a *GPS-based bandwidth lookup service*. For the solution presented in this paper, we extended the lookup service with support for storing information about different alternative networks (shown in figure 2). The following steps are performed:

- The client requests network and bandwidth availability information along its intended route. The route is known in advance, for example a commute route.

- The lookup service returns the positions of the available networks and a sequence of bandwidth samples for each point listed in the path description.

- During a streaming session, the receiver combines the measured, observed bandwidth with stored data in the database of the lookup service. Knowing network availability and bandwidth oscillations that have been measured by other clients before, the streaming system can calculate the estimated number of bytes that it can download during the remaining time of the trip. This technique is explained in detail in [17].

Using this approach, it is possible to predict the amount of data that can be downloaded in the future to smooth the video quality over the whole session.

3.2.1 Network and bandwidth logging

To provide the datasets of observed real-world network availability and their bandwidths to the streaming devices, we rely on crowd-sourcing. The idea is that the users themselves populate the database with their perceived performance at a given location [20]. Supporting this step is not restricted to this particular service – a client can contribute to the improvement of the database whenever it performs bulk data transfer. During each video streaming session, the roaming client monitors streaming performance, and this information is reported back to the lookup service server and stored in the lookup database.

3.2.2 Lookup database

The data points representing the expected throughput at different geographical locations are, as described above, collected by the users of the video service, and the network information is stored in a database with standardized geographic information system (GIS) extensions for handling location-based calculations. The database used in our first prototype is PostgreSQL using the PostGIS extensions [1].

All the information about the network and the performance from one measurement at a given time is stored as a single record in the database. This record includes network id, time, GPS coordinates and observed performance metrics like bandwidth, round-trip time and packet loss rate. Applications can then, for example, send the query

```
SELECT network_id, AVG(bandwidth)
FROM table_observed_performance
WHERE query_gps = gps AND time < 10-days-old
GROUPBY network_id
```

which returns the predicted average bandwidth for all available networks at a given GPS location based on measurements from the last 10 days.

The above information is sufficient if a user moves arbitrarily around. However, users often follows a given path, e.g., when commuting (our scenario), which can be used to perform long-term bandwidth availability prediction. Our database therefore defines a table for known paths, such as well-known commute routes in Oslo, returning a list of GPS coordinates and the respective time spent at given locations (for example within the vicinity of a GPS-coordinate or at a station). Thus, using the query above for every location, the media downloader can calculate the predicted amount of data that can be downloaded. It gains the ability to fill gaps in the stream that are caused by expected network outages, and it can schedule for a more stable video quality.

Information about the network provider of a given network ID is kept in separate table, and can be used to look up relevant data such as pricing. Although such a policy is not implemented in our prototype, the user can then for example choose the cheapest network at a given position.

3.3 Video streaming and quality scheduling

In our commute scenario, the location-based network and bandwidth lookup service predicts the available networks and calculates their historically observed bandwidths along the path. Based on this, the segmented adaptive HTTP streaming system can make a target schedule for the video quality of each segment, targeting continuous playout (even during network outages) and a stable perceived quality (even during heavy bandwidth oscillations). Connection handover and link selection is currently performed transparently by the roaming client and proxy.

Our streaming system provides two video quality schedulers (described in detail in [17]) a *reactive* and a *predictive* algorithm. The reactive algorithm is basically intended for sessions where predictions are unavailable, and the quality levels that are chosen are decided by current bandwidth and buffer fullness. E.g., when the buffer reaches a certain size for a given level, the system is allowed to increase the quality. Similarly, when draining the buffer, the selected quality is reduced if the buffer shrinks below a threshold. Here, the thresholds are defined to avoid quality oscillations [17].

The predictive algorithm takes the bandwidths predicted by the lookup service as input and calculates the highest quality level that can be used for the rest of the trip without getting a buffer underrun anywhere (according to bandwidth predictions). Then, to adapt to deviations between observed

---

[1]http://postgis.refractions.net/

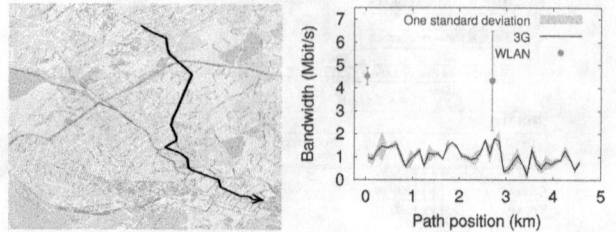

(a) Tram commute path   (b) Networks and bandwidths

Figure 3: Map and observed resource availability.

and predicted bandwidths, the schedule is recalculated occasionally to verify that the predicted resource availability matches the observed availability, and the selected quality adjusted if necessary. Additionally, to prevent too optimistic predictions, we use the reactive algorithm as a ceiling for the chosen quality. Also, if the transparent roaming client is forced to chose another network than the one with the highest stored bandwidth (which is used to create the segment quality schedule), a certain period of instability will occur until the HTTP streamer recalculates its schedule.

4. EXPERIMENTS AND RESULTS

To test our proposed solution, combining segmented adaptive HTTP streaming, multi-link and location-based QoS-information lookup services, we have performed real-world experiments on a tram commute route with different available networks in Oslo. Here, we present our results as a proof of concept.

4.1 Test scenario

Our real-world experiments was performed on a tram commute route between the University of Oslo (Blindern) and Oslo downtown, as shown in figure 3(a). Several networks with varying network availability depending on location are available along this route. Our client and server ran Linux 2.6.35, and the web server used was Apache 2. In our tests, the client was able to connect to the *Eduroam* WLAN [2], available at the University tram station and outside the Oslo University College, and the Telenor's [3] 3G network for the rest of the route. The predicted available bandwidths as a function of the distance from the start of the route are shown in figure 3(b). We observe that the WLAN has high bandwidth (compared to 3G), but it has a very limited range (tram stations only), whereas the 3G network was available everywhere along the path. To predict the duration of WLAN availabilities during our trip, we used the online traffic information systems Trafikanten to estimate the time until the arrival of the next tram.

For content, we used European soccer matches. These videos are encoded in 2-second segments where each segment is available in six quality levels for adaptation. The different quality levels range in average rates, from the lowest at 250 kbps to the highest at 3000 kbps.

4.2 Results

We performed three different sets of experiments: 1) 3G only, 2) switching between WLAN and 3G and 3) aggregating the WLAN and 3G bandwidths. For all tests, the performance of both video quality schedulers was evaluated. The

---

[2]http://www.eduroam.org
[3]http://www.telenor.no

first two sets of experiments were performed on the tram. Because any two runs will experience different conditions (for example, available bandwidth differ and the total travel time varies due to traffic), results using the other scheduler was simulated and plotted based on the gathered bandwidth traces. Thus, the real-world performance of the reactive scheduler was compared with simulated performance of the predictive scheduler, and opposite. This was done to get directly comparable results. Our bandwidth aggregation results were gathered using simulations.

4.2.1 3G only

3G was used as our base case and an average bandwidth of about 1000 kbps was observed. The 3G-network was available for the entire trip and it provided stable performance at all times of day. Thus, our prediction algorithm was able to improve the video quality significantly compared to the reactive scheduler, as shown in figure 4. The reactive scheduler, which resembles existing HTTP streaming solutions, followed the available bandwidth and gave a more unstable video quality than the predictive scheduler. With respect to the achieved quality, the video quality rarely exceeded level 4 at 750 kbps (level 5 requires about 1500 kbps).

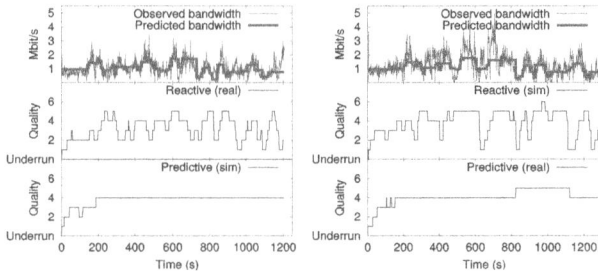

(a) Real-world: reactive   (b) Real-world: predictive

Figure 4: Only 3G

4.2.2 Switching networks (WLAN and 3G)

Figure 5 shows the results when the client switched between networks. The Eduroam WLAN always outperformed the 3G network, and was chosen whenever available. Both schedulers benefited from the increased capacity of the WLAN. The video quality was significantly higher than with 3G only (figure 4). With the predictive scheduler, the media player was allowed to stream at quality level 5 (1500 kbps) for most of the trip, compared to level 4 (750 kbps) when only 3G was used. The reason is that the higher bandwidth of the WLAN enabled the client to receive more data. Thus, it was able to work up a bigger buffer and could request segments in a higher quality. Also, the predictive scheduler achieved a much more stable video quality than the reactive scheduler.

As we described earlier, the handover was handled transparently, and with respect to handover performance, we have plotted the throughput for the streaming sessions from figure 5 in figure 6. From the plots, we can observe that the handover time is minimal and that the client receives data without any significant idle periods.

4.2.3 Aggregating networks (WLAN + 3G)

To evaluate the performance of aggregating WLAN and 3G, we simulated several streaming sessions. The simulated bandwidth of WLAN and 3G was based on traces from our real-world experiments. Because WLAN was only available

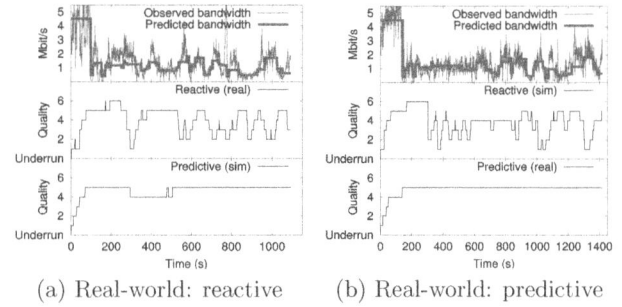

(a) Real-world: reactive   (b) Real-world: predictive

Figure 5: Switching between WLAN and 3G

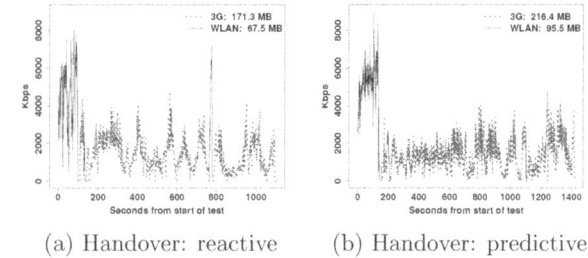

(a) Handover: reactive   (b) Handover: predictive

Figure 6: Achieved throughput and handovers

during the first minute or so of the route, the available bandwidth was most of the time equal to that of 3G.

The results from one representative set of simulations is shown in figure 7. As expected, the performance improved when more bandwidth was available. For example, when the client could aggregate WLAN and 3G bandwidths, the predictive scheduler was able to avoid a dip in quality towards the end. Also, the additional bandwidth allowed a faster growth in video quality.

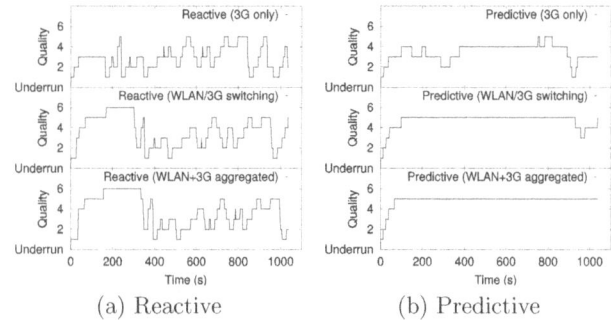

(a) Reactive   (b) Predictive

Figure 7: Perceived video quality: 3G only vs. WLAN/3G switching vs. WLAN+3G aggregated

4.3 Discussions

The solution and prototype implementation presented in this paper demonstrate the potential of combining adaptive HTTP-based video streaming with a predictive video quality scheduler, a location-based resource lookup service, transparent handover and bandwidth aggregation. However, there are still many issues that must be addressed.

The performance of networks varies depending on external factors such as weather conditions, network outages, time-of-day and day-of-week (e.g., rush hour differences), inaccurate position measurements, and so forth. The prototype used in this paper does not take any such factors into account. This requires long-term observation studies that we plan perform in future work.

Also, the current evaluations are all based on the assumption that users commute along a fixed path. However, this is not always the case. For example, the user might be in the passenger seat of a car. We are currently investigating several alternative scenarios, looking at path prediction, per-hop (between stations) bandwidth prediction, and so forth.

In the network switching scenario (section 4.2.2), there are several possible policies of how to chose which network to use. We chose to prioritize WLAN due to its higher bandwidth, which resulted in the highest achievable video quality. Another policy might prioritize based on power consumption or based on network pricing (some users may have very expensive 3G-data plans). For example, several providers [4] offer subscribers free access to WiFi-hotspots. By using these when they are available, a user can save both money (after an initial amount of data has been received, the user is charged per MB) and bandwidth (many providers reduce the bandwidth over 3G when a transfer cap is reached).

5. CONCLUSION

In this paper, we have presented a video streaming solution aimed at roaming clients that is able to reduce the effect of fluctuating bandwidth. Our solution enables the use of multiple networks, if available, and performs seamless handover if the client is within range of a network with a higher priority. Network selection is based on lookups in a QoS-database filled with GPS coordinates and corresponding bandwidth measurements. The database is populated by crowd-sourcing, and enables the video streaming client to predict bandwidth and schedule video quality.

The performance of a prototype was evaluated on a popular commute route. The results from the real-world experiments show that our proposed solution can increase perceived video quality. Also, we performed several simulations to determine the potential of bandwidth aggregation, with positive results. However, the are many challenges left to solve, and ongoing work includes the evaluation of various policies for changing and prioritizing networks, various factors such as time of day and bandwidth variation, more advanced techniques for path prediction and implementing bandwidth aggregation in our prototype.

6. REFERENCES

[1] BALASUBRAMANIAN, A., MAHAJAN, R., AND VENKATARAMANI, A. Augmenting mobile 3g using wifi. In *Proc. of ACM MobiSys* (2010), pp. 209–222.

[2] CARO, G. A. D., GIORDANO, S., KULIG, M., AND VANINI, S. Mobility across heterogeneous networks.

[3] CURCIO, I. D. D., VADAKITAL, V. K. M., AND HANNUKSELA, M. M. Geo-predictive real-time media delivery in mobile environment. In *Proc. of MoViD - ACM MM workshops* (Oct. 2010), pp. 3–8.

[4] DIAZ-ZAYAS, A., MERINO, P., PANIZO, L., AND RECIO, A. M. Evaluating video streaming over GPRS/UMTS networks: A practical case. In *Proc. of IEEE VTC Spring* (Apr. 2007), pp. 624–628.

[5] EVENSEN, K. R., KASPAR, D., GRIWODZ, C., HALVORSEN, P., HANSEN, A. F., AND ENGELSTAD, P. E. Improving the Performance of Quality-Adaptive Video Streaming over Multiple Heterogeneous Access Networks. In *Proc. of ACM MMsys* (2011), pp. 57–69.

[6] GUO, F., AND CHIUEH, T.-C. Device-transparent network-layer handoff for micro-mobility. In *Modeling,*

Analysis & Simulation of Computer and Telecommunication Systems (2009), pp. 1–10.

[7] HORSMANHEIMO, S., JORMAKKA, H., AND LÄHTEENMÄKI, J. Location-aided planning in mobile network-trial results. *Wireless Personal Communications 30* (2004), 207–216.

[8] JOHANSEN, D., JOHANSEN, H., AARFLOT, T., HURLEY, J., KVALNES, A., GURRIN, C., ZAV, S., OLSTAD, B., AABERG, E., ENDESTAD, T., RIISER, H., GRIWODZ, C., AND HALVORSEN, P. DAVVI: A prototype for the next generation multimedia entertainment platform. In *Proc. of ACM MM* (2009), pp. 989–990.

[9] JOHNSON, D., PERKINS, C., AND ARKKO, J. Mobility Support in IPv6. RFC 3775 (Proposed Standard), June 2004.

[10] KASPAR, D., EVENSEN, K., HANSEN, A. F., ENGELSTAD, P., HALVORSEN, P., AND GRIWODZ, C. An Analysis of the Heterogeneity and IP Packet Reordering over Multiple Wireless Networks. In *Proc. of IEEE ISCC* (2009).

[11] KIM, K.-H., AND SHIN, K. G. PRISM: Improving the Performance of Inverse-Multiplexed TCP in Wireless Networks. *IEEE Transactions on Mobile Computing* (2007).

[12] LIVA, G., DIAZ, N. R., SCALISE, S., MATUZ, B., NIEBLA, C. P., RYU, J.-G., SHIN, M.-S., AND LEE, H.-J. Gap filler architectures for seamless DVB-S2/RCS provision in the railway environment. In *Proc. of IEEE VTC Spring* (May 2008), pp. 2996–3000.

[13] MOVE NETWORKS. Internet television: Challenges and opportunities. Tech. rep., Move Networks, Inc., Nov 2008.

[14] NI, P., EICHHORN, A., GRIWODZ, C., AND HALVORSEN, P. Fine-grained scalable streaming from coarse-grained videos. In *Proc. ACM NOSSDAV* (2009), pp. 103–108.

[15] PANTOS, R., BATSON, J., BIDERMAN, D., MAY, B., AND TSENG, A. HTTP live streaming. http://tools.ietf.org /html/draft-pantos-http-live-streaming-04, 2010.

[16] PERKINS, C. IP Mobility Support for IPv4. RFC 3344 (Proposed Standard), Aug. 2002. Obsoleted by RFC 5944, updated by RFC 4721.

[17] RIISER, H., ENDESTAD, T., VIGMOSTAD, P., GRIWODZ, C., AND HALVORSEN, P. Video streaming using a location-based bandwidth-lookup service for bitrate planning (accepted for publication). *ACM Transactions on Multimedia Computing, Communications and Applications* (2011).

[18] RIISER, H., HALVORSEN, P., GRIWODZ, C., AND HESTNES, B. Performance measurements and evaluation of video streaming in HSDPA networks with 16QAM modulation. In *Proc. of IEEE ICME* (June 2008), pp. 489–492.

[19] SUN, J.-Z., SAUVOLA, J., AND RIEKKI, J. Application of connectivity information for context interpretation and derivation. In *Proc. of ConTEL* (2005), pp. 303–310.

[20] WAC, K., VAN HALTEREN, A., AND KONSTANTAS, D. Qos-predictions service: Infrastructural support for proactive qos- and context-aware mobile services (position paper). Springer Lecture Notes in Computer Science (vol. 4278). 2006, pp. 1924–1933.

[21] WAC, K., VAN HALTEREN, A., AND KONSTANTAS, D. QoS-predictions service: Infrastructural support for proactive QoS- and context-aware mobile services (position paper). In *Proc. of OTM Workshops*. 2006, pp. 1924–1933.

[22] ZAMBELLI, A. Smooth streaming technical overview. http://learn.iis.net/page.aspx/626/smooth-streaming-technical-overview/, 2009.

[23] ZINK, M., KÜNZEL, O., SCHMITT, J., AND STEINMETZ, R. Subjective impression of variations in layer encoded videos. In *Proc. of IWQoS* (2003), pp. 137–154.

---

[4]AT&T in the US and Telia in several European countries (through their Homerun-service) are two examples.

The Impact of Inter-layer Network Coding on the Relative Performance of MRC/MDC WiFi Media Delivery

Rohan Gandhi[1], Meilin Yang[1], Dimitrios Koutsonikolas[2],
Y. Charlie Hu[1], Mary Comer[1], Amr Mohamed[3], and Chih-Chun Wang[1]

[1]Purdue University, [2]University at Buffalo, SUNY, [3]Qatar University

{gandhir, yang144, ychu, comerm, chihw}@purdue.edu dimitrio@buffalo.edu amrm@qu.edu.qa

ABSTRACT

A primary challenge in multicasting video in a wireless LAN is to deal with the client diversity – clients may have different channel characteristics and hence receive different numbers of transmissions from the AP. A promising approach to overcome this problem is to combine scalable video coding techniques such as MRC or MDC, which divide a video stream into multiple substreams, with inter-layer network coding. The fundamental challenge in such an approach is to determine the strategy of coding the packets across different layers that maximizes the number of decoded layers at all clients. In [7], the authors showed that inter-layer NC indeed helps the delivery of MRC coded media over the WiFi, and proposed how to efficiently search for the optimal coding strategies online.

In this paper, we study (1) how NC can help with WiFi delivery of MDC media, and (2) in particular, due to the different decoding requirements of MDC from MRC, whether WiFi delivery of MDC media can benefit more from NC compared to that of MRC media. Our simulation results are somewhat surprising. Even though MDC is generally shown to outperform MRC in lossy channels, most of the benefit of MDC over MRC is lost after applying NC to both schemes.

Categories and Subject Descriptors

C.2.1 [**Computer Communication Networks**]: Network Architecture and Design—*Wireless Communication*

General Terms

Design, Performance

Keywords

streaming media, MDC, MRC, network coding, WiFi

1. INTRODUCTION

As both media content (e.g. youtube videos) over the Internet and wireless devices (e.g. smartphones) become increasingly popular, scalable delivery of rich media content over wireless hetero-geneous links, e.g., with varying Packet Delivery Ratios (PDRs), is quickly becoming one of the most important applications today.

A promising approach to dealing with receiver diversity is to exploit source-coding techniques such as Multi-Resolution Coding (MRC) [2] (also referred to as layered coding) and Multiple Description Coding (MDC) [4]. In contrast to a conventional media coder that generates a single bitstream, MRC and MDC encode a media source into multiple substreams and reception of more substreams generally improves the video quality. MRC divides the video into a base layer and multiple enhancement layers. The base-layer can be decoded to provide a basic quality of video while the enhancement layers are used to refine the quality of the video. If the base-layer is corrupted, the enhancement layers become useless, even if they are received perfectly. In contrast, in MDC, the substreams (or descriptions) are mutually refining, equally important, and independent. When the decoder receives more descriptions, the quality can be gradually increased no matter which description is received first.

In case of multiple clients, with diverse network conditions, the individual clients can independently decide how many substreams (layers or descriptions) to receive from the server according to their individual available bandwidth from the server. In a wireless network, however, all substreams transmitted share the medium; sending higher layers or more descriptions reduces the bandwidth available for sending lower layers/fewer descriptions.[1]

A promising approach to overcome the client diversity problem in delivering media content over WiFi is to combine using MRC/MDC streams with inter-layer network coding (NC) to maximize the number of useful layers that can be retrieved by the wireless receivers. In [7], the authors showed that inter-layer NC indeed helps the delivery of MRC coded media over the WiFi, and proposed how to efficiently search for the optimal coding strategies online.

The fundamental reason that inter-layer coding improves the number of decoded layers even for a single receiver is that it allows retrieving useful layers from more combinations of received transmissions; a scheme without coding could decode more layers by adjusting individual transmissions based on feedback after each transmission, which is costly and impractical when there are multiple clients. Further, this fundamental reason implies that inter-layer coding can also improve the case for multiple clients, which may have different combinations of received transmissions.

1.1 Related work

Several performance comparisons between MRC and MDC have been reported in the literature (e.g., [12, 11, 14, 8]). Summarizing

---

[1]For simplicity, we will use the term "layer" for both MRC layers and MDC descriptions in the remaining of the paper.

the findings from these studies, one can conclude that MDC outperforms MRC for networks with no feedback, long RTTs, or high loss rates.

MRC combined with network coding has been studied in the early years of the development of network coding. Recent analytical results focus on sustaining the largest possible rates for the MRC video applications with intra-layer (e.g [13]) or inter-layer network coding, both centrally [1] and distributively [6]. However, most results have focused on the wireline networks (or they convert the wireless network into its equivalent wireline counterpart), an approach which does not take into account randomness, one of the critical features of a wireless network. Recently, there have also been a few practical works that demonstrated the effectiveness of combining MRC video streaming with network coding in multihop wireless networks [3, 5], using simple heuristic coding strategies. In [7], the authors showed that such simple heuristics can perform poorly even for a single client, and proposed how to efficiently search for the optimal coding strategies online.

In contrast to MRC, to our best knowledge, almost no effort of combining MDC with network coding has been reported so far, with the exception of two recent, preliminary works [10, 9] focusing on wireline networks.

1.2 Problem Formulation

In this paper, we study (1) how NC can help with WiFi delivery of MDC coded media, and (2) in particular, due to the different decoding requirements of MDC from MRC, whether WiFi delivery of MDC media can benefit more from NC compared to that of MRC media. Intuitively, this appears to be the case; since there is no inter-layer dependence in MDC, receiving any K layers can lead to better quality of video compared to receiving less than K layers. In contrast, in MRC, receiving the Kth layer is only helpful if the previous $K - 1$ layers have been received. This second question is of particular interests as it will answer the question of practical importance: *whether MDC coupled with NC can lead to more efficient video delivery compared to MRC combined with NC.*

2. BACKGROUND

In popular video coding schemes such as H.264/AVC, the video content is partitioned into sequences of pictures, referred to as groups of pictures (GOPs), each beginning with an independently decodable intra-coded picture. A typical duration for a GOP is 1 to 2 seconds. Each GOP contains many pictures or frames. A GOP is divided into a sequence of packets for delivery over the network. Although a single frame may span multiple packets, or a single packet may contain more than one frame, we can assume that there will be multiple packets for a GOP, and in the case of constant bitrate video coding, the number of packets per GOP will be constant throughout a sequence.

We focus on network coding within each GOP. Let L be the number of layers/descriptions (typically 2-6) and Q be the number of packets per layer in a GOP. The value of Q depends on the streaming rate of the video. For example, an HD video of 12 Mbps coded in 4 layers, using 1000-byte packets corresponds to 375 packets per layer per (1-second) GOP.

Since Q can potentially be large, we divide up the Q packets per layer per GOP into multiple segments, so that the number of packets per segment (per layer) N is on the order of 8. This ensures that even when we code the packets from segments from all layers, the total number of packets is in the order of 32 (e.g. for 4 layers), which will not result in high coding/decoding overhead. Let X be the total number of transmissions the AP can have within the deadline of frames corresponding to the $N \cdot L$ packets for the L layers.

2.1 NC Helps Delivery of MRC

In [7], the authors showed that inter-layer network coding helps the delivery of MRC coded media over the WiFi, and proposed how to efficiently search for the optimal coding strategies online. We briefly review these results below.

Efficient Search of Optimal Strategies under MRC The primary challenge in combining inter-layer coding with MRC for WiFi delivery is how to find the optimal inter-layer coding strategy for a given channel condition, determined by the number of transmissions the AP can send before the deadline of a set of frames, and the packet deliver ratio (PDR) at the receiver(s). The most intuitive heuristic is to estimate the number of layers that can be decoded based on the expected number of received transmissions, and code packets from those many layers for all transmissions. While this strategy is expected to be optimal for the average cases (of reception outcomes), when dealing with small numbers of transmissions, due to the binomial distribution of reception outcomes, a carefully chosen strategy can outperform this simple though intuitive strategy.

[7] shows the naive way of searching all strategies for the optimal strategy has a complexity of $2^{LX} \cdot 2^X \cdot O((N \cdot L)^3)$. [7] then presents several optimizations that together enable efficient search of the optimal inter-layer coding strategies in real time, for practical scenarios, i.e., 4 layer segments with 8 packets per segment.

We first observe that since the X transmissions are assumed to be independent Bernoulli trails, the ordering in sending individual packets does not matter. Hence, two strategies are equivalent if their matrix presentations are the same after some row swapping. This suggests we just need to search among all the strategies that are not equivalent. Since there are only 2^L possible row vectors, or "bins", the total number of nonequivalent strategies is the same as the number of unique ways of assigning X transmissions to the 2^L bins, $\binom{X - 1 + 2^L}{2^L - 1}$. This is a drastic reduction from 2^{LX}.

Optimization 1: The main optimization is instead of searching for all possible 2^L coding strategies for each of the X transmission, we only need to consider the following L ways of coding packets from the L layers: the kth way being coding the first k layers, for $k = 1, ..., L$. Such a scheme can be denoted as $(x_1, ..., x_L)$, where $\sum_{i=1}^{L} x_i = X$, and x_i denotes the number of packets that code the first i layers. This optimization reduces the number of strategies to be searched down to $\binom{X - 1 + L}{L - 1}$. We will call a scheme that only considers the triangular canonical form of strategies **Canonical triangular scheme (Canonical-L)** in the remaining of the paper.

Optimization 2: The second optimization is to consider group transmission into groups of R packets, with each group always assigned the same coding strategy. This further reduces the number of coding strategies to $\binom{Z - 1 + L}{L - 1}$, where $Z = \frac{X}{R}$.

Optimization 3: The final optimization is to avoid Gaussian Elimination in calculating the number of layers that can be decoded for each outcome, using a simple calculation with a complexity of $O(L^2)$. This optimization takes advantage of the fact that all transmissions follow the canonical triangular coding scheme. [7] shows with these three optimizations, the time to search the optimal strategy is 0.13 seconds for $(L, N, X, R) = (4, 8, 64, 4)$.

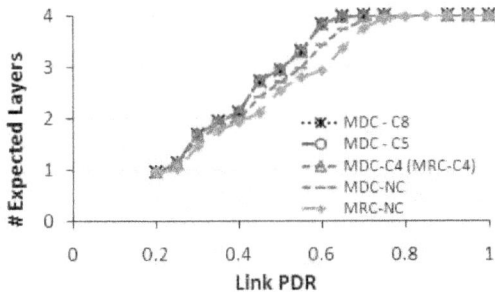

Figure 1: Performance comparison of different schemes for varying PDRs.

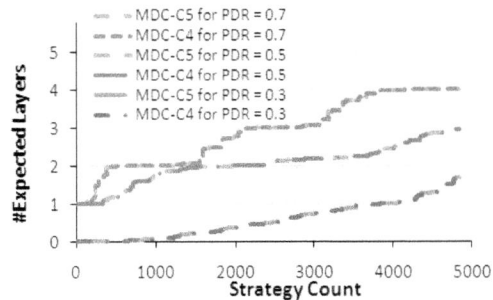

Figure 2: CDF for all the strategies at PDR = 0.7, 0,5 and 0.3 for MDC-C4 and MDC-C5.

3. HOW TO APPLY NC TO MDC

We first consider the case where the AP is trying to delivery an MDC video to a single client only. We then consider the case with multiple clients in the next section.

3.1 MDC vs. MRC

We first compare the performance of the two video encoding schemes without NC. We consider $(L, N, X, R) = (4, 8, 64, 4)$, (*i.e.,* we assume the two schemes have the same coding efficiency) and vary the PDR p at the client.

The two lower curves of Figure 1 (MRC-NC and MDC-NC) plot the average (out of all possible reception outcomes) number of decoded layers under the best transmission strategy, using MRC and MDC, respectively, with **N**o (Network) **C**oding. We observe that MDC outperforms MRC by as much as 17%. In MDC, there is no inter-layer dependency, and hence, receiving any K layers can lead to better quality of video compared to receiving less than K layers. In contrast, in MRC, the Kth layer is only helpful if the previous $K-1$ layers have been received.

Given that (i) MDC outperforms MRC and (ii) NC improves the performance of MRC ([7]), intuitively one would expect NC to also boost the performance of MDC and most importantly, MDC to benefit more from NC compared to MRC. In the following, we are we are trying to answer these two questions.

3.2 Adding NC to MDC

The intuition for the optimal coding strategy under MRC being of canonical triangular form comes from the very nature of MRC encoding: as mentioned before, receiving the Kth layer is only helpful if the previous $K-1$ layers have been received. For example, there is no need to deliver the second layer by itself, since if the first layer is received, delivering coded first and second layers is no different from delivering the second layer by itself; and if the first layer is not received, delivering the second layer is useless.

The above reasoning does not work for MDC, as receiving any descriptions contributes to the final quality of the video. Therefore, in principle, we need to consider all strategies, which can be prohibitively costly to search. We propose two heuristic schemes, in addition to **Canonical-L**, that exploit the nature of MDC to search more strategies than the canonical triangular scheme.

Canonical-(L+1): This scheme considers $(L+1)$ ways of inter-layer coding: in addition to the L canonical ways of coding, *i.e.,* the first K layers each, for $K = 1, ..., L$, it also considers layer 2 alone. The rational is to exploit the delivery of layer 2 by itself, since receiving layer 2 is as productive as receiving layer 1, under MDC. Complexity-wise, there are a total of $\binom{X+L}{L}$ unique

ways of assigning X packets to the $(L+1)$ ways of generating the coded packets in this scheme.

Canonical-(L+4): This scheme considers $(L+4)$ ways of inter-layer coding: in addition to the L ways in Canonical-L, it also considers layer 2 alone, layer 3 alone, coded layers 1 and 3, and coded layers 2 and 3. Complexity-wise, there are a total of $\binom{X+L+3}{L+3}$ unique ways of assigning X packets to the $(L+5)$ ways of generating the coded packets in this scheme. For the typical values of $(L, N, X, R) = (4, 8, 64, 4)$, the above three schemes will explore 969, 4845, 245157 strategies, respectively.

Comparing different NC schemes for MDC We first compare the performance of different NC schemes with MDC for a single client. The goal is to evaluate the benefit of considering more strategies for NC-based MDC videos. We denote MDC combined with Canonical-4, Canonical-5, and Canonical-8 as MDC-C4, MDC-C5, and MDC-C8, respectively. The three upper curves of Figure 1 plot the average (out of all possible reception outcomes) number of decoded layers under the best transmission (coding) strategy, using MDC-C4, MDC-C5, and MDC-C8, respectively. We observe that, the performance benefit of MDC-C5 and MDC-C8 over MDC-C4 is negligible; the maximum gain is less than 0.5%.

The reason for the negligible performance gain of MDC-C5 and MDC-C8 over MDC-C4, in spite of considering many more coding strategies, is that, for every PDR, *the maximum number of decoded layers with MDC-C4 is the same (or almost the same) as the maximum number of decoded layers with MDC-C5 for at least one strategy*. This is observed in Figure 2, which plots the average number of decoded layers for each MDC-C4 and MDC-C5 strategy under three different PDRs. MDC-C5 strategies cover all the MDC-C4 strategies and each MDC-C4 strategy is plotted against the MDC-C5 strategy it matches. Since the graphs overlap for a given PDR, there is no performance benefit in using MDC-C5 than MDC-C4.

Does NC help MDC? Figure 1 shows that NC helps MDC but the gains are moderate. MDC-C4 outperforms MDC-NC by 0-13.25%.

Does NC help MDC more compared to MRC? We saw that, when applying NC to MDC videos in the case of a single client, it is sufficient to use the triangular scheme Canonical-4 which has been shown in [7] to be optimal for MRC videos. This observation has an important implication. **Assuming that MDC and MRC have the same coding efficiency, i.e., they share the same parameters L and N per delivery segment within which we perform NC, the benefit of applying NC is the same for both schemes.** In other words, MDC-C4 is exactly the same as MRC-C4 and the results for MDC-C4 apply in the same way to MRC-C4 too. This can be explained by the properties of the canonical scheme. If any higher numbered layer is decoded by MDC-C4, all layers below it are also

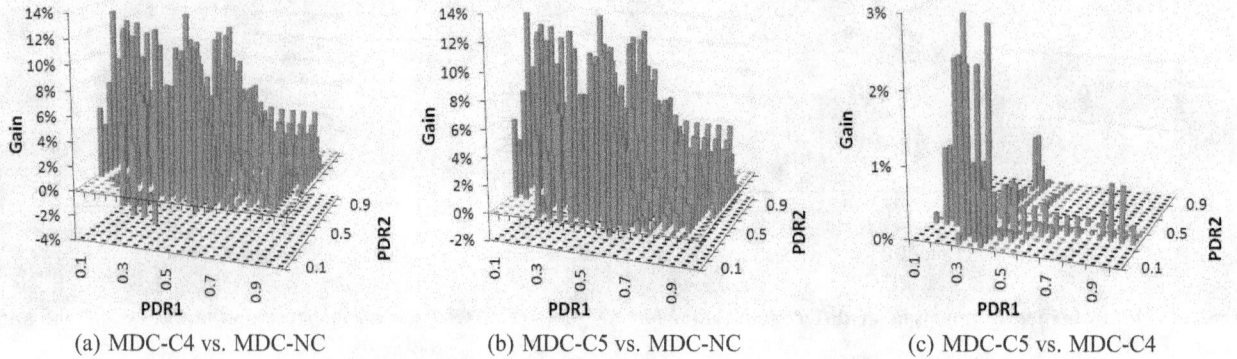

(a) MDC-C4 vs. MDC-NC   **(b) MDC-C5 vs. MDC-NC**   **(c) MDC-C5 vs. MDC-C4**

Figure 3: The benefit of applying NC to MDC in the case of 2 clients.

decoded due to NC, which is true for MRC-C4 too. In the rest of the paper, the results for MDC-C4 also apply to MRC-C4 with the same efficiency. Hence, *the benefit of MDC over MRC in the case of a single client is lost when we apply NC to both schemes.* In Figure 1, we have included MRC-C4 in parentheses next to MDC-C4. From now one, we will use these two terms interchangeably.

The next question is whether these conclusions hold when a video is multicast to more than one client with a diverse set of PDRs. In such a cases, for an MRC video, we are still limited to the Canonical-4 scheme. However, for an MDC video it may be worth using a higher complexity coding scheme (Canonical-5 or Canonical-8) which provides more strategies to choose from and hence, greater flexibility in dealing with heterogeneous clients.

4. MULTIPLE CLIENTS

In case of multiple clients, we multicast the network coded packets using 802.11 broadcast. As the PDR can be different for different clients, the number of decoded layers will also be different. This is effectively a multi-objective optimization problem as suggested in [7]. The server scans through all the strategies and selects a strategy that maximizes the objective function. In this paper, we consider the objective function of maximizing the sum of decoding layers for all the clients.

4.1 Does NC help MDC more with multiple clients than with a single client?

Figures 3(a) and 3(b) compare the performance of MDC-C4 over MDC-NC and MDC-C5 over MDC-NC, respectively, in the case of two clients. The height of each bar shows the gain in terms of the average number of decoded layers under the best coding strategy (*i.e.,* the one that optimizes the sum of the decoded layers for the two clients) for a given PDR pair.

MDC-C4 vs. MDC-NC. From Figure 3(a) we observe that MDC-C4 outperforms MDC-NC for most PDR pairs with the performance benefit being as high as 13%. Generally, this is consistent with Section 3.2, where we saw that the gain of MDC-C4 over MDC-NC varies from 0-13.5% for a single client. However, it should also be noted that MDC-C4 performs worse than MDC-NC for some PDR pairs, especially at low PDRs.

MDC-C5 vs. MDC-NC From Figure 3(b), we observe that the performance gain of MDC-C5 over MDC-NC can be as high as 13%, *i.e.,* similar to that of MDC-C4 over MDC-NC. However, overall the performance is improved and MDC-C5 outperforms MDC-NC for most of the PDR pair where MDC-NC outperforms MDC-C4.

This is because, MDC-C5 has an additional option to transmit layer 2 packets alone at the lower PDRs, which is similar to MDC-NC.

4.2 Does NC help MDC more than MRC with multiple clients?

In the case of a single client, we have seen that the benefit of MDC over MRC is lost when we apply NC to both schemes. Figure 3(c) compares the performance of MDC-C5 vs. MRC-C4 (which is equivalent to MDC-C4) for two clients. We observe that the conclusion for the single client case generally holds true for two clients as well. The benefit of MDC-C5 over MRC-C4 is always less than 3%. As we saw in Figure 2, the additional strategies considered by MDC-C5 do not provide any significant benefit for any PDR compared to the best MDC-C4 strategy. MDC-C5 only performs slightly better than MRC-C4 at lower PDRs. At the lower PDRs, the server mostly sends packets with 1 or 2 layers coded. To send 2 layers, MRC-C4 needs to code packets from layer 2 and layer 1, whereas MDC-C5 has an additional option to send layer 2 packets without coding with packets from layer 1. This way, MDC-C5 behaves more or less like MDC-NC.

5. ONLINE WIFI MULTICAST OF MDC MEDIA USING NC

In the previous two sections we assumed that the AP had perfect knowledge of the PDR of each client and the transmission budget X. In practice, the AP learns these parameters through feedback from the clients. In this section, we evaluate the benefits of applying NC to MDC in an online multicast system. In [7], the authors presented an online video delivery scheme, Percy, deployed at a proxy behind the AP of a WLAN. The proxy in real time collects loss rates for different clients, searches for the optimal NC strategy (assuming MDC or MRC coded video), and generates coded packets for the AP to broadcast. In Section 5.1, we give a brief overview of Percy's main components. We then describe the evaluation methodology in Section 5.2, and evaluate the performance of Percy with MDC and MRC videos using simulations in Sections 5.3 and 5.4.

5.1 Percy overview

Percy consists of 3 main building blocks:

PDR feedback from clients The AP transmits each packet it receives from the proxy using 802.11 broadcast. The clients periodically send feedback to the proxy to allow it to obtain an estimate of their PDRs. We use a lightweight scheme in which each client reports every 200 ms the *total* number of packets since the last report. These feedback messages are forwarded by the AP to the proxy.

Online Estimation of X and PDRs The proxy (1) continuously monitors the number of transmissions X' it can make in each GOP. The total transmission X' is divided equally among the segments constituting the GOP, i.e., X per segment; and (2) receives the periodic PDR feedbacks from each client, which are sent back to the proxy at fixed instants during every GOP.

At the end of GOP i, the proxy uses the measured X and PDRs as the predicted values for GOP $i+1$, to calculate a Strategy Performance Table (SPT) that lists the number of layers decoded for all possible strategies for the given L and X, using resolution $R = 4$, for all PDRs ranging from 5% to 100% with increments of 5%. As shown in [7], this calculation can be finished in less than 0.13 sec for typical values of (L, N, X, R), e.g. (4,8,64,4).

Calculating the optimal coding strategy For any given objective function, e.g., the sum of the layers that can be retrieved at each client, the proxy scans through all the coding strategies in the SPT, and finds the one that maximizes the objective function for the set of clients, based on their PDRs. This strategy is then used for all the segments consisting the next GOP.

5.2 Evaluation Methodology

We used the Glomosim simulator [15]. We placed an AP in the center of the simulation area and the clients uniformly on a circle around the AP. To evaluate the performance of the protocols under different loss scenarios, the clients were placed close to the AP and we generated link loss rates in a controlled manner, by artificially dropping packets at each client following a Bernoulli model.

We used the 802.11 MAC layer with a fixed bitrate of 5.5Mbps and RTS/CTS disabled, as in most operational networks. Data packets were broadcast at the MAC layer. The feedback messages sent by Percy clients were unicast at the MAC layer for increased reliability.

The video stream was a constant bit rate (CBR) traffic over UDP at 2.56 Mbps for a duration of 100 sec. The GOP duration was set to 1 sec. The stream consisted of $L = 4$ layers. Each layer included 80 1000-byte packets and was divided into 10 segments of $N = 8$ packets each.

5.3 Evaluation with a Single Client

Figure 4 shows the average number of decoded layers under different media coding schemes (MDC or MRC), with or without NC. We make the following observations: (i) Without network coding, MDC outperforms MRC. The gain of MDC-NC over MRC-NC is 0-25.08%. (ii) NC improves the performance of MDC. The gain of MDC-C4 and MDC-C5 over MDC-NC is 24.3% and 28.7% respectively. These gains are higher than the gains we observed in Section 3. (iii) The gain of MDC over MRC is lost when we apply NC to both schemes. The gain of MDC-C5 over MRC-C4 is at most 4.3%. Even though this is slightly higher compared to the offline gain in Section 3, it is still too low to justify using MDC-C5 instead of MDC-C4.

5.4 Evaluation with Multiple Clients

Applying NC to MDC Figures 5(a), 5(b) show the gain of MDC-C4 and MDC-C5 over MDC-NC, respectively. In Figure 5(a), we observe that MDC-C4 outperforms MDC-NC by up to 19%. This is higher than the offline analysis gain (up to 13.5%) in Section 4. Similar to Figure 3(a), there are a few cases where MDC-NC performs better than MDC-C4 by up to 3.28%. Figure 5(b) shows that MDC-C5 improves the performance in most of the cases where MDC-C4 performs worse than MDC-NC. However, the maximum

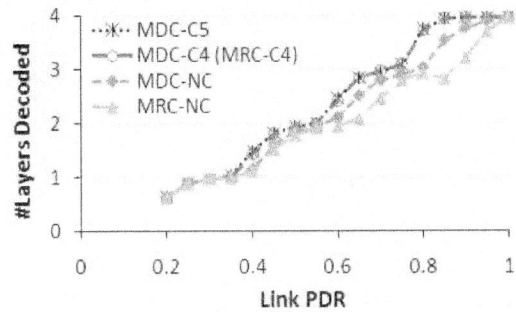

Figure 4: Performance comparison of different schemes in Glomosim for a single client.

gain of MDC-C5 over MDC-NC is 19%, equal to the maximum gain of MDC-C4 over MDC-NC.

Comparing different NC schemes for MDC Figure 5(c) shows the gain of MDC-C5 over MRC-C4. MDC-C5 outperforms MRC-C4 by up to 8.5%. Our offline analysis in Section 4 showed that the gain was always lower than 3%. Note that MDC-C5 outperforms MRC-C4 mostly at low PDRs. The lack of inter-layer dependency of MDC makes it more resilient to imperfect PDR and bandwidth estimation, which is unavoidable in an online system.

Of course, the 8.5% gain of MDC-C5 comes at the cost of increased complexity. Our measurements in [7] show that an SPT for MRC(MDC)-C4 can be constructed in less than 0.13 sec. The construction of an SPT for MDC-C5 takes much longer. However, in cases when the bandwidth does not change rapidly, one may not have to recalculate the SPT at the beginning of each GOP. In those cases, MDC-C5 can be used in place of MDC-C4 to increase performance by up to 8.5%.

Varying the number of clients We also evaluate the performance gain of network coding when the number of clients varies from 2 to 6 clients. For each case, we ran 100 different simulation scenarios; in each scenario the client PDRs are chosen uniformly randomly from the range [0.2, 0.9]. Figures 6(a), 6(b) and 6(c) plot the CDF of the gain of MDC-C5 and MDC-C4 over MDC-NC for 2, 4 and 6 clients respectively. Similar to 2 clients, MDC-C4 and MDC-C5 outperform MDC-NC for 4 and 6 clients but the benefit is small and it reduces with the number of clients (up to 18% for 4 clients and up to 13% for 6 clients). Also, the benefit of MDC-C5 over MRC-C4 is always negligible.

6. CONCLUSION

Motivated by the result of [7] (NC can help the delivery of MRC coded media over WiFi), in this paper, we studied whether NC can also help the delivery of MDC media, and in particular, if MDC combined with NC performs better than MRC combined with NC. Intuitively, this should be the case, as with no inter-layer dependency in MDC, receiving any K layers can lead to better quality of video compared to receiving less than K layers. Rather surprisingly, our simulation study shows that, even though MDC generally outperforms MRC without network coding, most of the benefit of MDC over MRC is lost after applying network coding to both schemes.

Note that, in this paper, our evaluation metric was the average number of decoded layers rather than the PSNR metric, which is traditionally used for video delivery schemes. However, since the two schemes deliver similar number of layers when combined with NC and MDC generally performs very poorly in terms of coding efficiency compared to MRC, the PSNR relationship can easily be

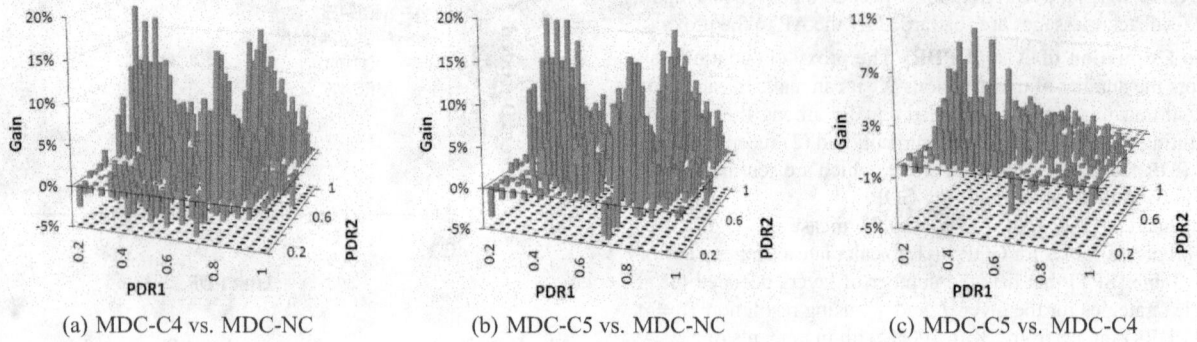

(a) MDC-C4 vs. MDC-NC   (b) MDC-C5 vs. MDC-NC   (c) MDC-C5 vs. MDC-C4

Figure 5: The benefit of applying NC to MDC in case of 2 clients in Glomosim.

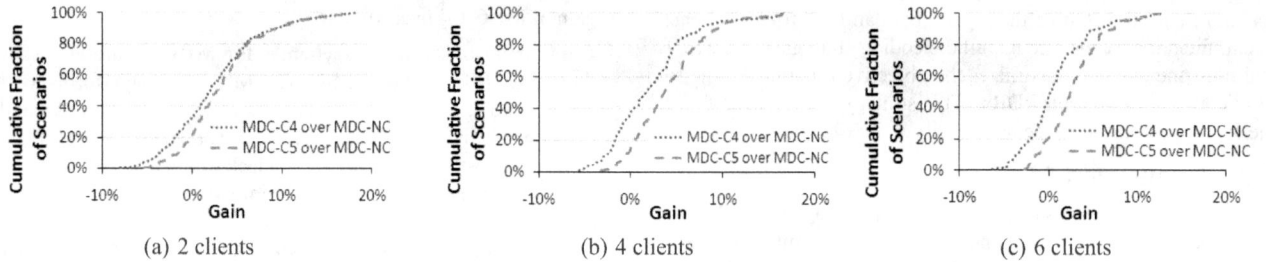

(a) 2 clients   (b) 4 clients   (c) 6 clients

Figure 6: CDFs of gain of MDC-C4 and MDC-C5 over MDC-NC for 2, 4 and 6 clients.

deduced by our results, i.e., for the same capacity, MRC with NC will typically deliver higher PSNR than MDC with NC.

Acknowledgment

This work was supported in part by NSF grants CCF 0845968, CNS 0905331, and Qatar National Research Fund (QNRF) No.08-374-2-144.

7. REFERENCES

[1] S. Dumitrescu, M. Shao, and X. Wu. Layered multicast with interlayer network coding. In *Proc. of IEEE INFOCOM*, 2009.

[2] M. Effros. Universal multiresolution source codes. *IEEE Trans. on Information Theory*, 47(6), 2001.

[3] S. Gheorghiu, L. Lima, J. Barros, and A. L. Toledo. On the performance of network coding in multi-resolution wireless video streaming. In *Proc. of IEEE NetCod 2010*, 2010.

[4] V. Goyal. Multiple description coding: compression meets the network. *IEEE Signal Processing Magazine*, 18:74–93, Sept 2001.

[5] M. Halloush and H. Radha. Practical network coding for scalable video coding in error prone networks. In *Proc. of Picture Coding Symposium (PCS)*, 2009.

[6] M. Kim, D. Lucani, X. shi, F. Zhao, and M. Médard. Network coding for multi-resolution multicast. In *Proc. of IEEE INFOCOM*, 2010.

[7] D. Koutsonikolas, Y. C. Hu, C.-C. Wang, M. Comer, and A. Mohamed. Online wifi delivery of layered-coding media using inter-layer network coding. In *Proc. of IEEE ICDCS*, 2011.

[8] Y.-C. Lee, J. Kim, Y. Altunbasak, and R. M. Mersereau. Layered coded vs. multiple description coded video over error-prone networks. *Elsevier Signal Processing: Image Communication*, 18:337–356, 2003.

[9] H. H. Maza'ar and H. N. Elmahdy. Multiple description coding based network coding. *International Journal of Computer Applications (IJCA)*, 6(9), 2010.

[10] A. K. Ramasubramonian and J. W. Woods. Multiple description coding and practical network coding for video multicast. *IEEE Signal Processing Letters*, 17(3), 2010.

[11] A. Reibman, Y. Wang, X. Qiu, Z. Jiang, and K. Chawla. Transmission of multiple description and layered video over an EGPRS wireless network. In *Proc. of IEEE ICIP*, 2000.

[12] R. Singh, A. Ortega, L. Perret, and W. Jiang. Comparison of multiple description coding and layered coding based on network simulations. In *SPIE Conference on Visual Communication Image Processing*, 2000.

[13] N. Sundaram, P. Ramanathan, and S. Banerjee. Multirate media stream using network coding. In *Proc. of 43rd Annual Allerton Conference on Communication, Control, and Computing*, 2005.

[14] Y. Wang, S. Panwar, S. Lin, and S. Mao. Wireless video transport using path diversity: multiple description vs. layered coding. In *Proc. of IEEE ICIP*, 2002.

[15] X. Zeng, R. Bagrodia, and M. Gerla. Glomosim: A library for parallel simulation of large-scale wireless networks. In *Proc. of PADS Workshop*, May 1998.

A Measurement Study of Resource Utilization in Internet Mobile Streaming

Yao Liu[1]   Fei Li[1]   Lei Guo[2]   Songqing Chen[1]
[1]Department of Computer Science   [2]Microsoft Corporation
George Mason University   Mountain View, CA, USA
{yliud, lifei, sqchen}@cs.gmu.edu   leguo@microsoft.com

ABSTRACT

The pervasive usage of mobile devices and wireless networking support have enabled more and more Internet streaming services to all kinds of heterogeneous mobile devices. However, Internet mobile streaming services are challenged by the inherently limited on-device resources, device heterogeneity, and the bulk amount of streaming data.

In this paper, focusing on resource utilization and streaming quality on mobile devices, we investigate 10 deployed Internet mobile streaming services that employ client-server, client-proxy-server, and P2P architectures from a client's perspective. We find that (1) existing Internet mobile streaming services mainly use the client-server architecture and commonly adopt burst traffic delivery that can save battery power consumption on mobile devices; (2) to deal with device heterogeneity, some streaming services have already utilized intermediate nodes (often the user's home computer) for online transcoding with a client-proxy-server architecture, but currently they lack power-friendly design for mobile devices; (3) a mobile device in P2P streaming consumes significantly more battery power mainly due to the inevitable P2P control traffic and uploading traffic to other peers. These findings provide us new insights to further optimize Internet mobile streaming in the future.

Categories and Subject Descriptors

C.2.4 [**Distributed Systems**]: Distributed applications

General Terms

Experimentation, Algorithms

Keywords

Mobile Streaming, Battery, Power, Resource Utilization, QoS

1. INTRODUCTION

Recent years have witnessed the rapid development and wide deployment of the 802.11 and the third generation wireless networks. For example, Jupiter Research estimated 65% of households in the United States have home-deployed WiFi access points (APs) [1]. Meanwhile, the smartphone market is also growing very fast. By September 2010, over 58.7 million people in the US owned smartphones [2]. With the most recent technology advancements, people today are more inclined to use their mobile devices to access the Internet.

In tandem with pervasive mobile Internet accesses, the Internet media streaming services are widely accessed with the rich and fast growing Internet bandwidth and streaming media content. For example, according to Comscore, 146.3 million viewers watched more than 2 billion videos on Youtube in October 2010 [3]. Many P2P/overlay based systems, such as PPLive [4] and PPStream [5], have enabled easy and highly scalable live streaming in practice and have attracted millions of users daily [6].

Naturally, under these two trends, there is a quickly increasing demand for Internet streaming to mobile devices (Internet mobile streaming hereafter). For this purpose, both iOS and Android have native support for YouTube. Targeting this market, more and more content providers now allow their customers to access multimedia content on their mobile devices via wireless connections. Most recently, Netflix [7] started to provide streaming services to subscribed iPad, iPhone, and iPod Touch users. However, delivering high quality Internet streaming to mobile devices faces several challenges due to inherent constraints of mobile devices.

First, compared to the traditional desktop computers, mobile devices commonly have limited resources, such as slower CPU speed, smaller memory and storage sizes, and limited battery power. Among these resources, the battery power poses a fundamental constraint. For Internet streaming, it often involves bulk and continuous data transmissions with stringent timing requirements. As a result, it demands continuous operations of the mobile device, including the wireless network interface card (WNIC) to receive the data, the CPU to decode the received data, and the screen to display the media content.

Second, mobile devices are very heterogeneous, differing from each other and from traditional desktop computers on not only the uploading/downloading bandwidth capacities, but also the screen sizes, the color depths, etc., which we refer to as *multi-dimensional heterogeneity*. Thus, most of the current popular Internet streaming content must be customized to the appropriate image resolution, size, frame rate, and bit rate for each mobile device. Such customizations could be done in advance or at runtime. For example, for pre-recorded video clips, it is possible to pre-code various versions of the same content. On the other side, if the customization is done at runtime, it demands a great deal of CPU cycles at either the server or the client side.

Despite these technical difficulties, Internet mobile streaming services are booming. For example, CTV [8], CCTV [9], WTV [10], ImgoTV [11], and NHKworld [12] all allow iOS users to access their live TV programming content via 3G or WiFi network. SPBtv [13] supports more diverse platforms including iOS, Android, and WebOS. It also provides a great variety of live TV channels from different countries. Orb [14] and AirVideo [15] allow users to access media content stored on their home computers. Justin.tv [16] even enables users to watch live streaming content broadcasted by other users. While these services become more and more popular on the Internet and potentially contribute a significant portion of Internet traffic, it remains unclear how they have addressed the aforementioned problems and how effective their schemes are in practice.

In this paper, we investigate these Internet mobile streaming services from an end user's perspective. In particular, we focus on the resource consumption on mobile devices and the streaming quality received at the client side. For this purpose, we conduct Internet measurements on 10 different Internet mobile streaming services using client-server, client-proxy-server, and P2P architectures. Our measurement and analysis show that (1) existing Internet mobile streaming services mainly use the client-server architecture and commonly adopt burst traffic delivery techniques that can save the power consumption on mobile devices; (2) to deal with device heterogeneity, some streaming services have already utilized intermediate nodes (often the user's home computer) for online transcoding with a client-proxy-server architecture. While the intermediate proxies provide great convenience for heterogeneous mobile devices, currently they lack power-friendly design for mobile devices; (3) a mobile device in P2P streaming consumes significantly more battery power mainly due to the inevitable P2P control traffic and uploading traffic to other peers, although the P2P architecture is most scalable. Based on these findings, we can further optimize existing Internet mobile streaming systems.

2. INTERNET MOBILE STREAMING AND MEASUREMENT METHODOLOGY

In this section, we briefly illustrate the three typical architectures of existing Internet mobile streaming applications, and then describe our measurement methodology.

2.1 Internet Mobile Streaming

Today Internet mobile streaming applications mainly use three different architectures: client-server (C/S), client-proxy-server (C/P/S), and peer-to-peer (P2P).

2.1.1 Client-Server (C/S) Architecture

C/S is the most traditional and popular architecture. Typically, within this architecture, a mobile device requests streaming data from a dedicated server using standard HTTP protocols. HTTP live streaming was made available on iOS 3.0 in July 2009 [17].

In C/S based streaming applications, we evaluate CTV, CCTV, W.TV, Imgo.TV, Justin.tv, SPBtv, and NHKworld.

In these applications, the media content is encoded as MPEG-4 audio and video, and transported via TCP using MPEG-2 Transport Stream (MPEG2-TS). A `.ts` file typically contains 10 second media content. For streaming access, the client queries the server for streaming content about every 10 seconds and the server replies with links to several `.ts` files, each of which contains media content for the next a few (typically 10) seconds in MPEG2-TS format. These files are reassembled after being downloaded and fed into the Media Player for playback.

2.1.2 Client-Proxy-Server (C/P/S) Architecture

Recently, placeshifting streaming services are getting popular. A placeshifting streaming system generally employs a C/P/S architecture, where an intermediary unit, referred to as a transcoding proxy, is needed for content customization. In addition, the placeshifting service provider may also set up a relay proxy to relay the content between the placeshifting server and the mobile device.

In our study, we examine Orb and AirVideo, both of which use personal computers as the placeshifting server and the transcoding proxy. In Orb, a user can set up the placeshifting server at home and register its available multimedia content with the Orb relay proxy. To access streaming services, the placeshifting server with a built-in transcoding proxy would transcode the video content based on its uploading bandwidth, the downloading bandwidth of the mobile device, and the supported codec on the mobile device. Unlike Orb that has been initially released in 2005, AirVideo does not have good support for remote accesses.

2.1.3 Peer-to-Peer (P2P) Architecture

Lots of Internet streaming systems today have adopted P2P techniques. While different protocols have been extensively studied, in practice, most systems use a pull based mesh structure, in which peers need to frequently exchange control messages [6], such as buffermaps, in order to determine the data chunks to exchange with each other.

In this study, we investigate TVUPlayer [18], which uses a peer-to-peer architecture to distribute live streaming content. To the best of our knowledge, TVUPlayer is the only P2P based live streaming application available on iOS at the time of this measurement. Instead of using TCP, it uses UDP for streaming delivery.

2.2 Methodology

In the experiments, we use the second generation iPod Touch (iTouch) running firmware version 3.1.2 to receive streaming services. The device is jailbroken to install essential tools for logging performance statistics. The iTouch is instructed to access 10 Internet mobile streaming services.

In the measurement, we record all incoming/outgoing data to/from our testing device at the data link layer by setting up Wireshark to listen on the same channel as the iTouch in promiscuous mode. For performance analysis, we also have logged both statistics of battery power consumption and CPU usage. We take a snapshot of battery state directly from battery every 30 seconds and we log kernel I/O statistics and CPU usage every 15 seconds. In order to minimize disturbance during the measurement, we mute the speaker on the device. We also set the screen backlight to 35 (max 127) and disable auto-adjustment.

As we do not have access to the server logs, we run our devices to access these streaming services repetitively. The reported results in this paper are based on experiments conducted from 03/20/2010 – 05/10/2010. Since we run experiments without plugging the device to a power source, for a single run, the longest session lasts for the lifetime of a fully charged battery. As we mainly focus on the relationship between resource consumption and perceived quality at the client side, we conduct all C/S and C/P/S based measurements at non-peak time, mostly from midnight to 6 AM in the morning unless noted otherwise. For P2P, we have conducted experiments at both peak time (8:00 PM in the evening) and non-peak time (midnight to 6 AM in the morning). All experiments are conducted with a dedicated AP running 802.11g deployed in a lab on a university campus in order to minimize traffic contention. We disable all other connections (e.g., bluetooth) on the iTouch.

For accessing each of these streaming services, two types of tests have been conducted. The first is *Stress Test* to examine how long video streaming can last. Basically, we start the streaming with a fully charged battery and keep the application running until the device battery is exhausted. The second is *1-Hour Test* for more detailed analysis as presented below, where we log all statistics for one hour immediately after the application is started.

3. MEASUREMENT RESULTS

In this section, we present our measurement results of Stress Tests. Among the 10 services we have investigated, we present the representative ones for brevity, namely SPBtv (a client-server (C/S) architecture), Orb (a client-proxy-server (C/P/S) architecture), and TVUPlayer (a P2P architecture). Some results of other services are collectively presented or presented for comparisons.

3.1 Overview

Figure 1(a) shows the CPU usage and battery consumption while the iTouch runs SPBtv to watch a video channel with a fully charged battery. In this figure, the left-y axis shows the CPU usage breakdown of user, system, and idle. The right-y axis shows the remaining battery (in terms of percentage) along the playback. The streaming rate of this video channel is 464 Kbps. All data are received from a dedicated server in Oregon, USA. As is shown in this figure, starting from a fully charged battery, the streaming lasted for about 6.4 hours. Note that Apple announced that the battery on 2nd generation iPod Touch can last 6 hours for video watching [19]. Our test here confirms this. On the other hand, we also notice that the CPU is mostly (about 80%) idle in this session.

Figure 1(b) shows the result of iTouch running Orb to watch episodes stored on a personal computer at home. With a fully charged battery, it can watch the program of 297 Kbps for a total of 4.3 hours. Compared to C/S based SPBtv, the watched video has a lower quality (297 Kbps vs. 464 Kbps), meaning 36% lower streaming rate. But a fully charged battery only works for about 67% of time duration in the C/S based SPBtv. It is also surprising that the user level CPU usage is as high as 50%. Given that the CPU also consumes a lot of battery power, this may explain the earlier exhaustion of battery power in C/P/S based Orb with a lower streaming rate. We will further analyze this later.

Figure 1(c) shows the result of using TVUPlayer, which uses P2P architecture for streaming delivery. The streaming only lasts for about 3 hours watching a 281 Kbps channel. We also notice that the CPU usage at user level is even higher than in the C/P/S based Orb, fluctuating between 60% and 80%.

The results above shows a mobile device in C/S based SPBtv and C/P/S based Orb consume much less energy compared to in P2P based TVUPlayer, even without considering the streaming rate difference. We next examine the potential reasons, focusing on two major power consumption sources: CPU and the network interface card.

3.2 CPU Usage Study

Since iOS 3.2.1 does not support multi-tasking, the CPU cycles in a streaming session could mainly be used for two purposes: decoding the received data and transcoding for the mobile device. Decoding is to decode the received data in the proper format for the MediaPlayer. The CPU cycles used for decoding depend on the video format, supported codec, the bit rate, the frame rate, the resolution, etc.

Transcoding is different and often consumes much more CPU cycles. In mobile streaming, mobile devices have different screen size, color depth, resolution rate, etc. from desktop computers, so not all streaming content can be directly played on mobile devices. An intuitive solution to address this heterogeneity issue is to provide different versions of the same video content for different platform/devices. Youtube uses this approach. Another more flexible solution is called online transcoding, which conducts content adaptation at runtime based on the device type, downloading bandwidth etc. This process, although very desirable, consumes a lot of CPU cycles at runtime.

We first investigate in SPBtv how the CPU cycles on our iTouch were spent. Via reverse-engineering, we find that CPU cycles are mainly spent on decoding the video content. For SPBtv, the video is encoded in H.264 standard, which can be decoded by hardware. H.264 has the native support on iTouch and iPhone as we discussed in section 2. This is confirmed by Figure 1(a) as about 80% CPU cycles are idle.

On the other hand, using a software decoder could consume more CPU cycles. Figure 1(b) shows that about 40% more CPU cycles are spent in Orb on decoding the media data for playback. The video content of Orb is encoded into `flv` format. Decoding flv on iTouch simply relies on the software embedded in the MediaPlayer on iTouch. Note that here the extra CPU cycles are not used for transcoding on iTouch, since transcoding is done by the transcoding proxy, co-located with the placeshifting server. The data received by iTouch has been transcoded.

Compared to SPBtv, Figure 1(c) shows that TVUPlayer consumes even more CPU cycles. To investigate how TVUPlayer use these CPU cycles, first, we set to examine video codec of TVUPlayer streaming content. Given that on the same P2P overlay, peers on Mac OS and iOS receive the same streaming data, we start a TVUPlayer client on Mac OS. As the playback starts, we examine all active local TCP connections and locate the port that the MediaPlayer downloads streaming data from. We then start a HTTP connection that downloads data from that port to a file. A closer examination of this file shows that it is encoded with Advanced Systems Format (ASF). However, neither Mac OS nor iOS supports such a video format. Therefore, it is clear

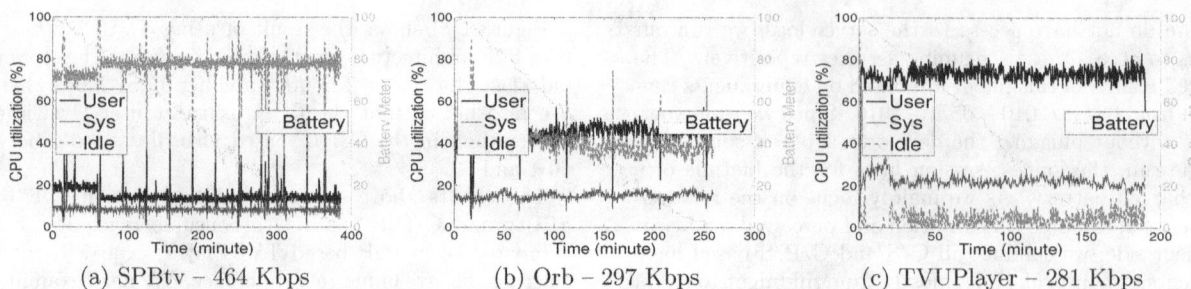

(a) SPBtv – 464 Kbps   (b) Orb – 297 Kbps   (c) TVUPlayer – 281 Kbps

Figure 1: Stress Test: CPU and Battery Usage

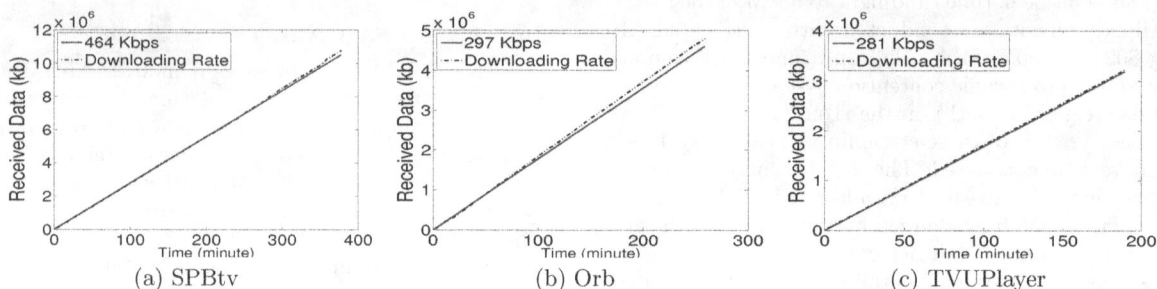

(a) SPBtv   (b) Orb   (c) TVUPlayer

Figure 2: Stress Test: Data Receiving vs. Playback

that TVUPlayer performs online transcoding from ASF to the supported codec at the client side.

The results in this section show that the hardware- and software-based decoding and transcoding can lead to significant difference in the CPU usage, and thus incur different amount of battery power consumption.

3.3 Battery Power Consumption By Transmission

Aside from the battery power consumed by the CPU, it is believed that the wireless network interface card (WNIC) is one of the largest drains of the battery power on mobile devices and the power saving mode (PSM) is commonly used in practice. In this subsection, we further study how the battery power is consumed by the WNIC on the iTouch in these streaming sessions.

Since we log packets at the data-link layer, we are able to extract frame control information from IEEE 802.11 header. One of the flags in the frame control field is `Pwr Mgt`. It indicates the Power Management mode that the device will switch to after this frame is transmitted. Basically, the mobile device would either sleep or stay active.

First, we plot the total duration of the mobile device in the power saving mode based on its power management activity. For each application, we present the median of the runs we had conducted (we ran 1-Hour Test for each application between 5 to 12 times). Figure 3 shows the percentage of time of the WNIC in the power saving mode. As shown in this figure, the WNIC in C/S based streaming commonly has the longest sleeping time: it spends about 80% of total streaming time in the power saving mode. In C/P/S based Orb, the WNIC also spends about 70% of time in the power saving mode, while in AirVideo, it can sleep more with the more efficient packetization scheme (details are omitted due to page limit). However, in P2P based TVUPlayer, the WNIC operates in the power saving mode for as little as 38% of the session time.

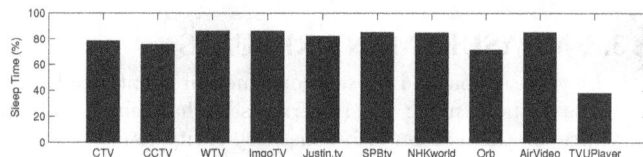

Figure 3: Sleep Time (%) of the WNIC

While the above results show that the power saving mode does take effect on iTouch in all the three Internet mobile streaming delivery architectures, the results also indicate the sleep time of the WNIC varies, which may be affected by the number of packets transmitted, packet size, inter packet delay, etc. Next, we investigate from these aspects in order to understand the underlying reasons.

3.3.1 Bursty traffic delivery saves battery power consumption

In the 802.11 power saving mode, the WNIC on a mobile device would wake up periodically and listen for Traffic Indication Map (TIM). If it does not have data buffered at the Access Point (AP), it will go to sleep. Otherwise, it will retrieve buffered data. In the PSM adaptive mode, if no data has arrived during last beacon interval (typically 100 ms), the WNIC can operate in the power saving mode until the next scheduled beacon interval. Thus we first study inter packet delay, and analyze its impact on energy consumption.

Figure 4 shows the corresponding inter packet delay distribution of the *Stress Test* we have studied. While `Inter Packet` considers all incoming/outgoing traffic to/from the mobile device, `Inter Streaming Packet` considers only ingress streaming data packets. In this figure, for SPBtv, we observe that both the Inter Packet delay and the Inter Streaming Packet delay show a clear bimodal pattern: about 5% packets arrive (both ingress and egress) over 20 ms after the previous packet, most of them are even over

36

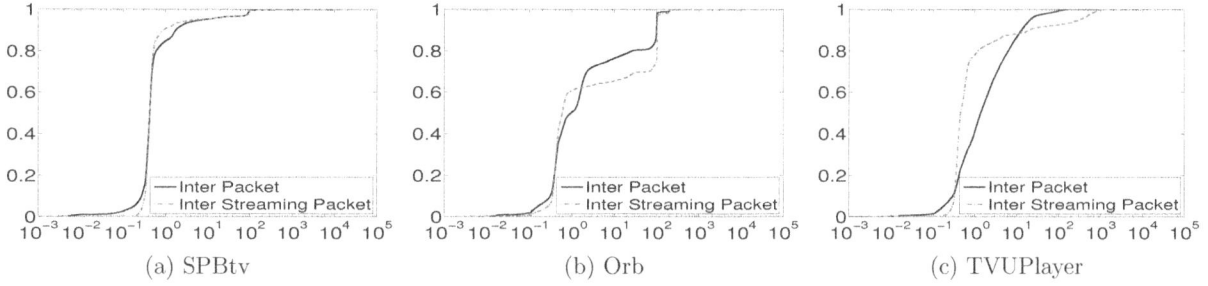

(a) SPBtv   (b) Orb   (c) TVUPlayer

Figure 4: Stress Test: Inter Packet Delay (ms) (CDF)

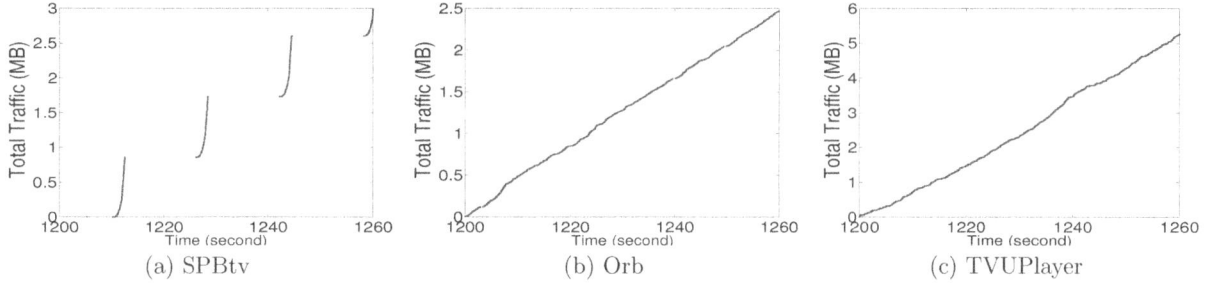

(a) SPBtv   (b) Orb   (c) TVUPlayer

Figure 5: Stress Test: Traffic Pattern

100 ms, leaving great opportunity for WNIC to sleep for power saving. On the other hand, the majority (over 85%) of packets arrive within very short time interval (less than 5 ms), resulting in bursty traffic as shown in Figure 5(a). Note Figure 5 shows the traffic pattern in 60 seconds only for clear visual effect. The traffic pattern in other time durations is similar. This indicates that the SPBtv server has considered the power saving on mobile devices by adopting the traffic shaping and delivery techniques.

On the other side, in C/P/S based Orb, the bimodal distribution of the inter packet delay is less pronounced. Compared to SPBtv, Figure 5(b) shows the traffic in Orb is almost at the constant streaming rate delivered by the proxy. This implies two things: 1) the sender in Orb does not use any traffic shaping technique; 2) the battery power saving simply relies on if the inter packet delay is larger than 100 ms or not. As shown in Figure 4(b), there are still 30% packets falling into this range, leading to battery power saving.

Similarly, Figure 4(c) shows that under P2P, only about 2% of packets have an inter packet delay larger than 100 ms, resulting in even less battery power saving during streaming. Figure 5(c) confirms that in P2P streaming, the streaming rate is almost constant and the streaming traffic is not delivered in bursts.

3.3.2 Inefficient packetization increases battery power consumption

Both SPBtv and Orb use TCP to transmit streaming data. However, their traffic patterns are significantly different due to the adoption of traffic shaping techniques in SPBtv. In this subsection, we further examine if other factors have contributed to the less power saving in Orb.

Figures 6(a) and 6(b) show the packet size distribution for SPBtv and Orb. As shown in the figures, nearly 20% packets in SPBtv are TCP ACKs. They are constantly 52 bytes, and contain no payload. The rest (about 80%) packets are streaming packets, whose size is the same as maxi-

mum transmission unit (MTU) in Ethernet (1500 bytes). In Orb, however, only about 50% packets are streaming packets with a size of 1500 bytes. Besides the 35% control packets (TCP ACKs), the rest 15% packets are streaming packets with smaller sizes: varying from about 100 bytes to 1500 bytes. This increases the number of packets transmitted as such small packets could have been combined to large packets. Potentially, this further reduces the inter packet delay, dis-allowing the WNIC from switching to the power saving mode. Given high speed connection at both the first-mile and the last-mile, this is less likely due to the congestion. Rather, it means the deficiency in Orb design without considering the power consumption on the mobile device.

3.3.3 P2P control and uploading traffic leads to excessive battery power consumption

For P2P based TVUPlayer, Figure 6(c) shows that only less than 30% packets are streaming packets with a size of 1300 bytes, with about 70% of packets having a size less than 100 bytes. Note that most P2P streaming systems today use UDP to transmit packets. Thus, these small packets can only be the control traffic of P2P protocol, such as buffermap information exchanged with other peers. Since P2P streaming systems require peers to exchange control messages with neighbors frequently, this is not a surprising result. However, these control packets significantly change the traffic pattern, resulting in less opportunities for the WNIC switching into the power saving mode.

In P2P streaming, besides the impact of the control traffic, the amount of uploading traffic is also important since a peer is required to upload streaming data to other peers during streaming. This can further aggravate the power consumption on a mobile device. For example, Figure 7 shows the uploading traffic in the Stress Test of TVUPlayer. In this figure, we can see that the uploading rate could reach as high as 1000 Kbps, 3 times more than the downloading rate of streaming data (281 Kbps) in the first half an hour.

| (a) SPBtv | (b) Orb | (c) TVUPlayer |

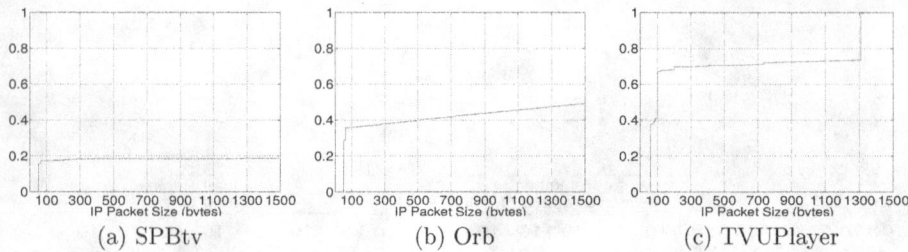

Figure 6: Stress Test: Packet Size (CDF)

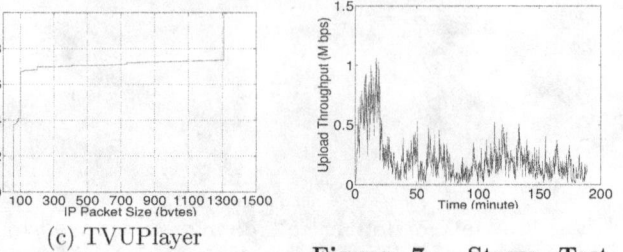

Figure 7: Stress Test: Upload Traffic in TVU-Player

Our measurement results show that some C/S and C/P/S based Internet mobile streaming services have adopted techniques to deal with battery power constraints and device heterogeneity. However, the existing P2P streaming service lacks power-efficient design and device heterogeneity handling capabilities, and deserves further optimization.

4. OTHER RELATED WORK

For media applications over wireless connections, Chandra studied typical Internet streaming services in 2002 and concluded that 802.11 PSM does not save energy if the streaming is over 56 Kbps [20]. Accordingly, history-based prediction [20] and linear prediction [21] schemes were proposed to schedule the WNIC into sleep or active modes. PSM-throttling leverages traffic shaping from the client side in order to allow the WNIC to sleep for longer time [22]. Targeting Internet P2P streaming, Tan et al. designed SCAP [23] in order to reduce the power consumption on wireless devices by caching the uploading traffic at the AP. Xiao et al. studied the power consumption of mobile Youtube [24].

5. CONCLUSION

Despite the fundamental constraints of limited available resources, device heterogeneity, and bulk data transmissions, Internet mobile streaming is becoming more and more popular. In this paper, we examine the resource utilization with a focus on battery power consumption on mobile devices in receiving such streaming services from a client's perspective. Our measurement and analysis show that mobile devices have different power efficiency in receiving Internet streaming services under existing architectures. Our study provides some new insights into effective power saving on mobile devices in Internet streaming and calls for future systems that can minimize battery power consumption while be scalable and efficient in heterogeneity handling.

6. ACKNOWLEDGEMENT

We appreciate constructive comments from anonymous referees. The work is partially supported by NSF under grants CNS-0746649 and CCF- 0915681, and AFOSR under grant FA9550-09-1-0071.

7. REFERENCES

[1] V.Bychkovsky, B.Hull, A.K. Miu, H.Balakrishnan, and S.Madden, "A Measurement Study of Vehicular Internet Access Using In Situ Wi-Fi Networks," in *Proc. ACM MOBICOM*, 2006.

[2] "Sep. 2010 U.S. Mobile Subscriber Market Share," http://www.comscore.com/Press_Events/Press_ Releases/2010/11/comScore_Reports_September_ 2010_U.S._Mobile_Subscriber_Market_Share.

[3] "Top U.S. Online Video Content Properties by Unique Viewers," http://www.comscore.com/Press_Events/ Press_Releases/2010/11/comScore_Releases_ October_2010_U.S._Online_Video_Rankings.

[4] "PPlive," http://www.pplive.com.

[5] "PPStream," http://www.ppstream.com/.

[6] X. Hei, C. Liang, J. Liang, Y. Liu, and K. Ross, "Insights into PPLive: A measurement study of a large-scale P2P IPTV system," in *Proc. of IPTV Workshop*, May 2006.

[7] "Netflix," http://itunes.apple.com/app/id363590051.

[8] "CTV," http://itunes.apple.com/app/id340381556.

[9] "CCTV," http://itunes.apple.com/app/id331259725.

[10] "W.TV," http://itunes.apple.com/app/id318676629.

[11] "ImgoTV," http://itunes.apple.com/app/id349448995.

[12] "NHKworld," http://itunes.apple.com/app/id350732480.

[13] "SPBtv," http://itunes.apple.com/app/id356830174.

[14] "OrbLive," http://itunes.apple.com/app/id290195003.

[15] "Air Video," http://itunes.apple.com/app/id306550020.

[16] "Justin.tv," http://itunes.apple.com/app/id358612216.

[17] "HTTP Live Streaming Draft," http://tools.ietf. org/html/draft-pantos-http-live-streaming.

[18] "TVUPlayer," http://itunes.apple.com/app/id323640984.

[19] "iPod touch (2nd generation) - Technical Specifications," http://support.apple.com/kb/SP496.

[20] S. Chandra, "Wireless network interface energy consumption implications of popular streaming formats," in *Proc. of MMCN*, 2002.

[21] Y. Wei, S. M. Bhandarkar, and S. Chandra, "A client-side statistical prediction scheme for energy aware multimedia data streaming," *IEEE Transactions on Multimedia*, vol. 8, no. 4, 2006.

[22] E. Tan, L. Guo, S. Chen, and X. Zhang, "Psm-throttling: Minimizing energy consumption for bulk data communications in wlans," in *Proc. of IEEE ICNP*, October 2007.

[23] E. Tan, L. Guo, S. Chen, and X. Zhang, "Scap: Smart caching in wireless access points to improve p2p streaming," in *Proc. of IEEE ICDCS*, June 2007.

[24] Y. Xiao, R. Kalyanaraman, and A. Yla-Jaaski, "Energy consumption of mobile youtube: Quantitative measurement and analysis," in *Proc. of NGMAST*, September 2008.

Understanding Demand Volatility in Large VoD Systems

Di Niu
Department of Electrical and
Computer Engineering
University of Toronto
dniu@eecg.toronto.edu

Baochun Li
Department of Electrical and
Computer Engineering
University of Toronto
bli@eecg.toronto.edu

Shuqiao Zhao
Multimedia Development
Group
UUSee, Inc.
shuqiao.zhao@gmail.com

ABSTRACT

Bandwidth usage in large-scale Video on Demand (VoD) systems varies rapidly over time, due to unpredictable dynamics in user demand and network conditions. Such bandwidth volatility makes it hard to provision the exact amount of server resources that matches the demand in each video channel, posing significant challenges to achieving quality assurance and efficient resource allocation at the same time. In this paper, we seek to statistically model time-varying traffic volatility in VoD servers, leveraging heteroscedastic models first used to interpret economic time series, with the goal of forecasting not only traffic patterns but also traffic volatility. We present the application of volatility forecast to efficient resource allocation that provides probabilistic service level guarantees to user groups. We also discuss volatility reduction from diversification, and its implications to new strategies for cost-effective server management. Our study is based on monitoring the workload of a large-scale commercial VoD system widely deployed on the Internet.

Categories and Subject Descriptors

C.4 [**Performance of Systems**]: Modeling Techniques; C.2.3 [**Network Operations**]: Network Monitoring; Network Management

General Terms

Measurement, Performance, Reliability

Keywords

Video-on-Demand, Volatility, Traffic Forecast, Demand Prediction, GARCH, Measurement, Resource Allocation, Diversification

1. INTRODUCTION

A large-scale video on demand (VoD) system on the Internet involves millions of users streaming movies, TV episodes, and other on-demand media from a huge library of video channels. However, Internet VoD largely remains a best-effort service, where either a large amount of extra unused server capacity is provisioned with low utilization, or the user experience is at risk. To enjoy smooth playback, a user needs to download at an average rate greater than the video playback rate. It is therefore necessary to ensure the right amount of outgoing bandwidth is available at the servers to meet the instantaneous demand.

To avoid the complication and vast cost in hardware maintenance, more content providers choose to rent public server resources, such as content delivery networks (CDNs), for video streaming. When a VoD application shares the underlying infrastructure with other applications in a "multi-tenant" environment, it is inevitably exposed to random congestion and variance in bandwidth availability. Providing quality assurance to bandwidth-intensive VoD services while not over-provisioning the resources becomes one of the most challenging issues for CDN servers.

As video access patterns exhibit clear trends and periodicity with time-of-day effects [2, 6, 8, 9], the expected bandwidth demand for each video is highly predictable by monitoring the usage history [5, 6]. Demand forecast enables the elastic adjustment of bandwidth allocation to match instantaneous user demand. We envision that a proactive "match strategy" for elastic bandwidth reservation in the presence of time-varying demand is a critical enabling technology to offer service-level assurance to VoD users, while making efficient utilization of resources. Nevertheless, since demand forecast is subject to errors due to unpredictable user dynamics, fast-changing network conditions and inherently noisy traffic, a "risk premium" must be accommodated on top of the expected future demand to tolerate fluctuations, or *volatility*.

In this paper, we argue that in order to elastically book resources for a VoD service, forecasting demand volatility is as important as predicting the expected demand. We seek to statistically model traffic volatility in large-scale VoD systems by analyzing the operational traces of 173 popular video channels collected from UUSee Inc. [1], one of the leading commercial Internet video solutions based in China. Inspection of real-world traces suggests that server bandwidth usage in each video channel exhibits alternating phases of relative tranquility and high variation around its expected value. We thus introduce GARCH [3], a heteroscedastic model originally used to characterize economic time series, to quantify the changing variance in large-scale VoD traffic, with the goal of forecasting volatility. We apply GARCH-based volatility forecasts to bandwidth allocation that economically books resources for each video channel with probabilistic bandwidth guarantees.

As real-world systems typically host very large video libraries, we proceed to study the volatility of the aggregate or mixed traffic of multiple video channels, and observe the volatility reduction phenomenon attributed to diversification. We discuss the implications of such an observation to cost-effective server management and load direction based on financial management tools such as hedging and diversification in real-world VoD systems, which may run a large collection of streaming channels over geographically distributed servers.

1.1 Relation to Prior Work

The importance of bandwidth demand estimation to capacity planning in Internet VoD systems has been recognized recently. It is shown that estimating time-varying demands in a large-scale IPTV network can help the system optimally place content on its geographically distributed servers [2]. Toward this goal, the recent demand history is used as an estimate of future demand in each video channel [2]. Apparently, this simple method does not yield accurate forecasts. [6] introduces linear stochastic time series models to capture the periodicity, trends and autocorrelations that exist in the demand history, achieving a high accuracy in demand forecast.

However, traditional forecast methods assume a constant forecast error variance and fail to capture the changing volatility in data. In fact, measurements show that bandwidth demand is subject to rapid changes in some periods, while remaining tranquil and highly predictable in other periods. We therefore introduce GARCH models [3] originated from econometrics to model the volatility persistence phenomenon — the bandwidth demand at a certain time period tends to exhibit similar volatility as in recent time periods.

Volatility reduction in the mixed traffic of multiple channels is similar to the idea of statistical multiplexing and resource overbooking [7] in shared hosting platforms, where the resources are booked to satisfy a certain percentile of demand in each application instead of its worst-case demand, so as to enhance resource utilization. However, the volatility reduction discussed here is novel in three aspects. First, we are concerned with forward-looking resource allocation and volatility forecasts for future demand, while in [7] the resource usage of each application is profiled in an offline and fixed manner, ignoring the change of demand patterns over time. Second, our study focuses on *large-scale* VoD systems, where the concurrent number of users can ramp up by several hundreds or thousands in tens of minutes. In this scenario, any fixed resource usage profiling for small video channels (*e.g.*, those with a user population of 20 in [7]) will be insufficient. Last but not least, we do not assume independence between the demands of channels. Instead, we accurately quantify the conditional demand variance in each channel, which enables the use of financial instruments such as hedging and diversification to achieve cost-effective server management with service level guarantees.

2. TRADITIONAL DEMAND FORECAST: APPLICATIONS AND LIMITATIONS

This research is based on our extensive experiences with UUSee, a real-world on-demand media streaming system widely deployed on the Internet. As one of the leading commercial P2P multimedia solution providers in China, UUSee simultaneously broadcasts tens of thousands of video channels to millions of users distributed across over 40 countries. It implements an optimized peer-assisted delivery structure where users can upload media data to each other, alleviating the server burden. However, servers are still responsible for a large part of the upload and play a critical role in compensating bandwidth shortage and controlling the quality provided [8]. It is worth noting that the observations and mechanisms presented in this paper also apply to any general streaming systems that do not involve peer assistance.

The data for validation in this paper feature the traces collected from 173 popular video channels over 21 days during the 2008 Summer Olympics. The maximum online population in each channel varies from 200 to 8000. The dataset contains server bandwidth consumption in each video channel sampled at a 10-minute frequency, so that there are 144 samples in a day.

From the traces, we note that UUSee users demonstrate diurnal access patterns with time-of-day effects [6, 8], and the popularity of most videos exhibits gradual downward trends after they are released. We can therefore use the so-called Box-Jenkins method [4] to predict the future evolution of server bandwidth demand by learning the trend, periodicity and autocorrelation exhibited in usage history. An accurate prediction of bandwidth requirement can help with server capacity planning and resource provisioning to meet user demands. We now briefly review and generalize a time-series modeling technique specifically tailored for VoD systems first described in [6], and point out its deficiency in handling volatility.

2.1 Forecasting the Expected Demand

Given a time series of interest $\{Y_t\}$, define the backward shift operator $B(\cdot)$ by $BY_t = Y_{t-1}$ and the lag-1 difference operator $\nabla(\cdot)$ by $\nabla Y_t = Y_t - Y_{t-1} = (1 - B)Y_t$. Powers of B and ∇ are defined in the obvious way, *i.e.*,

$$\begin{cases} B^j Y_t = Y_{t-j}, \\ \nabla^j Y_t = \nabla(\nabla^{j-1} Y_t), & \text{for } j \geq 1, \quad \text{with } \nabla^0 Y_t = Y_t. \end{cases}$$

We further introduce the lag-d difference operator ∇_d defined by

$$\nabla_d Y_t = Y_t - Y_{t-d} = (1 - B^d)Y_t.$$

The gist of the Box-Jenkins modeling of non-stationary series is to remove periodicity and trends in $\{Y_t\}$, using various differencing transformations, to obtain a stationary series $\{\tilde{Y}_t\}$ that can be modeled by an autoregressive moving-average (ARMA) process [4].

For a particular series $\{Y_t\}$ in VoD systems, *e.g.*, the server bandwidth usage in a video channel, we first apply transformation $\log(\cdot)$ to $\{Y_t\}$ to equalize the fluctuation, and apply ∇_{144} to $\{\log Y_t\}$ to remove daily periodicity. We then difference $\nabla_{144} \log Y_t$ for d times to remove the trend, obtaining a stationary series $\tilde{Y}(t) = \nabla^d \nabla_{144} \log Y_t$, which is well explained by an ARMA(p, q) process. The corresponding seasonal ARIMA model [4] for the original series $\{Y_t\}$ is thus

$$\phi(B)\nabla^d \nabla_{144} \log Y_t = \theta(B)Z_t, \quad d \in \{0, 1\}, \tag{1}$$

where $\{Z_t\} \sim \text{WN}(0, \sigma^2)$ denotes the uncorrelated white noise with zero mean, and $\phi(B) = 1 - \phi_1 B - \ldots - \phi_p B^p$ and $\theta(B) = 1 + \theta_1 B + \ldots + \theta_q B^q$ are polynomial operators in B of degrees p and q. The difference order d is chosen from $\{0, 1\}$, depending on whether a trend exists in the daily population variation.

Given $\{Y_1, \ldots, Y_t\}$, let $P_t Y_{t+h}$ ($h > 0$) denote the h-step-ahead *conditional mean prediction* for Y_{t+h}, *i.e.*, the expected value of Y_{t+h} given observations up to time t. Once the parameters of (1) are learned from the training data, $P_t Y_{t+h}$ is derived as follows. First, we obtain $P_t \tilde{Y}_{t+h}$, the minimum mean square error (MMSE) predictor for $\tilde{Y}_{t+h}$. $P_t Y_{t+h}$ is then calculated by retransforming $P_t \tilde{Y}_{t+h}$ using the inverse of the corresponding operators ∇^d, ∇_{144} and $\log(\cdot)$, *i.e.*,

$$P_t Y_{t+h} = (\nabla^d)^{-1} \nabla_{144}^{-1} \exp(P_t \tilde{Y}_{t+h}). \tag{2}$$

As an example, we make 10-minutes-ahead (one-step) prediction of the server bandwidth $\{S_t\}$ consumed by a popular video channel released at time period $t_0 = 264$ (2008-08-10 10:47:39). The channel has a maximum online population of 2664. The server consumption series of the first 3 days is used as the training data, excluding the initial 80 time periods after the release of the video which may not conform to later evolution patterns. The prediction is tested on the data of 3 days following the training period. We fit model (1) to the training data and obtain parameter estimates through a maximum likelihood estimator [4]. As shown in Fig. 1a, with $d = 0$, $p = 20$,

(a) One-step-ahead prediction of S_t

(b) Prediction errors

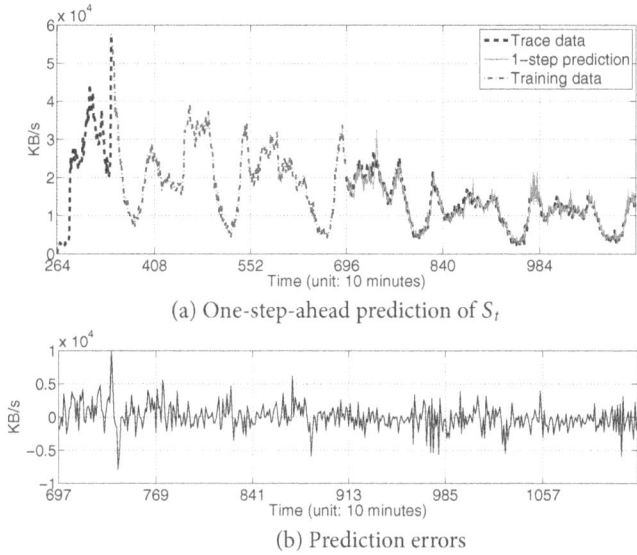

Figure 1: 10-minutes-ahead prediction for the server bandwidth consumption S_t of a popular video channel A55FF released at time period 264, compared against the trace data.

$q = 20$, model (1) can yield prediction results that are close to the real server bandwidth required by the channel.

2.2 Applications and Limitations

Demand forecast based on past observations enables the system to allocate a right amount of bandwidth to match the demand. A lightweight online bandwidth monitoring and reservation framework, as shown in Fig. 2, can be unobtrusively implemented in current operational systems. It monitors the server bandwidth consumed by a particular video channel periodically, *e.g., every 10 minutes*, learns models to forecast future demand, and judiciously decides the amount bandwidth to be provisioned in the next time period. As server bandwidth usage of each channel is readily available in server logs, there is no need to collect statistics from users.

However, as the MMSE predictor in Sec. 2.1 only forecasts the conditional mean demand, or the expected demand, the real demand may vary around this predicted conditional mean. The resulted prediction errors have a mean of zero and are plotted in Fig. 1b. Due to the existence of prediction errors, we need to provision an additional "risk premium" to tolerate demand fluctuation, which apparently depends on the variance of prediction errors. A further look into Fig. 1b suggests that forecast errors of server bandwidth consumption do not have a constant variance: there are periods where the prediction is relatively accurate alongside periods with less trustworthy forecasts. In other words, the server usage evolves smoothly and is highly predictable in some periods, but also becomes highly variable and unpredictable in other periods.

The changing volatility in resource consumption poses great challenges to efficient server provisioning. As traditional time-series techniques assume a constant variance for the disturbance Z_t, the risk premium provisioned will be a function of the fixed forecast error variance averaged over the long run. However, such an approach will necessarily result in over-provisioning when the demand is less volatile, but lead to insufficiency when the demand is liable to unpredictable changes. To achieve efficient resource allocation, we need a *conditional variance* forecast mechanism to estimate the time-changing variance of demand around its expected value (conditional mean), and adjust the amount of risk premium provisioned accordingly.

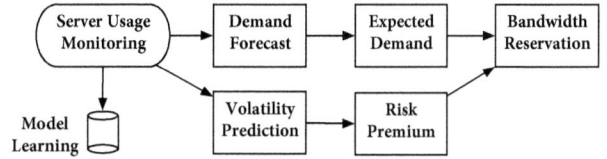

Figure 2: Online server bandwidth monitoring and reservation. The reserved bandwidth should match the sum of the expected demand and a risk premium that tolerates volatility.

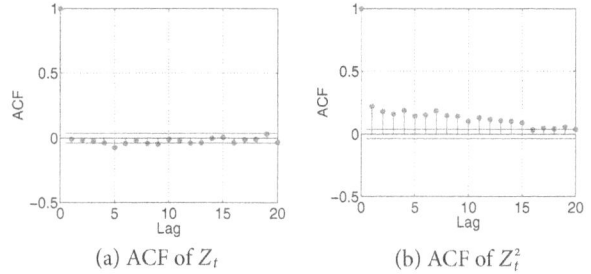

(a) ACF of Z_t (b) ACF of Z_t^2

Figure 3: The ACFs of the disturbance Z_t and Z_t^2 obtained from fitting the seasonal ARIMA model (1) with $d = 0$ and $p = q = 20$ to server bandwidth consumption $\{S_t\}$ in video channel A55FF.

3. MODELING DEMAND VOLATILITY

As a system operator, one may be interested in estimating the conditional variance in server bandwidth demand based on past observations, which is critical to deciding the "risk premium" provisioned to accommodate demand fluctuation. Such a "risk premium" should increase when we are less certain about the accuracy of the conditional mean demand forecast, and decrease otherwise, when the conditional variance of future demand is low. In contrast, the unconditional variance, *i.e.*, the long-run estimate of forecast error variance averaged over time, would not be important if we care about the instantaneous "risk premium" needed.

Although the seasonal ARIMA model (1) is a good conditional mean model that predicts the expectation of server bandwidth consumption S_{t+h} conditioned on $\{S_t, S_{t-1}, \ldots\}$, it fails to capture the serial dependency within the disturbance series $\{Z_t\}$ obtained from fitting (1) to $\{S_t\}$. To check such dependency, we plot the autocorrelation functions (ACFs) of Z_t and Z_t^2 in Fig. 3. We can see that although $\{Z_t\}$ is an uncorrelated white noise, it is not IID — the variance term Z_t^2 clearly depends on $Z_{t-1}^2, Z_{t-2}^2, \ldots$. In fact, we can observe a persistence of volatility for Z_t from Fig. 1b: Z_t tends to exhibit a similar conditional variance as in recent periods.

To include past variances in the explanation of future variances, we model Z_t using the GARCH (generalized autoregressive conditional heteroscedasticity) process [3], which has been successfully applied to modeling the volatility of stock data for the past decade. Specifically, we model the disturbance Z_t obtained from fitting model (1) to $\{S_t\}$ as a GARCH(P, Q) process:

$$\begin{cases} Z_t = \sqrt{h_t}e_t, & \{e_t\} \sim \text{IID } \mathcal{N}(0,1), \\ h_t = \alpha_0 + \sum_{i=1}^{P} \alpha_i Z_{t-i}^2 + \sum_{j=1}^{Q} \beta_j h_{t-j}, \end{cases} \quad (3)$$

where $\alpha_0 > 0$ and $\alpha_j, \beta_j \geq 0, j = 1, 2, \ldots,$ and h_t is the conditional variance of Z_t given its history $\{Z_s; s < t\}$. The GARCH model reflects the evolution of the variance in data by incorporating correlation in the sequence $\{h_t\}$ of conditional variances.

Taking channel A55FF as an example, we fit a GARCH$(1, 1)$ model to the one-step-ahead prediction errors for server bandwidth usage $\{S_t\}$ shown in Fig. 1b. The model parameters are obtained using

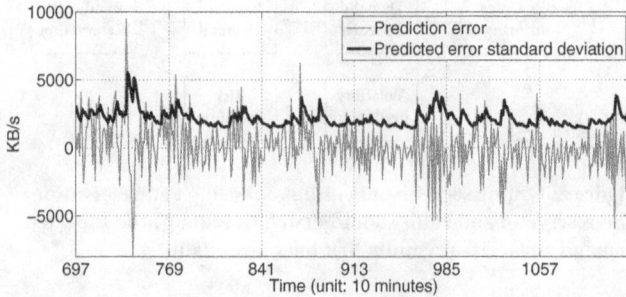

Figure 4: One-step-ahead forecast errors for server bandwidth consumption S_t in the video channel A55FF, and predicted conditional standard deviations for the forecast errors.

maximum likelihood estimation (pp. 417, [4]) based on the prediction errors of model (1) during the training period. We predict the conditional standard deviations $\{\sqrt{h_t}\}$ of the prediction errors for the test period using the trained model, and plot the results in Fig. 4. We can see that the predicted error standard deviation is larger when the demand prediction errors are highly variable.

With the GARCH model, we are able to forecast how much real data will deviate from the predicted conditional mean produced by model (1). It allows us to quantify our certainty about bandwidth consumption forecast so that server provisioning can leverage this fact to enhance resource utilization. When we are certain about the S_t in the next time period, the server bandwidth reserved for the channel should be close to the predicted conditional mean consumption. On the other hand, during periods where S_t is subject to rapid changes and less predictable, we need to provision a higher risk premium to tolerate the demand volatility in the channel.

4. VOLATILITY AND RESOURCE ALLOCATION

In this section, we present the application of volatility forecasts to resource allocation. To achieve service level guarantees to users without over-provisioning, the resource allocated should match the future demand with a conditional mean forecast plus a "risk premium" that tolerates traffic volatility.

In general, the effectiveness of a resource allocation scheme can be evaluated by two performance metrics: 1) *insufficiency ratio e*, which is the ratio of time periods where the booked resource is lower than the actual demand over all the test periods; and 2) *time-averaged utilization* $\overline{U}$, which is the average utilization of the allocated resource over all the test periods.

To provide quality assurance to users, it is expected to maintain the insufficiency ratio e to a low level. On the other hand, for the cost-effectiveness of servers, the cloud service providers expect to keep the average utilization $\overline{U}$ at a high level by booking resources sparingly. Striking a balance between the two conflicting objectives, the key to successful resource booking is to decide the minimum necessary "risk premium" R_{t+1} at time period $t+1$ given observations up to time t that achieves a target insufficiency ratio, *e.g.*, $e \leq 2\%$, under an appropriate volatility model.

4.1 Comparing Five Volatility Models

We propose five proactive server bandwidth reservation schemes for VoD systems, each based on a different volatility model including GARCH and other heuristics. To reserve bandwidth for a video channel at time $t + 1$, all these schemes periodically monitor the server bandwidth usage $\{S_1, \ldots, S_t\}$ of this channel by checking server logs (*e.g.*, at a 10-minute frequency), and predict the con-

ditional mean demand $P_t S_{t+1}$ using the same method described in Sec. 2. However, they incorporate different volatility models to determine the "risk premium" provisioned. Specifically, assuming $e = 2\%$, these schemes are described as follows:

Constant variance (baseline method) assumes a constant variance σ^2 in demand forecast errors, which can be learned from training data. As demand forecast errors exhibit Gaussian distribution in the traces, the risk premium is the 98th percentile of the normal distribution $\mathcal{N}(0, \sigma^2)$, *i.e.*, the value below which 98% of samples from the distribution $\mathcal{N}(0, \sigma^2)$ fall.

Probabilistic GARCH predicts the conditional variance h_{t+1} for the demand forecast error using the GARCH model. The risk premium is the 98th percentile of the normal distribution $\mathcal{N}(0, h_{t+1})$.

Deterministic GARCH predicts the conditional variance h_{t+1} for the forecast error using the GARCH model. The risk premium is $\eta\sqrt{h_{t+1}}$, where η is a positive constant determined as the η that achieves an insufficiency ratio $e = 2\%$ in the training data.

Recent variance is a heuristic method that calculates the sample variance σ_τ^2 of demand forecast errors in the recent τ time periods. The risk premium is the 98th percentile of the normal distribution $\mathcal{N}(0, \sigma_\tau^2)$.

Maximum absolute error is a heuristic method that decides the risk premium as the maximum absolute error of demand forecasts in recent τ time periods.

We test the performance of the above schemes in terms of resource utilization and insufficiency ratio through simulations driven by the real-world traces of 169 popular video channels. For each channel, we train the conditional mean model (1) and conditional variance model (3) based on the data of 1.5 days from the 50th to the 266th time period after the channel is released. The first 500 minutes (50 time periods) are excluded from training as the initial demands may not conform to the later evolution patterns. To test the generalizability of our proposed methods to any VoD demands, we only assume a simple seasonal ARIMA model (1) with $d = 0$, $p = q = 1$ for demand forecast. For the two GARCH-based methods, we train a GARCH(1,1) model for demand forecast errors in the training data. We then use the above 5 methods with the trained parameters to perform one-step-ahead bandwidth reservation in each channel for a test period of 2 days following the training period.

We calculate the average resource utilization $\overline{U}$ and insufficiency ratio e in each of the 169 channels over its corresponding test period, and plot the empirical cumulative distribution functions (CDFs) of these $\overline{U}$'s and e's in Fig. 5a and Fig. 5b, respectively. We can see that "constant variance," as the baseline method, achieves the lowest resource utilization as well as the lowest e, because it aggressively books a high risk premium assuming a large constant variance for demand forecast errors. In contrast, "probabilistic GARCH" can adjust the risk premium dynamically based on the changing forecast error variance. From Fig. 5b, we see that it achieves an insufficiency ratio $e \leq 2\%$ in 80% of the 169 channels, which is close to "constant variance," and an insufficiency ratio $e \leq 4\%$ in more than 90% of the channels, which is even better than "constant variance." In the meantime, "probabilistic GARCH" achieves a markable enhancement in resource utilization, shown in Fig. 5a as it only books the necessary risk premium to tolerate the instantaneous demand volatility instead of the long-run variance.

Although "deterministic GARCH" further enhances utilization by booking the risk premium more conservatively, its average e exceeds the target of 2%. Furthermore, the "recent variance" and "maximum absolute error" heuristics, when compared with the first three methods, enjoy an advantageous position, as they are fully adaptive during the test period, while the first three use fixed model parameters estimated from the training data for prediction. Even in such

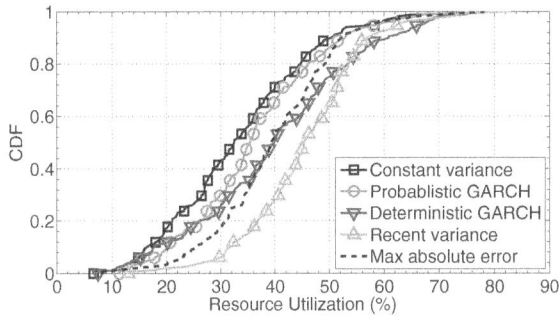

(a) CDF of resource utilization $\overline{U}$ in 169 channels

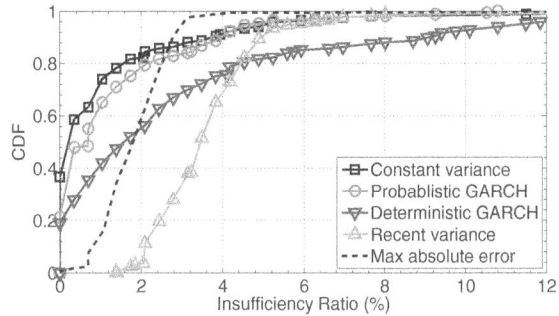

(b) CDF of bandwidth insufficiency ratio e in 169 channels

Figure 5: The empirical CDF of the utilization of booked bandwidth and the ratio of time periods where the booked bandwidth is insufficient. Bandwidth reservation is performed in 169 popular video channels independently, each with a test period of 2 days.

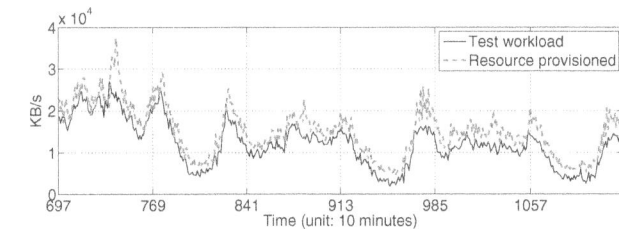

(a) The bandwidth reserved by "probabilistic GARCH."

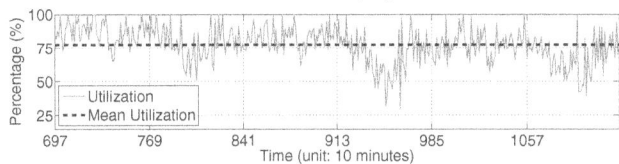

(b) Utilization of the reserved bandwidth.

Figure 6: Bandwidth reservation with "probabilistic GARCH" in channel A55FF, tested on a period of 3 days.

an unfair comparison, both heuristics perform worse than GARCH-based methods, resulting in an e way beyond the target of 2%. As they inherently lack a mechanism to quantitatively tune the trade-off between $\overline{U}$ and e, they are not appealing for the sake of quality assurance. We conjecture that a fully online version of ARIMA and GARCH, which adaptively relearns model parameters as the simulation proceeds in the entire test period, can yield even better utilization while being able to constrain e within the target range.

4.2 Utilization as a Volatility Indicator

From the above comparison, we find that the best bandwidth reservation scheme that strikes a balance in the $\overline{U}$-e tradeoff is "probabilistic GARCH," thanks to its superior ability to adjust the risk premium provisioned as the volatility changes. As an example, we apply "probabilistic GARCH" to a popular channel A55FF over a test period of 3 days, which represents the same test workload as in Fig. 1 in Sec. 2 and Fig. 4 in Sec. 3, with models learned from the preceding 3 days. The bandwidth demand is forecasted as a seasonal ARIMA process with $d = 0$, $p = q = 20$ driven by GARCH(1,1) forecast errors. We plot the bandwidth provisioned by "probabilistic GARCH" in Fig. 6a and the achieved utilization in Fig. 6b under a target insufficiency ratio of $e = 5\%$. The achieved e is 3.71% and $\overline{U} = 75.04\%$ on the test data.

Just as traffic volatility limits the resource utilization efficiency, the best achievable utilization $\overline{U}$ produced by one-step-ahead resource booking, given a target insufficiency ratio e (e.g., $e = 2\%$), is essentially a quantitative indicator of traffic volatility in the long

term. A high $\overline{U}$ means that less "risk premium" is needed and the traffic is likely to evolve smoothly with tractable variation. In contrast, a low $\overline{U}$ implies that the traffic is inherently liable to rapid and unpredictable variations, and thus more "risk premium" must be booked to tolerate demand fluctuation. In other words, $\overline{U}$ evaluates volatility by the ratio of the actual bandwidth usage over the sum of expected usage and the volatile part of usage. Therefore, in the following analysis, we use the time-average utilization $\overline{U}$ achieved by resource booking based on "probabilistic GARCH" to evaluate the demand volatility in the long run.

5. VOLATILITY REDUCTION THROUGH DIVERSIFICATION

In this section, we consider the combined or mixed traffic of multiple video channels. We observe that the aggregate traffic volatility decreases as the number of channels to be combined increases. Furthermore, such volatility reduction is not merely a consequence of a higher volume of traffic, but more importantly is due to traffic mixing between channels that may exhibit diverse variations. From the previous section, we see that $\overline{U}$ evaluates volatility by computing the ratio of the actual bandwidth usage over the sum of the expected usage and usage uncertainty. Therefore, in this section, we evaluate the demand volatility of mixed channels by the achievable $\overline{U}$ in one-step-ahead resource booking, given a target of $e = 2\%$.

To study how the number of combined channels affects traffic volatility, we conduct a series of bandwidth reservation simulations driven by the traces of 173 video channels in UUSee over 21 days. We divide the entire 21 days into 7 periods, each of 3 days, and study the traffic volatility of random combinations of video channels in each 3-day test period (except the first 3 days, which are only used for model training).

Now we illustrate the test with the second 3-day period (days 4-6). Suppose that the number of channels to be combined is n. We *randomly* choose n channels that exist in this test period and its previous 3-day training period, and consider their aggregate traffic. We perform bandwidth reservation based on "probabilistic GARCH" in this test period (days 4-6), using the models trained from the previous 3 days (days 1-3). We assume a simple conditional mean model (1) with $d = 0$, $p = q = 1$ and a conditional variance model (3) of GARCH(1,1). We calculate $\overline{U}$ and e in this test period of days 4-6. For this particular value of n, the above experiment is repeated for 60 times to allow for different combinations of channels. The mean and standard deviation of the achieved 60 $\overline{U}$'s and e's are calculated. The above procedure applies to the other 3-day test periods, each with its preceding 3 days as the training period.

From Fig. 7, we see that as bandwidth is reserved for an increasing

(a) Mean of utilization $\overline{U}$ (b) Standard deviation of $\overline{U}$

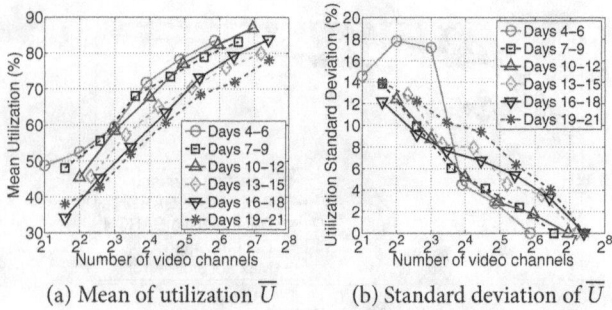

Figure 7: The mean and standard deviation of $\overline{U}$ when different numbers of video channels are randomly combined for bandwidth reservation. The achieved average e is less than 4% in all cases.

number of combined video channels, the mean of the achieved $\overline{U}$'s increases significantly up to close to 90%, and the standard deviation of $\overline{U}$'s decreases in all of the test days 4-21. As the resource utilization in one-step-ahead bandwidth reservation essentially evaluates the degree of volatility in data, the above phenomenon implies that the aggregate traffic of multiple channels demonstrates less volatile. Bandwidth provisioned to multiple channels can thus match the demand more closely. A further check into Fig. 7b shows that when the number of channels is small, the $\overline{U}$'s have a high standard deviation. This means that although all channels follow diurnal evolution in trend, there exist different degrees of correlation between the demand forecast errors of different channels: the volatility of the combined traffic is amplified when they are positively correlated and suppressed when they are negatively correlated.

To verify that volatility reduction is not a consequence of an increased amount of total traffic, but because of mixing different channels, we perform bandwidth reservation for all the 93 channels in a test period from time 697 to 1127, which is the same test period as in Fig. 1, Fig. 4, and Fig. 6a, where bandwidth reservation is performed for a single channel A55FF. However, instead of considering the aggregate traffic all 93 channels (including channel A55FF), we consider a mixture of them by taking 1/10 of user requests from each channel and adding them up. Comparing Fig. 8a with Fig. 6a, we see that the resulted mixed traffic is roughly the same in size as that of the single channel A55FF. But the mixed traffic evolves more smoothly, and its forecast errors shown in Fig. 8b not only have a smaller variance than that of channel A55FF shown in Fig. 4, but also exhibits less heteroscedastic property, *i.e.*, less time variation in terms of variance.

6. CONCLUSIONS AND FUTURE WORK

In this paper, we focus on demand volatility forecasts in large-scale operational VoD systems, with the objective of dynamically and efficiently provisioning bandwidth resources in VoD servers. We introduce GARCH models originated from econometrics to predict demand volatility based on server usage monitoring. We propose and compare five volatility-aware resource provisioning schemes, based on GARCH modeling and other volatility heuristics. It is shown that GARCH models yield the best tradeoff in terms of resource utilization and the service level provided to users. We further study the volatility reduction due to diversification when traffic of multiple video channels is mixed. As a result, allocating resources for a well diversified collection of video channels can improve resource utilization by up to 3 times as opposed to single-channel allocation.

The volatility reduction phenomenon observed in UUSee traces has laid a foundation for using modern portfolio theory such as

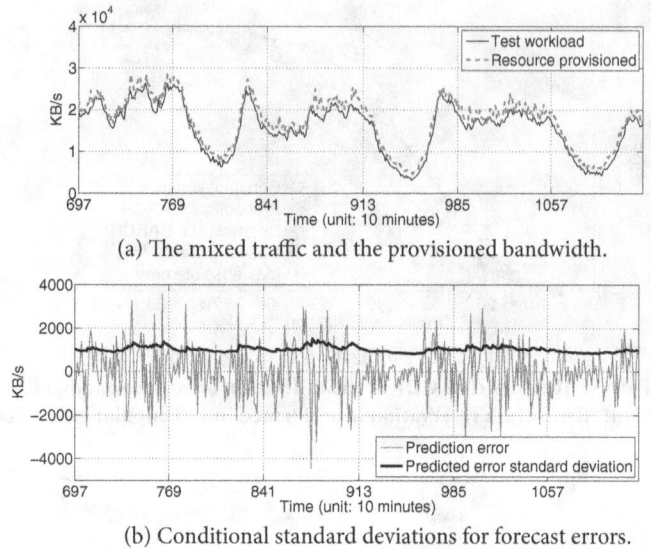

(a) The mixed traffic and the provisioned bandwidth.

(b) Conditional standard deviations for forecast errors.

Figure 8: Bandwidth reservation with "probabilistic GARCH" for the mixed traffic of all the 93 channels in the 6-day period from time 264 to 1127. The first 3 days are the training period, and the other 3 days (time 697-1127) are the test period.

hedging and diversification to achieve cost-effective server management, as the server cost directly links with both the mean and volatility of its usage. In our on-going work, we consider geographically distributed video servers, such as CDN nodes, and explore the use of hedging to enhance resource efficiency and to reduce usage fluctuation by mixing the video channels with negatively correlated demands.

7. REFERENCES

[1] UUSee Inc. [Online]. Available: http://www.uusee.com.

[2] D. Applegate, A. Archer, V. G. S. Lee, and K. Ramakrishnan. Optimal Content Placement for a Large-Scale VoD System. In *Proc. of ACM CoNEXT*, Philadelphia, USA, November, 2010.

[3] T. Bollerslev. Generalized Autoregressive Conditional Heteroskedasticity. *Journal of Econometrics*, 31:307–327, 1986.

[4] G. E. P. Box, G. M. Jenkins, and G. C. Reinsel. *Time Series Analysis: Forecasting and Control*. WILEY, 2008.

[5] G. Gürsun, M. Crovella, and I. Matta. Describing and Forecasting Video Access Patterns. In *Proc. of IEEE INFOCOM '11 Mini-Conference*, Shanghai, China, April 11-15 2011.

[6] D. Niu, Z. Liu, B. Li, and S. Zhao. Demand Forecast and Performance Prediction in Peer-Assisted On-Demand Streaming Systems. In *Proc. of IEEE INFOCOM '11 Mini-Conference*, Shanghai, China, April 11-15 2011.

[7] B. Urgaonkar, P. Shenoy, and T. Roscoe. Resource Overbooking and Application Profiling in Shared Hosting Platforms. In *Proc. of the 5th Symposium on Operating Systems Design and Implementation (OSDI)*, Boston, Massachusetts, December 9-11, 2002 2002.

[8] C. Wu, B. Li, and S. Zhao. Multi-Channel Live P2P Streaming: Refocusing on Servers. In *Proc. of IEEE INFOCOM '08*, Phoenix, Arizona, 2008.

[9] H. Yin, X. Liu, F. Qiu, N. Xia, C. Lin, H. Zhang, V. Sekar, and G. Min. Inside the Bird's Nest: Measurements of Large-Scale Live VoD from the 2008 Olympics. In *Proc. of Internet Measurement Conference (IMC)*, Chicago, Illinois, November 4–6 2009.

Sharing Social Content from Home:
A Measurement-driven Feasibility Study

Massimiliano Marcon, Bimal Viswanath, Meeyoung Cha[†], Krishna P. Gummadi

MPI-SWS
{mmarcon,bviswana,gummadi}
@mpi-sws.org

[†]KAIST
meeyoungcha@kaist.edu

ABSTRACT

Today, OSN sites allow users to share data using a centrally controlled web infrastructure. However, if users shared data directly from home, they could potentially retain full control over the data (i.e., what to share, whom to share with). This paper investigates the feasibility of alternative decentralized architectures that allow users to share their data directly from home. Specifically, we (a) characterize social content workloads using data gathered from the popular Flickr and YouTube social networks and (b) characterize home networks using data gathered from residential gateways deployed in a number of households. We use the data from these measurements to evaluate the potential for delivering social content directly from users' homes.

Categories and Subject Descriptors

C.4 [**Performance of Systems**]: Design studies

General Terms

Measurement, Performance, Design

Keywords

User-generated content, social content, content distribution

1. INTRODUCTION

Online social networks (OSNs) like Facebook, MySpace, and YouTube have become extremely popular. According to Nielson Online [12], OSN sites are visited by 75% of all active Internet households, for an average of 6 hours and 13 minutes a month. One of the primary activities of OSN users is sharing content with friends (e.g., status updates, web links, photos, videos) [1]. Because OSNs have made it easy for anyone to create, publish, distribute and consume content, the amount of data shared on such sites has grown massively. For instance, Facebook users uploaded more than 15 billion photos to date and continue to upload 220 million new photos every week. In fact, Facebook is the biggest photo-sharing site on the web [8], demanding 1.5 petabytes

of storage and 25 terabytes of additional storage every week. Given the trends, we expect that personal data shared on OSNs would account for a significant fraction of the entire Internet traffic.

Personal data that is shared on OSNs—which we call *social content*—is different from other web content. When people publish content on the web, typically their intent is to make the content accessible to Internet users everywhere. In contrast, *social content* has a limited intended audience. In some cases the audience is explicitly determined by the user or the site's policy (e.g., content can only be seen by friends). At other times, the audience is implicitly limited by the nature of the content. For example, a user's vacation pictures will be of interest primarily to people in the user's social circle.

1.1 The current data sharing architecture

Despite the fundamental differences between social and web content, OSN users today share data using content delivery architectures that were designed for traditional web content. Typically, users upload their content to centrally managed OSN servers in remote data centers, where the content is stored, often after having been converted to a lower-quality format that suits OSNs' storage requirements. Like content uploads, content downloads in OSNs also rely on the traditional web content delivery architecture. For instance, pictures uploaded to Facebook are delivered to users by the Akamai content delivery network (CDN), whose caches are deployed over geographically diverse regions in order to provide satisfying response times to users.

While the traditional web infrastructure scales well, it has several drawbacks when used for social content. One immediate drawback is that users *lose control* over their data [11, 13]. Several aspects contribute to this loss of control, including:

1. *Constraints on content shared:* OSN users sharing personal data are often subject to various site-specific constraints. Some sites allow particular types of contents to be shared but not others (e.g. Facebook and Flickr allow pictures and videos but not music). OSNs like Facebook and YouTube constrain the size and the resolution at which multimedia content can be shared.

2. *Ownership and copyrights:* Users who upload personal content to OSNs are often subject to complex (and dynamically changing) terms of ownership rights. For ex-

ample, many OSNs like Facebook demand fairly broad rights to use the content shared on their sites.[1]

3. *Privacy:* The last but perhaps most widely recognized concern with sharing data using OSNs is the associated loss of privacy. OSNs are known to change their privacy settings for uploaded content in ways that often catch ordinary users off-guard and compromise the privacy of the data they share [9, 14].

Another drawback is that managing the deluge of social content is becoming increasingly challenging and expensive for the OSN service providers [8]. The traditional web delivery infrastructure is optimized to serve highly popular content that lends itself to performance improvements through CDN caching. Social content, however, is of interest to a small audience and hence unlikely to become very popular. In fact, in Section 2, our study reveals that up to 97% of all photos shared over the Flickr social network and 44% of all videos shared over the YouTube social network are never accessed during the course of a given week. This translates to huge amounts of wasted storage capacity in data centers. Furthermore, the 3% of photos and 56% of videos that are accessed are only requested a small number of times, which reduces the effectiveness of CDN caching.

1.2 Exploring alternative architectures

In light of the above drawbacks with traditional centralized delivery architectures, researchers have started exploring alternative content sharing designs. One particularly appealing proposal is to share social content directly from users' homes. With home-based sharing, users can regain control over their social content. Furthermore, recent trends such as the availability of large, inexpensive home storage devices and always on, high-speed broadband connectivity bode well for a future where data is shared from homes. Finally, because most social content is generated by users in their homes, home-based sharing eliminates the need for uploading content to remote data centers.

Recent proposals for home-based content sharing include PeerSon [2], which sketches a social network that runs on a peer-to-peer (P2P) network, where individual users manage their own storage and run the distributed hash table (DHT) to route content. In addition to purely distributed designs, there are also hybrid designs that utilize home networks as well as external network entities. One such example is Vis-a-Vis [13], a system that relies on users' desktop machines and the cloud computing architecture to exchange content. Another example is Diaspora [5], a recent project that aims to create a fully-decentralized OSN entirely controlled by end-users. Diaspora is a network of personal servers that can run in end-users' homes or other infrastructure.

1.3 Our goals and contributions

While the above proposals have attracted a lot of attention, it is still unclear how well they would work in practice. Unlike centralized infrastructures like data centers and CDNs that are well provisioned and well managed by expert operators, home networks have limited resources (both storage and bandwidth) and are managed by lay users. Consequently, there are several unresolved concerns about the availability and performance of home-based content sharing architectures.

---

[1] Facebook terms of use: http://www.facebook.com/#!/terms.php?ref=pf

In this paper, we address these concerns by presenting a measurement-driven feasibility study of sharing social content from homes. To conduct this study, we first needed to understand (a) *the characteristics of OSN workloads*, i.e., patterns of social content uploads and downloads, and (b) *the characteristics of home networks*, i.e., the availability and utilization of residential access links. To this end, we gathered and analyzed detailed real-world traces from OSNs and home networks. Later, we used these traces to analyze the extent to which social content can be stored and delivered from users' homes.

To summarize our key findings here: (1) We found that the vast majority of OSN users upload a relatively small amount of content (in the order of a few gigabytes), and that a large fraction of the content is requested rarely. (2) Broadband links are scarcely utilized and have high availability. However, in order to achieve high availability an always-on device is required, like for example a home gateway. (3) When OSN workloads are served from an always-on home gateway, most of the content can be successfully delivered. However, resources in restricted home environments may not be sufficient to deliver a small fraction of content that is highly popular. Such bandwidth-demanding content might be better served by a centralized architecture. Overall, our study indicates that *it is feasible to deliver most social content directly from user homes.*

2. SOCIAL CONTENT WORKLOADS

OSNs have changed the way content is shared on the Internet. In this section we study the characteristics of OSN content using real traces gathered from popular OSN sites, and focus on the differences between OSN and the traditional web content.

2.1 Datasets

We implemented a web crawler for flickr.com and youtube.com, which are popular sites that allow people to share content with their friends. Our crawler gathered detailed information about the uploads and downloads of publicly available content from these sites.

- **Flickr:** We randomly chose 11,715 users from the list of 2.5 million users gathered by [4]. We crawled the profile pages of these users daily for 19 consecutive days. In total, these users had uploaded 1,324,080 publicly accessible photos. For each photo, we recorded the number of daily views received, as well as metadata, like photo size, tags, and favorite markings.

- **YouTube:** We randomly chose 77,575 users from the list of YouTube users gathered by [3]. We collected information about the videos uploaded by these users. In total, these users had uploaded 1,251,492 publicly accessible videos. We collected the number of daily views for all of these videos over a period of 166 days using the "StatisticsAndData" feature in YouTube.

Ideally we would have liked to include data from an OSN site like Facebook, but obtaining data from such sites is hard because most of the shared content is private. In contrast, all the data we gathered from Flickr and YouTube is publicly accessible. Furthermore, these two sites provide mechanisms for searching and featuring popular content. Hence, our analysis of content *consumption* patterns is likely to overestimate the popularity that content would have reached

(a) Objects

(b) Bytes

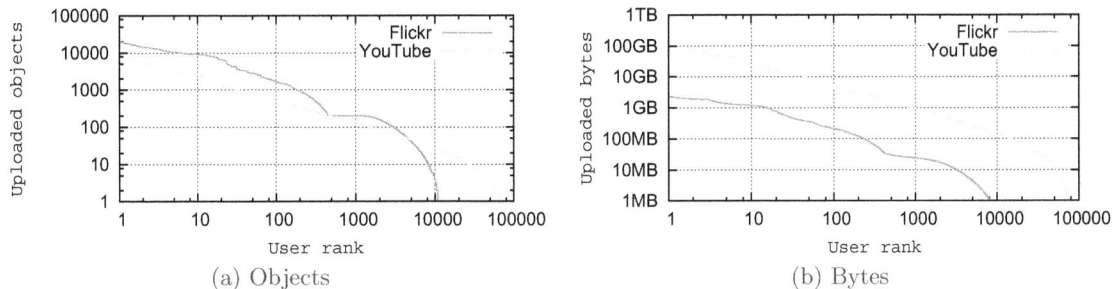

Figure 1: Content production patterns: (a) users ranked by number of uploaded objects and (b) by the total size of uploaded content.

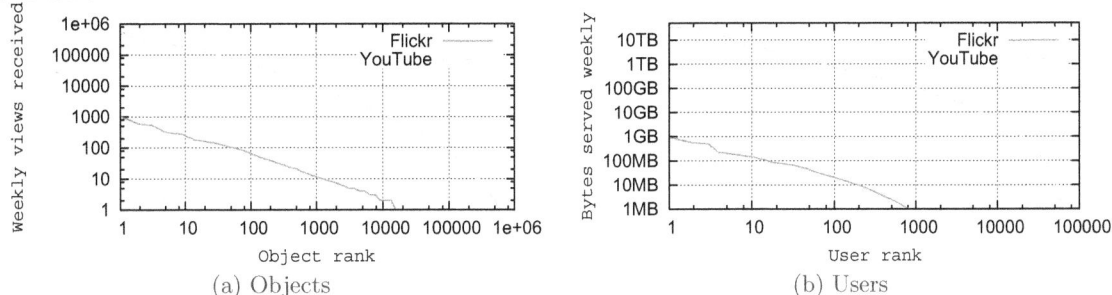

(a) Objects

(b) Users

Figure 2: Content consumption patterns: (a) objects ranked by the number of weekly requests and (b) the total amount of content served by Flickr and YouTube on behalf of content uploaders.

had it been shared on an OSN site like Facebook. On the other hand, the content *production* patterns are likely to be similar to the ones in Facebook.

2.2 Content production patterns

In order to understand the storage requirements for sharing OSN content from home, we study the content production patterns of Flickr and YouTube users. We examine the total amount of content shared by each user in our dataset since they joined Flickr and YouTube. The average user in our dataset has been in the system for over 4 years.

Figure 1(a) shows the rank of each user against the total number of objects (photos and videos) they shared, in a log-log plot. Flickr shows a plateau at 200 pictures, as a consequence of the limit imposed on the number of photos visible in a free account. The content production rate is generally low; users uploaded on average 111 photos (median=29) and 16 videos (median=6). Only 10 Flickr users (accounting for 0.08% of all users) uploaded more than 10,000 pictures. Likewise, only 40 YouTube users (0.05%) uploaded more than 1,000 videos.

Figure 1(b) shows the same trend as a function of the total size of uploaded content. Because we are interested in the storage requirements for active users, we only show users who uploaded more than 1MB. While a small fraction of users uploaded more than 100GB of videos, the remaining users' uploads remain small in size. Users on average uploaded 13.3MB to Flickr and 103MB to YouTube. Even the most prolific user on Flickr uploaded less than 3GB. This amount of data can easily fit into a small storage device, e.g., a USB-stick attached to a home gateway. Our analysis indicates that while the total amount of content that is shared by all users on an OSN is massive, *individual users only share a limited amount of content* and this content can fit on affordable storage devices.

2.3 Content consumption patterns

Next, in order to understand how frequently requests arrive for OSN content, we study content consumption patterns. We examine the number of requests each shared object and each uploader receive in a typical week. Due to space limitation, we present the request patterns based on the last week of our data. However, we did not observe significant changes when we examined other randomly chosen weeks.

Figure 2(a) shows the number of requests each shared object in Flickr and YouTube received during the one week period. YouTube videos in general receive more requests than Flickr photos. Many factors may contribute to this disparity such as the different popularity of the two sites—according to alexa.com, 22% of global Internet users visit YouTube, while only 2.5% visit Flickr.

With respect to the popularity of OSN content, we make two observations from Figure 2(a). First, not all 1,324,080 Flickr photos and 1,251,492 YouTube videos were requested during a week period. Rather, *a substantial fraction of objects did not receive a single request* during an entire week. More precisely, 97% of Flickr photos and 44% of YouTube videos were never requested during the one week period. These results suggest that the number of objects that need to be made readily available to web servers and CDNs can, at least potentially, be drastically reduced.

The second observation is that even the content that was requested received only a few requests during the one week period. Almost all Flickr photos received less than 1,000 requests. YouTube contained about 1,000 very popular videos, which were viewed over 10,000 times. However, the remaining videos (99% of all videos, or 88% of all videos with at least one request) each received no more than one thousand requests. The fact that many objects are unpopular is promising for the feasibility of a decentralized architecture, because it reduces the resource demand on home networks.

Finally, in order to see how popular objects are distributed across users, in Figure 2(b), we show the total amount of bytes that Flickr and YouTube served on behalf of the uploaders. This number is important because it represents how much data users would need to serve from their homes. More than 75% of YouTube users need to serve 1GB/week or less. This corresponds to an average bandwidth of 13Kbps, and is thus a demand that home connections can potentially meet. The bandwidth demands for Flickr photos are roughly two orders of magnitude smaller.

3. HOME NETWORK ENVIRONMENTS

Compared to well-provisioned and maintained centralized infrastructures like data centers and CDNs, most home network environments are resource-constrained and are managed by lay users. This raises a concern about the reliability of sharing content from home. In this section, we characterize the reliability of home network environments based on real measurements.

3.1 Methodology

For this work, we custom built home servers using NetGear wireless routers and deployed them in a number of households.

3.1.1 Customizing home gateways as servers

We turned the NetGear WGT634U home router into a home server. This router is equipped with a 200 MHz MIPS CPUs.[2] We attached a 2GB USB-based external flash drive for storing content, as shown in Figure 3, then installed OpenWrt, an open source Linux distribution for embedded devices, and ran a lightweight HTTP server to serve content stored on the drive.[3]

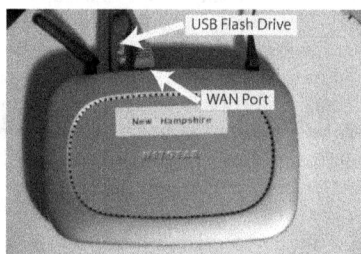

Figure 3: Wireless router equipped with USB storage used in testbed.

Our home servers are inexpensive and require only a limited amount of power. The cost of a home router comparable to the one we used is around $60. The cost of a 2GB flash drive today is $9. If additional storage is needed, it is possible to attach external USB hard disks that provide several hundred gigabytes or even terabytes of storage space. The wireless router is powered by an adapter whose maximum power output is 12 watts. Even assuming constant maximum power consumption, the router would consume about 100KWh over an entire year, which translates into a yearly cost of $18 (using electricity retail prices in the New York area in February 2010 [7]). Hence, we claim that an always-on home server is an affordable solution for most users.

---

[2]Specification of the NetGear WGT634U router `http://tinyurl.com/33vpnun`
[3]`http://www.openwrt.org`, `http://www.lighttpd.net/`

3.1.2 Deployed testbed

We deployed our home gateways in 10 households in 2 different continents: Europe (Germany, Spain, and Italy) and Asia (Korea). The gateways are connected to 9 different Internet Service Providers (ISPs).

The data from these gateways was collected over 79 consecutive days from April 1st to June 18th, 2010.

We instrumented the router to run a measurement daemon which performed the following three tasks: (1) sending minute-by-minute heartbeat messages to a remote tracking server, in order to infer the availability of gateways; (2) monitoring all traffic sent through the gateway, in order to measure utilization of the residential Internet links and detect the presence of any local devices accessing the Internet; and (3) periodically fetching media files (pictures and videos) from randomly selected routers in the testbed as well as from Facebook, in order to compare the performance of a decentralized architecture with that of Facebook. The media files exchanged and the logs of all the results were stored on the USB storage devices. In order to prevent our measurements from interfering with users' Internet traffic (such as Web or Skype), our gateways upload the media files at strictly lower priority than the traffic generated by locally connected devices.

While the number of deployed gateways in our testbed may seem small, especially when compared to prior studies of residential networks [6], no prior study has ever gathered such detailed performance measurements about home network environments over several months. Such data is necessary to evaluate the content delivery capacity of home networks. Moreover, we observed that network usage across the households in our deployment is quite varied and ranges from scarcely used network connections to very active subscribers.

Average connected time	98%
Median unavailability period	11 minutes
Unavailability period (90th percentile)	12 hours
Longest unavailability period	3.6 days
Average # of disconnections per day	0.1
Average # of IP changes per day	0.4

Table 1: Statistics about the availability of gateways in our testbed.

3.2 Availability of home gateways

We used data from the heartbeat messages to infer the availability of gateways. We consider a router to be *unavailable* if the tracking server misses five consecutive heartbeat messages from the router, i.e., does not hear a heartbeat over a period of five minutes. By waiting for five consecutive message losses, we reduce the chance of misinterpreting occasional packet losses as router unavailability.

Table 1 reports the availability of home gateways. Overall, the availability of gateways is generally high—around 98%. Unavailability periods are typically short; the median unavailability period is just 11 minutes. Occasionally, the unavailability periods lasted from several hours to a few days. Anecdotal evidence suggests that this happened when users turned off the power and left their home for a long time. The longest unavailability period lasted 3.6 days. However, in 90% of cases, the unavailability lasted less than 12 hours.

Another potential cause of unavailability are ISPs periodically resetting the home Internet connection to reassign the IP address of home gateways. However, Table 1 shows that

Transfer outcome	Served by Akamai			Served from home		
	Photo	Video	All	Photo	Video	All
OK	99.8%	98.7%	99.7%	93.1%	82.8%	93.0%
Not found	0.001%	0.9%	0.01%	0.4%	0%	0.4%
Server internal error	0.0002%	0%	0.0002%	2.4%	2.6%	**2.4%**
Empty response	0.003%	0%	0.003%	2.0%	2.4%	**2.0%**
Connection failed	0.02%	0.1%	0.02%	1.8%	2.0%	**1.8%**
DNS resolution failed	0.2%	0.2%	**0.2%**	0.01%	0.02%	0.01%
Total	1,517,406	12,521	1,529,927	1,060,027	8,700	1,068,727

Table 2: Summary of the outcome of content downloads: Akamai's failed transfers are dominated by DNS resolution errors, whereas failures in the testbed are dominated by a single faulty gateway and failed connection attempts due to disconnected gateways.

IP changes were infrequent. In fact, this happened for only 1 of the 9 ISPs we monitored. Also, when the connection was reset, the loss of connectivity lasted significantly less than five minutes and was thus never registered as an unavailability period. Overall, these results demonstrate that it is possible to achieve high reliability from home gateways.

	Photo download time (sec)	
Percentile	Akamai	From home
10th	0.11	0.58
50th	0.36	1.91
80th	0.81	2.91
95th	1.38	5.32
99th	4.69	10.33

Table 3: Time required to download a photo.

3.2.1 Availability of home devices

How would the availability be affected if, instead of home gateways, we used laptops and desktop computers as servers? To understand the availability of these home devices, we measured how long home devices are connected to the gateways. On average 3.1 different local devices were connected to each gateway at some time. While most home networks had multiple devices, 73% of the time there was no device connected to the gateway. In fact, even the most available local device (i.e., the device that remained connected to the gateway the largest fraction of time) was connected only 62% of time. The availability of home devices compares poorly with that of gateway servers (with average availability of 98%). This suggests that serving content directly from home devices might not be a viable solution.

3.3 Utilization of home access links

Residential Internet access links are known to have limited capacities [6]. Furthermore, a home gateway server can only rely on access link bandwidth that is not being used by home devices. A crucial question therefore is *how often are access links of home networks utilized and to what extent?*.

To answer this question, we analyzed the data collected from monitoring home network traffic. We computed the average utilization of all links over each 5-minute interval. We found that upstream links are not used more than 80% of the time, while the downstream links are not used more than 40% of the time. Furthermore, for 95% of the time, the link usage was below 230Kbps and 15Kbps for the downstream and upstream directions, respectively. We also looked at the hourly usage of individual upstream links and found that usage is very bursty and very low (below 50Kbps) when averaged over one-hour periods. Since all the access links had a downstream capacity of several Mbps and an upstream of several hundreds of Kbps, the results show that even when the access links were being used, they had plenty of spare capacity left for other traffic.

4. PERFORMANCE OF HOME-BASED CONTENT SHARING

In order to assess the performance of sharing content from home gateways, we stored 20 JPEG pictures and 1 MPEG4 video file on the USB storage of each gateway and measured the performance of fetching each file from other gateways. For comparison purposes, we uploaded the same media files to Facebook. The size of the files were between 80KB and 130KB for pictures and 18MB for the video.

Every 10 minutes, each gateway requests the pictures from a randomly chosen gateway and from the Akamai URL [4] used by Facebook to deliver the files. The same is done for the video file, although only once every hour. For each download, we recorded the completion times and any error and HTTP response codes.

On average, each home gateway in our experiments serves more than 4GB per week, which is more than the weekly data served today on behalf of 75% of YouTube users and 100% of Flickr users (see Section 2.3 and Figure 2 (b)). Therefore, our results here suggests that most social content can be served using home gateways.

4.1 Successful content downloads

We discuss how often the media file downloads were successfully completed. Table 2 displays the statistics for the content downloads. Overall, the percentages of successful downloads using home servers and Akamai are comparable (93% using home servers and 99.7% using Akamai), although Akamai is clearly preferable if one needs a highly reliable service. Given that content sharing is not a mission-critical service, the slightly lower reliability offered by home servers might be acceptable for many users.

Table 2 also reports the major sources of errors that caused content downloads to fail. The major sources of error for Akamai were failed DNS resolutions, where the client could not successfully resolve the Akamai URL. In the case of content served from the testbed, the major sources of errors were internal server errors and empty responses. After inspecting the logs, we found that a lot of these errors were generated by a single gateway with faulty USB storage. Excluding this outlier, the main source of error was failed connections to the server. This accounted for a small 1.8% of the cases, which well matches the 98% availability of the gateways presented above.

4.2 Performance of photo browsing

Next we look at the time taken to complete the photo downloads. Table 3 displays the percentile of download times

---

[4]Before every transfer, the gateway resolves the Akamai URL with a DNS query to obtain the current Akamai server's IP.

in the experiments. Even when photos were served from home gateways, 80% of the downloads took less than 3 seconds, a performance likely to be acceptable for many users. Optimized versions of the system could prefetch photos in the same photo album to hide fetch latency from the user. Prefetching seems to be useful since users are likely to spend a few seconds viewing a photo before requesting the next one. Thus, the results suggest that users can obtain acceptable performance when sharing their photos with friends directly from their homes.

4.3 Performance of video streaming

Unlike photos, which are typically looked at after being downloaded, videos are often watched as on-demand streams. So when evaluating the performance of video sharing, we looked at download bandwidths rather than download completion times.

Figure 4 reports the average bandwidths achieved during the media streaming experiments. The testbed cannot compete with the performance of the Akamai servers. However, 95% of transfers achieve an average bandwidth higher than 200Kbps (which correspond to low-bit rate streams), while 66% of transfers achieve an average bandwidth higher than 400Kbps—an encoding rate that is higher than a majority of YouTube videos [10]. The transfer bandwidths are by and large limited by the upstream capacities of home Internet connections.

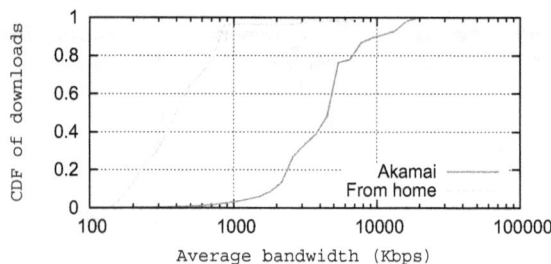

Figure 4: Bandwidth achieved by video downloads.

High average bandwidth alone does not guarantee that video streaming was uninterrupted. To understand whether a user would be able to watch a video streamed from home servers without interruption, we recorded the bandwidth achieved in every 1-second interval of streaming downloads and used the data to compute how many playbacks with a certain encoding rate would complete uninterrupted. In the computation, we assumed that all videos have a duration of 140 seconds. We also considered different pre-buffering times (i.e., the time between the begin of the video download and when the first frame is shown to the user).

Figure 5 shows the fraction of uninterrupted media playbacks for gateways whose upstream capacity is at least as high as the streaming bit rate. For low bit rates (100-200Kbps), two seconds of pre-buffering are sufficient for most playbacks to end without interruptions. These bit rates are more than enough for high-quality MP3 audio files, thus showing that music can be effectively streamed from home. For YouTube-like bit-rates (400Kbps), a consistent amount of pre-buffering is needed to lower the fraction of uninterrupted playbacks. For example, if the content is pre-buffered for 5 seconds (equal to 3% of the video duration), almost 80% of playbacks succeed. At higher bit-rates, no reasonable amount of pre-buffering can reduce the fraction of interrupted playbacks.

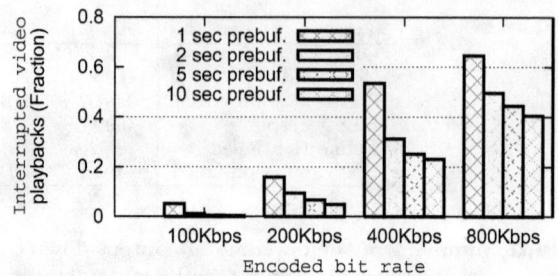

Figure 5: Fraction of interrupted playbacks across varying pre-buffering times and encoding rates.

5. CONCLUSIONS

Sharing personal and social content with friends has become an extremely popular activity for many OSN users. However, current OSN content delivery architectures require users to give up control over the data they share on OSNs. In this paper, we examine the feasibility of sharing social content directly from user homes. By sharing data from home networks, which they own and control, users can regain control over their data. Our analysis using measurements of OSN workloads and home network environments suggests that it would be possible to deliver most social content from users' home networks.

6. REFERENCES

[1] F. Benevenuto, T. Rodrigues, M. Cha, and V. Almeida. Characterizing user behavior in online social networks. In *ACM IMC*, 2009.

[2] S. Buchegger, D. Schiöberg, L. H. Vu, and A. Datta. PeerSoN: P2P social networking - early experiences and insights. In *ACM Social Network System Workshop*, 2009.

[3] M. Cha, H. Kwak, P. Rodriguez, Y.-Y. Ahn, and S. Moon. I tube, you tube, everybody tubes: Analyzing the world's largest user generated content video system. In *ACM IMC*, 2007.

[4] M. Cha, A. Mislove, and K. P. Gummadi. A measurement-driven analysis of information propagation in the flickr social network. In *WWW*, 2009.

[5] Diaspora OSN. http://www.joindiaspora.com.

[6] M. Dischinger, A. Haeberlen, K. P. Gummadi, and S. Saroiu. Characterizing residential broadband networks. In *ACM IMC*, 2007.

[7] Average retail price of electricity, U.S. Energy Information Administration, 2010. http://tinyurl.com/525u28.

[8] Facebook engineering. needle in a haystack: Efficient storage of billions of photos, 2009. http://tinyurl.com/cju2og.

[9] Nick Bilton, Price of Facebook privacy? start clicking. NYTimes, 2010. http://tinyurl.com/39nyzfb.

[10] P. Gill, M. Arlitt, Z. Li, and A. Mahanti. Youtube traffic characterization: A view from the edge. In *ACM IMC*, 2007.

[11] M. M. Lucas and N. Borisov. Flybynight: mitigating the privacy risks of social networking. In *ACM Workshop on Privacy in the Electronic Society (WPES)*, 2008.

[12] Nielsen Online Report. Social networks & blogs now 4th most popular online activity, 2009. http://tinyurl.com/cfzjlt.

[13] A. Shakimov, A. Varshavsky, L. P. Cox, and R. Cáceres. Privacy, cost, and availability tradeoffs in decentralized OSNs. In *ACM SIGCOMM WOSN*, 2009.

[14] J. Sun, X. Zhu, and Y. Fang. A privacy-preserving scheme for online social networks with efficient revocation. In *IEEE INFOCOM*, 2010.

Load-Balanced Migration of Social Media to Content Clouds[*]

Xu Cheng
School of Computing Science
Simon Fraser University
British Columbia, Canada
xuc@cs.sfu.ca

Jiangchuan Liu
School of Computing Science
Simon Fraser University
British Columbia, Canada
jcliu@cs.sfu.ca

ABSTRACT

Social networked applications have been more and more popular, and have brought great challenges to the network engineering, particularly the huge demands of bandwidth and storage for social media. The recently emerged content clouds shed light on this dilemma. Towards the migration to clouds, partitioning the social contents has drawn significant interests from the literature. Yet the existing works focus on preserving the social relationship only, while an important factor, user access pattern, is largely overlooked.

In this paper, by examining a large collection of YouTube video data, we first demonstrate that partitioning the network entirely based on social relationship would lead to unbalanced partitions in terms of access. We further analyze the role of social relationship in the social media applications, and conclude that user access pattern should be taken into account and social relationship should be dynamically preserved. We formulate the problem as a constrained k-medoids clustering problem, and propose a novel Weighted Partitioning Around Medoids (wPAM) solution. We present a dissimilarity/similarity metric to facilitate the preservation of the social relationship. We compare our solution with other state-of-the-art algorithms, and the preliminary results show that it significantly decreases the access deviation in each cloud server, and flexibly preserves the social relationship.

Categories and Subject Descriptors

H.3.4 [**Information Storage and Retrieval**]: Systems and Software—*Distributed Systems*

General Terms

Algorithms, Measurement, Performance

Keywords

Social Network, Content Cloud, Clustering

[*]This research is supported by a Canada NSERC Strategic Project Grant, an NSERC Discovery Grant, an NSERC DAS Grant, and an MITACS Project Grant.

1. INTRODUCTION

Social networked applications and services have been dominating the Web 2.0 world in the recent years. The most popular applications include YouTube[1] for video sharing, Facebook[2] for online social networking, and Twitter[3] for micro-blogging. Besides these representatives, many other user-generated content (UGC) applications have emerged and been developing extremely fast.

Generally, it is difficult if not impossible to predict the impact and the development of any UGC application in advance. The provision of resource is thus a great challenge, because any application is possible to grow to the similar scale to YouTube and Facebook, and any one is possible to fail. The applications have brought great challenges to the network engineering, and social media faces a much greater challenge because of the huge resource demands of bandwidth and storage. The recently emerged content cloud service sheds light on this dilemma. Clouds provide "pay-as-you-go" service that allows designers to start small and easy to grow big [1]. A migration that moves the current non-cloud contents, particularly video contents, into clouds is essential for the benefit of the social networked application's development and competition.

To move such application into content clouds, one of the most important steps is to partition the social media contents and assign them into a number of cloud servers. Different from traditional web contents that are isolated, social media contents have connections among each other, and thus the partition is non-trivial. There are some existing works trying to solve this problem, e.g., SNAP [2] and SPAR [15]. Aiming at preserving the social relationship, they are quite effective tools to partition the social network.

However, considering the cloud scenario, one important factor, user access pattern, is largely overlooked in the previous studies. If the videos are assigned into cloud servers entirely based on social relationship, a possible result is that some servers hold many very popular videos but some hold many very unpopular ones, even if the load-balance in terms of the video number is considered. By the evidence of our measurement study on a large collection of YouTube video data, we demonstrate the existence of this phenomenon, which would cause great problem in cloud computing, from the perspective of network engineering. Specifically in the client/server architecture scenario, some cloud servers with many popular videos would be accessed much more fre-

---

[1]http://www.youtube.com
[2]http://www.facebook.com
[3]http://twitter.com

quently than the other servers with many unpopular videos, and this behavior would decrease the utilization of cloud computing [1]. Even worse, one cloud server may not handle the computation and transmission of the intensive data, while workloads of others are extremely low. The unbalanced partition would also lead to network traffic problems, thus further degrading the quality of service.

On the other hand, partitioning the social media is not simply isolating the popular videos and evenly distributing the others. Taking YouTube as an example, we analyze the role of social relationship in the application, and argue that the social relationship should be dynamically preserved.

In this paper, we formulate the problem as a constrained k-medoids clustering problem, and present a dissimilarity/similarity metric to facilitate the preservation of the social relationship. We propose a novel Weighted Partitioning Around Medoids (wPAM) algorithm to partition the social networked video repository, focusing on load-balance in terms of access. We evaluate our solution on YouTube data, comparing with state-of-the-art algorithms. The preliminary results show that wPAM achieves extremely low deviation of load in terms of the popularity, and flexibly preserves the social relationship under different requirements.

2. RELATE WORK

Web 2.0 UGC applications are emerging in the recent years, and there have been numerous related measurement studies, particularly on understanding YouTube for video sharing [16][5][16], Facebook, MySpace and LinkedIn for online social networking [12][3], Twitter for micro-blogging [9], and etc. Most of them focus on the social structure, user behaviors, and network usage.

There are some works trying to detect the communities and partition social networks. Newman et al. studied a set of algorithms for discovering community structure [13]. The algorithms iteratively remove edges, identified by "betweenness" measure, from the network to split it into communities. Mishra et al. introduced a new criterion that overcomes the limitations that clusters typically do not overlap, by combining internal density with external sparsity in a natural way [11]. SNAP [2] is a tool for analyzing and partitioning small-world network, and it introduces a series of algorithms trying to maximize the modularity of the graph in a parallel manner. SPAR [15] is a work similar to ours, as it considers the cloud scenario. SPAR replicates linked nodes in the same server, and tries to minimize the replications. But as mentioned, while the social relationship is an important factor to the efficiency of the cloud computing, user access pattern is overlooked in their work. Also, different from their work, we focus on the migration to clouds, and thus the maintenance such as adding and removing nodes and edges, adding and removing cloud servers, is not our focus in this paper.

3. MOTIVATION

In this section, we argue that partitioning the social media entirely based on social relationship is not enough, as user access pattern should be taken into account. By examining YouTube video data, we show the correlation between the social relationship and the user access pattern. We also discuss the role of social relationship in social media applications, and conclude that a dynamic preservation of social relationship is preferred.

3.1 Understanding User Access Pattern

User access pattern is yet to be considered while partitioning the social media. We show strong evidence that partitioning entirely based on social relationship would lead to unbalanced partitions in terms of popularity.

We have crawled YouTube videos and obtained a dataset containing over $40,000$ videos. The methodology of the data collection can be referred to our previous work [5]. We focus on the information of video ID, popularity (the number of views), and IDs of the related videos in the dataset. YouTube video graph is a directed graph, and the dataset only records the top-twenty outgoing related video IDs for each video, yet the incoming videos can be easily found within the dataset, and the number might be much greater than 20. We are particularly interested in the number of views and incoming links.

Figure 1 shows the scatter plot of the video's popularity against the number of incoming links. There is a clear trend that videos with more incoming links have greater number of views. This is because videos with more incoming links have more chances to be accessed through related videos. Yet videos with few incoming links might also be very popular, because our measurement dataset is not the entire YouTube video repository. Nevertheless, videos with many incoming links are mostly popular.

We further study the correlation between the video's popularity and the neighbors' popularity. We calculate the mean of neighbors' views, and plot in Figure 2, which clearly shows the positive correlation. Figure 3 further shows the CDF of the ratio of neighbors' popularity and its own popularity. Most of the videos have the comparable number of views as their neighbors' (ratio between 0.1 and 10). This characteristic indicates that if a video is popular, its neighbors are probably also popular, and vice versa.

In summary, a popular video's social neighbors are probably also popular, and they are likely to be clustered based on social relationship only.

3.2 Social Relationship Is Not Enough

From the measurement above we know that partitioning the social media entirely based on social relationship would lead to unbalanced partitions, i.e., some cloud servers have many very popular videos, but others have many very unpopular videos. This behavior would cause great problems in the content clouds as we discussed.

Figure 4 gives a simple example: 8 nodes, each with a weight in terms of popularity as shown, constitute a social graph, which is divided into two parts. As a result, the number of inter-connections is 2 on the left graph, but the standard deviation of the total weight in each part is as great as 348; while on the right graph that we take popularity into account, although the number of inter-connections is 4, the standard deviation is as small as 23.

3.3 Beyond Social Relationship

It is intuitive to preserve the social relationship when partitioning the social graph, but we raise our question: is social relationship that important? Towards answering this question, we analyze the role that social relationship plays in social media applications.

We take the representative YouTube as an example, and discuss videos' social relationship in particular. Each YouTube video has a list of related videos, which constitute

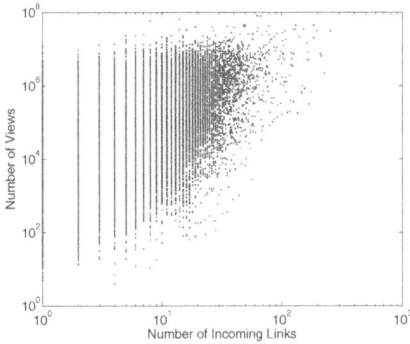

Figure 1: Popularity against incoming links

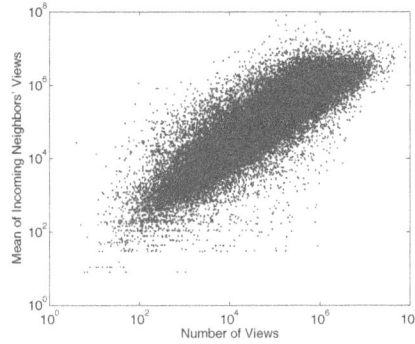

Figure 2: Mean of neighbor view against number of views

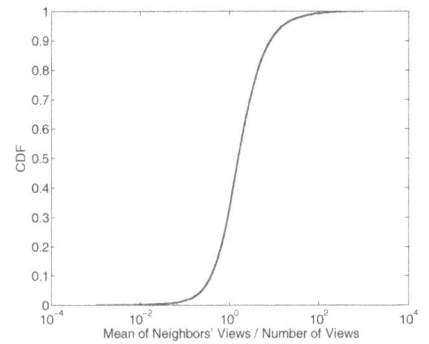

Figure 3: CDF of mean of neighbors' views over number of views

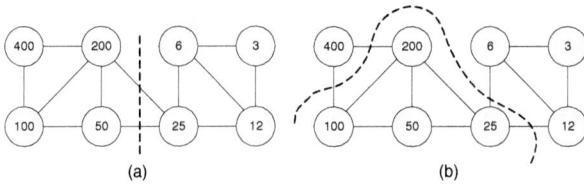

Figure 4: Example of different partitions based on (a) social relationship only, (b) both social relationship and popularity

a social graph. Two videos that have similar titles, tags, descriptions are likely to be linked to each other. The related videos can also be considered as the recommendation from the YouTube system [16]. As studied, one related video is possible to be requested after the user finishes the current video [5][16]. If two related videos are held by the same cloud server, the system can quickly locate the second one to achieve a smooth transition; if the two videos are held by two different cloud servers, this process would take longer, and thus delay would occur. Therefore from this perspective, preserving social relationship is beneficial.

However, the social relationship among videos is not so important that preserving it should be the top priority. As the measurement study shows, about 30% of the overall views are referred from the related recommendation, which is the most important view source [16]. This characteristic indicates that the system's recommendation has a great influence on user's viewing behavior, and thus the system can easily adapt to the situation where related videos are in different cloud servers, e.g., by lowering the rank of the recommendation of the videos that are in different cloud servers. In fact, Zhou et al. suggested utilizing YouTube recommendation to help increase the diversity of video views in aggregation, which encourages users to discover more videos of their interest rather than the popular videos only [16].

Furthermore, a pre-fetching mechanism, where the next video is predicted and being fetched while the user is watching the first video, has been proposed to reduce the startup delay for social media sharing [4]. Considering a system utilizes such a mechanism, sending the two videos at the same time from the two respective cloud servers works better, because it takes advantage of the cloud computing and better utilizes the network resource. Thus from this perspective,

breaking the social relationship is beneficial, which seems counter-intuitive but is the case under this circumstance.

In summary, the importance of preserving social relationship is not so significant, and thus it should not be the top priority. Some systems can easily adapt to the situation where related videos are held by different cloud servers, and if the systems utilize a pre-fetching mechanism, it is even better to break the social relationship.

4. PROBLEM STATEMENT

In this section, we first formulate the problem statement, and then introduce a new distance metric used in the problem. We also discuss the details about weight constraint.

4.1 Formulation

Consider a social graph with N nodes $n_1, n_2, \ldots, n_N$, each node n_i has a weight w_i.

We try to partition the nodes into k clusters (cloud servers), $C_1, C_2, \ldots, C_k$. Each cluster C_j has a weight W_j, which is the summation of all the weights of the nodes in cluster C_j, $W_j = \sum_{n_i \in C_j} w_i$.

We suppose there is a representative node o_j in each cluster C_j. We denote $d(n_s, n_t)$ as a distance metric between the two node n_s and n_t. The problem is to find a partition which minimizes

$$E = \sum_{j=1}^{k} \sum_{n_i \in C_j} d(n_i, o_j)$$

subject to

$$|W_{j_1} - W_{j_2}| < \Delta$$

for $j_1, j_2 = 1, 2, \ldots, k$, where Δ is a weight difference constraint.

The problem can be considered as a k-medoids clustering problem with constraint. k-medoids problem is related to k-means problem, except that k-means calculates the mean in each cluster as the center yet k-medoids selects a representative node in each cluster as the center. k-medoids method is more robust than k-means in the presence of noise and outliers, because a medoid is less influenced by outliers or other extreme values than a mean [6].

4.2 Node Distance – Dissimilarity/Similarity

In the previous studies, several metrics for measuring social networks are used, such as betweenness [13], con-

53

ductance [11], modularity [2], and number of replicas [15]. Since k-medoids problems generally use Euclidean distance as the metric, we initially considered using integral number of shortest path length between nodes as the metric. After further consideration, we found that the range of the integral path length is however too small. Studies have shown that the shortest path length for YouTube dataset is about 8 [5], and that individuals are separated by six degrees of social contact, known as "six degree of separation" [10]. Furthermore, to compute the path length between two nodes requires the whole knowledge of the social graph, which is very costly.

We thus introduce a new metric, dissimilarity/similarity. It provides a much larger range of calculation than integral number of path length, and computing it only requires the knowledge of the adjacent nodes, which is much more efficient than requiring the information of the whole graph.

We define the similarity metric as follows: consider two nodes n_s and n_t, each has a set of adjacent nodes A_s and A_t. Let $A_s^* = A_s \cup n_s$ and $A_t^* = A_t \cup n_t$. The similarity is calculated as

$$\mathbf{sim}(n_s, n_t) = \frac{|A_s^* \bigcap A_t^*|}{|A_s^* \bigcup A_t^*|}.$$

Different from Jaccard similarity coefficient [7], we include the node itself in the adjacent node set, because we take the relationship between the two target nodes into account as well. Take Figure 5 as an example, both n_s and n_t have four adjacent nodes, yet they are not adjacent on the left while they are on the right. If we do not include the node itself in the adjacent node set, i.e., the similarity is calculated by Jaccard similarity coefficient as $\frac{|A_s \bigcap A_t|}{|A_s \bigcup A_t|}$, the results are 1 and 0.6, respectively, but the right graph is closer to our concept of "similar". By our definition of similarity, the results are 0.67 and 1, respectively.

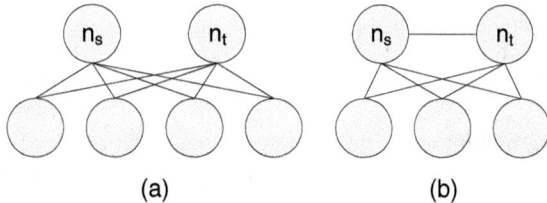

Figure 5: Similarity calculation

To cluster the similar nodes, we require the smaller distance indicating closer nodes, and thus we use dissimilarity as the metric, which is defined as

$$\mathbf{dissim}(n_s, n_t) = 1 - \mathbf{sim}(n_s, n_t).$$

Therefore, the dissimilarity/similarity metric has the unique advantage: we can either use dissimilarity as the metric to preserve the social relationship, or use similarity as the metric to break the social relationship, i.e., to cluster the dissimilar nodes.

4.3 Weight Constraint

In this application, the weight of a node is the number of views of the video, which reflects the possibility of being accessed by the users.

We do not utilize standard deviation for the constraint, because the mathematical formula of the standard deviation would make the problem difficult if not entirely infeasible to solve (we will calculate the standard deviation for the evaluation results). Since it is nearly impossible to decrease the standard deviation to zero, i.e., all the clusters have the same weight, it is much better to use a threshold. In our problem statement, the difference between the total weight of any two clusters should be less than Δ.

Clearly, the smaller the threshold is, the tighter the constraint is, and the less the social relationship will be preserved. Thus there exists a trade-off between social relationship preservation and load-balancing, and we will examine it in the evaluation by testing different value of Δ.

5. SOLUTION

To solve the problem, we propose a wPAM algorithm in this section, and explain the modifications from the original PAM algorithm. We also discuss methods to improve its efficiency and scalability.

5.1 wPAM

Both k-medoids and k-means clustering problems have already been proven to be NP-hard, and a variety of heuristic algorithms have been proposed. PAM (Partitioning Around Medoids) was one of the first k-medoids algorithms introduced [8]. We develop a Weighted PAM algorithm (wPAM) based on PAM, and Algorithm 1 shows the pseudo-code.

Algorithm 1 wPAM

Input:
N nodes $n_1, n_2, \ldots, n_N$ with weight $w_1, w_2, \ldots, w_N$,
cluster number k,
weight constraint threshold δ.
Output:
a set of k clusters satisfying the weight difference constraint: $|W_{j_1} - W_{j_2}| < k \cdot \delta$.
Method:
(1) arbitrarily choose k nodes as the initial representative nodes (medoids);
(2) **repeat**
(3)   assign each remaining node with weight w, to the first nearest cluster with weight W_j, if satisfying $W_j + w < \overline{W} + \delta$, where $\overline{W}$ is the average weight of all the clusters;
(4)   randomly select a non-representative node, n';
(5)   compute the total cost, $S = E' - E$, of swapping representative node, o_j, with n';
(6)   if $S < 0$ then swap o_j with n' to form the new set of k representative nodes;
(7) **until** no change;

Step (3) is the only modification from the original PAM, and there are two major differences. First, in PAM, the distance is between the target node and the representative node in the cluster. We found that there is a great chance that the target node has no mutual neighbors with any representative nodes, and thus using dissimilarity/similarity metric would not get the nearest one. To address the problem, we not only calculate the distance between the target node and the representative node, but also the distance between the target node and the set of nodes that are in the cluster. Specifically, the target node is n_t, and the set of nodes in the cluster is A_s; we apply the distance calculation in Section 4.2, and further calculate the mean of the two distances.

Second, in PAM, each node is just assigned to the nearest cluster. Since we have weight constraint, when assigning the node, we need to ensure that the resulted cluster's weight will not exceed the maximum. In the perfect case, each cluster has a weight $\overline{W}$; considering all clusters but one have weight $\overline{W} + \delta$, which is the maximum result from the algorithm, the last cluster thus has weight $\overline{W} - (k-1) \cdot \delta$. The difference between the last cluster and the others is $k \cdot \delta = \Delta$, which is the weight difference threshold in the problem statement.

Step (5) is the same as the original algorithm, but we explain it in detail here. This step calculates the difference of E if a current representative node is replaced by a non-representative node,

$$E' - E = \sum_{n_i \in C_j} d(n_i, n') - \sum_{n_i \in C_j} d(n_i, o_j).$$

If this total cost is negative, then n_j is replaced or swapped with n' since the actual E would be reduced; if the total cost is positive, the current representative node, n_j, is considered acceptable, and nothing is changed in the iteration. In our experiment in Section 6, the number of iteration turns out to be under 5 in most cases.

5.2 Improving Efficiency

The complexity of iteration in PAM is $O(k(n-k)^2)$, where k is the number of clusters and n is the number of nodes. Therefore, it does not scale well for large dataset.

A sampling-based method, CLARA (Clustering LARge Applications), was introduced to deal with larger dataset [8]. The idea is taking a small portion of the data into consideration, choosing medoids from the sample using PAM. If the sample is selected fairly random, it should closely represent the original dataset, and the medoids chosen would likely be similar to those that would have been chosen from the whole dataset. The complexity of each iteration becomes $O(ks^2 + k(n-k))$, where s is the size of the sample.

CLARANS (Clustering Large Applications based upon RANdomized Search) was further proposed [14]. Unlike CLARA, CLARANS draws a sample with some randomness in each step of the search, and it has been experimentally shown to be more effective than both PAM and CLARA.

Both CLARA and CLARANS are based on PAM, and thus we can utilize either method based on our wPAM algorithm to solve the problem without any further modification. More details about CLARA and CLARANS can be referred to [8] and [14], respectively.

6. EVALUATION

We implement wPAM algorithm to evaluate its performance. For weight difference constraint, we test Δ being $0.1 \cdot \sum W$, $0.01 \cdot \sum W$ and $0.001 \cdot \sum W$, and the number of clusters (cloud servers) k being 4, 8, 16, 32, 64 and 128.

To compare, we also implement pLA algorithm in SPAN [2] and SPAR algorithm [15], as well as a random algorithm that assigns each video to a random cluster without considering social relationship. Briefly, pLA algorithm is a greedy aggregation algorithm to merge the nodes/clusters that increases the overall modularity score, and SPAR algorithm assigns each node to a cluster that needs to generate the fewest replicas. More details about the two algorithms can be referred to the papers [2][15]. Because all the algorithms are randomized, we run each algorithm five times and calculate the average results and their standard deviations.

Our top priority is load-balance, and hence we first look at the result of the standard deviation of each cluster's weight. The cluster's weight is the summation of all the videos' weight (popularity) in the cluster, and reflects the possibility of being accessed. The results against the number of clusters are shown in Figure 6. We normalize the result by dividing the total weight of all the videos in the dataset. Note that both axes are in logarithmic scale. pLA algorithm performs worst, because it tends to detect the popular community, and moreover, pLA does not consider load-balance in terms of the video number in each cluster, and thus the weight deviation is extremely high when the number of clusters is small. Random algorithm performs well, because videos are randomly assigned and thus load-balance is partly achieved. SPAR algorithm performs worse than random algorithm. The reason is the same as that of pLA, yet SPAR strictly balances the number of videos in each cluster, and thus it performs better than pLA. When the weight difference constraint is loose and the number of clusters is small, wPAM algorithm performs similar to SPAR, and becomes better when the number of clusters increases. When the constraint is tight, wPAM outperforms all the compared algorithms, as the green and blue solid lines shown in the figure, thanks to the strict constraint when clustering (step 3) in Algorithm 1.

Supposing the system requires to preserve the social relationship as much as possible, we run wPAM using dissimilarity metric. To test how well the social relationship is preserved in the resulted partition, we generate 10 test cases, each contains $10,000$ YouTube video viewing transactions, which are used in work [4]. If two consecutive videos are held by two different cloud servers, we define it as one *transition*, and thus the less the number of transitions is, the better the social relationship is preserved. Because SPAR replicates all the linked nodes (called slave node) of a master node, the next video of a master video is always in the same server. Therefore, only if the next video of a slave video is in a different server, the number of transitions increases. We calculate the percentage of the transitions by dividing the total number $10,000$.

Figure 7 shows the results. Not surprisingly, random algorithm performs worst, because it does not take social relationship into account at all. On the other hand, SPAR performs best, since replicas are always in the same cloud server. Our wPAM performs similar to pLA, and with looser weight difference constraint, it performs better as expected, but the difference is not big. Although SPAR outperforms wPAM in terms of preserving social relationship, it requires much more space to store the replicas, about 4 to 12 times more than wPAM for different values of k. Nevertheless, wPAM achieves a rather good performance, even though our priority is load balance.

One advantage of wPAM is that we can break the social relationship to cluster the dissimilar videos, using similarity as the metric, which other algorithms are not capable to do. Figure 8 shows the result using the same test cases as above, and we compare it with the same random algorithm. As a result, when the number of clusters increases, wPAM outperforms random algorithm, and nearly achieves 100% transitions, i.e., the next video is always in a different server.

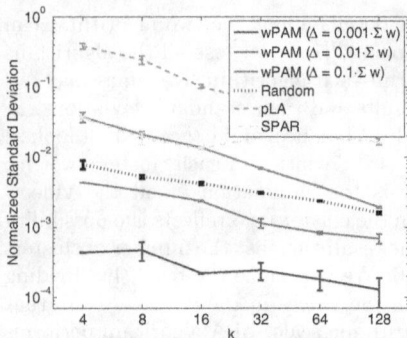

Figure 6: Comparison of normalized weight deviation

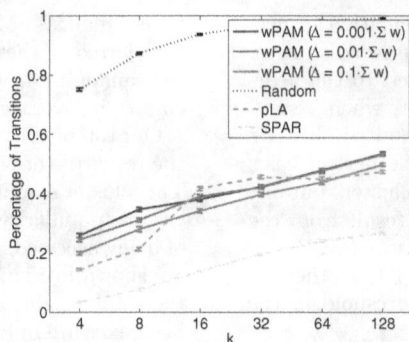

Figure 7: Comparison of percentage of transitions (preserving social relationship)

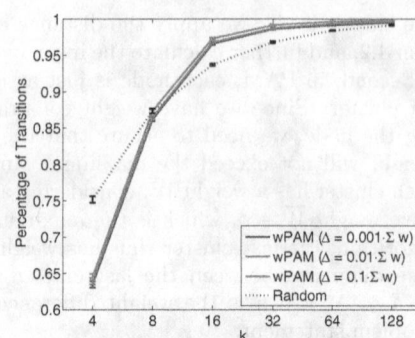

Figure 8: Comparison of percentage of transitions (breaking social relationship)

Looser weight difference constraints do not significantly improve the result. Therefore, considering the performance in terms of load-balance, we suggest using tight constraint when the system requires to break the social relationship.

7. CONCLUSION AND FUTURE WORK

In this paper, we took user access pattern into account in the problem of partitioning social contents, especially social media, in the cloud scenario. By examining YouTube video data, we have demonstrated that partitioning social media content entirely based on social relationship leads to unbalanced access, which would cause great problems to cloud computing. We concluded that a dynamic preservation of social relationship is preferred, by analyzing the role of social relationship in the social media applications. We have formulated the problem as a constrained k-medoids clustering problem, and proposed wPAM algorithm, which significantly decreases the deviation of access in each cluster, and flexibly preserves the social relationship.

Although preliminary results show positive performance of wPAM, we are doing more experiments to validate, in particular with larger datasets. We are also trying to find a more efficient solution to solve the problem. In addition, we are doing the same research on other types of social networked applications, such as Twitter and Facebook. In this paper, we only considered the client/server (C/S) architecture, yet peer-to-peer (P2P) architecture worths investigating as well. The difference between the two scenarios is that, from the server perspective, unpopular videos would be more likely to be requested in P2P, as opposite to C/S, because popular videos are more likely to be shared among peers. P2P scenario is more complicated, as the key issue is how to assign weight to each video to apply the wPAM algorithm.

8. REFERENCES

[1] M. Armbrust, A. Fox, R. Griffith, A. D. Joseph, R. H. Katz, A. Konwinski, G. Lee, D. A. Patterson, A. Rabkin, I. Stoica, and M. Zaharia. Above the Clouds: A Berkeley View of Cloud Computing. Technical report, University of California at Berkeley, 2009.

[2] D. A. Bader and K. Madduri. SNAP, Small-world Network Analysis and Partitioning: An open-source parallel graph framework for the exploration of large-scale networks. In *Proc. of IPDPS*, 2008.

[3] F. Benevenuto, T. Rodrigues, M. Cha, and V. Almeida. Characterizing user behavior in online social networks. In *Proc. of IMC*, 2009.

[4] X. Cheng and J. Liu. NetTube: Exploring Social Networks for Peer-to-Peer Short Video Sharing. In *Proc. of INFOCOM*, 2009.

[5] X. Cheng, J. Liu, and C. Dale. Understanding the Characteristics of Internet Short Video Sharing: A YouTube-based Measurement Study. *IEEE Transactions on Multimedia*, 2011.

[6] J. Han and M. Kamber. *Data Mining Concepts and Techniques (2nd Edition)*. Morgan Kaufmann, 2006.

[7] Jaccard Index. http://en.wikipedia.org/wiki/Jaccard_index.

[8] L. Kaufman and P. J. Rousseeuw. *Finding Groups in Data: An Introduction to Cluster Analysis*. Wiley, 1990.

[9] H. Kwak, C. Lee, H. Park, and S. Moon. What is Twitter, a Social Network or a News Media? In *Proc. of WWW*, 2010.

[10] S. Milgram. The Small World Problem. *Psychology Today*, 2(1):60–67, 1967.

[11] N. Mishra, R. Schreiber, I. Stanton, and R. Tarjan. Clustering Social Networks. In *Algorithms and Models for the Web-Graph*, volume 4863 of *Lecture Notes in Computer Science*, pages 56–67. Springer Berlin / Heidelber, 2007.

[12] A. Nazir, S. Raza, and C.-N. Chuah. Unveiling Facebook: A Measurement Study of Social Network Based Applications. In *Proc. of IMC*, 2008.

[13] M. E. J. Newman and M. Girvan. Finding and Evaluating Community Structure in Networks. *Physical Review E*, 69(2):026113, 2004.

[14] R. T. Ng and J. Han. Efficient and Effective Clustering Methods for Spatial Data Mining. In *Proc. of VLDB*, 1994.

[15] J. M. Pujol, V. Erramilli, G. Siganos, X. Yang, N. Laoutaris, P. Chhabra, and P. Rodriguez. The Little Engine(s) That Could: Scaling Online Social Networks. In *Proc. of SIGCOMM*, 2010.

[16] R. Zhou, S. Khemmarat, and L. Gao. The Impact of YouTube Recommendation System on Video Views. In *Proc. of IMC*, 2010.

Improving HTTP Performance Using "Stateless" TCP

David A. Hayes
Centre for Advanced Internet
Architectures,
Swinburne University of
Technology
Melbourne, Australia
david.hayes@ieee.org

Michael Welzl
Department of Informatics,
University of Oslo, Norway
michawe@ifi.uio.no

Grenville Armitage,
Mattia Rossi
Centre for Advanced Internet
Architectures,
Swinburne University of
Technology
Melbourne, Australia
{garmitage,mrossi}@swin.edu.au

ABSTRACT

TCP is quite a heavyweight protocol when serving very small web pages. We introduce a server-side kernel modification which enables a web server to perform HTTP over a UDP socket while the kernel provides a regular TCP interface 'on the wire' to remote clients. We show that our "stateless" TCP modification can greatly reduce a server's CPU usage ($> 20,\%$) and TCP related memory requirements($> 90\%$), potentially enabling it to serve small web pages even under extreme overload conditions.

Categories and Subject Descriptors

C.2.4 [**Computer Systems Organization**]: Distributed Systems—*Network operating systems*

General Terms

Performance

Keywords

HTTP, TCP, stateless TCP, FreeBSD

1. INTRODUCTION

A key challenge for HTTP-based content distributors is scaling their HTTP servers to handle growth in client-initiated load. The number of inbound connections per second may spike upwards for many different reasons – an active and successful marketing campaign, a denial of service attack, the so-called *Slashdot effect*, and so on. Traditional mitigation techniques include using load balancing to spread client-initiated TCP connections across identical servers, redirecting connections to caches geographically closer to individual clients (to both spread load and minimize the round trip times experienced by individual client connections), and simply adding more processing capacity to each web server.

In this paper we explore a server-side approach that can reduce the processing load per connection, and might conceivably be deployed alongside most existing load mitigation

techniques. Our approach is built on a number of observations about client-initiated web traffic today.

Many websites are constructed from relatively small pages (blocks of HTML or related code) that themselves trigger the retrieval and display of many additional, yet also small, web objects. Thus the reply to a typical GET request is often a small number of Kbytes long. Because the maximum segment size (MSS) of TCP connections is often between 1400 and 1460 bytes (allowing for tunnels and other overhead along the IP path), such answers will fit within a handful of TCP/IP packets. Given TCP's traditional "Initial Window" (IW) of three packets, and recent proposals to increase the IW to ten packets [2][1], a typical GET request is likely to be answered before TCP's congestion control can play any role.

We suggest that TCP's congestion control and reliability mechanisms play little part in the efficient transfer of small web objects in response to HTTP GET requests. In this paper we explore what benefits may be achieved by running web servers over a stripped-down transport protocol that looks like TCP 'on the wire' (so remote client TCP stacks remain happy), but keeps minimal state information within the server's kernel. Our "Stateless" form of TCP (*statelessTCP*) for HTTP reduces the kernel resources required per TCP connection, and consequently increases the number of client-initiated HTTP connections per second a given combination of hardware and operating system can handle.

statelessTCP is only suitable for servers serving up small web objects. Sites with a mix of small and large web objects should structure their sites so that large objects are served by machines running a regular TCP stack.

The rest of this paper is structured as follows: after a discussion of related work in the next section, we present the design of statelessTCP for HTTP traffic in Section 3, and our test web server in Section 4. Then, in Section 5 we present some test results. Section 6 concludes.

2. RELATED WORK

The intention behind our work is to minimize a web server's load. This is important when a server is receiving more requests than it can handle, such as when it is the victim of a Distributed Denial-of-Service (DDoS) attack. Because this is a severe problem and administrators of many important servers are so far still unable to cope with it (cf. the recent

---

[1]Such larger-than-the-standard-allows IW values are already being used in practice [16].

Pro-Wikileaks attacks on Visa and Mastercard), most of the related literature focuses on DDoS mitigation.

SYN cookies are a particularly well known method to reduce the load of a server that is being sent a lot of (fake) SYN packets. Normally, the server would be required to immediately create local state for each and every one of these packets – but with SYN cookies, the necessary information is only encoded in the server's response. This can be done by using the TCP header's sequence numbers [1] that the client reflects (increased by 1) in the acknowledgement field; this method shares with statelessTCP that it reduces the server's load with a server-only code change. However, statelessTCP reduces state for a whole connection, not just the SYN, and the server-side-only SYN cookie method also has some disadvantages (not being able to support TCP options, and lack of space in the sequence numbers). An extension to the TCP standard to solve these problems has recently been published [14]. SYN cookies are the best known, but not the only approach to mitigate SYN flooding attacks; a survey of known countermeasures is given in [3].

"Slowloris" [12] is an example of an attack that exploits server side state without having to send requests at a high rate; it forces a server to keep connections open by sending it partial HTTP requests on a regular basis. Common mitigation methods include limiting the number of concurrent connections per IP address, increasing the total number of concurrent connections allowed, and applying load balancers. statelessTCP cannot help against this attack because it does not address the issue that is being exploited: a vulnerability that is due to the way HTTP is specified.

"Not-A-Bot" (NAB), described in [6], attempts to detect the activity of humans as opposed to robots, akin to CAPTCHAs [18] but without requiring human involvement. Such automated systems can be used for a variety of purposes other than DDoS attack mitigation for web servers – e.g. spam detection and click-fraud mitigation. There is thus some overlap in the literature for these different purposes. Proposals such as NAB, the stateless TCP replacement "Trickles" [13] or the "Traffic Validation Architecture" (TVA) [19] however require a change to the client behavior, which is a key disadvantage over a scheme like statelessTCP which can improve a server's scaleability by only applying a local software update.

In contrast with our approach, none of the above overload mitigation strategies disable the server's congestion control. This has, however, been done for "normal" small web transfers for a long time now: Google has proposed using a larger initial window of 10 packets [2], and both Google and Microsoft were found to already apply this method even though it conflicts with the standard [16]. Even for hosts that use the standard initial window of 3 packets, a similar effect is attained by most web browsers, as they open a number of connections in parallel – the cumulative effect being the same as using a much larger initial window. statelessTCP can therefore be judged to be safe for deployment provided that its maximum file size is limited to at least 3 (conservative tuning) and at most 10 (progressive tuning) packets.

What we term 'statelessTCP' was originally[2] proposed (somewhat tongue-in-cheek) by Geoff Huston as a means to mitigate a potential performance issue faced by DNS servers

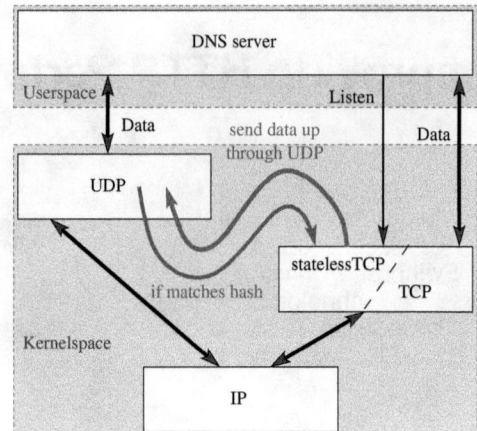

Figure 1: TCP as UDP

seeing a rise in DNS queries arriving over TCP. (The theory being that as more and more requests are expected to use IPv6 and DNSSEC, UDP responses will often exceed the commonly configured 512-byte packet size limit, requiring clients to switch to TCP for DNS queries [8].) We subsequently re-implemented this idea directly in the FreeBSD kernel and demonstrated significant potential performance improvements for DNS servers handling 100s of thousands of queries per second [7]. We have now leveraged our prior work to explore the potential of statelessTCP to support servers handling thousands of small HTTP transactions too.

3. "STATELESS" TCP FOR HTTP

Algorithms 1 and 2 show the basic operation of statelessTCP; it consists of a few simple rules for reacting to incoming control packets, and some additional behavior for dealing with application data. A timer ensures that we close the connection if the other side does not; we will explain in Section 3.3 why a RST flag is included in all FIN packets.

We translate the packets completely in kernel-space, passing only UDP packets with HTTP commands to the web sever which runs in user-space. The same applies for UDP packets generated by the web server – the translation to TCP occurs completely in kernel-space. Figure 1 illustrates the basic architecture.

The operation of statelessTCP is application-specific, in that it assumes a certain transaction sequence of the application protocol – algorithm 2 would never become active unless information from a previous incoming packet is available. This matches the behavior of HTTP, where a web server responds to incoming HTTP requests (typically HTTP GET commands). While the necessity to store some information prohibits statelessTCP from being strictly stateless, this is a very small amount of data compared to the state requirements of "normal" TCP – statelessTCP only uses the already existing SYN cache (also for its timer), and it neither requires a per-connection socket nor the `in_pcb` and `tcb` data structures. Packets are not buffered for retransmission. We implemented statelessTCP in FreeBSD 9.

3.1 statelessTCP and HTTP 1.0

Initially we tested statelessTCP using our test web server (see section 4) accepting only HTTP 1.0 type connections (no persistent connections). We installed it together with

---

[2][17] describes an older, but very vague description of a roughly similar idea – albeit for a special "simple document server" instead of a standard service such as HTTP or DNS.

Algorithm 1 statelessTCP algorithm outline: incoming

Capture every TCP packet arriving at port 80 and perform the following operations, using a raw socket:

1. If it is a TCP SYN packet, send back a TCP SYN/ACK

2. If it is a TCP DATA packet,

   (a) store the acknowledgement number (and some more information) of the incoming packet and start a timer

   (b) send a TCP ACK packet back to the sender carrying no payload, and correct sequence and acknowledgement numbers based on the incoming packet's header

   (c) send the TCP payload to the server via a UDP socket

3. If it is a TCP FIN packet, send back a TCP FIN/ACK/RST and remove the data stored at 2a, including the timer.

4. If it is none of the above packet types, drop the packet

Algorithm 2 statelessTCP algorithm outline: outgoing

Event 1: *upon a local UDP socket send request at port 80, perform the following operations, using a raw socket:*

1. Check whether the source and destination addresses used in the socket call match any of the information stored at incoming/2a. If they do not match, let UDP carry on normal processing; otherwise continue:

2. Depending on the size of the response, create one or multiple TCP packets:

   (a) For the first TCP packet, set the sequence number to the value stored at incoming/2a

   (b) For each additional packet, add the size of the previous packets payload to the previous packets sequence number and set the resulting value as the sequence number

Event 2: *if the timer from incoming/2a fires, perform the following operations, using a raw socket:*

1. Send a TCP FIN/RST to the host and port identified via the information that was stored with the timer, and remove the data stored at incoming/2a, including the timer.

---

statelessTCP on a FreeBSD desktop PC in our lab's LAN and accessed it from other PCs in the same LAN using the browsers listed above. We found that it works without any problems, using some static web pages containing small images. No packets were lost in this setup. Consistently, all web browsers requested HTTP 1.1, and, because our server announced HTTP 1.0, the browsers submitted a HTTP GET request for every object. These requests were actively terminated by the browsers, i.e. a FIN packet was sent by the client. This was accordingly answered with a TCP FIN/ACK/RST by statelessTCP (the RST played no role in these tests).

3.2 statelessTCP and HTTP 1.1

Persistent connections, which were introduced in HTTP 1.1, allow a web browser to issue multiple consecutive requests over a single TCP connection, thereby eliminating the connection setup/teardown overhead and delay. Restricting a web server to HTTP 1.0 is therefore at the cost of efficiency for the client. With HTTP 1.1, a connection can theoretically be closed by either side after a timeout [4]. However, we found that, if we let our web server announce HTTP 1.1 with persistent connections, browsers generally assume the server will close the connection after a while. This strikes us as an obvious strategy: keeping a connection available as long as possible for future use is in the interest of the browser, whereas it is in the interest of the server to close connections after a while in order to minimize the amount of state that is kept. This indeed matches the behavior exhibited by common web servers such as Apache.

An early version of statelessTCP did not include the timer that is described in Algorithms 1 and 2. With this version, persistent connections worked, but they were never closed. This resulted in the browser indicating ongoing download activity (the visualization depends on the browser, e.g. Firefox showed an animated symbol on the left side of the web page tab). We therefore needed to change statelessTCP to close

the connection after a timeout. Luckily, the TCP SYN cache already includes a timer for every entry, which is normally used to issue another SYN/ACK in case it was never responded to. We reuse it to send a FIN/RST instead, which is correctly answered with a FIN/ACK by the client, causing the transaction to be terminated on both sides at the application level (i.e. the browser animation stops). Again, the RST played no role.

3.3 statelessTCP and packet loss

Since data is never retransmitted by statelessTCP, packet loss in the network can become a problem. As previously noted, statelessTCP is primarily for servers that must remain up under heavy loads; under such conditions, it allows access to web sites that could otherwise not be seen, and the risk of packet loss with its detrimental effects on the client side is outweighed by the ability to sometimes show a page at all. Nevertheless, we strived to minimize the problems caused by packet loss. To see what happens to a web client when packets are lost, we used dummynet to create various amounts of random loss on our web server. We saw that browsers generally display as much as they receive – but here, subtle differences between various browsers became evident. For example, Internet Explorer never showed images that were only partially available (instead, it showed a textual placeholder), whereas missing packets that make up a part of an image caused Firefox to partially display the image (with lines missing at the bottom). Figure 2 shows a screenshot of Safari displaying a page when some packets were lost.

Since a packet loss before a FIN causes the client's TCP to wait until any missing intermediate packets are received before it processes the FIN, we saw the browsers indicate ongoing download activity until the browser's "stop" button was pressed in our first tests. This was solved for most browsers by changing statelessTCP to always send a RST when it

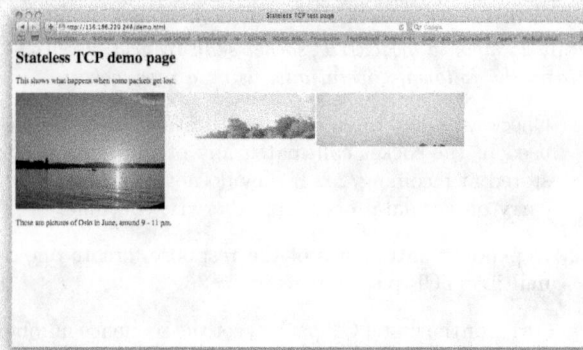

Figure 2: Safari displaying a page with packet loss

Figure 3: Test bed setup

sends a FIN, and this never created any additional problems. If the lost packet was a HTML page, the FIN/RST caused browsers to display an error message (e.g. "The connection to the server was reset while the page was loading." in case of Firefox or "Safari can't open the page [url] because the server unexpectedly dropped the connection." in case of Safari), but if the browser was only waiting for an image or parts of an image, the download terminated. This seems to be a more appropriate behavior to us than showing that the download is still active when it really is not, but for service providers who disagree with this view, including RST flags on FINs could easily be made a configurable option.

4. TEST WEB SERVER (HTTPUDPD)

A web server operating with statelessTCP opens both TCP and UDP sockets to listen for requests. Client-initiated web requests received on the external TCP port are then handled by statelessTCP in the kernel. statelessTCP responds to TCP control packets, but sends data packets to the application via the UDP socket, created at initialization by the web server. It is assumed that the web server issues only one UDP transmission in response to the HTTP request. If it tries to send more data than would fit into a PathMTU-sized TCP packet, statelessTCP will (using the MTU information cached in the operating system) fragment it into multiple TCP packets. The total length of this data is limited by the maximum UDP packet length, which is 65507 byte – assuming the aforementioned common TCP MSS of 1460 byte, this would mean sending 45 packets, which is well beyond the number of packets that would be acceptable to send without doing congestion control. Thus, the UDP message length imposes no limitation on statelessTCP (but the maximum accepted amount of data should be set accordingly for the socket, e.g. via the `net.inet.udp.maxdgram` variable in case of FreeBSD).

To test statelessTCP we developed "httpudpd" (based upon "micro_httpd" by Jef Poskanzer)[3], and a variety of browsers (the latest versions of Firefox, Safari, Internet Explorer, Opera and Chrome as well as Gnu wget). micro_httpd is an exercise in creating the smallest possible web server in C – it is designed to run from inetd, i.e. it does not need

to explicitly support parallel transactions and uses the stdin and stdout streams to communicate with a TCP socket. It has 286 lines of code (including comments and empty lines). We enhanced micro_httpd in several ways, yielding 520 lines of code:

- It listens on TCP, or TCP and UDP ports.
- It starts a fixed number of processes with `fork()` at initialization to handle parallel incoming http requests and avoid performance loss due to IOwaits.
- For TCP, it uses `select` with FreeBSD's accept filtering[4] [11, 10] (similar to Apache) to provide high performance HTTP request handling.
- For UDP, it uses `select`.
- It supports HTTP 1.1 with UDP.
- Apart from socket reads and writes, processing is identical for TCP and UDP.

5. PERFORMANCE TESTS

A simple testbed, shown in Figure 3, was used to test the relative performance of TCP and statelessTCP. Two instances of httperf [9] run on the (Linux) client, which also emulates a 15 ms delay in both directions using netem [5]. The client and server are connected on a 100 Mbps link through a switch. httpudpd (see Section 4) and statelessTCP run on the (FreeBSD) server. httpudpd starts 10 processes at initialization to handle incoming requests. The FreeBSD server runs with default parameters with the following two exceptions:

- the maximum UDP datagram size is set to 64000 B (net.inet.udp.maxdgram=64000),
- and the TCP SYN cache size is set to 2048 B. (net.inet.tcp.syncache.hashsize=2048)

The httperf clients request a single file from the httpudpd web server using HTTP 1.0 (non-persistent connections). Requests are made by each httperf instance at exponentially distributed random intervals (the request rate has a Poisson distribution). We measure:

- the average http request rate as determined by httperf,
- the load of the kernel process,
- the load of the httpudpd process[5],
- and the memory used by the kernel zone allocator [15].

The load of the kernel and httpudpd processes is measured using `ps -x`. The accumulated CPU time given by ps is sampled every 20 s, (21 times in total) with the difference between the samples used to plot the graphs. The

---

[3]statelessTCP, including httpudpd, is available from http://caia.swin.edu.au/ngen/statelesstcp/http and micro_httpd is available from http://acme.com/software/micro_httpd/

[4]Incoming TCP connections are accepted by the kernel, and only presented to the application program when the first data packet arrives
[5]The accumulated CPU time given by ps for a user process includes user + system time. Therefore the httpudpd measurement will include a portion of the kernel process CPU

Zone	Description
socket	memory used by the UNIX sockets.
tcp_inpcb	memory used to store network layer state (IP) for TCP connections.
tcpcb	memory used for the TCP control block.
tcptw	memory used to store the compressed TCP information for connections int the Time-Wait state
syncache	memory used in the TCP SYN cache

Table 1: Monitored memory use

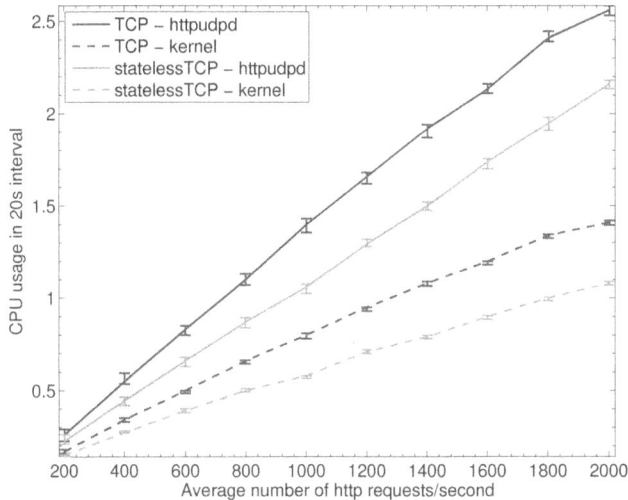

Figure 4: Httpudpd and Kernel load measured in accumulated CPU time in 20 s intervals

memory usage is sampled every 10 s (42 times in total) using `vmstat -z` to compare the average memory used in the communication process by statelessTCP and TCP. Specifically we look at the memory used by `socket`, `tcp_inpcb`, `tcpcb`, `tcptw`, and `syncache`.

Experiments are run with httperf parameterized for average http request rates of 200, 400, 600, 800, 1000, 1200, 1400, 1600, 1800, and 2000 requests per second. Results are plotted against the achieved request rate as reported by httperf. Graphs show the 10th, 50th, and 90th percentiles (marker at the median, and error bars spanning the 10th to 90th percentiles).

5.1 Results

The relative loads for the http server are shown in Figure 4 for both normal TCP and statelessTCP modes. The httpudpd load is shown with a solid line, and the kernel load is shown with a dashed line. statelessTCP provides benefits for both kernel processing and the httpudpd process. At the higher loads, where the performance difference stabilizes, there is a 18–20 % improvement in the load due to the httpudpd process, and a 15–18 % improvement in the kernel process performance.

Memory consumption is another important issue for highly loaded web servers. Figure 5 shows the sampled memory usage for the memory zones outlined in table 1. Notice that `tcptw` does not increase with load in the both the TCP and statelessTCP plots (Figures 5(a) and 5(b)). After an

IP address / port number combination has been used, it is placed in a TIME-WAIT state which prevents this combination from being used again for a period of time. FreeBSD has a default limit of 5150 previous connections whose state is stored in this way. In the normal TCP test, this limit is reached and maintained at all of the rates tested, resulting in the static memory use shown for these two elements. For statelessTCP, the very small amount of TIME-WAIT induced state is due to the test management script's interaction with the http server, not the HTTP requests. statelessTCP does not create and maintain full TCP state, so connections do not enter the TIME-WAIT state.

For the TCP tests, `tcpcb` and `socket` (and to a lesser extent `syncache`) increase with load, both containing the state necessary for active connections. `Tcpcb_inpcb` also does, though it is masked by the large proportion of `tcpcb_inpcb` state due to connections in the TIME-WAIT state.

Figure 5(b) shows that `syncache` dominates the statelessTCP memory usage.[6] Note that the graph scale is an order of magnitude smaller than in the TCP graph. statelessTCP extends the life of the SYN cache entries to enable the response to be returned to the client. `Syncache` entries use 144 B of memory, compared with 880 B for `tcpcb`.

A comparison of the total connection related memory usage is shown in Figure 5(c) with a two scale split y-axis. TCP's memory usage is in the order of 10^6 B, while statelessTCP's memory usage in the order of 10^4 B. Even without the huge static memory used by TCP due to the TIME-WAIT state, statelessTCP's memory increases much more slowly than TCP's memory. TCP requires `tcpcb` (880 B) + `tcpcb_inpcb` (336 B) + `socket` (680 B) for active connections, compared to statelessTCP's `syncache` (144 B) requirement.

6. CONCLUSION

We have introduced statelessTCP and shown that it greatly reduces the CPU usage ($> 20 \%$) and TCP related memory requirements ($> 90 \%$) of web servers hosting very small files. It could be used to provide access to pages that could not normally be shown within a reasonable time frame, e.g. when a server is a target of a DDoS attack or when flash crowds occur, e.g. in emergency situations. As such, by removing the strict reliability requirement of TCP, it seems that statelessTCP can in fact increase the overall reliability of the web – but further work is needed to study the behavior of a more realistic web server (e.g. Apache) under extreme loads.

We have first applied statelessTCP to DNS and then made it work with HTTP with only a handful of minor changes; this leads us to believe that statelessTCP could just as easily be used in support of any other transactional application protocol.

Acknowledgment

This work has evolved from earlier work made possible in part by grants from APNIC Pty Ltd and Nominet UK, and subsequent valuable discussions with Geoff Huston. The work has also been supported in part by a grant from the Cisco University Research Program Fund at Community Foundation Silicon Valley.

---

[6] The `tcpcb`, `tcpcb_inpcb` and `tcptw` memory consumption for statelessTCP is an artifact of the testing mechanism.

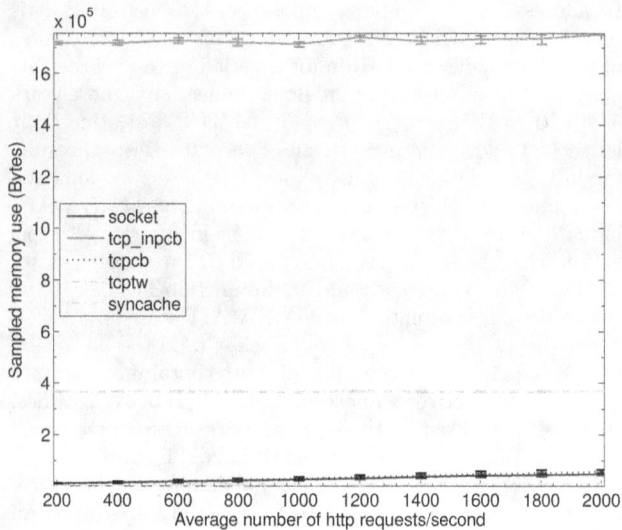

(a) TCP

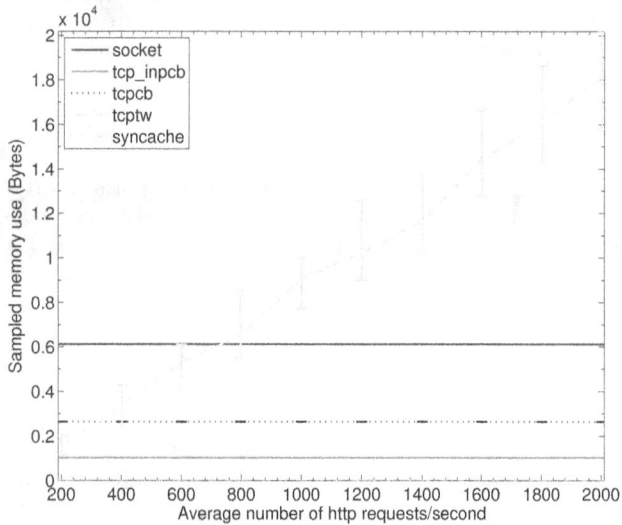

(b) statelessTCP

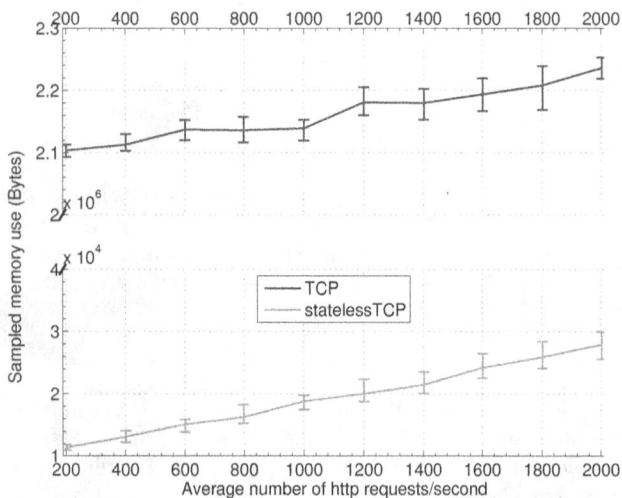

(c) Combined memory usage

Figure 5: Sampled memory usage for statelessTCP

7. REFERENCES

[1] D. Bernstein. SYN cookies.
http://cr.yp.to/syncookies.html.

[2] N. Dukkipati, T. Refice, Y. Cheng, J. Chu,
T. Herbert, A. Agarwal, A. Jain, and N. Sutin. An
argument for increasing TCP's initial congestion
window. *ACM SIGCOMM CCR*, 40:26–33, June 2010.

[3] W. Eddy. TCP SYN Flooding Attacks and Common
Mitigations. RFC 4987 (Informational), Aug. 2007.

[4] R. Fielding, J. Gettys, J. Mogul, H. Frystyk,
L. Masinter, P. Leach, and T. Berners-Lee. Hypertext
Transfer Protocol – HTTP/1.1. RFC 2616, June 1999.

[5] L. Foundation. Netem — network emulation.
http://www.linuxfoundation.org/collaborate/
workgroups/networking/netem, Nov. 2009.

[6] R. Gummadi, H. Balakrishnan, P. Maniatis, and
S. Ratnasamy. Not-a-bot: improving service
availability in the face of botnet attacks. In *USENIX
NSDI*, pages 307–320, Berkeley, CA, USA, 2009.

[7] D. Hayes, M. Rossi, and G. Armitage. Improving DNS
performance using "Stateless" TCP in FreeBSD 9.
Technical Report 101022A, Centre for Advanced
Internet Architectures, Swinburne University of
Technology, Melbourne, Australia, 22 October 2010.

[8] G. Huston. Stateless and dnsperate! The ISP Column,
http://www.potaroo.net/ispcol/2009-11/stateless.pdf,
November 2009.

[9] D. Mosberger, T. Jin, S. Eranian, and D. Carter.
Httperf homepage.
http://www.hpl.hp.com/research/linux/httperf/, Feb.
2009.

[10] A. Perlstein. ACCF_DATA — buffer incoming
connections until data arrives. FreeBSD Man 9, Nov.
2000.

[11] A. Perlstein, S. Hearn, and J. R. van der Werven.
ACCEPT_FILTER — filter incoming connections.
FreeBSD Man 9, June 2000.

[12] RSnake. Slowloris. http://ha.ckers.org/slowloris/,
June 2009.

[13] A. Shieh, A. C. Myers, and E. G. Sirer. A stateless
approach to connection-oriented protocols. *ACM
Trans. Comput. Syst.*, 26:8:1–8:50, September 2008.

[14] W. Simpson. TCP Cookie Transactions (TCPCT).
RFC 6013 (Experimental), Jan. 2011.

[15] D.-E. Smorgrav and J. R. van der Werven. ZONE —
zone allocator. FreeBSD Man 9, Oct. 2010.

[16] B. Strong. Google and Microsoft cheat on slow-start.
Should you?
http://blog.benstrong.com/2010/11/google-
and-microsoft-cheat-on-slow.html, November 2010.

[17] supercat. Stateless tcp/ip server.
http://www.halfbakery.com/idea/
Stateless_20TCP_2fIP_20server, October 2004.

[18] L. von Ahn, M. Blum, N. Hopper, and J. Langford.
Captcha: Using hard AI problems for security. In
EUROCRYPT 2003. Springer, 2003.

[19] X. Yang, D. Wetherall, and T. Anderson. A
DoS-limiting network architecture. In *SIGCOMM '05*,
pages 241–252, New York, NY, USA, 2005. ACM.

A DTN Mode for Reliable Internet Telephony

Christian Hoene and Patrick Schreiner
Universität Tübingen, Interactive Communication Systems (ICS)
Sand 13, 72076 Tübingen, Germany
hoene|schreiner@uni-tuebingen.de

ABSTRACT

IP telephony suffers from the well-known fact that the Internet does only provide a best-effort service. Thus, minimum transmission quality cannot be guaranteed and, especially during times of network congestion or occasional link failures, UDP-based VoIP becomes unusable. To overcome these limitations, we have developed a rate-adaptive transmission system for highly scalable speech and audio codecs that uses the Delay Tolerant Networking (DTN) approach for very low bit rates. In this way, as soon as the available transmission capacity falls below the minimum coding rate, our system switches to a Push-To-Talk (PTT) like conversational mode. Subjective conversational quality tests have shown that the algorithm allows for a good and effective conversation (MOS-CQS is 3.5) even in cases where traditional UDP based VoIP telephony fails (MOS-CQS is 1).

Categories and Subject Descriptors

B.4.1 [**Input/Output and Data Communications**]: Data Communication Devices; C.2.2 [**Computer-Communication Networks**]: Network Protocols

General Terms

Algorithms, Human Factors, Measurement, Reliability

1. INTRODUCTION

Every regular user of Internet telephony knows only too well that the quality of VoIP calls is sometimes bad or even unacceptable. Already in 2003, Jiang and Schulzrinne measured a call abortion rate of 2% on typical VoIP connections in unmanaged networks because of network problems [14]. The authors also stated that this call abortion rate is significantly higher than the call abortion rate of classic PSTN systems. Thus, to allow for reliable high-quality VoIP-services, a well-managed IP network is suggested, which either gives VoIP a higher transmission priority or is overprovisioning capacity [11]. Of course, neither PSTN phones nor well

managed networks are always available even if important calls need to be made. Thus, effective voice conversations should work reliably even in unmanaged networks.

A similar problem can be observed for cellular networks. Wireless access networks intermittently show link failures, for example, when the user is driving through a tunnel or when a handover is taking place.

Connections using TCP recover from those temporary link outages. Either they lower throughput if the link quality is bad or soon after reestablishing connectivity, TCP goodput goes up again and retransmissions occur to recover lost TCP segments. In UDP-based VoIP, the situation is different: The speech quality of VoIP connections suffers and the service can become unusable for the duration of the outage. The conversational flow is interrupted and the talker has to repeat himself.

To overcome VoIP's quality problems with bad links, numerous approaches have been proposed in scientific literature: The playout time of the audio signal can be varied to cope with increased delay [19]. Packet losses can be concealed to limit the perceptual distortions. Forward error correction can be added to increase the loss robustness at the cost of delay and quality [6]. Packet interleaving might be applied to cope with bursty loss events (at the cost of delay). Transmission paths can be changed [21]. Packets can be dispersed over multiple paths [16]. Selected calls can be dropped to allow a reasonable quality of the remaining [23]. Alternatively, any combination of these algorithms can be used (e.g. [7]).

However, all of these techniques fail if the available bandwidth is significantly lower than the minimal coding rate (e.g. half). In these cases, traditional VoIP becomes unusable and making a call is pointless. In this publication, we introduce a scalable IP-based audio and speech transmission system that allows for a usable conversation even if bandwidth is scarce. We continue with a description of the algorithm in Section 2 and address the problem of what shall happen if the available bandwidth falls below the minimal coding rate. We describe the implementation of the system in Section 3. To judge the quality of the proposed algorithm, we have conducted subjective conversational tests that show that our approach still allows for good quality even if other VoIP methods fail.

The presented algorithms are of particular importance for emergency calls and other mission critical situations when Internet phone calls have to be understandable despite a high conversational delay.

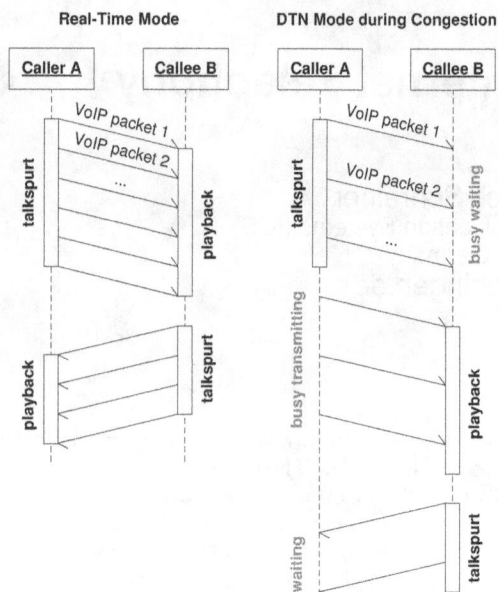

Figure 1: Message sequence diagram displaying two talkspurts. Left: conventional real-time VoIP mode. Right: DTN mode with delayed playback and optical busy indication.

2. RELIABLE AND SCALABLE AUDIO AND SPEECH TRANSMISSION

Our idea is simple yet effective. We extend VoIP clients by a transmission protocol like DCCP (as done by others before) and use DCCP to measure the momentary end-to-end throughput. As soon as the throughput is so low that a real-time VoIP transmission is not possible anymore, we switch to a push-to-talk like mode. Push-to-talk works similar to walkie-talkies supporting a half-duplex, delayed voice transmission. To avoid misunderstandings, we visually inform the phone users about the push-to-talk operational mode. They change their conversational patterns and interestingly, they perceive the push-to-talk mode as much better as a bad real-time VoIP mode, as the our subjective conversational tests have shown.

Figure 1 compares the traditional real-time mode and the proposed DTN mode: A question/answer conversation is displayed consisting of two talkspurts, one from caller A to callee B and one vice versa. In real time mode, A is sending VoIP packets to B, which are played out immediately after a dejittering delay of a few milliseconds. If the network is congested and the transport protocol notifies the senders about the available transmission rate, the senders lower their VoIP packet sending rates and buffer unsent packets until they can be transmitted safely. As a consequence, the talkspurt cannot be played back immediately but the receivers have to wait until they are going to receive them fully. As in streaming media, playback may start before receiving the end of the talkspurt.

It is believed that phone calls require a mouth-to-ear transmission delay of below 150 ms to be of good quality and below 400 ms to be still acceptable [2]. Within this publication we want to show that this delay boundary does not hold and that effective conversations are possible even with much higher delays. To achieve this, we notify the listeners that they have to wait for a talkspurt and we ask the talkers whether they want to speak (e.g. via a push-to-talk button). This way, the phone users become more tolerant about transmission delays as they can easily adapt their communication behavior to the current network constraints, as the conversational listening tests in the following section show.

Our algorithm extends a traditional VoIP client: A VoIP sender consists of an A/D converter and signal processing units, an encoder, and the RTP/UDP protocol stack. The encoder generates speech frames which are queued for sending via socket calls. If a network connection is given, the operating system transmits the UDP packets immediately. In the described setup, the encoder schedules the sending times and defines the sending rate. We extend this design by a transport protocol that supports congestion control and that measures the momentary throughput. But then the question arises as to what shall happen if network throughput is lower than the coding rate (plus the overhead caused by packet headers). In this case, we consider the following four mechanisms:

First, supernumerary packets are enqueued in a FIFO queue controlled by the transport protocol (and typically placed in the kernel of the OS). Those queues have a limited, application controlled capacity. If network conditions remain bad for a longer period of time, the queue fills up and packets are dropped. Dropping many speech frames is not advisable because then the speech quality degrades and conversation is not possible anymore. Second, if the network condition is worse for a longer period (e.g. multiple frame durations), a rate control unit can lower the coding and frame rate of the encoder. As a result, packets are enqueued at a rate that is lower than the one they are transmitted at. Thus, the queue is emptied and packet dropping can be avoided. Third, if the encoder is already operating at the lowest rate, a discontinuous transmission mode (DTX) is switched on which lowers the number of VoIP packet frames sent during periods of silence. And last, if the sending queues are still filling up, the algorithm presented in this publication switches automatically to a push-to-talk like mode. Then, speech frames are transmitted only if the transport protocol indicates a transmission opportunity. In addition, the VoIP sender may interrupt the talker or–alternatively–the talker may have to press a button to indicate his wish to talk.

Since the first three mechanisms are state of the art and supported by many modern VoIP clients, we do not describe them further. To support the fourth mechanism, we add a *send ueue* to the VoIP transmission components (see red parts in Fig. 2). The size of the send queue has to be large enough to store multiple minutes of audio. Nowadays, memory is not a limiting factor.

A sender-side rate control unit decides when to turn on the DTN mode and when to go back to normal operation mode. The DTN mode can be transmitted to the receiver but this is not necessarily required because the receiver can figure out the DTN state by observing the rate of the incoming packets. If frames are received at a rate lower than their actual frame rate, it can be assumed that the sender has switched to DTN.

If the VoIP sender operates in DTN mode, the acoustic input signal is first stored in the send queue. Only if the transport protocol triggers transmission opportunities, the encoder dequeues an audio block, compresses it and puts it

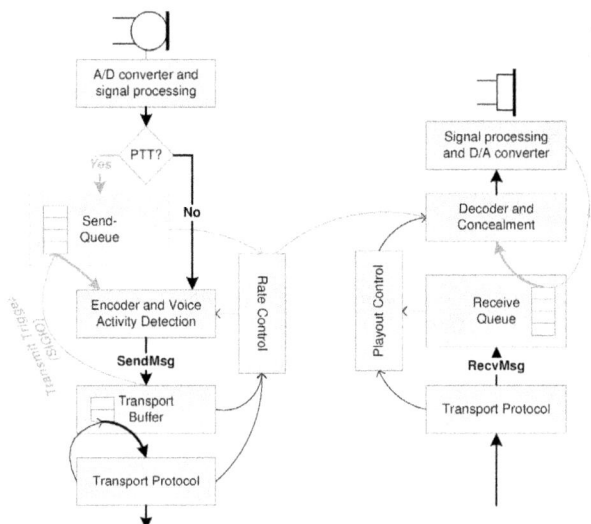

Figure 2: Modified VoIP design

in the transmission buffer. If despite large storage the send queue is filled up, the talker will be notified via an optical or acoustic signal so that he can stop talking until the send queue has free capacity again.

The playout of speech frames has to be adapted accordingly. Thus, the VoIP receiver has to be changed, too. Again, we assume a typical VoIP receiver having a transport protocol, a playout buffer and a decoder. The decoder includes packet loss concealment algorithms and an algorithm to speed up or slow down the playout of speech concealment. Conveniently, packet concealment, time stretching and time shrinking can be implemented in the same unit because similar algorithms to detect pitch periods, to extrapolate, and to mix speech signals are applied.

If packets arrive at a low rate or if DTN mode has been signaled to the VoIP receiver, the following steps are taken:

First, if a packet does not arrive on time, the receiver has to assume either a packet loss or a late packet. In both cases, the receiver performs an extrapolation of the audio signal to conceal the loss or to stretch the audio signal. It needs not to decide whether to conceal losses or to slow down the playout, yet. This decision has to be only made after a new packet has arrived. Second, if the receiver notices that many packets continuously arrive late or if the sender has indicated DTN mode, the receiver interrupts the playout and stores the packets in the playout buffer. Ideally, the listener should be informed that the sender is in DTN mode to be able to adapt his conversation pattern to the new situation. If the receiver detects an end of a talkspurt in DTN mode, it plays out the stored speech frames at a normal pace.

The latter mode is advantageous because neither are late packets dropped nor is the speech quality significantly reduced due to extensive time stretching. Thus, the conversational effectiveness is maintained even though conversational turnaround times are higher.

3. IMPLEMENTATION

We implemented the algorithm described above to study its performance. As audio codec, we used Bluetooth's SBC

audio codec [13] and as transport protocol DCCP with the TFRC congestion control mode [22].

The SBC codec is of low complexity and has a wide operational range. It supports sampling frequencies f_s of 16, 32, 44.1 or 48 kHz and one and two channel mode. In addition, different frame rates are supported. The algorithmic delay can be selected to be very low (a few milliseconds). For this reason, it can support distributed ensemble performances which work well with overall one-way delays of about 25 ms. In other coding modes, it is good to compress wideband speech (this is for example used for Bluetooth wideband headsets). Since the Bluetooth SBC standard does not include packet concealment algorithms, we implemented a concealment algorithm that uses a pitch replication method and supports time stretching and shrinking [13].

In this implementation, we switched only between three SBC coding modes–extending our rate control algorithms to take advantage of all possible modes is subject of future studies. What all the applied modes have in common are the SBC mono mode, loudness mode, 16 blocks, 8 subbands, 32 bit in the bitpool, and one frame per packet. We varied the sampling frequency selecting a value of 16, 32 or 48 kHz. Thus, the frame rates were 125, 250, or 375 Hz. The SBC frame has a size of 72 byte. To the gross packet size the headers of Ethernet (18 byte), IP (20 byte), DCCP (12 byte), and a custom protocol similar to RTP (20 byte) are added. If one assumes a frame length of 1136 bit, the gross bit rates are 142, 284, and 426 kbps.

As transport protocol, we selected the Linux kernel implementation of DCCP and the TFRC congestion control algorithm. TFRC adjusts more slowly to changing transmission capacities than TCP-like congestion control which makes it more suitable for applications in need of a more constant data throughput, like VoIP. To achieve a fair distribution of bandwidth between TCP-based and DCCP-based applications, TFRC uses TCP's throughput equation which estimates a sending rate as a function of loss event rate and round-trip-time [10]. Via the Berkeley Socket API, the application accesses DCCP-specific information by calling the `getsockopt` function. If provided with the options `DCCP_SOCKOPT_GET_CUR_MPS`, `DCCP_SOCKOPT_CCID_RX_INFO` or `DCCP_SOCKOPT_CCID_TX_INFO`, the `getsockopt` function returns the current maximum packet size (application data size in byte) or detailed information on the current estimations of the bidirectional transmission path. The given parameters are the same as described in the TFRC specification [10] and include the other side's estimates of sending rate, round-trip-time, and loss event rate, as well as the computed own transmit rate, the filtered RTT, the current loss event rate, and the inter-packet sending interval.

The VoIP sender uses these parameters in its rate control unit to select the SBC coding parameters and to decide whether to switch to DTN mode. SBC's sampling frequency is adapted on the fly to the currently estimated transmit rate so that the coding rate is lower than the transmit rate (minus headers). Experiments have shown that the transmit rate varies strongly even if the physical bit rate remains constant. Thus, a smoothing of the estimated bandwidth is applied before changing the codec parameters. We use the average of ten different estimated transmit rates. Based on this value, a suggested sampling rate $f_{suggested}$ is calculated.

To select the actual sampling rate f_{actual}, we follow the principle of additive increase and multiple decrease (AIMD) that is typically used in TCP-like congestion control algorithms. We switch to a lower sampling frequency faster than to a higher one because we want to avoid extensive losses and we want to ensure stable transmission quality. Thus, if network congestion occurs and frames are lost, the rate control tries to limit the period of loss by reacting promptly.

We define t_{now} as the current time, $t_{lastdrop}$ as the time of the last drop, and $t_{lastincrease}$ as the time of last increase of the sampling rate. If the suggested sampling frequency is lower than the actual one and the last sampling rate decrease has occurred at least one second ago, the sampling rate is lowered to the suggested rate (Algorithm 1).

If the suggested value is larger than the actual one, the algorithm typically checks whether the last increase has been at least t_{gap} seconds ago. If this applies, the suggested sampling rate is set to the actual sampling rate. In addition, the algorithm checks whether the last decrease has been less than one second ago. In that case, we assume that the last increase of the sampling rate has been too hasty and that t_{gap} is too low. Consequently, t_{gap} is increased. On the other hand, if the last decrease event has been at least twenty seconds ago, t_{gap} is decreased.

Algorithm 1 Smoothed rate selection

```
unsigned adapt_rate(unsigned t_now, unsigned f_suggested)
{
  static unsigned t_lastdrop = 0, t_lastincrease = 0, f_actual = 0;
  if(f_suggested < f_actual && t_now + 1s ≥ t_lastdrop) {
    f_actual = f_suggested; t_lastdrop = t_now;
  } else if(f_suggested > f_actual) {
    if(t_now + 1s < t_lastdrop)
      t_gap = min(t_gap + 1, 20s);
    else if(t_now > t_lastdrop + 20s)
      t_gap = max(t_gap - 1, 3s);
    if(t_now > t_lastincrease + t_gap) {
      f_actual = f_suggested; t_lastincreae = t_now;
    }
  }
  return f_actual;
}
```

In our experimental tests, we have also noticed that the distribution of bandwidth between communication partners should be fair that is to say that the quality should be equally good in both directions as they both shared the same bottleneck. Thus, if $f_{suggested}^{to}$ is equal to 48 kHz and if the receiver sees a sampling rate of $f_{suggest}^{from} = 16$ kHz, we set the sending sampling rate to 32 kHz.

As soon as the available bandwidth falls below the codec's minimum bitrate, the adaptive VoIP-System changes to DTN mode. In this implementation, data is collected while the user holds down a button. The entire data is compressed and sent as soon as the user releases the button. The receiving side starts to play out the entire DTN talkspurt after having received the last frame of the talkspurt. This is similar to a walkie-talkie except that both users are able to hold down a button and to talk at the same time or to receive messages from their communication partner while doing so. Another difference is the fact that the message a user hears is as old as the time it took to record it.

During DTN mode of operation we transmit two types of packets that are either normal speech frames or just mode flags. If the receiver gets a frame with DTN flag set, it switches to DTN mode. All the speech frames are stored until an empty packet without speech frames is received. Then, the receiver decodes and plays out all of the stored

speech frames. If the receiver does not play out any speech frame, it sends out a busy tone to inform the user that he has to wait.

4. TEST RESULTS

To evaluate the Quality of Experience of our adaptive VoIP system in general and of the DTN mode in particular, we conducted subjective conversation tests following ITU-T recommendation P.805 [1].

The subjects were asked to have a series of conversations. Each conversation was used to test a different network scenario. After each particular scenario, the subjects were supposed to answer seven questions about speech quality, understandability, effort and any noticed distortions. These questions were answered on an absolute rating scale from 1 to 5 where 1 corresponded to the worst quality and 5 to the best one. Then the MOS-CQS of every question was calculated.

The test subjects were located in two separate quiet rooms. The subjects were wearing high quality head-sets that were connected to PCs. On the PCs, two different softphone implementations were running: a constant VoIP connection based on UDP and wide-band SBC and the adaptive VoIP algorithm described in the previous sections of this publication.

To simulate different conditions on a wide area network, we used the network simulator WANem[18]. In a first network setup, the network simulator did not restrict the bandwidth–the links were only limited by their physical transmission capacity (Fast Ethernet). Next, we added a random packet loss rate of 20%. Thirdly, a one-way bandwidth limit of 50 kbps was enforced. That way, losses only occurred because of full queues. Finally, both 15% random losses and a 50 kbps bandwidth limit were enforced.

A summary of the test conditions is given in Table 1.

Table 1: Test conditions: summary

Parameters	Values
Subjects	18 naive, 1 experienced, and 1 expert subjects. 7 female, 13 male.
Age	between 22 and 32, mean: 27.2
Groups	2 subjects per group
Rating scales	ACR: 1 (bad) to 5 (excellent)
Objective of the test	push-to-talk vs. classic VoIP under varying transmission bandwidths and packet loss rates.
Setup	headset, network simulator, softphone
Environment	quiet, separate rooms

4.1 Conversation test results

Figures 3 to 7 provide the MOS ratings of the conversational tests. In the case of unlimited bandwidth, both adaptive and constant VoIP show ratings that are not significantly different from each other. Both are equally good besides the fact that our implementation named AVoIP can use a fullband coding mode.

If suffering from 20% packet losses, both approaches have a speech quality of about 3.2 (Fig. 3). Understandability, listening effort and conversational effort are at about 4 (Figures 4, 5, and 6). Overall, the conversational quality is rated at 3 (Fig. 7). If a bandwidth limit of 50 kbps is applied, the adaptive VoIP solution has a speech quality of 3.5 compared to a value of about 1 for a constant mode. In the presence of additional packet losses, these values do not show any significant differences to the test case without loss. Under bandwidth limits, the understandability of AVoIP remains good; using UDP, speech cannot be understood anymore. The effort to talk back and forth is rated at 2.5 and 1.5, respectively. The most interesting test results are the ratings of the overall quality. In the presence of bandwidth limits, AVoIP has a value of about 2.9 (fair) without loss and of about 2.2 (poor) with loss as compared to about 1 (bad) for the UDP tests.

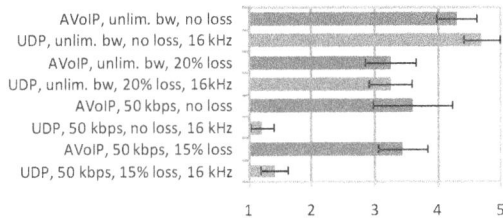

Figure 3: Speech quality: How would you assess the sound quality of the other person's voice?

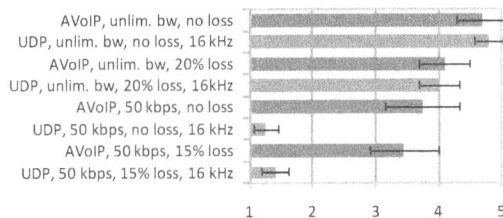

Figure 4: Understandability: How well did you understand what the other person was telling you?

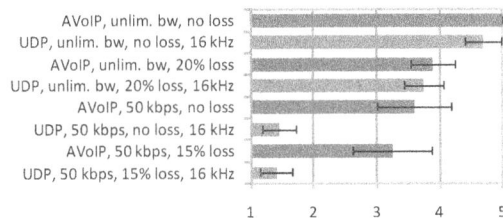

Figure 5: Listening effort: What level of effort did you need to understand what the other person was telling you?

4.2 Adapting coding modes

As mentioned in the previous section, DCCP does not provide stable bit rate estimates even if the simulated bandwidth remains stable. Thus, we studied how often the coding mode is changed and which modes are used at a given gross bandwidth.

The experimental setup was similar to the previous one. However, we tested the AVoIP application in an emulated network varying the gross one-way bandwidth from 200 kbps

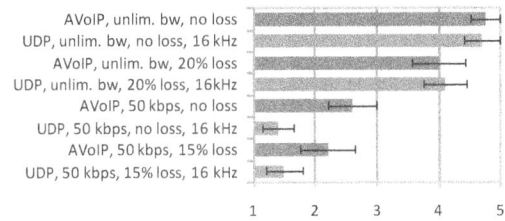

Figure 6: Conversational effort: How would you assess your level of effort to converse back and forth during the conversation?

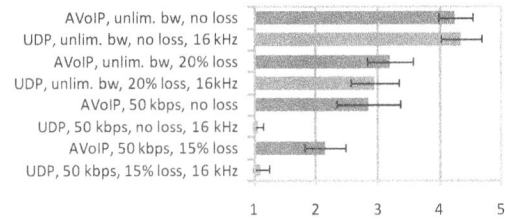

Figure 7: Overall quality: What is your opinion of the connection you have just been using?

to 700 kbps in steps of 50 kbps. Each particular test lasted one minute.

If the DCCP-estimated transmit rate is used to select the codec mode, mode changes occur frequently (Fig. 8). Using our rate control algorithm, the frequency of those hearable distortions is reduced.

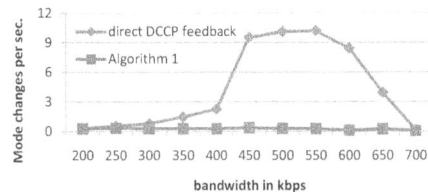

Figure 8: Mode changes per second in respect to the gross bandwidth.

Using the smooth rate control, the mode still changes from time to time. Figure 9 shows the distribution of the modes depending on the emulated bandwidth. First the DTN mode is dominant, then the wideband, followed by the superwideband, and finally, at high rates, the fullband mode is used most of the time.

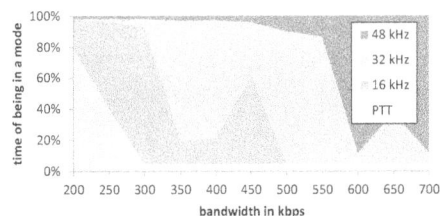

Figure 9: The percentage of the test duration remaining at the particular sampling frequencies with smoothed DCCP feedback

5. RELATED WORK

Modern VoIP receivers include a sophisticated jitter buffer management which controls the decoding of speech frames. For example, the 3GPP TS 26.114 specification [3] describes a speech receiver that includes a network analyzer, a play-out buffer adaption logic and sophisticated concealment algorithms that conceal besides frame loss also changes in the playout time. In addition, it also has a sender-side rate control to cope with varying network conditions. Rate control is achieved by means of RTCP feedback.

If a VoIP transceiver uses a transport protocol other than UDP–more precisely, a transport protocol that supports some flow and congestion control–the encoder's rate control can be based on the feedback from the transport protocol. Variable rate VoIP has been studied in–for example– [17, 20]. Typically, the VoIP transceiver switches to a better coding mode at a high bit rate if more transmission capacity is available. However, to the best of our knowledge, the question of what shall happen if the transmission capacity is lower than the least coding rate has not been addressed yet.

Traditionally, push-to-talk voice services have been used for half-duplex connections such as walkie-talkies. Nowadays, push-to-talk services are available for public safety radio communication systems [5], cellular phones [4], air traffic control [8], car communication [12], or social many-to-many wireless communication [15]. The conversational quality of PTT services has hardly been studied. Fernandez has compared normal and push-to-talk like conversations. Interestingly, PTT was more efficient than PSTN because the conversational task has been solved faster [9].

6. CONCLUSIONS

The subjective conversational tests have shown that the push-to-talk mode is advantageous if available transmission bandwidth is (too) low. In an unmanaged network, the DTN mode is the only approach to achieve a fair conversational quality and should therefore be included in VoIP phones–especially for the rare but not unimportant cases of flash crowds, catastrophic events, or bad weather conditions, when transmission bandwidth becomes scarce but communication remains important.

Furthermore, in this publication we have shown that the traditional delay requirements of telephony are conservative estimates. The maximum mouth-to-ear latency must not be below 150 or 400 ms but can be much higher if a proper user interface is designed and a push-to-talk mode is applied.

7. REFERENCES

[1] Subjective evaluation of conversational quality. ITU-T P.805, Apr. 2007.

[2] The E-model: a computational model for use in transmission planning. ITU-T G.107, Apr. 2009.

[3] 3GPP. IP multimedia subsystem (IMS). TS 26.114, June 2009. v8.3.

[4] T. Ali-Vehmas and S. Luukkainen. Service diffusion strategies for push to talk over cellular. In *ICMB 2005*, July 2005.

[5] N. Aschenbruck, M. Gerharz, M. Frank, and P. Martini. Modelling voice communication in disaster area scenarios. In *IEEE LCN 2006*, Nov. 2006.

[6] J.-C. Bolot, S. Fosse-Parisis, and D. F. Towsley. Adaptive FEC-based error control for internet telephony. In *IEEE INFOCOM '99*, New York, NY, Apr. 1999.

[7] C. Boutremans and J.-Y. L. Boudec. Adaptive joint playout buffer and FEC adjustment for internet telephony. In *IEEE INFOCOM 2003*, San Francisco, CA, Apr. 2003.

[8] A. Burgemeister. Packetized voice: A new communications concept for air traffic control. In *IEEE/ I 25th Digital ionics Systems Conference*, Oct. 2006.

[9] R. Fernandez, T. Lucht, K. Rodriguez, and D. Schlangen. Interaction in task-oriented human-human dialogue: The effects of different turn-taking policies. In *IEEE Spo en Language Technology Wor shop*, Dec. 2006.

[10] S. Floyd, M. Handley, J. Padhye, and J. Widmer. TCP Friendly Rate Control (TFRC): Protocol Specification. IETF RFC 5348 (Informational), Sept. 2008.

[11] C. Fraleigh, F. Tobagi, and C. Diot. Provisioning IP backbone networks to support latency sensitive traffic. In *IEEE INFOCOM 2003*, Mar. 2003.

[12] C.-H. Gan and Y.-B. Lin. Push-to-talk service for intelligent transportation systems. *IEEE Transactions on Intelligent Transportation Systems*, 8(3), Sept. 2007.

[13] C. Hoene and M. Hyder. Considering bluetooth's subband codec (SBC) for wideband speech and audio on the internet. Technical report, Universitätsbibliothek Tübingen, Germany, Oct. 2009.

[14] W. Jiang and H. Schulzrinne. Assessment of VoIP service availability in the current internet. In *M 2003*, San Diego, CA, Apr. 2003.

[15] K. Lee, A. Lippman, and T. Santos. Cocktail party on the mobile. In *IEEE ISM 2008*, Dec. 2008.

[16] H. Levy and H. Zlatokrilov. The effect of packet dispersion on voice applications in IP networks. *IEEE/ CM Transactions on Networ ing*, 14(2), Apr. 2006.

[17] C. Mahlo, C. Hoene, A. Rostami, and A. Wolisz. Adaptive coding and packet rates for TCP-friendly VoIP flows. In *IST2005*, Shiraz, Iran, Sept. 2005.

[18] M. Nambiar, H. K. Kalita, D. Mishra, and S. Rane. WANem - the wide area network emulator. http://wanem.sourceforge.net/, 2009.

[19] P. Noll, V. Leesemann, and G. Wessels. *a etorientierte Sprachü ertragung*. 86-05. Deutsche Versuchsanstalt für Luft- und Raumfahrt, 1986.

[20] G. Sarwar, R. Boreli, and E. Lochin. Performance of VoIP with DCCP for satellite links. In *IEEE ICC '09*, June 2009.

[21] S. Tao, K. Xu, A. Estepa, T. Gao, R. Guerin, J. Kurose, D. Towsley, and Z.-L. Zhang. Improving VoIP quality through path switching. In *IEEE INFOCOM 2005*, Mar. 2005.

[22] H. Vlad Balan, L. Eggert, S. Niccolini, and M. Brunner. An experimental evaluation of voice quality over the datagram congestion control protocol. In *IEEE INFOCOM 2007*, May 2007.

[23] J. Widmer, M. Mauve, and J. P. Damm. Probabilistic congestion control for non-adaptable flows. In *IEEE NOSSD V 2002*, Miami, FL, May 2002.

Inferring the Time-zones of Prefixes and Autonomous Systems by Monitoring Game Server Discovery Traffic

Mattia Rossi, Philip Branch, Grenville Armitage
Swinburne University of Technology
Melbourne, Australia
{mrossi,pbranch,garmitage}@swin.edu.au

ABSTRACT

Geolocation of IP addresses is used for determining authenticity of webpages, delivering specific country or location related content and advertisements, or to add security for online transactions. Although IP geolocation databases exist, it is sometimes useful to validate their entries or create new, independent databases using independent sources of information. We propose and demonstrate a method whereby collecting and analyzing online game server discovery traffic over short periods of time can allow us to detect in which timezone a certain prefix or AS is located. Our method provides very good estimates of various AS timezones which we verify using publicly available IP geolocation databases.

Categories and Subject Descriptors

C.2.5 [**Computer-Communication Networks**]: Local and Wide-Area Networks—*Internet*

General Terms

Measurement, Experimentation

Keywords

Autonomous System, Timezone, Geolocation, Gameserver Discovery, First Person Shooter

1. INTRODUCTION

Many webpages including well-known services such as Google, Youtube and Facebook deliver advertisements tailored to the country their users connect from. Large portals also improve content delivery by redirecting connections to servers geographically close to the end hosts. The methods used for determining the country consist in either checking the user's browser language and locale settings or determining the IP address geolocation.

As the browser language and locale settings can be easily changed by a user, and do not necessarily reflect the country the user is currently located in, IP geolocation is the preferred method.

IP geolocation is not only a useful tool for delivering location dependent content but also to protect against malicious man in the middle attacks and phishing [1].

The IP address location in geolocation databases is extracted from various databases which correlate information such as a user's mail address with an IP address. An example of such a database is the *whois* [2] database which is maintained by Domain Name registrars. The information contained in *whois* is the country and mail address of the owner of the domain name and prefix. However this provides little information about the actual location of prefixes or the location of a user of an IP address, which can be located in a different area or country than that of the registrar. Additionally, the information can become inaccurate over time, given that updates in the *whois* database depend solely on updates by the registrars.

We propose a novel method of identifying the timezones of Autonomous Systems (ASes) and prefixes [3] using game server discovery traffic collected over time of certain first person shooter (FPS) games. We show that it is possible to identify prefixes within a certain AS which are located in a different timezone from the majority of prefixes in the AS. We also suggest ways in which the information could be used to help validate information found in the *whois* database or existing geolocation databases.

During the last decade, online First Person Shooter (FPS) games have become increasingly popular. It is now quite feasible for households with a broadband access link to both play and host such games. A single game server attracts a large number of UDP packets (probes) from clients all over the world, without the clients actually playing on the server. An analysis of this probe traffic shows that game traffic from particular ASes and address prefixes demonstrates strong 24 hour periodicity. The peaks in packet arrival rate appears to be strongly correlated with the time zone the packets originate from.

By calculating the phase shift between two such ASes or prefixes, it is possible to determine the difference in hours, and thus detect the timezone in which such an AS or prefix is located. This information can also be used to identify a country, if the timezone is specific to it.

In this paper we report on statistics of probe traffic observed at our game server. We demonstrate that it is possible to identify the timezone of the AS or prefix using the probe traffic.

Although we report on game traffic probes, the approach

could possibly be applied to any server that receives increased traffic at a particular time of day. For example news sites may observe peaks during the early morning.

The paper is organized as follows. In Section 2 we discuss previous work on game server discovery traffic. Section 3 details the game server setup and data collection, while Section 4 explains the basic method used for evaluating the data. In Section 5 we show an example of AS timezone detection and in Section 6 we further extend the method to prefixes and verify the results. We summarize our work and suggest future research in Section 7.

2. BACKGROUND

There are many multiplayer online FPS games that rely on enthusiast-hosted game servers to provide the online environments within which people play. For example there are tens of thousands of game servers such as Valve's *Counter-Strike: Source* available online at any given time. FPS game clients locate playable game servers by first querying a Master Server (usually hosted by the game's publisher) which returns to the client a list of IP address and port numbers of currently registered game servers. Each client typically then probes game servers to determine the round trip time (RTT) to each server and to retrieve additional server information [4]. This information is used by the client to create a ranked list of available/reachable game servers from which the player makes a selection.

A side effect of this server discovery process is that registered game servers experience a continuous influx of UDP-based probe traffic 24 hours a day from game clients around the planet [5, 6]. Furthermore, this influx of probe traffic fluctuates over time, with traffic from different parts of the planet typically peaking in the afternoon and evening at the origin. This phenomenon suggests that an IPv4 address, or a range of IPv4 addresses could be assigned to a certain geographical region by simply analyzing the oscillation of probe traffic volume. In this paper we provide such an analysis.

3. DATA COLLECTION

We have set up a *Valve* Counter-Strike:Source game server [7] (CS:Source) collecting probes using tcpdump, and used a Quagga [8] BGP speaker to access BGP routing table information for extracting AS and prefix information.

Apart from the ease of running a CS:Source game server, the reason we used this game is because of its popularity as observed at *GameTracker.com* [9].

3.1 Game Server Deployment

We ran the CS:Source game server on a single machine deployed at the Centre for Advanced Internet Architectures at Swinburne University of Technology, Melbourne, Australia, and connected to the Internet by a 100 MBit/s connection. The game server was password protected (allowing clients to discover the server, but not permit game play on it) and registered with the Steam [10] master server so it can be found by clients across the globe.

3.2 Collecting the Data

At the game server side, traffic has been collected passively using *tcpdump* for 75 days (25 Dec 2009, 00:00 to 09 Mar 2010, 23:59 AEST). The collected data has been filtered to remove probes arriving at a constant rate with short

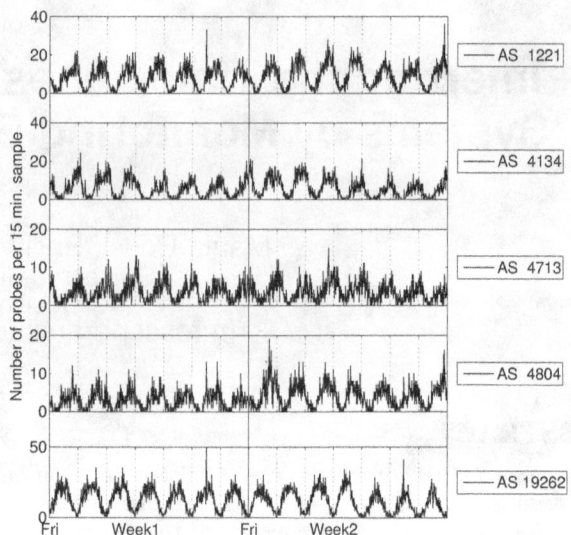

Figure 1: Activity curve for 5 selected ASes over 14 days using a 15 minute sampling window

AS number	Company	Country
1221	Telstra	AU
19262	Verizon	US
4134	Chinanet	CN
4804	Microplex	AU
4713	OCN NTT	JP

Table 1: AS numbers, company names and country codes for the example ASes used. Information gathered from the *whois* database.

intervals (typically machined-triggered probing used to provide publicly available statistics, such as 'GameTracker' [9]). The IPv4 addresses extracted from the resulting probes have then been matched to their respective AS numbers and prefixes extracted from the BGP table.

4. ANALYSIS OF RAW DATA

In order to extract the 24 hour cycles, we have used a sampling window of 15 minutes, extracting the IPv4 addresses of the probes. Multiple probes originating from a single address have been discarded. Such probing might be generated by multiple hosts behind a gateway, using Network Address Port Translation (NAPT, commonly referred to as NAT). Or they may be generated by users repeatedly pressing their client's "refresh" button over a short period of time, biasing the data.

Figure 1 shows the activity of five selected ASes over the first 14 days. These ASes are a representative sample having identifiable activity curves, regardless of the total amount of probes received from each AS. Table 1 shows the companies and locations of each AS according to *whois* [11].

Although there is an obvious 24 hour cycle of probe traffic it becomes even more apparent when we examine the autocorrelation function (ACF) of the traffic flows. The ACF is a function which measures the similarity of a signal to itself at a particular displacement (the lag). If the signal has a strong periodic component the ACF will also be periodic. It will have a low value when measured at a lag of half a cycle,

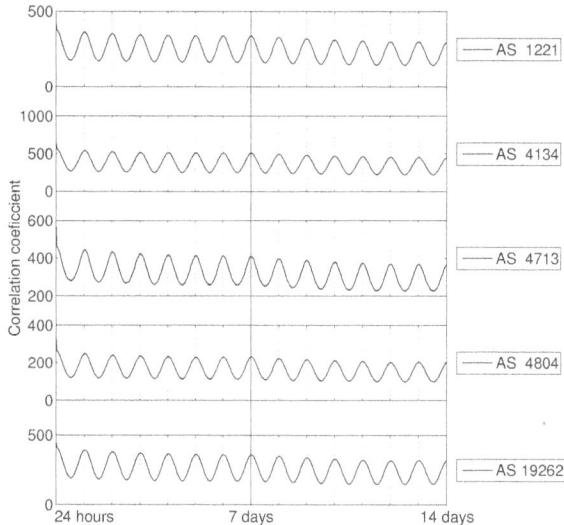

Figure 2: The auto-correlation function for each AS shows peaks at exactly 24 hours and multiples of it

since the signal will be most different and will have a large value at a full cycle. In Figure 2 we plot the ACF for each of the selected ASes. We see a well defined 24 hour period in each ACF.

5. IDENTIFYING TIMEZONE OFFSETS FOR AUTONOMOUS SYSTEMS

In this section we demonstrate that the peaks in activity enable us to estimate in which timezone the addresses in an AS are located. If we assume that the peak of activity occurs at the same local time for each AS then by comparing the relative position of the peaks we can estimate the difference in timezone. Of course this is a substantial assumption, but we see in the data that follows that it appears to be a reasonable one.

We illustrate the approach by using AS 1221 (Telstra, Australia) as a reference AS and examining the difference in peak packet rates with the other ASes. AS 1221 covers all three timezones of Australia, however the population is concentrated on the east coast of the country, with about 60% in Victoria (Melbourne), New South Wales (Sydney) and the Australian Capital Territory (Canberra) [12], which all share the same timezone. We can therefore plausibly locate AS 1221 in that timezone as reference. Figure 3 shows a 24 hour plot of the activity of AS 1221 and AS 19262.

There is an obvious difference in the time at which activity peaks within the two ASes. However, the actual peak is difficult to identify from a single 24 hour period. We see that it is approximately six to eight hours. A more effective approach is to calculate the cross-correlation function (CCF) over many days of the two functions representing the arrival rate for each AS. The CCF between two functions gives a measure of similarity between two signals at a particular phase shift. The phase shift where the CCF is at a maximum is our estimate of the timezone difference

In Figure 4 we plot the CCF between AS1221 and AS19262. The peak occurs at a phase shift that corresponds to a time difference of seven-and-a-half hours.

This can be interpreted in a number of ways. One expla-

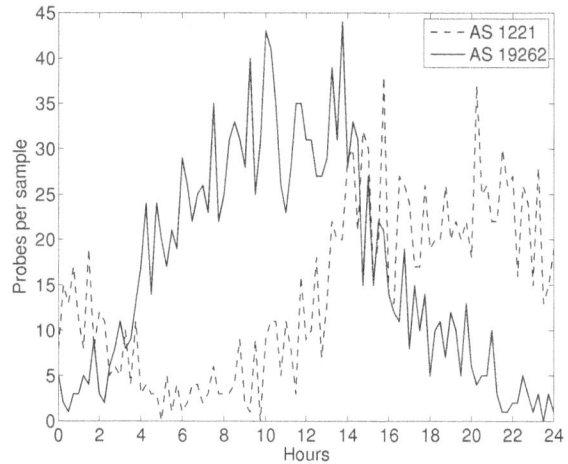

Figure 3: A 24 hour extract of the raw data of AS 1221 and AS 19262.

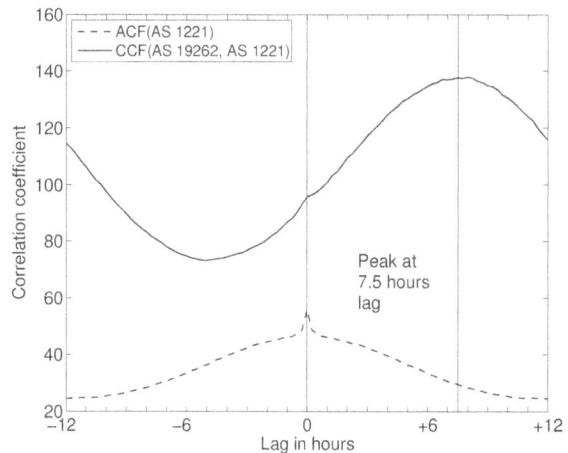

Figure 4: CCF between AS 1221 and AS 19262. The lag of the peak is also the timezone offset

nation is that people in Australia begin game play half an hour earlier in their day than in the US. Given the cultural similarities between the countries, this is unlikely. Another interpretation is that we are seeing activity across several timezones in the US but that the bulk of game players is located on the East coast of the US. Since AS 19262 is the AS of Verizon, a national US carrier this is the more likely explanation.

5.1 Workday vs. Weekend traffic

Although users seem to start game play at similar hours of the day in different countries, there is a substantial difference in the probe traffic between weekends and weekdays.

We have performed cross correlation between AS 1221 and AS 19262 using samples of one to five consecutive days. The samples have been extracted starting at every possible day within the 75 day period, but had to contain only weekdays data in the first test and include a weekend on the second test. To increase the accuracy and eliminate outliers we have summed every 24 hour cycle into a single 24 hour cycle within each sample.

The resulting datasets for each sampling period have then

been cross correlated and the lag plotted as a boxplot. Figure 5 shows the results using weekdays only. The boxes delimit the median, and the upper and lower quartile, while the whiskers delimit the 5th and 95th percentile. Outliers are marked with crosses.

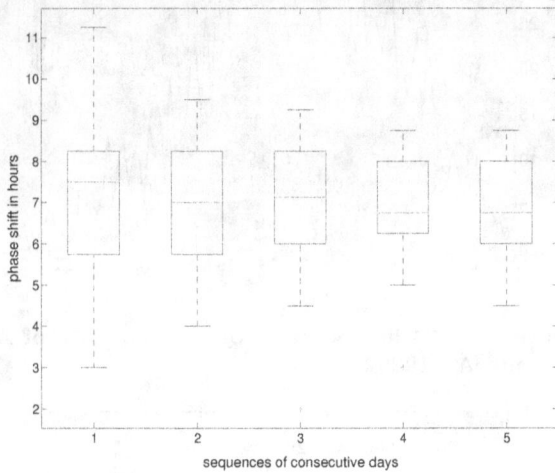

Figure 5: **AS 19262 cross correlated to AS 1221: Time zone offset calculated using a maximum of 5 consecutive days using only weekdays traffic**

Figure 6 shows the results for the sequences containing a weekend.

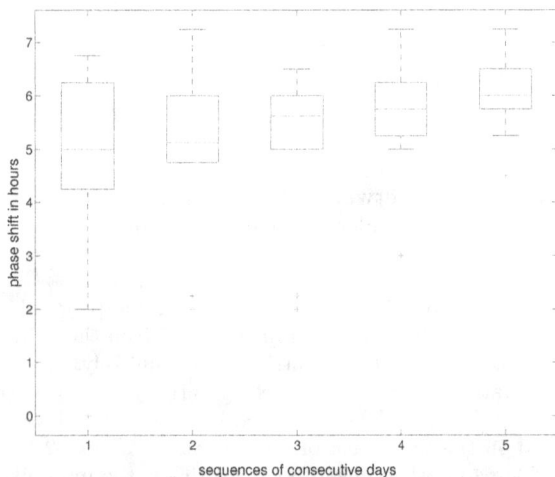

Figure 6: **AS19262 cross correlated to AS 1221: Time zone offset calculated using a maximum of 5 consecutive days, always including weekends.**

The boxes show a smaller lag for one or two consecutive days, and increases if more days are included. This happens for two possible reasons:

- Users in the US start game play much earlier on the weekend than in Australia

- Users in Australia play games longer on the weekend

A mix of both reasons can not be excluded.

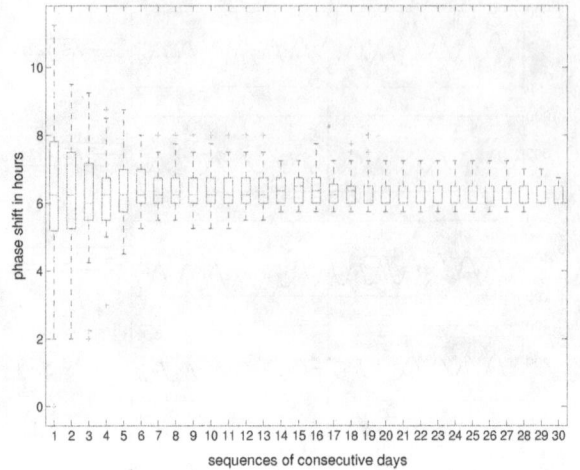

Figure 7: **AS 19262 cross-correlated to AS 1221: Timezone offset per sequences of consecutive days of data.**

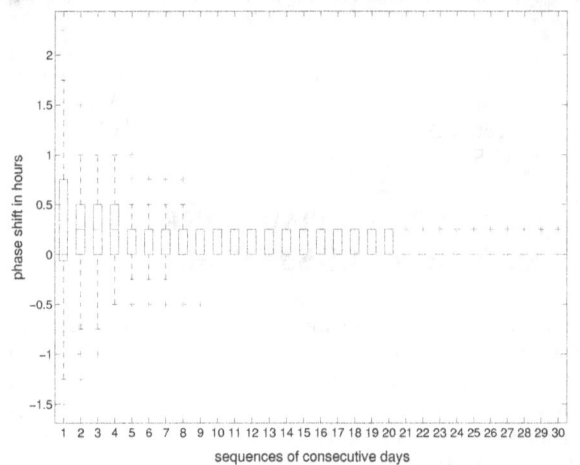

Figure 8: **AS 4804 cross-correlated to AS 1221: Timezone offset per sequences of consecutive days of data.**

5.2 Testing for consistency

Given the difference in weekends and weekdays data, it is most likely necessary to use a larger dataset than 5 consecutive days to achieve consistent results. We have further analyzed samples of 1 to 30 consecutive days within the 75 day period. The samples have been extracted starting at every possible day within the 75 day period, resulting in 74 samples for a sampling period of 1 day up to 44 samples for a sampling period of 30 consecutive days.

Using the same method as in Section 5.1 we have cross correlated AS 1221 and the other four example ASes. The results are shown in Figures 7, 8, 9 and 10.

AS 19262 yields an offset between six and eight hours, confirming previous results. The variation is most likely caused by the bulk of game playing slightly shifting from the US East coast to the West coast on certain days.

The cross correlation of AS 4804 and AS 1221 demonstrates that the method presented in this paper can be quite accurate. With 20 days of data, we can see that the offset is mostly zero hours. That is the two ASes are located within the same time-zones.

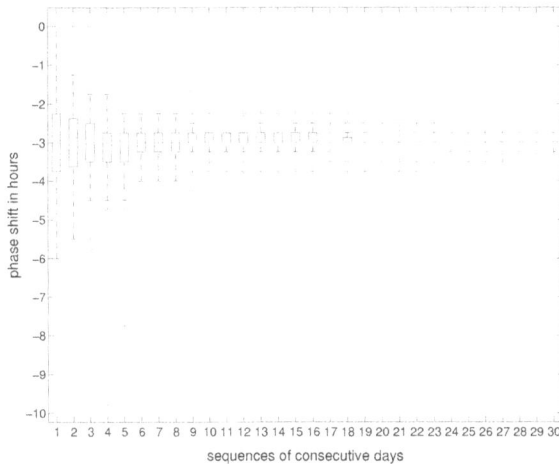

Figure 9: AS 4713 cross-correlated to AS 1221: Timezone offset per sequences of consecutive days of data.

The cross correlation of AS 4713 and AS 1221 converges to an offset of -3 hours. However, since the AS is located in Japan we would expect an offset of two hours. This is obviously an area for future research, as the one hour difference is not caused by adoption of daylight saving. However it might be explained by the comparatively small number of probes received from this AS.

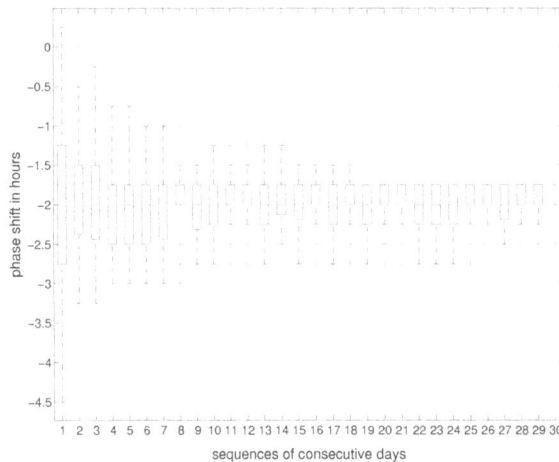

Figure 10: AS 4134 cross-correlated to AS 1221: Timezone offset per sequences of consecutive days of data.

We see a similar effect in the CCF between AS 1221 and AS 4134 (China Telecom, and China has a single country-wide timezone centered on Beijing). This suggests a phase shift of around two hours, whereas we might expect a phase shift of three hours, again not caused by daylight saving. Also the graph does not converge to a single value, suggesting there may be some informal adoption of local timezones across China. Again this is a topic for further investigation when additional data is obtained.

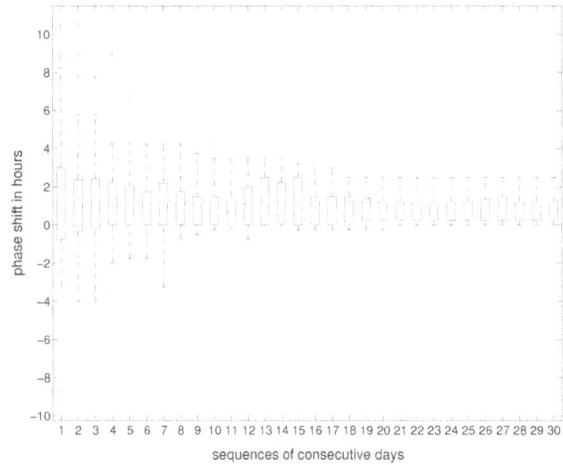

Figure 11: Prefix 139.168.0.0/16 cross-correlated to AS 1221: Timezone offset per sequences of consecutive days of data.

6. TIMEZONE OFFSETS FOR PREFIXES WITHIN AN AUTONOMOUS SYSTEM

Timezone offsets can also be calculated for prefixes within an AS. Using the same cross-correlation method as for the AS timezone offsets, we show in Figure 11 that we are able to find a prefix within AS 1221 that is offset with a spread between zero and one hour.

The only one hour time difference that can be found in Australia in the period of data collection, is between the state of Queensland with capital Brisbane and the states of New South Wales (Sydney), Victoria (Melbourne) and the Australian Capital Territory (Canberra). While all 4 states are located at the east coast of Australia and should share the same timezone, Queensland doesn't observe daylight saving, thus has a time offset of one hour. Within the one hour spread anyhow, we find an additional timezone in Australia, belonging to South Australia with capital Adelaide. The timezone of south Australia has an offset of half an hour from the most populous cities covered by the AS (Sydney and Melbourne).

Calculating prefix timezone offsets with the data we gathered risks inaccuracy. For prefix 139.168.0.0/16 only 355 addresses out of the approximately 65,500 possible addresses[1] probed our server. This results in a relatively noisy ACF as shown in Figure 12, which could bias the results.

As with ASes, large prefixes like 139.168.0.0/16 are not always bound to single areas within a country. It is more likely, that smaller subsets (such as /24 blocks) are used for specific areas. Analyzing such /24 blocks, the signal is even more noisy, as the number of addresses probing can drop below 10 addresses. Nevertheless, we can demonstrate how the timezone of a particular prefix within an AS can be identified. Figure 13 cross correlates prefix 139.168.193.0/24 which contains probes from only 5 addresses with AS 1221.

Although there is a great deal of variability in the CCF the offset appears to be approximately half to one hour, suggesting the South Australian timezone. By carrying out a Traceroute on five randomly chosen addresses within this

_____

[1]The exact number of available addresses depends on how the prefix is subdivided by the ISP

73

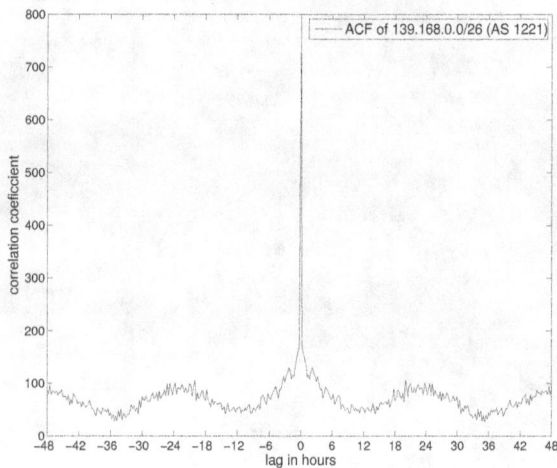

Figure 12: ACF of prefix 139.168.0.0/16

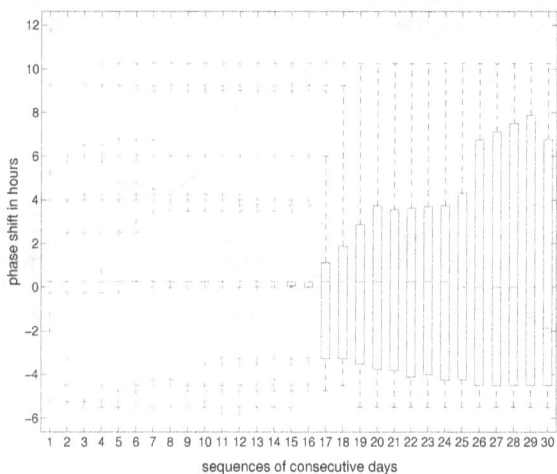

Figure 13: Prefix 139.168.193.0/24 cross correlated to AS 1221: Timezone offset per sequences of consecutive days of data.

prefix we find that all of them are located in Adelaide, capital of South Australia, thus confirming our supposition.

This information is an improvement to the information which can be extracted from the *whois* database. It is also consistent with the information provided by proprietary geolocation databases.

7. CONCLUSIONS

The immediate use of this technique is to confirm the geolocation information provided by existing databases. As noted earlier geolocation databases are currently updated manually, with consequent possibilities of error. Also, the technique provides information about the actual rather than the claimed distribution of IP addresses within an AS. It is possible than an AS may be registered in one timezone but most of its IP addresses are located in another timezone. This technique allows such situations to be identified. There is also the possibility of identifying the geolocation of IP prefix addresses within an AS enabling the internal structure of an AS to be determined. We require additional data to test the feasibility of this further idea.

Although we have concentrated on gameserver probes, the approach could be adapted to any website that receives sufficient volumes of traffic and is subject to daily human rhythms, such as e-mail access.

Future work in this area will include refining the statistical tools used for analysis, and using the technique to identify the geolocation of IP prefix addresses within an AS. This novel approach to IP geolocation has considerable potential, and is worth further exploration.

8. ACKNOWLEDGMENTS

This work has been made possible in part by a grant from APNIC.

9. REFERENCES

[1] D. Garrett, "Flagfox." [Online]. Available: https://addons.mozilla.org/en-US/firefox/user/235431/

[2] L. Daigle, "WHOIS Protocol Specification," RFC 3912 (Draft Standard), Internet Engineering Task Force, Sep. 2004. [Online]. Available: http://www.ietf.org/rfc/rfc3912.txt

[3] J. Hawkinson and T. Bates, "Guidelines for creation, selection, and registration of an Autonomous System (AS)," RFC 1930 (Best Current Practice), Internet Engineering Task Force, Mar. 1996. [Online]. Available: http://www.ietf.org/rfc/rfc1930.txt

[4] G. Armitage, M. Claypool, and P. Branch, *Networking and Online Games*. John Wiley & Sons, 2006.

[5] S. Zander, D. Kennedy, and G. Armitage, "Dissecting server-discovery traffic patterns generated by multiplayer first person shooter games," in *NetGames '05: Proceedings of 4th ACM SIGCOMM workshop on Network and system support for games*. New York, NY, USA: ACM, 2005, pp. 1–12.

[6] G. Armitage, "A Packet Arrival Model for Wolfenstein Enemy Territory Online Server Discovery Traffic," in *ICON 2007. 15th IEEE International Conference on Networks, 2007.*, Nov. 2007, pp. 31–36.

[7] Valve Corporation, "Games by Valve Software." [Online]. Available: http://www.valvesoftware.com/games.html

[8] K. Ishiguro, "Quagga Software Routing Suite." [Online]. Available: http://www.quagga.net

[9] GameTracker.com, "GameTracker - Online game server statistics." [Online]. Available: http://www.gametracker.com

[10] Valve Corporation, "Steam dedicated server update tool (hldsupdatetool)." [Online]. Available: http://store.steampowered.com/about/

[11] C. Small, "Small drop bear - autonomous system whois lookup." [Online]. Available: http://enc.com.au/itools/aut-num.php

[12] A. B. of Statistics, "Australian demographic statistics, jun 2010." [Online]. Available: http://www.abs.gov.au/ausstats/abs@.nsf/mf/3101.0/

GPU-based Fast Motion Estimation for On-the-Fly Encoding of Computer-Generated Video Streams

Javier Taibo
CITIC, Univ. Corunna, SPAIN
jtaibo@udc.es

Victor M. Gulias
CITIC, Univ. Corunna, SPAIN
gulias@udc.es

Pablo Montero
CITIC, Univ. Corunna, SPAIN
pmontm@gmail.com

Samuel Rivas
CITIC, Univ. Corunna, SPAIN
samuelrivas@gmail.com

ABSTRACT

Motion estimation is known to be one of the most expensive tasks in video coding as it is usually performed through blind search-based methods. However, in the particular case of computer-generated video, the rendering stage provides useful information to speed up the process. In this paper, we propose a fast motion estimation algorithm, designed to run completely inside the GPU, to compute the optical flow required to estimate motion vectors at the same time as the graphical rendering process by using high-level information about the objects, viewpoints and effects that define each frame. The proposed method takes advantage of GPU parallelism and avoids bottlenecks in the CPU-GPU communication as the entire rendering and encoding process is performed completely inside the GPU. Avoiding search, motion estimation has very little overhead, negligible when compared with rendering and (the rest of the) video encoding costs while maintaining reasonably good quality.

Performance evaluation is done with a CUDA implementation for MPEG-2 video, though results are valid for other formats, and it has been tested as part of the rendering and encoding engine of a real-world system that provides server-side visually-rich interactive applications to lightweight clients equipped with standard MPEG video decoders.

Categories and Subject Descriptors

H.5.1 [**Information Interfaces and Presentation**]: Multimedia Information Systems—*Animations, Video*; I.4.2, I.4.8 [**Image Processing and Computer Vision**]: Compression (Coding), Scene Analysis—*Motion*

General Terms

Performance

Keywords

Motion Estimation, GPU, Rendering, Optical Flow

1. INTRODUCTION

With the increase in networked electronic media, several services will require the deployment of systems capable of generating a huge number of concurrent video streams in real-time for both natural (acquired with a camera) or synthetic (computer generated) content. Custom hardware video encoders do not scale at all and impose an unaffordable cost per video stream. Software encoders, on the other hand, are limited to encoding only a few streams concurrently, even on modern CPUs, as real-time video encoding is a demanding task, even more so with High Definition coming into play.

Motion estimation, the process that finds the optical flow between past (or even future) and present frames, is known as one of the most expensive tasks in video coding as it is usually performed through blind search-based methods. However, in the case of synthetic video, the rendering stage can provide additional information to improve performance of motion estimation. In this paper, we propose a fast motion estimation algorithm, designed to run completely in the GPU, for animated scenes rendered in real time. Motion information about camera and objects composing the scene, present in a computer animation system, can be exploited to help the motion estimation process. In addition, motion estimation can be performed at the same time as the graphical rendering process. The proposal takes benefit from GPU parallelism and avoids bottlenecks in CPU-GPU communication as the entire rendering and encoding process is performed completely inside the GPU. Avoiding search, motion estimation has very little overhead, negligible when compared with the cost of rendering and the rest of the video encoding, while maintaining a reasonable quality.

This work is part of a large-scale GPU-based video rendering and encoding system (*Synthetrick*) designed to offer interactive 3D applications for digital television (see figure 1). To meet the demanding system requirements of server-side on-the-fly video stream generation (in terms of both throughput and low latency), workload is distributed among a cluster of GPU-equipped nodes. Computing nodes run 3D applications and GPU computing power is exploited for both scene rendering and video encoding as a whole. Lightweight clients act on these 3D applications by using low latency RTP messages, mainly to encode user interactions (remote controller key strokes, for instance). A distributed

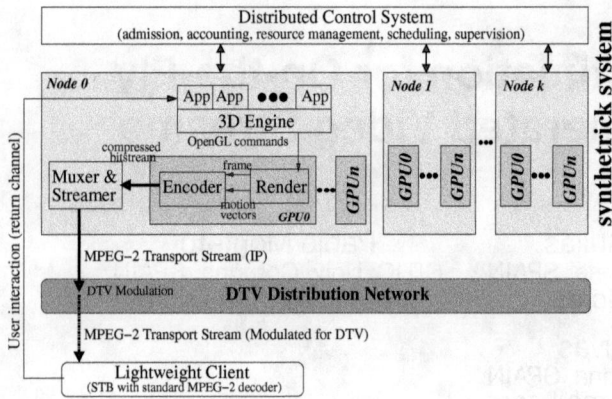

Figure 1: Overview of Synthetrick system.

control system is in charge of admission, resource management, scheduling and supervision of all the computing nodes and user sessions.

A GPU-based encoder is an interesting option for massive encoding of video streams at relatively low cost per stream. Mass-market dynamics have allowed modern GPU architecture trends with price-performance ratios unheard of a few years ago. Moreover, in the case of video streams encoded from computer-generated frames, the gain can be enormous as the target raw frame is generated in GPU memory, which eliminates the costs of transferring it from the CPU.

The video stream is supposed to be decoded by existing cheap (and low power) hardware devices such as DVB-C set-top boxes or hand-held devices. As the system is tested on real-world broadcasting networks based on MPEG-2 standard (both DVB-C and IPTV), the proposed technique is applied to an MPEG-2 CUDA-based video encoder tightly integrated with visually-rich OpenGL applications. MPEG-2 elementary streams are multiplexed in MPEG transport streams to be directly modulated and injected into digital television distribution (DTV) networks. Though the system is focused on CUDA, OpenGL and MPEG-2, it can be easily ported to other platforms such as OpenCL, for the encoding, or Direct3D, for the rendering. Moreover, our method can be applied to other video formats, such as H.264.

The paper is structured as follows. Section 2 summarizes previous work on encoding animated scenes. Section 3 outlines the render-based motion estimation algorithm. Section 4 discusses some open issues and their consequences, while experimental results are commented upon in section 5. Finally, section 6 presents the conclusions and outlines future work.

2. PREVIOUS WORK

Transform information to compute per-pixel motion estimation was explored in [5] to define a lossless compression method to encode computer animated scenes. The encoded video includes the transform matrices and additional per-pixel metainformation about the scene geometry; such huge overhead makes this work unsuitable for streaming and real-time processing; besides it does not address standard MPEG decoders. In [1], 2D transform matrices are bound to each pixel block for their use in the decoding process, allowing the management of translational as well as non-translational

motions; though this solves some limitations, it also does not address standard MPEG decoders.

Wallach et al. [9] described a method to compute the optical flow between consecutive frames of a scene using the graphics hardware capabilities, for some steps, in MPEG video encoding. It uses transformation (matrix-vector multiplication), scan conversion and Gouraud shading to render a frame containing the per-pixel motion vectors of the scene. The difference between consecutive frames is computed in the vertices of the models and the graphics hardware interpolates the rest of the pixels using Gouraud shading. The motion vector of each macroblock is computed as the mode of the motion vectors of the macroblock pixels; this motion vector is the starting point to refine the result using search. After rendering the per-pixel motion vectors, the remainder of the computations, including the mode and exhaustive search, are made in the CPU, which impose a performance penalty. Similarly, [3] described an encoding system that performs the rendering and computes per-pixel motion vectors in the GPU, performing the rest of the encoding in the CPU, including computing per-macroblock motion vectors. Transform matrices and per-pixel depth information are used to unproject the current pixel and reproject it with the reference frame camera projection. That has an important overhead, as it needs to store and access, for the reference frames, the depth buffer, an additional buffer with the rendered objects IDs, the transform matrices for each object and a map between object IDs and transform matrices.

A similar video stream generation system is presented in [7], a server-based 3D walkthrough system focused on lightweight devices based on MPEG-4 encoding. Scene is segmented in two layers (background-foreground) and encoded with different quantizer values. An estimation of the optical flow is computed for each macroblock and is used as the initial location for a refinement using logarithmic search. As client devices must compose both video layers, this solution has limited applicability with mass-market set-top boxes.

Our method adapts [9] to perform the whole rendering and encoding process in the GPU and puts emphasis on performance as it is targeted to large-scale on-the-fly video stream generation. In our experience, CPU-GPU communication is a bottleneck for such systems and only final bitstream should be transferred, rather than intermediate results such as motion vectors. Another difference with respect to other methods is that we must comply with standard MPEG decoders (in our test implementation, MPEG-2) to be used in large deployments of commodity hardware. Unlike previous work, motion estimation is computed in the vertex shader with excellent performance and quality good enough to avoid costly extra refinement. In addition, deformable objects are also considered (most of the state of the art restricts geometry to rigid bodies) with very little overhead by supplying the deformer parameters to the vertex shader.

A similar idea has been recently applied to natural video [2], using hardware sensors to compute camera movement and help improve the compression and speed performance. Our method, however, is not limited to global motion, as it also gathers the motion of every single object in the scene.

3. RENDER-BASED MOTION ESTIMATION

Motion estimation algorithms compute a 2-dimensional vector field describing the on-screen motion with respect to a reference frame with minimal distortion for each pixel. As it is costly, motion estimation is usually performed per block instead of per pixel, with the assumption that all the pixels in the block share the same motion. Most algorithms are based on blind search because no additional information is known about the sequence of frames to be encoded.

3.1 Search-based Motion Estimation

Most search-based motion estimation algorithms use the sum of absolute differences (SAD) as the distortion criterion between the current and reference frames, which can be described as the following equation for a given $N \times N$ block:

$$SAD(m,n) = \sum_{i=1}^{N} \sum_{j=1}^{N} | \; curr(i,j) - ref(i+m, j+n) \; |$$

where $curr(x,y)$ and $ref(x,y)$ are the values at position (x,y), with respect to the given block, for current and reference frames, respectively. Brute force exhaustive motion estimation scans all candidates within a $2P \times 2P$ search range, that is $-P \leq m < P$ and $-P \leq n < P$; though it returns the best quality solution, it is the most computationally intensive and, hence, different approaches such as fast search algorithms are proposed to reduce the candidates for lower computation using heuristics.

3.2 Exploiting High-Level Information

Instead of performing a search (or fast search) on the raw frame, we take advantage of render information to compute the per-pixel optical flow simultaneously with scene render. The overall steps of the rendering and encoding process, as shown in figure 2, are carried out entirely in the GPU.

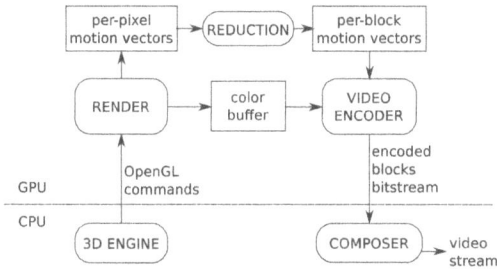

Figure 2: Overview of rendering and encoding.

3.2.1 Regular Rendering Pipeline

The 3D engine sends OpenGL commands that describe the camera and objects in the scene for each frame. Figure 3 (in black) shows a simplified view of the well-known real-time rendering pipeline. The vertex shader simply translates the vertex from object space to clip space using the model-view and projection matrices as well as other transformations, such as deformer operators, that produce per-vertex displacements. Then, vertices are used by the primitive assembly, clipping, perspective projection, face-orientation culling and finally by the rasterization stage that generates the fragments that potentially feed the frame buffer. When resulting vertices reach the rasterization stage, they carry some attached attributes (e.g., color, normal, texture coordinates) whose values are interpolated for each fragment.

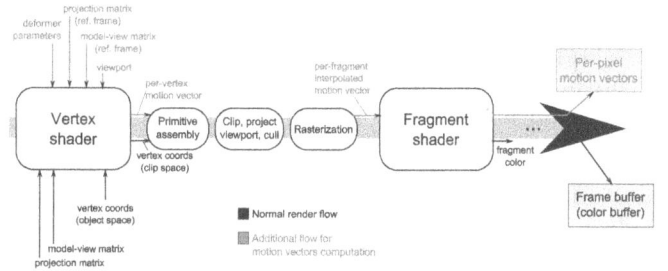

Figure 3: Modified pipeline to estimate motion.

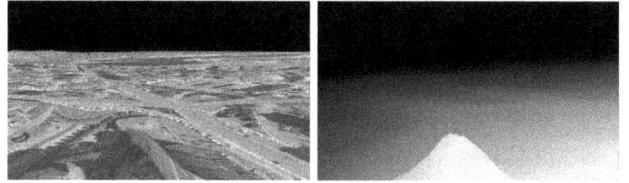

Figure 4: Sample color and per-pixel motion buffers.

3.2.2 Computing Per-Pixel Motion Vectors

The rendering pipeline is extended to compute in the GPU, using shaders, the per-pixel motion vector with respect to a reference frame in addition to the color buffer, as exemplified in figure 4; figure 3 (in red) shows the additional information required. First, the estimation of the vertex position in clip space for both current and reference (denoted with superscript r) frame is computed as:

$$\mathbf{v_c} = (x_c, y_c, z_c, w_c) = \mathbf{P} \times \mathbf{M} \times d(\mathbf{v_o})$$
$$\mathbf{v_c^r} = (x_c^r, y_c^r, z_c^r, w_c^r) = \mathbf{P^r} \times \mathbf{M^r} \times d^r(\mathbf{v_o})$$

where $\mathbf{v_o}$ and $\mathbf{v_c}$ are 3D vertex position at object and clip space, respectively, expressed in homogeneous coordinates using a 4-dimensional vector (x, y, z, w), $\mathbf{M}$ and $\mathbf{P}$ are the model-view and projection matrices, and function d is the deformer operator.

After computing clip space coordinates, perspective division is applied to compute the normalized device coordinates for current ($\mathbf{v_d} = \mathbf{v_c}/w_c$) and reference frames ($\mathbf{v_d^r} = \mathbf{v_c^r}/w_c^r$). Finally, the viewport and depth range transforms are applied to the normalized device coordinates to get the window space coordinates $\mathbf{v_w}$, measured in pixels, as:

$$\mathbf{v_w} = \left(X + W \times \frac{x_d+1}{2}, Y + H \times \frac{y_d+1}{2}, \frac{z_d+1}{2} \right)$$
$$\mathbf{v_w^r} = \left(X + W \times \frac{x_d^r+1}{2}, Y + H \times \frac{y_d^r+1}{2}, \frac{z_d^r+1}{2} \right)$$

where viewport has offset (X,Y) and size $W \times H$, in pixels. The z component of the window coordinates could be used to check the visibility of the surface at each point, as in [3], but it would need to store additional buffers and information for the reference frame. As we are not looking for high accuracy but for good quality/performance tradeoff, only x and y coordinates are required to estimate the per-vertex motion vector as $\mathbf{v_w^r} - \mathbf{v_w}$.

The fragment shader receives per-vertex motion vectors interpolated by the rasterizer. They are encoded as color values that must match the same pixel format as the main color buffer. These motion vectors are output to a second render target (considering the color buffer as the first one).

3.2.3 Computing Per-Macroblock Motion Vectors

MPEG compression uses a single motion vector for all the pixels in a macroblock. Hence, a transformation from per-pixel to per-macroblock motion vectors is required. In [9], mode is suggested for this reduction as it performs better than other operations such as mean. However, mode does not adapt well to GPU parallel computation, thus other options must be considered such as mean (efficiently computed using a CUDA kernel, as shown in [6]) or even the central pixels in the macroblock as a quick approximation to the mode. Experimental results in section 5 confirm that quality is similar but the performance improvement is noticeable.

3.2.4 Deformable Objects

Previous similar approaches have dealt only with rigid-body geometries. As vertex displacements are efficiently computed in the vertex shader, our proposal can take into account non-rigid bodies. The displacement for object's vertices in the reference frame has to be stored.

Deformer operations are usually implemented in GPU (in vertex shaders). In this case, the deformer parameters for the reference frame must be passed to the shader. For example, using blend shape deformers, only the weight for the different poses must be passed for the current frame as well as for the reference frame. This is very light, as they are per-object parameters. Per-vertex information (e.g., per-pose vertex displacement) is already stored in GPU memory.

4. OPEN ISSUES

The proposed technique is well suited to most situations, but there are some cases where motion vector computation is not possible. It is important to note, however, that most of these problems are also present in non-exhaustive search-based methods. The solutions to some of these problems (when feasible) are computationally expensive and not fit for our target application where efficiency of real-time encoding is prioritized over image quality. The strategy followed in the cases when a motion prediction is bad is to encode the block as intra or simply cope with the error. If there are significant changes (e.g., a scene cut, or a light is turned on), the whole frame can be encoded as intra. These decisions can be based on high-level information from the scene.

Hidden elements. One of the most difficult situations is when elements enter the frame (i.e. they were hidden in the reference frame and now they are visible). That occurs because the object was out of the viewing volume, it was occluded by another object or it was self-occluded (e.g. a rotation movement). In the first case, an invalid motion vector (out of frame) is computed; second and third cases produce valid motion vectors but with potentially bad matches. Regardless, as noted in [1], objects not visible in the reference frame will probably produce an incorrect motion estimation. Our strategy is to simply assume these errors, because not even a blind search would produce good results in this case.

Transparency. Semi-transparent objects can lead to incorrect motion vectors because the Z-buffer algorithm keeps the top-most surface motion vector but deeper surfaces are also visible. We address this issue by discarding the motion vector when alpha value trespasses a preestablished threshold (usually 0.5). As opaque geometry is rendered first and then transparent elements sorted back to front, this will keep the motion vector for the most visible element.

Multisampling. The use of multisampled frame buffers could degrade the quality of the motion vectors in the contours of objects. In these contours, different samples can fall in different objects that compute different motion vectors. The final value in the fragment will be an average of all the samples, so none of the partially valid motion vectors will be selected, but a combination of them all. This would be solved by not using multisampling in the motion vectors' render target, but this implies not using antialiasing for the render, as current graphics hardware forces all the images attached to a frame buffer object to have the same number of samples. The solution could be to render the scene in two passes, one for the color buffer with a multisampled frame buffer and one for the motion vectors with multisampling disabled. However, these multisampling issues are very unusual and only really noticeable in scenes with a large quantity of small randomly moving objects.

Lighting. The basic assumption of our technique is that a point of an object has the same aspect wherever it is in the scene. This is true in many cases, but not always, as there are some factors that affect the aspect of the point. The most important factor is lighting, though there are some others like fog (depth cueing) or other post-processing effects like motion blur or depth of field. In lighted scenes, the color of objects remains constant when objects are static, lights are static and only diffuse lighting is computed. Examples of applications where our motion estimation is very accurate are diffuse-lighted architectural walkthroughs or 3D GIS visualizations. The motion of objects and lights, and the variation of light parameters (e.g. color, intensity) does not produce substantial differences when these changes are not abrupt because frame to frame changes are relatively small. However, fast light variations as well as movement of objects and/or lights involved in shadow casting computations and strong specular reflections are much more difficult to deal with. Despite that these problems reduce the quality of the match, the estimated motion vectors are usually a fairly good approximation.

5. EXPERIMENTAL RESULTS

As we require computer-generated frames, commonly used video sequences do not apply. Some benchmarks were performed with computer-generated frame sequences from kernel and real-world (3D GIS visualizations) scenes, comparing results using different reduction strategies (mode, mean, central point) against the EPZS [8] implementation of the FFMPEG encoder and zero-motion vectors (good performance and a not-so-bad approach in many real-world examples where most blocks do not move). Per-pixel computations were implemented using OpenGL and GLSL. All the tests were measured in an Intel Quad Core Q6600@2.4GHz with an NVIDIA 8800GT GPU. Reduction and encoding times were measured using CUDA profiler. All experiments used the same fixed quantizer, thus we can assume constant video quality and observe the fitness of the motion vectors by measuring the size of the resulting compressed bitstream.

A kernel benchmark was designed to measure the general impact of different parameters that affect motion estimation: (a) percent of macroblocks with motion in the scene (as opposed to static background); (b) translational motion; and (c) rotational and zoom motion. It consists of a sequence with a richly textured moving quad over a static background; the quad varies in size, increasing the percentage of motion as well as other factors of interest like number of macroblocks with object boundaries. The translational motion starts at zero and increases in sub-halfpixel steps. Rotational motion was chosen because it is not considered by MPEG motion compensation model and, hence, only a blind search could reduce its impact by looking for a motion vector that minimizes distortion, so it becomes a good worst-case stress test for our proposed method. This simple kernel benchmark also features the hidden objects issue, as some parts of the background that were not visible appear when quads move.

5.1 Performance

For performace analysis, time consumed by the rendering, per-pixel motion estimation and per-pixel to per-macroblock reduction was considered. Motion estimation time was measured as the difference between render and encoding with and without motion estimation. As motion estimation shares some operations with rendering, it cannot be completely isolated for time measurement. We distinguish between per-pixel motion vector render and reduction because they present different behavior, as per-pixel motion vectors render scales with scene complexity while reduction operation only depends on frame resolution.

5.1.1 Per-pixel Motion Vector Rendering

The cost of the rendering part of the motion estimation is divided between GPU and CPU. The GPU computations are described in this work, mainly vertex processing, rasterization/interpolation and fragment processing. There is an additional CPU overhead for the scene graph traversal that must gather the inputs to the vertex shader (the transform matrices of each drawable object). In the kernel worst case scenario, it can be up to 10% of the total rendering time. However, this is by any means a common scenario: in every real-world example tested, the computing of the per-pixel motion vectors was neglectable because performance bottleneck appears first in other parts of the real-time render.

5.1.2 Pixels to Block Reduction

Mode implementation in CUDA resulted much more expensive than mean, ruining the quality/performance ratio even though it produces better motion vectors. Macroblock central point, on the other hand, is a good computationally efficient approximation of the mode. Using PAL frames (720x576), time spent for GPU render-based motion estimation using mean and block central point averaged 150 and 40 microseconds per frame, respectively, while EPZS algorithm in CPU averaged 1270 microseconds per frame. This makes our approach nearly 8.5 times faster using mean as reduction and over 30 times faster using central point.

It is important to point out that, in [4], the time for motion estimation was 53% of the total encoding of a predictive frame using mode as the reduction operation. Our approach, using central point, greatly decreases this impact.

5.2 Compression

5.2.1 Compression in Kernel Sequence

Each of the subfigures of figure 5 shows the average size of the compressed bitstreams for the kernel sequence modifying the parameters studied. In the figures, central point is considered instead of mode. Comparing mode with the

much more efficient central point approximation, differences were detected in an average of 14% of the blocks but its impact in the total bitrate was less than 1%, the mode always performing better than the central point.

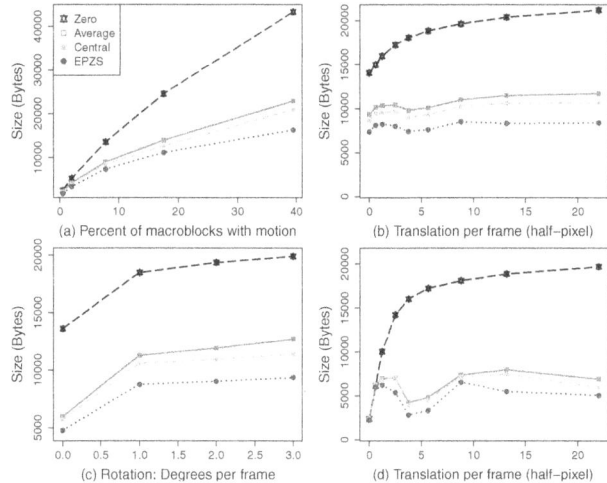

Figure 5: Compression analysis for kernel sequence.

As expected, compressed bitstream size grows almost linearly with the amount of motion in the scene. Our fast motion estimation behaves much better than zero-vector and it is a good approximation to EPZS. Averaging all the scenes tested (over 400), central point produces 17% larger compressed bitstreams than EPZS but it is 30 times faster. In almost every sequence, the central point method produces better results than the average because in macroblocks with object boundaries, computing the motion average is usually worse than using vectors of objects in the macroblock.

With translational motion, size grows very slowly because this kind of motion is fairly accurately calculated. Rotation produces the worst results because even though precise per-pixel motion vectors are computed, MPEG block motion compensation model cannot take advantage of that while EPZS search minimizes distortion with neighboring non-scene related blocks. Figure 5.d) shows the impact of translational motion in absence of rotational movement. In this case, our motion estimation produce perfect motion vectors for all the non-hidden objects; difference with EPZS in this case shows how important hidden objects are as search minimizes distortion with neighboring non-scene related blocks.

5.2.2 Compression in Real-World Scenes

To measure the quality of the vectors obtained in real examples, some tests were done with some flythrough sequences of a 3D terrain visualization system, similar to that shown in figure 4. The geometric model was texture-mapped with pre-lighted aerial image, so no real-time lighting computations are performed. Each sequence describes a different geometric model and camera motion at different speeds.

Figure 6 shows that the motion estimation of these typical real-world scenes behave better than our kernel sequence (9% in the worst case, 2.66% average). In fact, in *A6* sequence (real uniform camera movement for all the macroblocks in the scene), our proposal achieved better results.

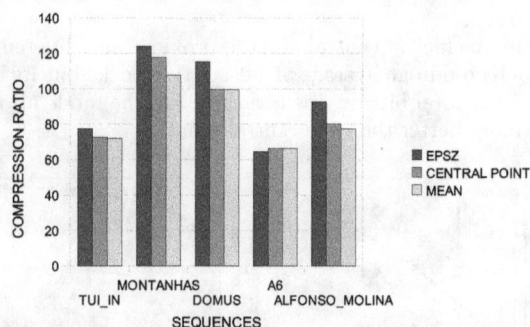

Figure 6: Compression in 3D terrain sequences.

5.3 Search Refinement

Vectors obtained with our proposal can be used as starting points for refinement with the aim of producing better compression ratio; minimizing distortion metric even though it does not necessarily match real motion. This helps to alleviate some of the errors that could occur using projection (e.g., objects that were occluded in previous frames).

When refining using search, the compression ratio is very close to EPZS, though the performance quickly drops. There is a tradeoff between speed and compression when using refinement. Even when using GPU-based search methods, its impact ruins the main advantage of our approach: transforming motion estimation into one of the lightest tasks of video encoding. Taking the efficient exhaustive search method proposed in [10] as a reference, figure 7 shows the decrease in performance and the improvement in compression ratio on an average of sequences when using refinement for different search ranges.

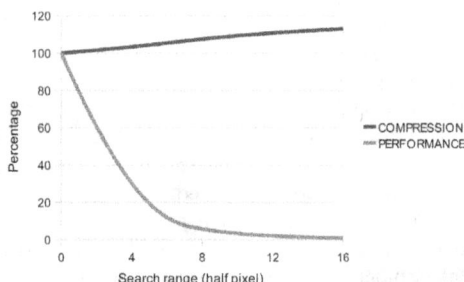

Figure 7: Speed-Compression Tradeoff.

6. CONCLUSION & FUTURE WORK

We have presented a method for fast motion estimation to be applied to computer-generated video sequences. It takes advantage of scene information, rendering pipeline, and GPU massive parallelism. The method is easily adaptable to existing 3D applications, simply adding a few operations to the shader and an additional render target. It has been integrated and tested into a large-scale GPU-based video rendering and encoding system designed to offer visually rich 3D interactive applications for digital television, where real-time encoding efficiency is required. Though the compression achieved is slightly worse than that obtained using popular search-based methods such as EPZS, it is good enough for this target application. As proposed fast estimation is so cheap, it is interesting to consider other encoding

formats, such as MPEG4, which allow using more than one reference frame, addressing some open issues such as hidden objects.

A future evolution is to consider mixing computer-generated and natural video. Natural video is mapped to a texture that changes from frame to frame but no high-level information is known about video motion. If natural video is already encoded, perhaps its own motion information can be used to re-estimate its projection on scene objects.

As another line of research, additional high-level scene information can help improve both performance and size/quality of compressed bitstream, for example by modifying the frame rate in still sequences or by changing the quantizer to pay more attention to important blocks. A modification of the rendering pipeline, as proposed in this work, can help speed up the process with the support of GPU parallelism.

7. ACKNOWLEDGMENTS

This work is partially supported by Spanish MICINN (TIN 2010-20959) and Xunta de Galicia (PGIDIT09TIC015CT).

8. REFERENCES

[1] M. Agrawala, A. C. Beers, and N. Chaddha. Model-based motion estimation for synthetic animations. In *Proceedings of the third ACM international conference on Multimedia*, MULTIMEDIA '95, pages 477–488, New York, NY, USA, 1995. ACM.

[2] X. Chen, Z. Zhao, A. Rahmati, Y. Wang, and L. Zhong. SaVE: sensor-assisted motion estimation for efficient h.264/AVC video encoding. In *Proceedings of the 17th ACM international conference on Multimedia*, MM '09, pages 381–390, New York, NY, USA, 2009. ACM.

[3] L. Cheng, A. Bhushan, R. Pajarola, and M. E. Zarki. Real-time 3D Graphics Streaming using MPEG-4. In *In Proc. IEEE/ACM Wksp. on Broadband Wireless Services and Appl*, 2004.

[4] W. Choi, B. Jeon, and J. Jeong. Fast motion estimation with modified diamond search for variable motion block sizes. In *ICIP03*, pages II: 371–374, 2003.

[5] B. K. Guenter, H. C. Yun, and R. M. Mersereau. Motion Compensated Compression of Computer Animation Frames. In *SIGGRAPH 93, (August*, pages 297–304, 1993.

[6] J. Nickolls, I. Buck, M. Garland, and K. Skadron. Scalable Parallel Programming with CUDA. *Queue*, 6(2):40–53, 2008.

[7] Y. Noimark and D. Cohen-Or. Streaming scenes to MPEG-4 video-enabled devices. *Computer Graphics and Applications, IEEE*, 23(1):58 – 64, jan/feb 2003.

[8] A. M. Tourapis. Enhanced predictive zonal search for single and multiple frame motion estimation. In *VCIP*, pages 1069–1079, 2002.

[9] D. S. Wallach, S. Kunapalli, and M. F. Cohen. Accelerated MPEG Compression of Dynamic Polygonal Scenes. In *Computer Graphics (SIGGRAPH '94 Proceedings*, page pages, 1994.

[10] S.-T. Yang, T.-K. Lin, and S.-Y. Chien. Real-time motion estimation for 1080p videos on graphics processing units with shared memory optimization. pages 297 –302, Oct. 2009.

SAS Kernel: Streaming as a Service Kernel for Correlated Multi-Streaming

Pooja Agarwal, Raoul Rivas, Wanmin Wu, Ahsan Arefin, Zixia Huang, Klara Nahrstedt
Department of Computer Science
University of Illinois at Urbana-Champaign
Urbana, Illinois, United States
{pagarwl, trivas, wwu23, marefin2, zhuang21, klara}@illinois.edu

ABSTRACT

This paper presents a novel paradigm of *Streaming as a Service (SAS)* to model correlated multi-streaming in Distributed Interactive Multimedia Environments. We propose *SAS Kernel*, a generic, distributed, and modular service kernel realizing SAS concept. SAS Kernel features high flexibility by employing a configurable interface to allow for input of correlated multi-streams (bundle of streams) from diverse types of sensory devices. It is also highly extensible by allowing user-controlled functions to be applied to bundle of streams in runtime. Experiments with real-world applications demonstrate that the SAS Kernel incurs low overhead in delay, CPU, and bandwidth demands.

Categories and Subject Descriptors

C.2.4 [**Computer Communication Networks**]: Distributed Systems—*Network Operating System*; D.4.7 [**Operating Systems**]: Organization and Design

General Terms

Design, Measurement, Performance

Keywords

Streaming as a Service, SAS Kernel, End Device Abstraction

1. INTRODUCTION

Cyber-Physical systems using large number of sensors are fast becoming ubiquitous. An example of multi-sensory system is Distributed Interactive Multimedia Environments (DIMEs). DIMEs allow real-time collaborative activities like interactive gaming, physical therapy, and sport activities across multiple, geographically distributed users. Some of the real applications include Physical Training [5], Virtual Gaming [16], and Teleimmersive Dancing [11].

DIMEs are comprised of input devices (e.g., cameras, microphones, body sensors, haptic devices) and output devices (e.g., displays, speakers, actuators). DIMEs make use of service gateways to transfer content from input devices to remote output devices over the Internet. Apart from streaming, DIME service gateways need to provide various functionalities like overlay routing, bandwidth management, QoS provisioning, synchronization, and monitoring.

Several architectures for streaming gateways interconnecting local area networks like Ethernet, Bluetooth, wireless access to the Internet exist in the literature. However, these service gateways [9], [10], [13], [14], [15] are limited to functionalities like relaying, multiplexing, translating, and managing local resources only, which fail to satisfy the requirements of DIMEs. There are some proprietary gateways developed at HP Halo, Cisco Telepresence, and Technicolor, however they are tailored to cater closed applications and their internal functionalities are publicly unknown.

DIME requirements differ from those of traditional gateways as:

1. Presence of multiple correlated sensors interacting in a DIME session requires support for *large scale correlated multi-streaming* as an inherent functionality.
2. High interactivity in DIME sessions requires *soft real-time delivery* of all streams.
3. *Advanced QoS services* across multiple spatially and temporally correlated streams need to be supported.
4. With end-devices dispersed across remote locations, *distributed resource management* is important in DIMEs.
5. Lack of standard stream formats across sensors from diverse vendors require *unified interface* with the end-devices.

Based on the above requirements, concepts of *correlated multi-streaming*, *device abstraction*, and *user-controlled services* need to be supported in DIMEs. Other important challenges include *flexibility*, and *scalability* of DIME frameworks.

In this paper, we envision a novel paradigm, *Streaming as a Service (SAS)* to model correlated multi-streaming service, where correlated multi-streams, also called *bundle of streams* are first class objects. We propose a SAS-based, generalized, distributed service kernel, *SAS Kernel* to setup, process, and control bundles of streams. We emphasize that SAS and SAS Kernel are not limited to just DIMEs but provide a fundamental foundation of modern service-oriented architectures for wide range of stream-based applications (e.g., 3D Streaming).

In summary our contributions in this paper are:

1. Formalization of the SAS paradigm (see Section 2);
2. Design of the SAS Kernel with properties:
   (a) Streams and bundles as first class objects (Section 3),
   (b) Unified interface for diverse end-devices (Section 5.1),
   (c) User-controlled runtime functions over streams and bundles (Section 3 and 5.2),
   (d) Integrated session and bundle management (Section 3),
   (e) Extensibility of SAS components (Section 5)
3. Quantitative evaluation in a real testbed (Section 6).

2. STREAMING AS A SERVICE (SAS)

We propose a generalized Streaming as a Service paradigm for platforms providing correlated soft real-time multi-streaming as the key service. The guiding properties of SAS are as follows:

- *Distributed Correlated Multi-Stream Support* - DIMEs are composed of distributed correlated multi-streams called *Bundle of Streams (BoS)* [1] sharing high spatial and temporal correlations. These bundles interact in synchronous and soft real-time manner. The current streaming protocols like RTP/RTCP, SIP, RTSP do not take into account efficiently the spatio-temporal dependencies among large sets of streams. To deal with this, the SAS model inherently supports: (1) large scale correlated soft real-time streaming, (2) end-to-end session management based on media correlations [8].

- *Universal Open Access* - Unlike the Internet Protocols which have become the lingua franca, there is a lack of well-agreed formats across emerging devices like 3D cameras and microphone arrays. To overcome the problem of implementing large sets of formats, SAS model supports universal access policy with well-defined interfaces to the end-devices. In SAS, varied types of streaming devices with different standards seemlessly connect and stream the data.

- *User-defined Functions* - SAS provides the flexibility of provisioning two types of run-time functions on streams: (1) system-defined functions like rate control, congestion control, and multi-stream synchronization, (2) user-defined functions like compression, encryption, and view management. These functions can be requested in an on-demand basis.

- *Availability* - It is anticipated that in the future, access to SAS will follow "always on" paradigm, like cable modem access is today. Thus, SAS is highly available at all times.

- *Robustness* - For SAS, the capability to monitor performance, isolate faults, and automatically recover from faults is critical. The robustness of SAS comes through (1) On-demand monitoring services with varied resolutions, (2) Fault localization and easy recovery mechanism.

- *Scalability* - It is anticipated that larger scale of sensors will enhance the Quality of Experience (QoE) of users. Thus, SAS provides scalability in terms of supporting large sets of streams. Also, extensibility of a SAS-based framework is important to support adding new functional services as need arises.

Thus, the goal of the SAS is to foster bundles of streams needing correlated multi-streaming support, universal access across diverse devices, and user-controlled runtime functions in future DIME systems. To realize the SAS paradigm, we present SAS Kernel, set of real-time integrated services that enforce *SAS properties* (as outlined above) at runtime.

3. SAS KERNEL FRAMEWORK

In DIMEs, distributed end-devices share streams and resources in real-time collaborative sessions. The SAS Kernel provides runtime system for easy setup, processing, management, and access of bundles of streams. The SAS Kernel implements the SAS properties as follows:

Strong distributed correlated multi-streaming support: SAS Kernel ensures correlated multi-streaming by (1) Managing and keeping states of streams, bundles, sessions, and resources, (2) Providing streaming policies for correlated soft real-time scheduling, co-operative congestion control, and overlay routing. The Management Entities (Figure 1) handle correlated multi-streaming.

Universal access and easy availability: SAS Kernel provides (1) Unified interface for end-devices, (2) Easily configurable stream specifications to describe device and stream characteristics. The SAS Interface (Section 5.1) provides universal access.

Runtime mechanisms and functions: (1) SAS Kernel follows the principle of *Separation of mechanism and policy* [6], i.e., the mechanisms only provide a unified framework for plugging-in the policies/functions and the actual functions are implemented at the user space, (2) SAS Kernel provides runtime loading of *user-defined functions* operating over streams or bundles. The Runtime Entities (Figure 1) and Function Manager (Section 5.2) provide functions and mechanisms. This design also allows easy availability.

Robustness: To ensure robustness (1) A cross-layer online monitoring interface is provided, (2) Runtime analysis of monitoring data to trigger recovery procedures is done. The Monitoring Manager (Figure 1) ensures robustness.

Scalability: SAS Kernel provides both device scalability and stream service extensibility via (1) User-configurable interfaces with varied end-devices, (2) Modular design of stream services to allow user-defined functions on streams, (3) Modular design of all SAS Kernel entities built on the principle of separation of concerns. The SAS Interface and Function Manager (Section 5) discuss the extensibility of the framework.

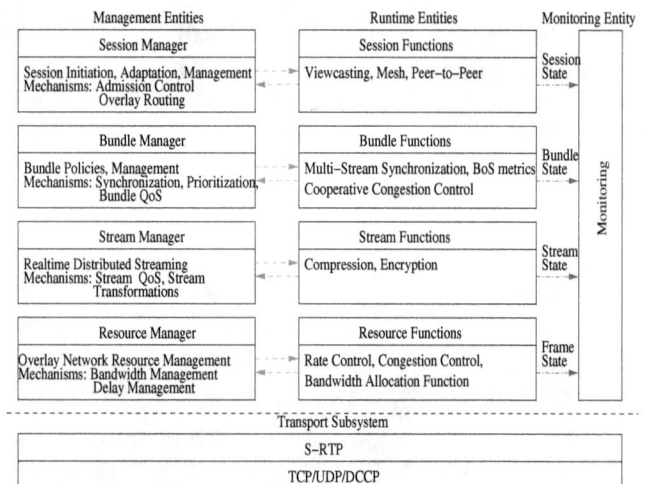

Management Entities	Runtime Entities	Monitoring Entity
Session Manager	**Session Functions**	Session State
Session Initiation, Adaptation, Management Mechanisms: Admission Control Overlay Routing	Viewcasting, Mesh, Peer–to–Peer	
Bundle Manager	**Bundle Functions**	Bundle State
Bundle Policies, Management Mechanisms: Synchronization, Prioritization, Bundle QoS	Multi–Stream Synchronization, BoS metrics Cooperative Congestion Control	
Stream Manager	**Stream Functions**	Stream State
Realtime Distributed Streaming Mechanisms: Stream QoS, Stream Transformations	Compression, Encryption	
Resource Manager	**Resource Functions**	Frame State
Overlay Network Resource Management Mechanisms: Bandwidth Management Delay Management	Rate Control, Congestion Control, Bandwidth Allocation Function	
Transport Subsystem		
S–RTP		
TCP/UDP/DCCP		

Figure 1: SAS Kernel Framework

In SAS Kernel, the SAS properties get implemented as management, runtime, and monitoring entities in the session subsystem on top of a transport subsystem. Since streams are first class objects in SAS Kernel, each of the entities keeps track of and controls streams and stream derivatives (e.g., bundles, frames). Figure 1 shows the layout of various entities over the transport subsystem. A brief description of each of them is as follows:

Management Entities: The management entities manage sessions, bundles, streams, frames, and their corresponding resources. They provide mechanisms for generic tasks like overlay routing and provide interfaces to dynamically load the runtime entities. There are four management entities:

1. Session Manager - It performs session initiation, membership control, and session management. It takes management decisions and provides mechanisms to load session level functions like overlay routing and admission control.

2. Bundle Manager - It handles the correlation between the streams and defines the policies to group multiple streams into correlated bundles of streams. It provides mechanisms for runtime functions over these correlated bundles of streams like cooperative congestion control, prioritization, view management, and bundle of streams (BoS) metrics [1].

3. Stream Manager - It keeps states about receipt and delivery of streams across sites and determines policies for streaming. It categorizes streams as InStreams (from input devices) and OutStreams (to output devices). Mechanisms for stream-based runtime functions like compression, encryption are also provided by this manager.

4. Resource Manager - It manages overlay network resources like bandwidth and delay to ensure real-time delivery of streams.

Runtime Entities: The runtime entities provide specific system/user-defined policies for the mechanisms like Mesh protocol for overlay routing. These entities are dynamically pluggable real-time functions operating over sessions, bundles, streams, frames, and network resources. These entities are open to be either implemented by SAS Kernel system-admins or the end-users. Examples of runtime entities at each level are shown in Figure 1.

Monitoring Entity: SAS Kernel implements a cross-layer event-driven monitoring entity. This entity provides real-time monitoring plane for overall system monitoring. The monitoring entity forms a feedback loop by communicating the states from the run-time functions to the corresponding managers, allowing the managers to take appropriate actions like adaptation, or policy switching. The monitoring entity also monitors for faults and failures.

Transport Subsystem: To ensure soft real-time delivery, the transport subsystem abstracts the underlying transport layer protocols allowing end-users to dynamically request appropriate protocols like TCP, UDP, DCCP based on application type and network conditions. The frames are encapsulated using our DIME specific S-RTP protocol (section 5.1.3) which adds semantic information (used by managers) like stream type, functions requested, device addressing, and streams in same bundle.

4. STREAM FLOW IN SAS KERNEL

Distributed SAS Kernel is realized through a set of multiple distributed SAS gateways and SAS interfaces as shown in Figure 2. SAS gateways take on the responsibility of hosting the SAS Kernel instances and the SAS interfaces (SASI) provide the connectivity between the end-devices and the SAS Kernel. We assume that all gateways and end-devices can be connected to each other via the Internet. Figure 3 shows the end-devices, SAS interfaces, and the functional placement of the SAS Kernel entities in a gateway. The streaming algorithm is as follows:

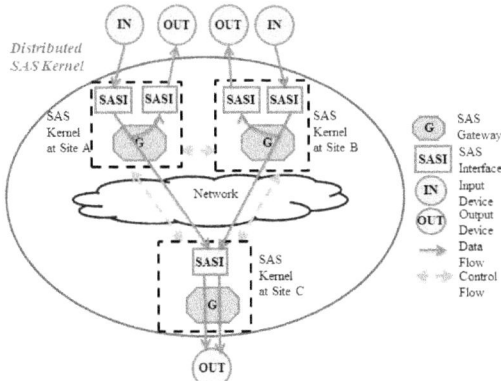

Figure 2: Distributed SAS Kernel Components

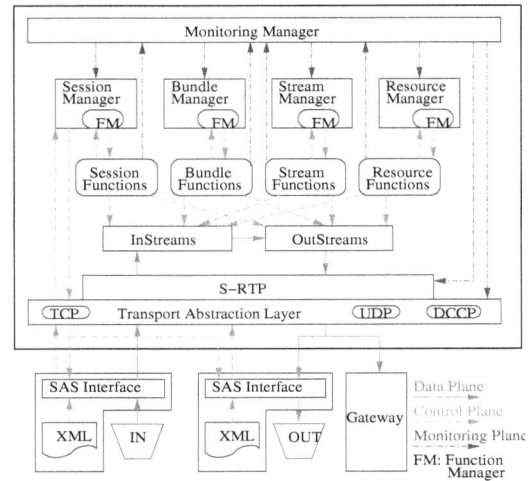

Figure 3: SAS Kernel Data, Control, and Monitoring Planes

1. Session Initiation: A streaming end-device first starts a connection with the SAS interface present at the end-device machine. The SAS interface initiates a session with the closest SAS gateway and requests the services specified in the user-defined XML configuration. The request is handled by the Session Manager in the gateway. It verifies if the requested services are supported and sends an *ACK* to the SAS interface. On positive *ACK*, Session Manager opens data and control connections with the end-device through the SAS interface. It also constructs overlay routing topology with other gateways, stores the meta-data about the new session, instantiates a Stream Manager for the joined stream, groups streams into bundles, and instantiates Bundle Manager.

2. End-to-End Streaming: An input device communicates its stream to the SAS interface. The SAS interface applies the S-RTP headers on each packet based on the information specified in the XML file. The packets are then sent over a chosen transport layer protocol to the corresponding InStream instantiated by the Stream Manager for this session. Once the InStream starts to get delivered in SAS Gateway, the Stream Manager creates corresponding sets of OutStreams based on number of requesting output devices. The InStreams are then connected to the respective OutStreams.

3. Runtime Functions: The run-time functions are loaded by the Function Manager (FM) present in each of the Managers. The InStreams and OutStreams are processed through the Bundle Manager to apply user-demanded bundle functions over bundles. The Stream Manager then applies stream based functions. For resource optimization, Resource Manager applies policies for bandwidth management and congestion control. It must be noted that streams pass through all these functions only when the user demands them. Thus, no extra overhead is incurred unless some functions are specified. This ensures fastest delivery of streams.

4. Monitoring: Each entity implements hooks and callbacks to send monitoring information like QoS performance, resource utilization, and faults to the Monitoring Manager. Based on the received information, Monitoring Manager takes appropriate QoS or fault tolerance measures.

5. SAS KERNEL DESIGN

The two main components of SAS Kernel are SAS Interface and Kernel Function Managers which are discussed in detail in the following subsections.

5.1 SAS Interface

The device-SAS Kernel interface provides universal open access (section 3) and faces the challenges of (1) Multiple non-standardized stream formats of end-devices, (2) Requirement to understand all the stream formats to allow functions over streams.

The above challenges severely affect the scability and flexibility of the service gateways. To address this issue, current solutions only implement a subset of these stream formats and thus, fail to support devices from diverse vendors. Instead, our approach relies on separating the stream formats from the main SAS Kernel using configuration mechanisms to specify the formats at runtime. Thus, SAS Kernel realizes four concepts: 1) End-to-End Tunneling, 2) Device Stream Specification, 3) Semantic data propagation through S-RTP, and 4) Service Negotiation.

5.1.1 End-to-End Tunneling

The idea behind SAS Kernel is that end-devices should interact agnostic of the SAS Kernel i.e. the end-devices do not know if they are communicating via SAS Kernel. The challenge in providing agnostic connection is that there should be *no source code modification at the end-devices*. To achieve this, POSIX socket API is used as an interface between end-devices and SAS Kernel.

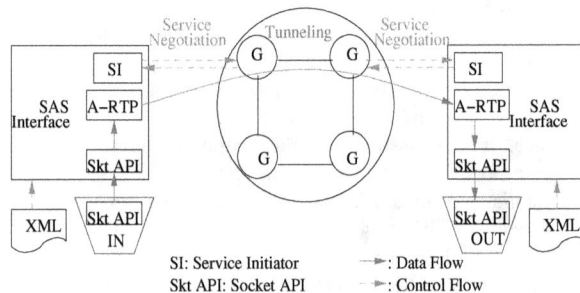

Figure 4: Socket Interface and Tunneling

The assumption behind using socket API is that the end-devices in DIMEs mostly follow client-server type of connections and they usually provide interface to specify the IP and port number of the remote device. Thus, the end-devices can be dynamically configured to connect to the SAS interface. The SAS interface, placed at each device, uses socket API to intercept the traffic from the input devices and send it via the SAS Kernel to the output devices. In addition, a peer-to-peer virtual tunnel is created between the devices where the virtual tunnel is supported by the underlying SAS Kernel. Figure 4 shows the socket interface and the tunnel.

5.1.2 Device Stream Specification

In order to apply functions on streams, SAS Kernel needs to understand the semantics of the stream, i.e. the packet structure. Thus, SAS interface requires end-users to provide a simple high-level specification of the stream semantics in a user readable language like XML. The specification is composed of two main parts: (1) Device Specification containing general metadata about the device, (2) Stream Specification containing stream format.

The Device Specification consists of a unique identifier for addressing the device in the originating site, the content type (e.g., video, audio), content subtype (e.g., for video point cloud, mesh) and the transport protocol the device uses (e.g., TCP, UDP). The Stream Specification specifies the format of the sequence of data packets as they appear within the stream. There are two general formats: fixed-size packets and variable-size packets. The fixed-size packets require only packet size to be specified while the variable-size packets require a fixed size header containing the packet size to

```
<DEVICE SPECIFICATION>
   ...
   <PROTOCOL_TYPE> TCP </PROTOCOL_TYPE>
   <TYPE> VIDEO </TYPE>
   <SUBTYPE> POINT-CLOUD </SUBTYPE>
</DEVICE SPECIFICATION>
<STREAM SPECIFICATION>
   <PACKET_FIXED>
      <HANDSHAKE> ON </HANDSHAKE>
      <PACKET_SIZE> 140 </PACKET_SIZE>
      <PACKET_COUNT> 1 </PACKET_COUNT>
   </PACKET_FIXED>
   <PACKET_VARIABLE>
      <HANDSHAKE> OFF </HANDSHAKE>
      <HEADER_SIZE> 10 </HEADER_SIZE>
      <HEADER_OFFSET> 6 </HEADER_OFFSET>
      <DATASIZE_TYPE> 4 </DATASIZE_TYPE>
      <PACKET_COUNT> -1 </PACKET_COUNT>
   </PACKET_VARIABLE>
</STREAM SPECIFICATION>
```

Figure 5: Device Stream Specification for a video stream

be specified. Other stream parameters like frame rate, color information are specified through *Handshake packets* between the end-devices. This specification allows for marking packets as *Handshake packets*. SAS Kernel forms a multicast network between the input devices and the output devices, requiring storing and replaying these *Handshake packets* when new output devices are added to the kernel. The packet count specifies how many of each type of packets are present consecutively in the stream.

Figure 5 shows an example XML configuration file used in the 3D Tele-immersion system in our lab for a video stream. The camera protocol is comprised of single fixed handshake packet of 140 bytes followed by all (packet count of -1 indicates possibly infinite) payload packets of variable size that have a header of 10 bytes, with packet size specified at byte 6 in the header. Moreover, this specification is easy to implement and flexible enough to allow a wide range of end-devices to interface with our SAS interface without modification or recompilation.

5.1.3 SAS Real-Time Protocol (S-RTP)

Each data packet read by the SAS interface is then encapsulated using the SAS Real-Time Protocol. S-RTP is similar to RTP but it is tailored to include DIME specific session semantics and lighter-weight. Through S-RTP, session semantics like device addressing, services requested, and groups of streams forming bundles are marked on each packet, allowing easy dissemination of each stream's state to all SAS components.

Bit Offset	0–31	32–47	48–63	64–95	96–127
0	Version	SID	RID	DID	TOS
128	Stream Type	Stream SubType		Frame Timestamp	
256	<BundleList>			Header	Payload(Variable)
256+64*C+64	... (Variable Payload)			Frame Number	

Figure 6: S-RTP Header Specification

The structure of the S-RTP packet is shown in Figure 6. The packet first specifies the version of the S-RTP protocol followed by a 64 bit unique stream identifier. The unique identifier uses a hierarchical addressing scheme composed of the DIME session ID (SID), the DIME site/room identifier (RID), and the device identifier (DID) within the room. The Type of Service (TOS), a 64 bit flag vector, specifies the requested functions, the state information about functions that were applied along the route in SAS Kernel, and a Handshake bit to specify Handshake packet.

The stream type and subtype together form a tuple to uniquely identify the type (video, audio, sensory data) and the data format (e.g. for video, mesh and point-cloud). Next, S-RTP packet contains a list of all stream IDs forming a bundle <BundleList>, timestamp of packet creation, fixed/variable payload, and frame number.

5.1.4 Service Initiation and Negotiation

After reading the stream specification and constructing an S-RTP packet, the SAS interface at the joining end-device initiates a session with the SAS Kernel. The Session Manager in the SAS Kernel handles the session initiation and service negotiation tasks. Remote procedure calls (RPC) and marshalling is used between SAS interface and SAS Kernel and simple session initiation and negotiation protocols are used as can be found in the literature. Our contribution in SAS Kernel is that the SAS Kernel allows dynamic pluggability of different correlations based admission control and bundle routing algorithms as need arises in the session and resource management.

The SAS interface sends a *JOIN* request message specifying desired transport protocol to use, the characteristics of the bundles and joining streams (e.g., periodic or aperiodic, variable or fixed packet sizes, payload type, payload sub-type, expected bandwidth usage), and the services requested (encryption, compression, congestion control). Upon receipt of the *JOIN* message, the SAS Kernel verifies whether it can support services requested, and if so, opens required data ports and returns an *ACK* containing the ports. The SAS Kernel renegotiates if it does not support any of the services with the SAS interface. The Session Manager in SAS Kernel then creates InStreams and Bundles accordingly, bookmarks the parameters, and uses the data channels for data transfer.

In case of output end-device join, the payload type and subtype tuple provides a hierarchical way for the SAS Kernel to determine which bundles should be routed to the output device by matching the payload type and sub-type of the possessed InStreams with those specified. For example, one may use two renderers to display the frontal and back camera streams respectively; although they all identify the "video" type, one renderer and the frontal cameras use the "frontal" sub-type, and the other renderer and the back cameras use the "back" sub-type.

The strategy for interconnection and exchange of streams between the SAS gateways depends on the chosen routing protocol in the SAS Kernel. Some useful routing protocols for DIMEs are application level multicasting [17] like Viewcasting, Mesh. The discussion of these routing algorithms is out of scope of this paper.

5.2 SAS Kernel Function Manager

In order to provide runtime stream-processing functions, i.e., user controllable functions (as discussed in section 3), each manager in SAS Kernel implements a Function Manager (FM) as shown in Figure 3. The function manager is responsible for: (1) Implementing mechanisms, and (2) Scheduling functions on bundles, streams, and frames.

To support extensible operations, SAS Kernel divides the execution plane in two spaces: *End-User Space* and *System Space*. User-controllable functions are in the End-User Space while all the other SAS Kernel functions and resource management remain in the System Space. New functions to be added to the SAS Kernel are compiled separately by end-users into dynamically linked libraries and these functions are loaded and linked at runtime by the FM. Functions interact with FM using system calls (Syscalls) and FM uses Upcalls to the functions. Figure 7 shows FM architecture.

The Syscalls provide direct access to the bundle and stream metadata, S-RTP packet format, and also to the raw payload implemented by the end-devices. Each function implements an object and FM keeps the state information, allocates memory and forks threads. This makes FM suitable for supporting parallel concurrent

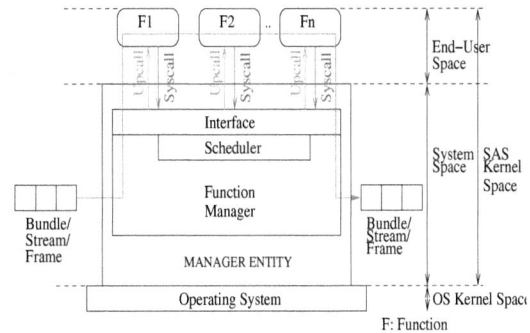

Figure 7: SAS Kernel Function Manager

functions. Functions are executed as a computing pipeline where the user can configure the order in which the operations are applied. A scheduler inside FM is responsible of context switching to the corresponding operation. FM thus provides the support for defining mechanisms at each level of data abstraction and load user-specific functions to implement these mechanisms. This ensures high extensibility of services in SAS Kernel.

6. EVALUATION

We evaluate the performance of SAS Kernel in a real 3D Teleimmersion (3DTI) DIME System at University of Illinois, Urbana Champaign. 3DTI typically includes 4 to 5 sites, each producing 4 to 5 streams comprising of 3D cameras and microphones. Each site spawns a gateway for the SAS Kernel. Each stereo camera produces a variable 3D video stream ranging between 6 to 10Mbps. The SAS Kernel is supported over both Linux and Windows. To evaluate the strength of the SAS framework, third-party softwares for 3D camera from UC, Berkeley and renderer from UC, Davis are used. No source code modification in these third party softwares was needed and these end-devices could easily interface with SAS Kernel by only specifing device configuration in simple XML file.

We compare the performance of SAS Kernel in terms of overheads incurred on a) End-to-End Delay, b) CPU, and c) Bandwidth. We perform two experiments: Experiment 1) SAS Kernel consists of one gateway with 1 to 6 bundles with 2 video streams each, Experiment 2) SAS Kernel consists of two gateways, each with 1 to 6 bundles with 4 video streams each, and 2 output devices (renderer and the other gateway). So, each gateway receives total 24 instreams and sends 24 corresponsing outstreams. It is to be noted that 12 and 24 streams per site is a large workload in DIME scenario in terms of bandwidth (120 to 240 Mbps), CPU (24 to 48 threads), and current applications. Thus, the evaluation highly stresses the system. Moreover, multiple gateways can be spawned to balance the load in the event of dramatic increase in streams. For repeatability, we use a recorded creative dance performance. For the gateway server, we use 4 Dell Precision 670 with dual Intel Xeon processor.

End-to-End Delay Overhead: The major goal of the kernel is to support real-time streaming even under heavy loads. We evaluate the total delay overhead added by the SAS Kernel wherein total delay is the difference between the entry time of a frame and the exit time of that frame from the SAS Kernel. Figures 8(a), 8(b) show that the total delay is less than 3 milliseconds even for 12 concurrent streams, and increases minimally on using 2 sites and 24 streams. This shows that SAS Kernel meets the soft real-time requirements of streaming while efficiently providing SAS.

CPU Overhead: It is important for SAS Kernel to scale in terms of CPU demands as large number of end-devices is added to the system. As shown in Figures 8(c), 8(d), the average CPU overhead ranges between 2% for 2 streams to 20% for 12 streams in Experiment 1. On doubling the number of sites and streams, the average

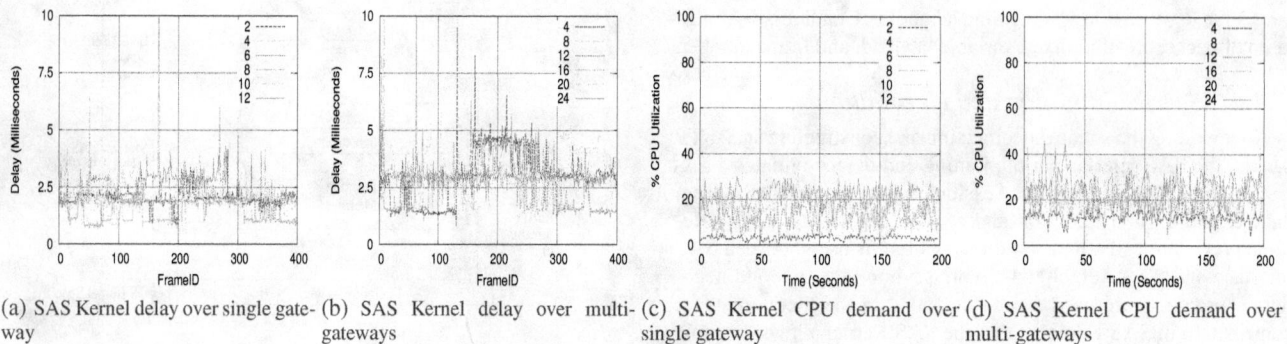

(a) SAS Kernel delay over single gateway (b) SAS Kernel delay over multi-gateways (c) SAS Kernel CPU demand over single gateway (d) SAS Kernel CPU demand over multi-gateways

Figure 8: SAS Kernel Evaluation

CPU requirement only increases to 10% for 4 streams and 30% for 24 streams. This emphasizes that SAS Kernel demands low CPU even when large number of sensors are connected to it.

Bandwidth Overhead: SAS Kernel adds S-RTP header on the data packets and uses Google Protobufs for marshalling S-RTP frames. Some DIME applications are bandwidth hungry, so it is important that SAS Kernel itself does not add too much bandwidth overhead. For the current implementation of the SAS Kernel, only a fixed cost of 22 bytes per frame is incurred as S-RTP header. The Google Protobuf only adds 4 bytes to the header. Thus, a total of 26 extra bytes per frame over frame size ranging from 2KB to 30KB for 3D-video frames and 140Bytes of audio frames is incurred.

7. RELATED WORK

SAS Kernel synthesizes ideas from service gateways, network services, and operating systems. We discuss the related work in these research areas. In [9], [10], [13], [14] general architectures for home, sensor, and streaming gateways, supporting small set of functionalities like protocol translation, media transcoding, admission control, data processing, synchronization are presented. These gateways focus on a small subset of the SAS requirements and hence fail to provide major SAS services.

In network services, OSGi [7] is a java-based service platform for home networks allowing service providers to dynamically load and deliver services to the end users. However, it is very cumbersome to build complex systems like multi-correlated streaming over low-level OSGi [3]. In [12], user-configuration is used for setting class of service policies in routers. Our approach however, focuses on using user configurations to manage multi-streaming sessions.

SAS Kernel also draws concepts from operating systems like application-level functions in [4] and interface for run-time functions in [18]. In [2], resource containers are presented to provide resource management over processes and threads for network servers. Compared to [2], our approach is at a higher level of abstraction spanning across sites, sessions and streams.

8. CONCLUSION

Our main thesis is that multi-streaming in DIMEs should be modeled as a real-time, generic, flexible, scalable, and robust Streaming as a Service (SAS) for highly correlated sensory data over the Internet. We introduce the concept of SAS and its implementation in the distributed SAS Kernel. SAS Kernel is a proof-of-concept architecture of this SAS model. SAS Kernel supports various types of sensors, transport and session protocols, as well as dynamically loaded functions such as congestion control, compression, and synchronization. Our experiments in a real DIME testbed indicate that SAS Kernel is successful at providing the service without much overhead time-wise (i.e., delay) and space-wise (i.e., bandwidth).

9. ACKNOWLEDGMENT

This research is supported by grants NSF CNS 09-64081, NSF CNS 08-34480, NSF CNS 07-20702, and NSF CNS 10-12194. The presented views are those of authors only.

10. REFERENCES

[1] P. Agarwal et al. Bundle of streams: Concept and evaluation in distributed interactive multimedia environments. In *ISM*, 2010.

[2] G. Banga et al. Resource containers: a new facility for resource management in server systems. In *OSDI*, 1999.

[3] H. Cervantes et al. Beanome: A component model for the osgi framework. In *Software infrastructures for component-based applications on consumer devices*, 2002.

[4] D. Engler et al. Exokernel: an operating system architecture for application-level resource management. In *SOSP*, 1995.

[5] G. Kurrilo et al. Immersive 3d environment for remote collaboration and training of physical activities. In *VR*, 2008.

[6] B. Lampson et al. Reflections on an operating system design. *Commun. ACM*, 19:251–265, 1976.

[7] D. Marples et al. The open services gateway initiative: an introductory overview. *IEEE Commun.*, 39(12):110 –114, 2001.

[8] K. Nahrstedt et al. Next generation session management for 3d teleimmersive interactive environments. *MTAP*, 51:593–623, 2011.

[9] S. Roy et al. A system architecture for managing mobile streaming media services. *Distributed Computing Systems*, 0:408, 2003.

[10] P. Schramm et al. A service gateway for networked sensor systems. *Pervasive Computing*, 3(1):66 – 74, 2004.

[11] R. Sheppard et al. Advancing interactive collaborative mediums through tele-immersive dance (ted): a symbiotic creativity and design environment for art and computer science. In *ACM Multimedia*, 2008.

[12] Y. E. Sung et al. Modeling and understanding end-to-end class of service policies in operational networks. In *SIGCOMM*, 2009.

[13] D. Valtchev et al. Service gateway architecture for a smart home. *IEEE Commun.*, 40(4):126 –132, 2002.

[14] M. Weihs. Design issues for multimedia streaming gateways. *Mobile Communications and Learning Technologies*, 0:101, 2006.

[15] W. Wu et al. Implementing a distributed tele-immersive system. In *ISM*, 2008.

[16] W. Wu et al. "i'm the jedi!" - a case study of user experience in 3d tele-immersive gaming. *ISM*, 2010.

[17] C. K. Yeo et al. A survey of application level multicast techniques. *Computer Commun.*, 27(15):1547–1568, 2004.

[18] G. Zhenyu et al. R2: An application-level kernel for record and replay. In *OSDI*, 2008.

Managing Home and Network Storage of Television Recordings

"I filled my DVR again! Now what?"

Raymond Sweha
Boston University
remos@cs.bu.edu

Donald E. Smith
Verizon Labs, Waltham MA
dsmith@verizon.com

James H. Drew
Verizon Labs, Waltham MA
jim.drew@verizon.com

ABSTRACT

In this paper we study the recording and watching patterns of DVR users using real traces. Many DVR users complain about running out of space. Thus, we propose the idea of adding extra storage on the network. Storing content in the network would create a new challenge, as most of users use their DVR during prime-time resulting in congesting the already strained network with unicast streams. We develop statistical models that learn the behavior of users and are most likely to make watched programs readily available for users each day. We develop a simple caching technique that captures the dominant factors of user behavior. Our verification, using real traces, shows that this technique performs as efficiently as more advanced statistical models, while requiring only a small state to be maintained. [1]

Categories and Subject Descriptors

H.3.2 [**Information Storage and retrieval**]: Information Storage; C.2.4 [**Computer-Communication Networks**]: Distributed Systems

General Terms

Algorithms, Design, Measurement

Keywords

Caching, Video Retrieval and Resource Management

1. INTRODUCTION

High-volume DVR users often find themselves filling their DVRs and having to delete content to make room for more recordings. One solution is to add more DVR storage. But this solution is not recommended from operational point of view, because more local storage means another device to

---

manage and maintain and it is susceptible to filling as well. [LRM08] [SDK+07] proposed caching the content in a P2P fashion between the DVRs. This approach raises legal challenges presented by copyright holders.

An alternative is extra storage on a network server that a service provider can allocate dynamically. Unless it is implemented intelligently, the network storage solution may use too much network bandwidth. For example, suppose the home DVR fills and then new recordings go on the network server. If the home DVR has mostly stale content, the subscriber might play most content from the network server, thereby loading the network with unicast streams in prime time when, according to our data, DVR playback and other traffic peaks.

This paper proposes and validates algorithms to manage a subscriber's home and network storage jointly, as a single virtual cache. The algorithms place in the home cache content the subscriber is likely to watch in today's busy hour. When the home cache fills, the algorithms move content from the home to the network that the subscriber is unlikely to watch. The algorithms also do the reverse: when there is space in the home storage, they bring back that content from the network storage the subscriber is most likely to watch.

The algorithms are based on actual user behavior. We obtained a set of anonymized logs showing two months of recordings and playbacks by 454 DVRs. We studied many factors governing future viewing. Some factors pertain to the behavior of the DVR user, which can be derived from her logs, e.g. how prompt does the user watch recordings? Others pertain to the user's viewing pattern of a series, e.g. John's watching pattern of American Idol verses Grey's Anatomy. Others pertain to the specific recording, e.g. whether or not the user had already watched the recording and the recording's age. We developed statistical methods to study the effects of those factors and converged to an algorithm that is both practical and achieves near optimal performance.

We developed a decision tree model and a proportional hazards model that incorporated all of these factors. We used the results to develop some simpler models that relied on fewer factors. We evaluated the models both by using statistical tests and a cost function. This cost function reflects the penalty of having to download a recording during prime time that resides in the network, but not in the home storage.

Our results show that using simple factors, such as whether or not the recording has already been watched and when was the last time the recording was used, leads to a uniformly well-performing algorithm. This is welcomed news, as a simpler algorithm maintains less state information, and henceforth, it is more practical to implement.

Paper organization: Section 2 describes the real world traces and their general characteristics. Section 3 introduces the problem of intelligent caching and provides a mathematical model of how to choose the recordings to be stored locally. Section 4 explains statistical models as well as practical models on how to best cache those recordings. Section 5 shows the experimental results of those models using our real traces and explains our findings. We conclude in section 6.

2. DESCRIPTIVE ANALYSIS OF THE DATA

Basic analysis shows some interesting observations of subscribers' recording and playback behavior, reinforcing the need for intelligent caching and suggesting how to make caching decisions.

2.1 Structure of the Data

Our raw data consisted of playback logs from 454 DVRs. Each record in the log corresponded to one DVR playing back one recorded program. A single record consisted of an integer DVR identifier, the program name, the program duration, the time the program recording began, and the time the playback stopped. We also determined each program's series name, e.g. American Idol. A series name, if exists, helps discern TV viewing patterns among users.

2.2 Large Scale Features

First, we analyzed features of the entire data set to formulate hypotheses about the best way to utilize a joint home and network DVR storage arrangement. Our major findings are in bold, followed by explanations.

DVR playback peaks in the late evening. Figure 1 shows the times of day when playback stopped in our entire data set. The rate at which playbacks finish grows quickly after 11 PM and reaches a peak at around 2 AM. Since most TV programs last at most an hour, mid to late evening is the prime time for DVR playback (our data does not include the times playback begins). The same time period happens to be the peak usage period for data in general and video-on-demand in particular. A Network DVR service that replaced home storage with network storage would put additional bandwidth demands on the network exactly when demand now peaks, which is the worst possible time. Therefore, any network DVR storage must be in addition to, and not instead of, home storage, especially with other unicast video, such as over the top video, growing. When there is home storage, we want to minimize cache misses from the home storage during prime time.

Users are mores likely to view newer recordings than older recordings. Figure 2 plots the delay density of our entire dataset on a logarithmic scale, while figure 3 shows the CCDF of it. By delay of a recording we mean the time that elapses from the beginning of recording until the end of any playback. That is, delay is the recording's age when playback ends. The figure shows delay in hours over a two week period. Several features of the density are noteworthy. First, the probability that a recording will "live" to an old age before playback declines rapidly with age. Some 20% of recordings have a delay less than an hour, 55% of recordings

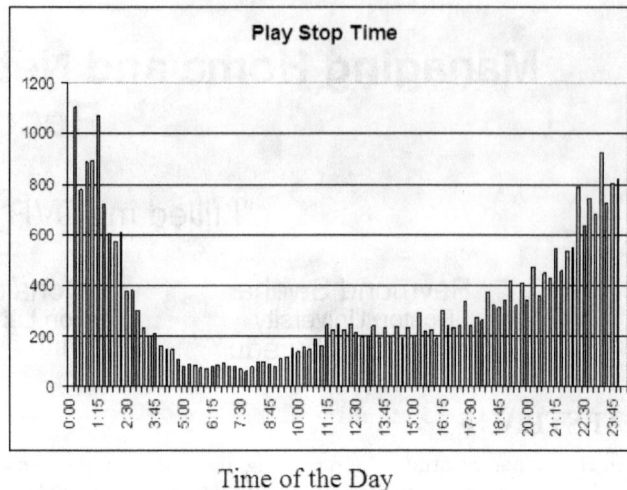

Figure 1: **A histogram showing the frequency of watching time over the time of the day.**

are played back within 24 hours, and 90% of delays are less than a week. The age of a recording is a key explanatory variable for selecting what content to place in home storage, but it is not the only one.

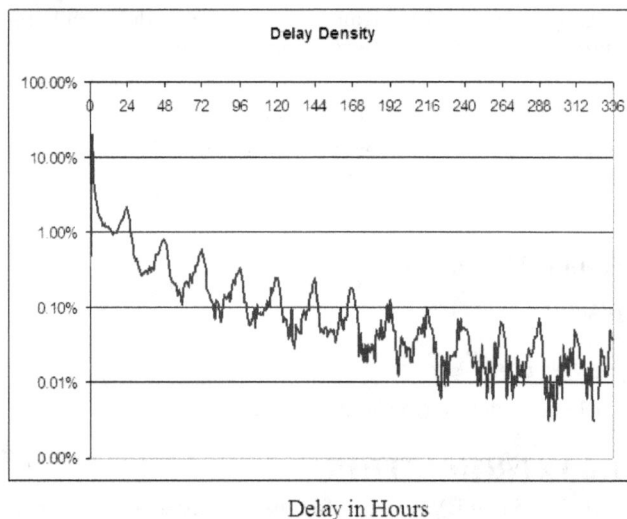

Figure 2: **The diminishing periodicity of the delay between recording and playback .**

Delays are most likely to be multiples of 24 hours. The other striking feature of Figure 2 is the oscillations with a period of 24 hours. The most likely delay after zero hours is 24 hours, then 48 hours, etc. The reason for the periodicity is most likely that people watch TV at set times and either watch a program live or watch something they recorded at roughly the same time on a previous day. Since most playbacks occur in the evening, this observation suggests that caching decisions can be implemented in the early morning and should not be made during the evening.

The delay distribution has a large probability mass near the origin. Since users are likely to watch newly

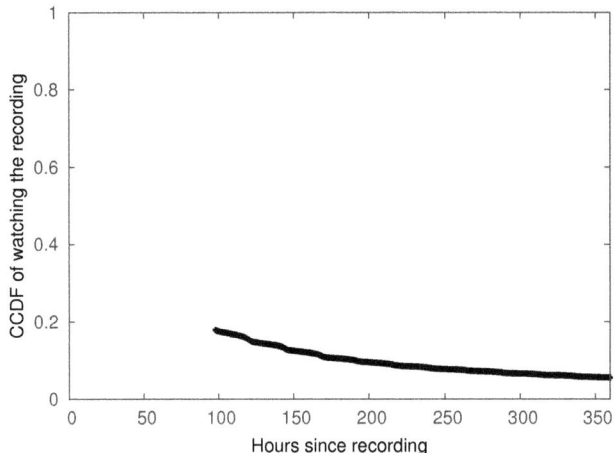

Figure 3: The Complementary Cumulative distribution function of the probability of watching as a function delay.

recorded material, there is little value in running our algorithm during the busy hour. Instead, we could reserve storage space for recordings made during the day and evening, thereby minimizing the need to move recordings to the network during prime time. If the home storage should fill, we can move recordings with previously calculated low viewing probabilities to the network without rerunning the algorithm, since new recordings are likely to have high viewing probabilities.

Only some users will need network storage, but many of those who do will require much dynamic caching. Although not every DVR owner uses it heavily, those who do require a dynamic caching technique.

3. COST MODEL

3.1 Viewing Probabilities

Our first goal is to develop algorithms that assign time-dependent viewing probabilities to recordings. The time-dependence reflects, for example, that aging or previous viewing may lower today's viewing probability.

In this paper, we assume the algorithms update viewing probabilities once per day, but they could run more often. Consider one user at an update time. Let R be the set of items that the user has recorded at the update time. Assume that the algorithm has calculated the viewing probabilities p_i for all $i \in R$. The question is how to use the viewing probabilities to assign recordings to the home storage or network storage.

3.2 Moving Costs

A home cache miss in prime time requires the network to transport a unicast video stream to the subscriber at a time when bandwidth is scarce. The miss (or a decision by a a subscriber to record a new program) may force the DVR to move an existing recording to network storage to make room for the new recording. The move uses upstream bandwidth at a bit rate greater than or equal to the bit rate of the new recording. We can reduce this cost by moving content to the network ahead of time (e.g., by maintaining

some empty space on the DVR or duplicating some recordings on the network allowing its space to be overwritten at any time) during low-usage periods and at low bit rates

In this paper, we will assume that the cost of moving a recording to the network is zero. The only cost is the cost of streaming a recording from the network during prime time. We next introduce notation and define the cost function formally.

Let S_i be the size of item i in bytes. Let c_i be the cost of streaming item i from network storage during prime time. Although the cost might depend on the streaming rate and the duration of the session as well as network utilization, we will set the cost equal to the file size $c_i = s_i$.

Rather than letting space in the home storage go unused, we will allow a portion of a recording to reside in the home and the rest in the network. To model this scheme, divide item i into s_i pieces each of size unity.

Let x_i^j be a binary decision variable that takes the value 1 if chunk j of item i is in the network and zero otherwise.

Define the random variable V_i to be 1 if the user views item i during prime time on the day the update occurs and $V_i = 0$ otherwise. Note that $E(V_i) = p_i$.

Assuming that recordings are watched in full, the probability of watching each chunk of item i is p_i We can now write the download cost as $\sum_{i \in R} \sum_{i \leq j \leq s_i} V_i x_i^j$. We want to minimize its expectation:

$$\text{Minimize} \sum_{i \in R} \sum_{i \leq j \leq s_i} p_i x_i^j$$

$$\text{subject to} \sum_{i \in R} \sum_{i \leq j \leq s_i} (1 - x_i^j) \leq b$$

where b is the storage available on the home DVR. The optimal solution is to select x_i^j where p_i is maximal until we fill the local DVR. In other words, put the chunks with the highest viewing probability in the home DVR. Note that all recordings on the home DVR, except possibly the one with the lowest viewing probability, will end up on the home DVR in their entirety. Thus, given a set of recordings $i \in R$ each with a probability p_i of viewing, the optimal solution is to save the recordings with the highest probability locally *regardless* of their size.

4. OPERATIONALIZING THE INTELLIGENT CACHING ALGORITHM

As detailed above, the key to the algorithm is the estimation of the probability that, on a given day a given subscriber will play a recording. Using characteristics of the DVR users and the recordings derived from a set of training data, we estimate the probability of that day's watching of the recording, and choose the recordings with the highest estimated probabilities to retain in the home, or retrieve from the network cache, up to the home storage's designated capacity. Note that the designated capacity could be smaller than the DVR's physical capacity, if we leave space for further subscriber recording.

Once an algorithm is developed, it will be evaluated in two distinct ways. First, its general fit to the training data will be evaluated using standard statistical procedures. Second, the algorithm will be applied to test data unused in development, and the cost of its incorrect decisions will be calculated and compared to simpler, intuitive models.

4.1 Model Development: Structuring the Training Data

The raw training data comprised a two-month period in 2010, and contained information on recordings recorded and later played back for a sample of 454 DVRs. For each recording, its dates and times of recording and playback were captured, as was the total duration of the recording. Many recordings were part of a series (e.g. American Idol or Lost) and the series name was also captured.

This information was re-structured to reflect the decision-making of the algorithm, and to account for the rather complicated time pattern of recording and playback over the data's time period. For each DVR and recording, an observation (a row in the dataset) is written for each day the recording is available for playback, and a separate 0/1 variable indicates whether the recording was watched on that day. Each observation thus contains the age of the recording on that day (which increases by 1 day per observation) and whether it was watched later that day. We suppose that the observation corresponds to the time at which the algorithm makes its caching decision (e.g. 4 AM), and we make the conservative assumption that downloading a recording from the network server will incur a bandwidth cost. Also, for testing purposes, we assume a recording watched on a particular day will remain on the DVR and be available for re-watching.

Other variables, summarized in table 1, were added to the resulting data set. The variables capture the behavior of the DVR users regarding all recording as well as regrading the recordings of a specific series, e.g. American Idol. It also has variables pertaining to the specific recording and others pertaining to the series as a whole.

Those variables were fed to the statistical models in order to predict which recordings the user is more likely to watch in a given day.

4.2 Model Development: Statistical Models

One useful statistical model is a decision tree [CG84], which recursively partitions the explanatory variables named above with the goal of constructing hypercubes of data where the playback probability is either 0.0 or 1.0. Because of its automation it can suggest variables to use in other models. Its hierarchical partitioning can indicate their relative importance. The model can be drawn as a tree, with the sequential variables splits shown as branches.

The data was edited before modelling. First, the variable "replays" was dichotomized into 0 (never previously watched) and 1 (already watched at least once). Then, the small numbers of missing values for Delay-prev and DVR-Delay were imputed. If Delay-prev was missing, that is, there was no previous history of watching this series, the average delay for that DVR, DVR-Delay, was substituted for the missing value. If DVR-Delay was missing, in which case there was no previous history of recording on that DVR, the median value for all DVRs was imputed. Modelling proceeded on this modified dataset. The figure below shows the uppermost branches of a tree constructed with training data. Note that the only variables found to influence the tree structure were the a) whether the recording has already been watched,

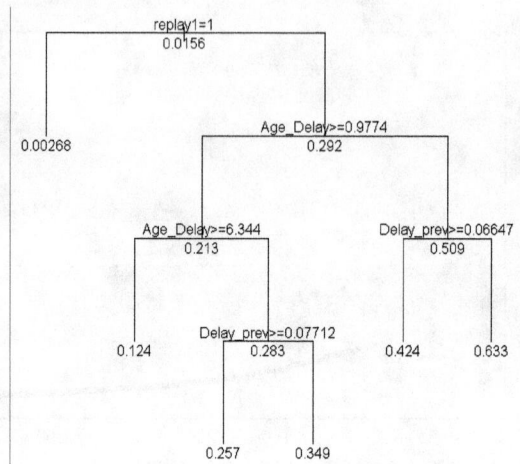

Figure 4: The decision tree deciding which probability of records at each leaf of the tree.

b) how old is the recording, and c) the average delay in watching this series for this DVR. Other variables seem to be of less importance. Our experimental results, mentioned later, shows that this model is inefficient. The reason is that it assigns the same probability to all the recordings in the same leaf of the tree. If most of the recordings are in the same leaf, only a random subset of them will be cached locally, resulting in performance loss.

To overcome this problem, we developed a proportional hazards model [Cox72] incorporating all these variables.

In addition to the editing and imputation indicated above, Age-Delay, the age in days of a series on a specific day in the dataset, is made an integer, and truncated at 15 days (i.e. age values greater than 15 days are labelled as 15). The

DVR specific variables	
DVR-Delay	The average delay between recording and playback for all recordings played by this DVR.
n-DVR-watched	The number of recordings of all types watched by this DVR to date.
Recording specific variables	
Age-delay	The time between recording and the day of observation.
Replays	Counts the number of times the recording was watched before the day of observation.
DoW-Recording	The day of the week when this was recorded
Series specific variables per DVR	
Delay-prev	The average delay taken by the DVR until previous recordings of this series were played back
n-series	The number of series episodes played to date by the DVR.
Series specific variables	
n-aired	The number of episodes of this series aired so far

Table 1: A summery of variables generated for each recording each day of simulation

resulting variable coefficients refer to their effect on log(-log(P)) where P is the probability of watching the recording in question. The baseline hazard function is contained in the coefficients for Age, and its fitted values show a rapid decrease in viewing probability as the recording ages.

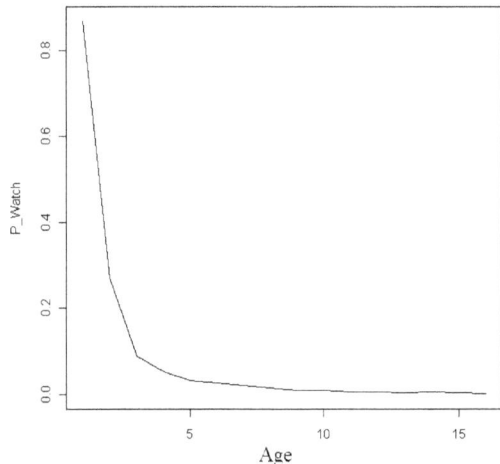

Figure 5: Fitting the CLL model against the *Age-Delay* of the recording .

4.3 Practical Models

Based on the results obtained from the decision tree model and the variables with the dominant coefficients in the proportional hazards model, we propose five practical algorithms

1. **Never Played**: filled the local DVR with recordings that was never played selected at random. If there were more space, it fills it with already played recordings at random. The rest of recordings are sent back to the server. This model requires only keeping a log of the recording that was already watched, thus it has minimal overhead.

2. **Least Recently Recorded (LRR)**: probability is inversely proportional to the Age of the recording on a subscribers DVR; hence place in the network recordings in reverse order of the time since recording, oldest first.

3. **Least Recently Used (LRU)**: probability is inversely proportional to the time since the recording time or the most recent playback, whichever comes latest.

4. **NP+LRR**: sort first by whether the recording was watched or not and then by the least recently recorded within that.

5. **NP+LRU**: sort first by whether the recording was watched or not and then by the least recently used within that. This model is inspired by the decision tree outcome.

5. COST ASSESSMENTS OF THE MODELS

Assessing our models as in the section above is useful from a statistical point of view, but is too crude to assess the performance of such models as caching algorithms. Unlike the usual statistical measures, which summarize the closeness of model fit at each prediction point, the models incur costs only when a recording is wrongly marked for placement in the network.

For each DVR, on each day of the test period, incorrect placement occurs when a recording is predicted to have a low probability of future viewing, and is put on a network server, yet is subsequently watched, thus requiring its downloading. Therefore, we care about the accuracy of a model's prediction for recordings with low viewing probability.

Costs of incorrect caching are calculated as follows. A model, which may explicitly predict viewing probability or may simply rank recordings by their relative viewing probability, sorts a DVR's daily recordings from least likely to most likely to be watched. For example, our statistical models produce predictions of viewing probability for each recording on the DVR, and the recordings are sorted by this prediction. For an algorithm such as LRU (see section 4.2), the recordings are ranked from most recently used to least recently used. The DVR has a particular capacity and for convenience with our data, this is measured in hours of programming. (In so measuring, we assume some constant relative split of SD and HD so hours of capacity could in principle be converted to bytes.) Cumulative hours of recording time are calculated for each DVR each day, using the sorting imposed by the caching algorithm, and the lower ranking recordings whose cumulative duration exceeds DVR capacity are stored on a network server (i.e. effectively removed from the DVR.) A cost is incurred if the recording is on the network server on the day it is played back, for this requires the recording to be downloaded. The cost is here measured for the duration, in minutes, of the downloaded recordings.

We calculate total costs for a set of data from 184 DVRs which were randomly selected to be held out from the training data used to build our statistical models. The chart below shows the caching cost (in minutes, as detailed above, for a 32-day period) for a variety of algorithms.

Figure 6 compares the cost of the five simple algorithms mentioned earlier. The costs associated with each of these algorithms was calculated for each of several DVR capacities, from 10 to 80 hours (typical DVR capacity is 320GB $\simeq$ 80 hours of SD recording). It shows that NP+LRU algorithm outperforms all the others. This is expected as it coincides with our results using the decision tree model. From now on, we will always use NP+LRU out of those five.

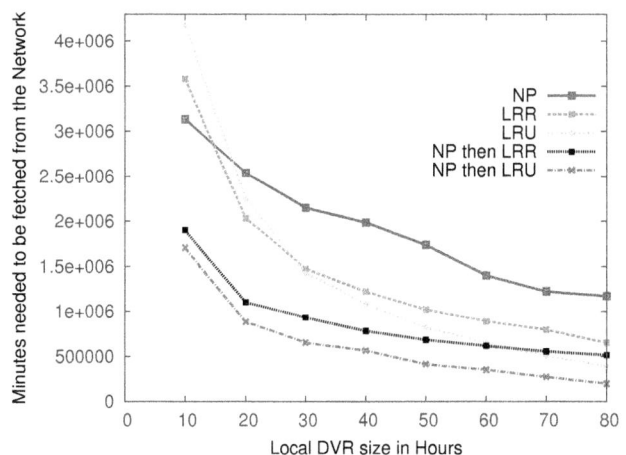

Figure 6: The performance comparison of Least Recently Used/Recorded and Never Played algorithms against an increasing DVR capacity .

The second experiment compares our practical model (NP+LRU)

against
1- **Random**: a baseline model which chooses recordings to store locally at random
2- **DT**: the decision tree model, where each recording is stored locally with the probability of the leaf it belongs to in the tree
3- **CLL**: the complementary log log value computed using the proportional hazard model. Figure 7 shows the result. Random performs pretty badly, indicating the utility of any intelligent caching algorithm. DT performs a lot better than Random but there is still room for improvement. The CLL and NP+LRU models essentially perform equally. This is an unexpected result as one would think knowing more about the users general habits or his habits concerning specific series would yield better results, but the simulation of real world traces shows that this is shadowed by more dominant factors, namely whether this recording is already watched or not and the time since it was last used.

Figure 8 shows the cost of NP+LRU against two com-

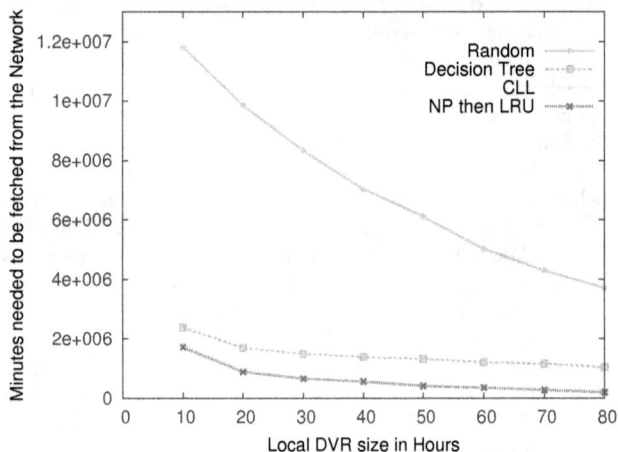

Figure 8: A table showing the similarity of different CLL models to NP+LRU.

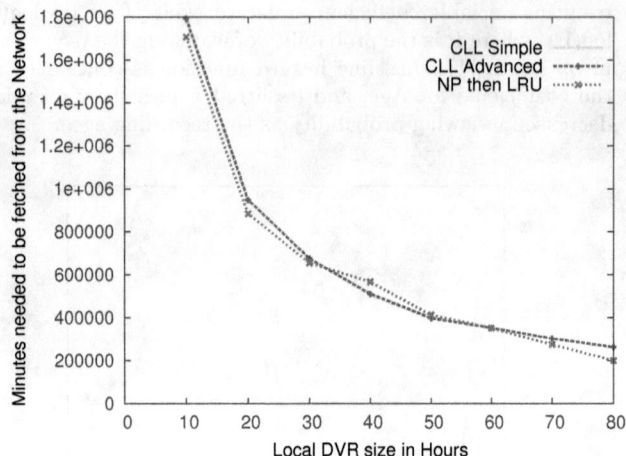

Figure 7: The performance comparison of different algorithms against an increasing DVR capacity.

binations of variable to compute the CLL model. Simple CLL utilized *Age-delay* and *Replays* while CLL Advanced has *Age-delay, Replays, Delay-prev, n-DVR-watched, Delay-prev:Replays, n-DVR-watched:Replays, Age-delay:Replays* and *DVR-delay*. All of them perform fundamentally the same, where the CLL models perform slightly better in medium range of the capacity and NP+ LRU model performs better at higher DVR capacities. Although adding information about the DVR behavior makes small improvements, the variants perform similarly. This is actually a positive result. As a simple and intuitive algorithm ,like NP+LRU which does not require maintaining a big state, performs very closely to more sophisticated models.

6. CONCLUSION

We studied the behavior of DVR users based on real traces of 454 users. Our characterization showed that users are more likely to record and watch recordings during prime-time. They are also more likely to watch recent recordings. If they do not watch recordings immediately, they tend to watch them after multiples of 24 hours.
One other observation was that some users often run out

of space on their DVRs. One solution to this problem is to add network storage accessible to the users where they can save their extra recordings. An intelligent caching technique is crucial to locally cache the recordings most likely to be viewed each day, particularly because users tend to watch recordings at prime-time, when the network is already congested. This minimizes the risk of flooding the network with unicast streams during prime-time. The statistical methods we used, namely recursive partitioning and proportional hazards models, indicate that the most dominant factors are whether or not the recording was watched and when was the last time this recording was used. Based on this observation, we built a simple algorithm, NP+LRU, and subsequently, ran it against a testing set. We found that it performs just as well as the statistical models that utilize more information about the usage history of users. This is encouraging, since our practical algorithm maintains only a small state about each recording, consumes little computational power to run and effectively predicts the user behavior
.

7. REFERENCES

[CG84] E. F. Cook and L. Goldman. Empiric comparison of multivariate analytic techniques: advantages and disadvantages of recursive partitioning analysis. *Journal of chronic diseases*, 37(9-10):721–731, 1984.

[Cox72] D. R. Cox. Regression models and Life-Tables. *Journal of the Royal Statistical Society. Series B (Methodological)*, 34(2):187–220, 1972.

[LRM08] Nikolaos Laoutaris, Pablo Rodriguez, and Laurent Massoulie. ECHOS: edge capacity hosting overlays of nano data centers. *SIGCOMM Comput. Commun. Rev.*, 38:51–54, January 2008.

[SDK+07] Kyoungwon Suh, C. Diot, J. Kurose, L. Massoulie, C. Neumann, D. Towsley, and M. Varvello. Push-to-Peer Video-on-Demand system: Design and evaluation. *IEEE Journal on Selected Areas in Communications*, 25(9):1706–1716, December 2007.

Moving Beyond the Framebuffer

Charles D. Estes
University of North Carolina at Chapel Hill
Brooks Computer Science Building, CB 3175
Chapel Hill, NC 27599-3175 USA
cdestes@cs.unc.edu

Ketan Mayer-Patel
University of North Carolina at Chapel Hill
Brooks Computer Science Building, CB 3175
Chapel Hill, NC 27599-3175 USA
kmp@cs.unc.edu

ABSTRACT

This paper explores a new abstraction to replace the framebuffer as the metaphor for a new display interface. Our novel approach aims to provide backward compatibility with applications that require a simple framebuffer, while also providing tremendous channel capacity savings to applications that exploit application level semantics to use the display interface in a more sophisticated way. The goal is to develop a versatile interface that scales from very large displays to small, low-power displays connected over wireless links.

Categories and Subject Descriptors

C.0 [**General**]: Hardware/software interfaces

General Terms

Design, Algorithms, Performance, Experimentation

Keywords

Display interface, framebuffer, scalable display

1. LEGACY OF THE FRAMEBUFFER

Since the rise of raster displays, the framebuffer, as a concept, has been the predominant abstraction for display interfaces. The earliest personal computers either adopted the television for display purposes or integrated a cathode ray tube (CRT) display as part of the computer. The framebuffer as an abstraction was a logical extension of the rowwise scanning of pixels performed in order to generate an analog signal compatible with existing television standards and CRT-based components.

The modular design of the IBM PC and its clones introduced the display adapter as an interface to the display as a peripheral resource. The software drivers for the display adapter formalized the framebuffer as a software construct. The separation of the display as a distinct and somewhat independent component was important because advances in CPU technologies generally outpace advances in

display technologies. This allows the CPU to be upgraded or replaced without requiring the purchase of a new display. Likewise, if and when display technologies advance, only the display adapter and monitor need be replaced.

Analog display technologies were slow to evolve because any advance in resolution and/or frame rate required the development and adoption of new signaling and cabling standards for the analog signal driving the display. IBM led the industry through a series of such advances in analog signaling with the development of CGA in 1981, EGA in 1984, VGA in 1987, and XVGA in 1991[9]. These analog display interface standards were so pervasive, that the earliest digital flat panel displays used the same interfaces *despite the fact that these displays were not analog devices.*

2. MODERN DISPLAY CHALLENGES

For the most part, digital display technologies such as liquid crystal displays (LCDs), digital light projectors (DLPs), and plasma displays have completely supplanted CRT-based analog displays. Modern digital display interface standards include Digital Visual Interface (DVI), High-Definition Multimedia Interface (HDMI)[4], and DisplayPort[1][15]. While these protocols directly support digital displays, they all essentially mimic their analog predecessors by continuously packaging the framebuffer and transporting it at the specified refresh rate. Unfortunately, like their analog predecessors, these standards will not be able to keep pace with trends in display technologies and emerging innovations in how displays are used. These challenges include:

- **Increased resolution** - While 1080p is a common native resolution for many displays, this particular spatial format is popular because it matches current high-definition video standards. Higher resolution displays are common in computer applications and there are few technical barriers to prevent the manufacture of digital displays with spatial formats as high as 3840x2400 (WQUXGA)[6].

- **Higher refresh rates** - Many LCD HDTVs today are advertised as being able to support refresh rates of up to 240 Hz.

- **3D television** - The HDMI 1.4a specification allows for 3D over HDMI, but it stops short of full 1080p at 60 Hz support[5]. True stereo 3D television will require a pair of images for each supported viewpoint. One can easily imagine future scenarios with tens of supported viewpoints.

- **Large-scale displays** - Scalable display walls and jumbotrons currently involve stitching together separate panels driven by individual display adapters[7][10][2]. The jumbotron in Cowboy's Stadium uses HDTV video sources to drive its panels despite the fact that the native format of these displays is more than 5x larger[8]. One of the reasons why such a large display is being under-utilized is the complexity and bandwidth involved in trying to drive it at a resolution that is at the same scale as its physical size. The Walgreen's billboard in Times Square, for example, requires a 48-drive RAID disc streaming data at 3.2 GB/s to drive its 17,000 square foot billboard at a spatial format of 10,000 x 4,000[3].

- **Low-power mobile displays** - Mobile displays face similar challenges on a different scale. A popular current example is HD video playback on tablets. A tablet with a 1280 x 800 pixel display and 16 bits per pixel will require 512 kB per frame. At 24 frames/sec, this requires a channel capacity of 400 Mbps, easily exceeding the capacity of mobile data links. Video compression combats this but at the cost of reduced battery life due to decoding the video at the tablet[11].

- **Remote displays** - Remotely connected display resources must overcome mismatches between the bandwidth required to transmit the framebuffer and the bandwidth available which is subject to fluctuating network conditions and congestion control. A common solution is to employ a remote display application such as Virtual Network Computing (VNC)[13] to avoid transmitting parts of the display that are not changing. This solution essentially requires integrating a computer in the display in order to execute the remote client. Similarly, kiosk displays are often driven by a dedicated collocated computer which is then managed remotely in order to transfer and control content.

In our opinion, the framebuffer as an abstraction for display resources has reached the limits of its scalability. In order to support future advances in spatial formats and refresh rates as well as innovative uses for displays, a new abstraction needs to be considered. We can no longer afford the cost of repeatedly copying out the entire framebuffer tens or hundreds of times per second inherited as the legacy of the framebuffer. This paper presents early work in progress for what such a new abstraction could look like. We start with a clean-slate design derived from first principles that incorporates lessons learned from the framebuffer's legacy. One of the key features of our proposed design is that it allows processes at higher levels of the system such as applications, GUI toolkits, graphics libraries, etc. to leverage high-level semantics in order to most efficiently and flexibly make use of display resources.

The rest of this paper is organized into seven additional sections, in which we explore our search for a new abstraction, outline the design principles that emerged from that search, detail our design, illustrate several use cases for our design, and present a key use case experiment and results.

3. CHOOSING A NEW ABSTRACTION

Consider the exercise of evaluating well-known software abstractions as candidates for a new abstraction for display

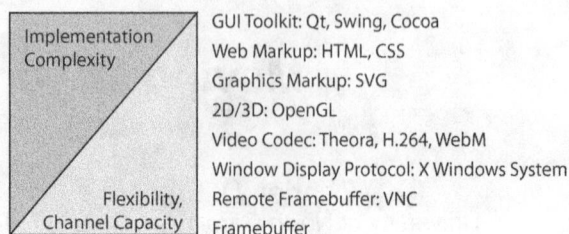

Figure 1: Sample software abstractions.

resources. Several possibilities are shown in Figure 1. First, we note that there is a general tradeoff between channel efficiency and flexibility against implementation complexity. High-level complex abstractions can communicate display updates efficiently for content that matches the data model for which that abstraction was designed for. However, flexibility is decreased such that any content that is outside of the data model becomes very difficult to communicate efficiently.

For instance, it is unreasonable to build a display based on HTTP, webkit, and Javascript for obvious reasons of complexity as well as the implicitly limited flexibility of such a display. While such a display abstraction might provide scalability and throughput savings for web-based applications, any advantage is quickly lost once outside of the abstraction's domain. For example, a high-performance video game.

Window managers based on X[14] represent another abstraction with high implementation complexity due to the need to support features such as z-ordering, blending, focus, and cursors. Furthermore, limited or highly variable bandwidth will severely affect performance.

One reasonably flexible abstraction is the popular remote display application, VNC, which requires that the host machine use a VNC server to monitor framebuffer changes. It sends those encoded changes to a remote VNC client leveraging the Remote Framebuffer (RFB) protocol. While very efficient for coherent display content where changes are concentrated into small areas, such an abstraction will not gracefully handle highly dynamic content such as video and/or gaming. Furthermore, VNC and RFB are still somewhat complex to implement, effectively requiring the display to utilize a microprocessor to support the VNC client.

Net2Display is a recent specification from VESA that provides an official standard for remoting displays, competing to replace VNC, Microsoft Remote Desktop Protocol (RDP), Citrix ICA, and others[12]. One of the key differentiators of the Net2Display standard, is that it accommodates dedicated display devices connected over an IP-based link. The Net2Display standard is primarily an architecture that specifies a minimum feature set in order to best encourage interoperability. While this "minimal feature set" may make Net2Display easier to embed in a display, it effectively makes these devices less capable[16].

4. DESIGN PRINCIPLES

In this section, we articulate a number of design principles that a new display abstraction should embody. A primary lesson from the legacy of the framebuffer is that major design shifts are infrequent. Thus, any such design needs to be reasonably simple and highly adaptable in order to accommodate a wide range of applications and future needs. It was to that end that we developed the following set of design principles.

4.1 No Computational State Machine

In considering other possible display interface abstractions, we find that most require some form of a computational state machine, whether it be a general purpose processor to support a VNC-like client or a highly specialized graphics/multimedia processor to support codecs and/or perform higher-order graphics commands. Specifying display hardware that leverages some form of a computational state machine can yield dramatic benefits, but it will consume far more power than a solution that employs simple digital logic. Power consumption may not be a major concern of large home theater displays, but it is a major constraint for a mobile displays using an energy efficient technology like electronic paper (EPD). Thus, the first design principle is that our new abstraction must not require a computational state machine.

4.2 Highly Parallel

While a state machine based design must address scalability by using ever increasing clock rates for the underlying processor, a design based on simpler digital logic scales easily if parallelism is brought to bear. Therefore we identify high parallelism as another key design principle. It should be possible to update every pixel on the display simultaneously via highly parallel digital logic.

4.3 Asynchronous

One consequence of forgoing a computational state machine and adopting high parallelism, is the ability to embrace asynchrony as a design principle. Allowing asynchrony decouples the data rate of the display interface and the refresh rate of the display panel. This is an important consideration because it supports use cases in which quality of service for the connection to the display is either constrained or highly variable. Furthermore, the system can be made more energy efficient by only performing calculations and updating the display when new display data arrives.

4.4 Framebuffer Compatible

The framebuffer abstraction is deeply established and will not be quickly abandoned as a supported abstraction. Its simple elegance and ubiquity in today's software makes it a compelling method for interacting with our new display interface as well. Furthermore, adopting framebuffer compatibility as a design principle better allows for a staged adoption of the new abstraction.

4.5 Progressive Benefit

Recalling the discussion in section 3, there is a general tradeoff between the complexity of an abstraction and the channel capacity required to support it. The more we leverage application knowledge about how display resources are being used, the more compactly we can describe and represent the data required to drive the display. Furthermore, this semantic knowledge can be used to help negotiate appropriate adaptations to fluctuating or constrained channel resources. Thus, another design principle that we espouse is that the proposed abstraction provide a progressive benefit when higher-level application semantics are known.

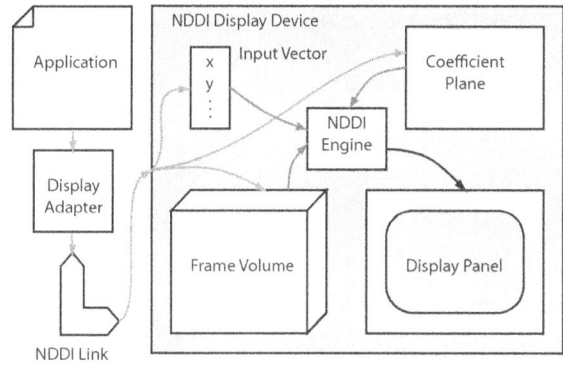

Figure 2: NDDI concept diagram.

5. N-DIMENSIONAL DISPLAY INTERFACE

In this section, we present the design of our proposed display abstraction, the n-Dimensional Display Interface (NDDI). The NDDI is comprised of the following components:

- The Frame Volume
- The Coefficient Plane
- The Input Vector
- The NDDI Engine

These components are illustrated abstractly in Figure 2. The application in this diagram represents an agent using the NDDI Display Device. The Display Adapter represents an interface layer that the application drives much in the same way current systems have a display adapter that provides an interface to the framebuffer. The NDDI Link represents the physical connection between the Display Adapter and the NDDI Device. This physical link and the protocol used to communicate over it are not described in this paper. While an actual realization of NDDI would, of course, require specification of this link, for the exploratory purpose of this paper, it can be thought of abstractly as a wired or wireless connection capable of transmitting and receiving data encapsulated within NDDI commands. The following subsections describe each of the NDDI components in turn.

5.1 Frame Volume

NDDI expands on the idea of a display with "memory" of its pixels. It does not utilize a fixed, two-dimensional framebuffer matching the format of the display panel. Instead it specifies that a display has a *frame volume*. This frame volume is a very large piece of memory that holds pixel values that can be mapped to the individual pixels on the display panel in a variety of ways.

The frame volume can be configured to any dimensionality. In its simplest representation, it can be configured as a two-dimensional framebuffer that represents the current contents of the display. Another configuration might add a third dimension that represents time, allowing a video stream to buffer on the actual display itself. Exactly how the frame volume is configured is one of the ways the NDDI provides applications driving the display to take advantage of higher-level semantic knowledge. In practice, applications may never use more than three or four dimensions, and so future implementations of NDDI may impose a limit.

5.2 Coefficient Plane

The dimensionality of the Frame Volume most often will not match the display panel, and so the pixel values from the Frame Volume must be mapped to the panel. NDDI accomplishes this through the *coefficient plane*. The coefficient plane is a two-dimensional grid of *coefficient matrices*. This grid matches the dimensions of the display panel. The coefficient matrix at a particular x and y location in the coefficient plane is used in conjunction with the *input vector* to pick a unique value from the Frame Volume in order to display on the panel at the same x and y location.

5.3 Input Vector

The update process is driven by the *input vector*. The input vector is a one-dimensional vector, with the first two values reserved for the x and y position of a pixel. The remaining values are optional and are specified by the application. The x and y values are not driven by the application, but rather by NDDI when it is computing output pixel values for the panel.

5.4 NDDI Engine

The three primary components of NDDI are effectively memory stores. The digital logic that drives the process of updating the display panel resides in the *NDDI engine*. Any time the data in the input vector, coefficient plane, or frame volume changes, the NDDI engine calculates the updates to the *display panel* in parallel. The process begins with the input vector. For each pixel, the NDDI engine 1) sets the x and y value in the input vector, 2) multiplies the input vector by the coefficient matrix at the corresponding x and y location in the coefficient plane to produce a tuple that matches the dimensionality of the frame volume, and 3) finally updates the display panel using the single pixel value from the frame volume addressed by the tuple.

The following illustrates the calculation for a pixel at location $(7, 8)$. The coefficient matrix at that location in in the coefficient plane is multiplied by the input vector with the x and y values set to 7 and 8 to produce the tuple $(8, 8, 2)$. The pixel value at this location in the frame volume is displayed.

$$\begin{bmatrix} 1 & 0 & 0 & 1 \\ 0 & 1 & 0 & 0 \\ 0 & 0 & 1 & 2 \end{bmatrix} \begin{bmatrix} 7 \\ 8 \\ 0 \\ 1 \end{bmatrix} = \begin{bmatrix} 8 \\ 8 \\ 2 \end{bmatrix}$$

The NDDI interface reflects the design principles we identified in section 4. The NDDI mapping mechanism requires only a simple set of matrix and addressing operations allowing it to be implemented directly with digital logic. The NDDI engine computes the value of each display pixel in precisely the same manner which makes the mechanism highly parallel. NDDI is driven exclusively by the contents of its various structures. Thus the NDDI engine only needs to recalculate output when data arrives, making it asynchronous. If necessary, the NDDI structures can be configured in order to mimic a framebuffer directly. This is done by simply configuring the frame volume to be a 2D structure that matches the size of the display and setting the coefficient planes to the identity matrix. Finally, NDDI provides a progressive benefit to applications that are able to employ higher-level semantics about how best to deploy and exploit the NDDI structures. Several use cases that demonstrate how this might be done are described in the next section.

6. USING APPLICATION SEMANTICS

While it is possible to configure an NDDI display as a simple framebuffer, it will not produce throughput savings beyond the benefit of being able to drive the display at framerate other than the fixed refresh rate of a traditional display. In order to realize a more dramatic throughput advantage, the application must configure the NDDI display leveraging higher-level semantics.

6.1 Example: Video Player

A video playback application might configure the frame volume in three dimensions, with the x and y dimensions matching the display panel and the z dimension representing a buffered queue of frames. The buffering of frames would allow the application to handle channel capacity fluctuations when a fixed quality of service is unavailable. Additionally, the application can use a previous frame in the frame volume as the basis for the next frame by utilizing an inexpensive copy command to copy the contents to another z plane and then updating that new frame with only the changed pixels, mimicking the way a video codec would handle P and I frames. The coefficient plane would consist of simple 3 x 3 identity matrices. The display updates would be driven by an input vector with the default x and y values and a third value representing the frame counter, c. The application only needs to update that frame counter to display the next frame.

$$\begin{bmatrix} 1 & 0 & 0 \\ 0 & 1 & 0 \\ 0 & 0 & 1 \end{bmatrix} \begin{bmatrix} x \\ y \\ c \end{bmatrix} = \begin{bmatrix} x \\ y \\ c \end{bmatrix}$$

6.2 Example: Windowed User Interface

An application representing a computer desktop with a windowed user interface might also configure the frame volume in three dimensions, with the third dimensions instead being used as a cache for various windows. The x and y dimensions of the frame volume would match the largest window dimensions allowed and the pixel values for each window would be stored at the origin of each xy plane in the frame volume. The task of configuring the coefficient plane would not be as simple as with the video player example, because portions of several windows can be displayed simultaneously. In this case, the input vector would instead have a 1 in the third value, and the coefficient matrices would be updated with a w, tx, and ty values to choose and translate the window.

$$\begin{bmatrix} 1 & 0 & tx \\ 0 & 1 & ty \\ 0 & 0 & w \end{bmatrix} \begin{bmatrix} x \\ y \\ 1 \end{bmatrix} = \begin{bmatrix} x' \\ y' \\ w \end{bmatrix}$$

6.3 Example: Web Tablet

A web tablet device could leverage NDDI to overcome several challenges for tablet computers. Tablets are constrained devices with large displays, diminished power supplies, limited processing power, and low-capacity wireless links. Their large displays bring a higher level of interaction for the user, so manufacturers strive to keep the web and multimedia content downloading, decoding, and rendering quickly. A web tablet using NDDI could eschew a high-power CPU/GPU and instead use an ASIC-based NDDI Engine combined with slow, low-power RAM and a wireless modem to create a thin-client. In a simple configuration, it could arrange the frame volume in three dimensions with the third representing tabs. The x and y dimensions could be larger than the display, allowing more content outside of viewport to be buffered and then rendered when the user scrolls the viewport. In this configuration, the tabs would be modal, and so they would be chosen and scrolled with b, tx, and ty.

$$\begin{bmatrix} 1 & 0 & tx \\ 0 & 1 & ty \\ 0 & 0 & b \end{bmatrix} \begin{bmatrix} x \\ y \\ 1 \end{bmatrix} = \begin{bmatrix} x' \\ y' \\ b \end{bmatrix}$$

7. PIXEL BRIDGE EXPERIMENT

Our first proof-of-concept prototype of an NDDI display is a software simulation using a driving application that we call "Pixel Bridge". Pixel Bridge is intended to interface existing legacy applications and as such is an important first step. Pixel Bridge is like VNC in that it monitors framebuffer changes in order to identify areas of the display that require updating. It does not employ higher-level application semantics, but can marshall NDDI resources in a number of different ways in order to be as efficient as possible. In this experiment, we recorded a number of computing sessions and replayed them using Pixel Bridge and measure the amount of throughput required.

7.1 Pixel Bridge Configurations

Pixel Bridge can be configured to operate in five different modes. The first three modes employ progressively more sophisticated configurations of the the NDDI display. The last two modes are calculations that bound the performance.

- **Framebuffer** - Configured as a 2D framebuffer

- **Flat Tiled** - Configured as a 2D, tiled framebuffer

- **Cached Tiled** - Configured as a cache of tiles

- **60 Hz** - Cost of full screen updates at 60Hz

- **Ideal Pixel Latching** - Cost of only changed pixels

7.1.1 Framebuffer Mode

When Pixel Bridge is in the *Framebuffer* mode, it configures the frame volume with a dimensionality matching the recorded computing session. The coefficient plane is initialized so that each pixel on the display corresponds to the pixel value in the frame volume at the same x and y location. The input vector only has the default x and y values. For each frame, the entire frame volume is updated. This is similar to the 60 Hz mode, except that the *Framebuffer* mode is only updated at the framerate of the recorded computing session.

7.1.2 Flat Tiled Mode

The *Flat Tiled* mode configures the frame volume and initializes the coefficient plane the same way as with the *Framebuffer* mode. However, it logically partitions the frames into tiles. A CRC32 checksum of each tile is computed and compared to the corresponding tile in the frame volume to determine if that tile has changed. Only new tiles are updated.

7.1.3 Cached Tiled Mode

The final NDDI mode is the *Cached Tiled* mode. This mode still logically partitions the frames into tiles, but it configures the frame volume and coefficient plane differently

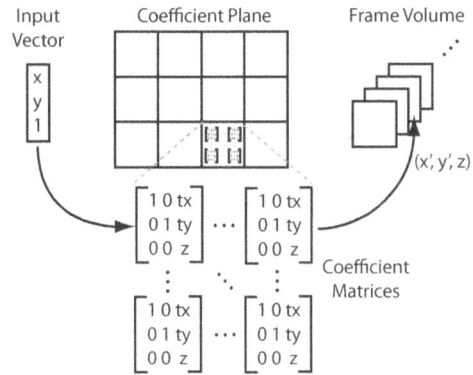

Figure 3: Cached tile mode NDDI configuration.

(see figure 3). The frame volume is configured in three dimensions, forming a cache of tiles. The x and y dimensions match the tile dimensions. The z dimension is set to a value representing the size of the cache. The coefficient plane is then logically partitioned into tiles. The coefficient matrix for each pixel in that logical tile maps to the pixel in the frame volume with the matching x and y coordinate and a z value for the particular tile in the cache.

The *Cached Tiled* mode shares the same advantages as the Flat Tiled mode, but adds the ability to leverage the cache to easily duplicate a tile at multiple locations on the display and to re-use older tiles in the cache.

7.1.4 60 Hz and Ideal Pixel Latching Modes

These non-NDDI modes are not implemented in Pixel Bridge as rendering modes, but rather are derived directly from the frame content and frame rate. The 60 Hz mode considers the number of frames and framerate of the original recorded session. It then calculates how many bytes are updated to the display if the display is updated at a constant 60 Hz rate. This should represent a worst-case performance boundary for Pixel Bridge. The Ideal Pixel Latching mode calculates only the number of bytes required to communicate just those pixels that change in value from one frame to the next. This mode completely disregards the obvious need to address pixel locations when updating a pixel value, and in doing so it serves as a theoretical, best-case boundary for Pixel Bridge.

7.2 Experiment Design

The following computing sessions were recorded and used as test vectors for the experiment:

- **office** - Document Editing

- **browser** - Web Browsing

- **eclipse** - Application Development using Eclipse

- **presentation** - Viewing a Presentation

- **video** - H.264 Video Playback

The first four sessions were recorded at 1280x1024 and 10 Hz. The relatively low framerate is justified because these computing activities do not produce highly dynamic changes to the display. The last session is an H.264 video playback

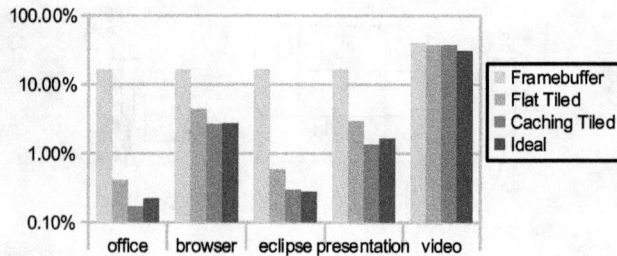

Figure 4: Preliminary Pixel Bridge Results.

at 656 x 352 and 23.98 Hz. Each of the five recorded sessions was tested with all five modes. Tile size was calculated dynamically, resulting in forty square tiles along the longest dimension. Each experiment tracked the number of bytes transmitted over the NDDI link without compression.

7.3 Results and Analysis

The results are shown in Figure 4, with each data point representing the ratio of the bytes transferred "over the wire" for that mode versus the 60 Hz mode. Recall that the 60 Hz mode represents the current status quo of transferring the entire framebuffer at a constant refresh rate. For the first four recorded sessions (i.e., not including video playback), Pixel Bridge demonstrates progressively better performance between *Framebuffer* mode to *Flat Tile* mode to *Cached Tiled* mode. Each of these modes employs NDDI resources in an increasingly sophisticated manner which is reflected in the improved performance. The *Framebuffer* mode illustrated the advantage of updating the display at a framerate that matches the source content instead a fixed refresh rate. The *Flat Tile* mode brought the advantage of only updating the changed regions of the display. The *Cached Tiled* mode showed the gains of filling the display with identical tiles as well as using previously cached tiles allowing it to outperform the *Ideal Pixel Latching* mode for some tests.

The results of the H264 video clip are quite contrary to the first four. Using a trivial, static tile size proved to be a poor approach to partitioning the screen. Furthermore, the frame content is so dynamic, that the caching was barely beneficial. The NDDI overhead of updating the coefficient plane negated most of the benefit from the cached tiling. This result was somewhat expected, since the *Cached Tiled* mode was conceived with the computing pixel bridge use cases in mind. Furthermore, full motion video represents highly dynamic content which does not match well with the title cache abstraction of Pixel Bridge. However, a more video-specific application that marshaled NDDI resources in a manner more in line with how video is compressed and represented may be more effective. This early experiment is meant only to serve as a proof-of-concept for the NDDI architecture.

8. CONCLUSIONS AND FUTURE WORK

Although the move to digital display interface standards was a significant step in developing higher capacity channels, it was largely an iteration on the same framebuffer abstraction for interfacing with a display. NDDI splits the framebuffer concept between application and display and uses a dramatically different approach to organizing that memory. Our initial Pixel Bridge experiment represents a "base case", bridging pixels from a computing session to an NDDI display. It showed increased savings as NDDI resources were marshaled in increasingly sophisticated ways despite not leveraging any application-level semantics. Our ongoing work will refine the Pixel Bridge experiment as well as explore new use cases in order to test our hypothesis that greater performance gains can be realized when application-level semantics are brought to bear.

9. REFERENCES

[1] Digital visual interface dvi revision 1.0. Digital Display Working Group, April 1999.

[2] S. Eilemann, M. Makhinya, and R. Pajarola. Equalizer: A scalable parallel rendering framework. *Visualization and Computer Graphics, IEEE Transactions on*, 15(3):436 –452, 2009.

[3] The insane hardware driving the world's biggest led billboard. website. http://gizmodo.com/#!5096475/the-insane-hardware-driving-the-worlds-biggest-led-billboard.

[4] High-definition multimedia interface specification version 1.3a. HDMI Founders, November 2006.

[5] High-definition multimedia interface specification version 1.4a extraction of 3d portion. HDMI Founders, March 2010.

[6] Ibm introduces world's highest-resolution computer monitor. Press Release, June 2001. http://www-03.ibm.com/press/us/en/pressrelease/1180.wss.

[7] B. Jeong, L. Renambot, R. Jagodic, R. Singh, J. Aguilera, A. Johnson, and J. Leigh. High-performance dynamic graphics streaming for scalable adaptive graphics environment. *ACMIEEE SC 2006 Conference SC06*, (November):24–24, 2006.

[8] Mitsubishi electric diamond vision is dallas cowboys' choice for new stadium. Press Release, April 2008. http://www.businesswire.com/news/home/20080416005327/er

[9] R. L. Myers. *Display Interfaces: Fundamentals and Standards*. Series in Display Technology. Wiley, 2002.

[10] Nirnimesh, P. Harish, and P. Narayanan. Garuda: A scalable tiled display wall using commodity pcs. *Visualization and Computer Graphics, IEEE Transactions on*, 13(5):864 –877, 2007.

[11] Nvidia tegra 2 specifications. website. http://www.nvidia.com/object/tegra-2.html.

[12] K. Ocheltree, S. Millman, D. Hobbs, M. McDonnell, J. Nieh, and R. Baratto. Net2display: A proposed vesa standard for remoting displays and i/o devices over networks. In *Proceedings of the 2006 Americas Display Engineering and Applications Conference*, Atlanta, GA, October 2006. ADEAC.

[13] T. Richardson, Q. Stafford-Fraser, K. R. Wood, and A. Hopper. Virtual network computing. *IEEE Internet Computing*, 2(1):33–38, 1998.

[14] R. W. Scheifler and J. Gettys. The x window system. *ACM Trans Graph*, 5(2):79–109, 1986.

[15] Vesa displayport: Version 1.1. Video Electronics Standards Association, April 2007.

[16] Vesa net2display remoting standard: Version 1. Video Electronics Standards Association, October 2009.

Systems Support for Stereoscopic Video Compression

Wu-chi Feng, Feng Liu, Yuzhen Niu, Scott Price

{wuchi, fliu, yuzhen}@cs.pdx.edu

Intel Systems and Networking Lab, Portland State University

Portland, Oregon, USA

ABSTRACT

In this paper, we propose a content-based, threaded stereoscopic video compression algorithm. We believe that it is likely future stereoscopic imaging systems will contain more than two lenses, allowing the display system to optimize the stereoscopic viewing experience. Furthermore, it will allow for the adjustment of framing (scene) composition errors that can arise from stereoscopic capture. Our proposed system uses 10 linearly aligned lenses. Upon capture, the images are run through a feature detection and matching algorithm in order to determine disparity between the stereoscopic images. During compression, the disparity measurements can be used to drive the selection of key frames within the image sets to provide better retrieval of data for display.

Categories and Subject Descriptors

H.3.4 [**Information Storage and Retrieval**]: Systems and Software

General Terms

Algorithms, Design, Experimentation

Keywords

Stereoscopic imaging, stereoscopic video compression.

1. INTRODUCTION

A recent trend in imaging and display devices has focused on stereoscopic video. For example, Blu-ray players, coupled with 3D display technology can give the user a more life-like image with depth. In typical stereoscopic 3D imaging, two images are taken at the same time. Then, using polarized, shuttered, or red-cyan filtered glasses, users are able to sense depth in the images. Movies such as Avatar are now available on Blu-ray devices that support shuttered glasses which alternate left and right images on a single screen. While it might seem that the problem of capture and display of stereoscopic images and video are essentially solved, this is far from the truth. As noted in a recent article, there are problems with such stereoscopic devices [14]. Professor Banks at UC Berkeley has pointed out that viewers can suffer "3D fatigue" from improperly produced sequences. Furthermore, most 3D viewing systems come with warnings that viewers may experience discomfort such as eye strain, eye fatigue, dizziness,

or nausea. The primary cause of such problems is the mapping of stereoscopic images on the display that can require the user's visual system to either cross or diverge for extended periods of time while trying to cope with the disparity between the images being displayed for the right and left eyes. For movies like Avatar, the filmmaker paid particular attention to reducing eye fatigue by drawing viewer focus on just one object at a time, with controlled depth of field.

The primary issues with stereoscopic imaging are the need to carefully capture the scene appropriately as well as managing the dependence of the viewing experience on the viewing scenario. By scenario, we mean the viewing distance (the distance between the user and display) and the screen size. Stereoscopic content intended for one viewing scenario may not be appropriate for another. The transformation of the stereoscopic content for the viewing scenario is limited by the fact that a common two-lens stereoscopic camera only provides images from two viewpoints. We envision that future stereoscopic cameras may be made of many linearly aligned lenses to provide a denser sampling of the viewpoints. With the knowledge of the display size and the viewing distance from the screen, the system can then render a stereoscopic image from a subset of the images taken to maximize viewing experience. This requires an underlying system to manage both the capture, compression, and display of stereoscopic imaging with multiple lenses.

In this paper, we propose a content-based, threaded stereoscopic compression algorithm for multiple-lens stereoscopic video. Optimizing the delivery of stereoscopic imaging to a display will require that the system to display the appropriate images from each stereoscopic image set (the linear set of images taken at the same time). Our proposed technique takes into account the *disparity* (horizontal difference of key objects) in the selection of the image frame type used in compression. Thus, we expect our system to be able to more quickly support viewing scenario optimization for stereoscopic images.

In the next section, we will briefly review some of the related and background work. This will include further motivation for stereoscopic video versus 3D and multiview video. Section 3 describes our proposed compression approach. Section 4 provides some experimental results for our proposed approach. Finally, we conclude with some discussion and directions for future research.

2. RELATED WORK

2.1 Stereoscopic Imaging

Stereopsis is the process in visual perception that leads to the perception of depth. Each eye can be thought of as an individual point of view. The brain perceives depth by processing the discrepancy between these views, which is known as retinal disparity. Objects that are far away have a small retinal disparity. As objects are brought closer, we perceive them as being closer because the disparity has increased. What this means is that our perceived depth is inversely proportional to the retinal disparity. The goal of stereoscopic imaging is to recreate depth perception in the brain.

To recreate depth perception, stereoscopic systems try to display the appropriate retinal disparity for the object being viewed. This is accomplished with two images of the same object that each represent the left and right eye point of view. The two images need to be delivered to the eyes separately. This is accomplished by using either red-cyan glasses, polarized light with different polarization for each eye, or shuttered glasses that quickly alternate covering each eye and changing the on screen image.

In a simple model of stereoscopic display, the retinal disparity depends on the interocular distance, the distance between the viewer and the screen and the on-screen disparity between two displayed images. The interocular distance is constant, roughly 2.5" for an adult. The on-screen disparity linearly depends on the raw disparity between two stereoscopic images and the screen size. A stereoscopic image pair designed for a certain viewing scenario (a certain viewing distance and screen size) may not be appropriate for another viewing scenario. The only adjustable parameter with a fixed user distance and display size is the raw disparity in the stereoscopic content. Assuming a fixed viewing distance, as the size of the screen increases, the retinal disparity will usually increase. In order to maintain the same perceived depth, the raw disparity will need to be decreased to maintain the on-screen disparity, thus, maintaining the retinal disparity. Similarly, assuming a fixed screen size, as the distance of the user from the screen increases, the retinal disparity will decrease. In order to maintain the same perceived depth, the raw disparity will need to be adjusted to compensate. The dependence of the retinal disparity on these factors is complicated. Readers interested in a more detailed description are referred to [1].

Unlike 2D content, stereoscopic images need to be adapted to different viewing scenarios for the proper experience [10]. Wang and Sawchuk developed a disparity manipulation system that combines image warping and data-filling techniques for novel view synthesis according to the new disparity map [15]. Lang et al. further discussed the important perceptual aspects of stereo vision and their implications for stereoscopic content creation, and then provided a set of basic disparity mapping operators to enable disparity map editing [6].

2.2 Multi-camera and 3D Video

The use of multiple cameras has been the subject of research for the last several years. Minimal overlap multi-camera systems have been used for tracking and management in surveillance and traffic monitoring systems. While some inter-camera overlap sometimes occurs, the focus of such systems typically are on the coordination amongst multiple cameras and not necessarily efficient compression (due to dissimilarity of content).

In the multimedia computing and networking community, multi-camera image systems have been used to create better immersion systems. Most notably, efforts from UNC's immersive tele-conferencing system [5] and UIUC's TEEVEE project [16] use multiple cameras pointed towards a small number of object. The purpose of these projects is to capture depth from multiple cameras in order to create 3D geometries of the objects being captured. This allows the remote participant to freely move around the objects being captured. The display in these systems is planar (i.e., displayed to a normal screen). Capturing 3D depths and texture can, in theory enable stereoscopic display. We focus, however, on systems primarily meant for stereoscopic display.

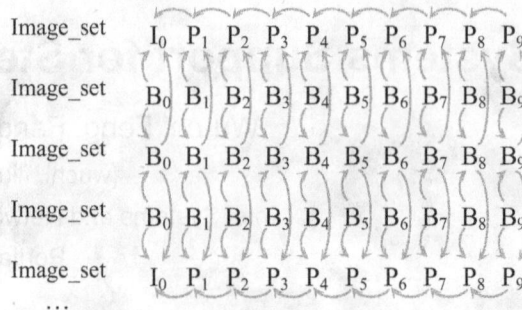

Figure 1 – Typical MVC coding example – This figure shows an example compression of multiview images that is typical in the literature. The image sets (horizontal rows) are images that are taken at the same time.

For our work, we are interested in stereoscopic capture and compression. For clarity, we refer to all the images taken at the same time as an image set. Thus, a stereoscopic video in our approach consists of a sequence of stereoscopic image sets. The goal, then, is to compress the image sets such that we (i) achieve good compression ratios, (ii) achieve good image quality, (iii), and provide a way for efficient retrieval of a small subset of each image set for view optimized display.

2.3 Multi-view Video Coding

Several efforts have focused on compression to take advantage of redundancy in multiple camera/video systems. Perhaps the closest work to ours is the recent introduction of 3D stereoscopic Blu-Ray players with content such as Avatar [7]. The underlying standard used for this type of video is the H.264/MPEG-4 AVC standard with amendment for multi-view video coding (MVC) [3]. There are two important points here with respect to our work. First, standards specify the format for a properly formatted stream, not how to get there. Thus, algorithms are still needed to compress the image data into a stream that is useful for the application. Second, current implementations (i.e., 2 channels) use as much compression between frames temporally and between channels as possible. The reason for this is that the entire stream is decompressed when played back so partial access to data is not required. Our proposed approach is expected to display only two substreams from the stored stream for display. Thus, being able to extract partial streams for streaming across a network will be an important part of our envisioned end system. Further details of H.264/MPEG4 AVC and MVC can be found in [9][13].

As an example, a typical compression model found in MVC compression papers typically have a compression structure similar to that found in Figure 1 and in [11]. In this figure, we see that the typical MVC compression approach is to maximize compression. Image_set$_0$ and Image_set$_4$ are key frames (i.e. I-frames of traditional MPEG-1 or MPEG-2 video streams). All other frames within the image sets are differentially coded. Image_set$_2$ is bi-directionally coded with respect to key framesets 0 and 4. Furthermore, image sets 1 and 3 use hierarchical B-frames, encoding with respect to a key-frame or the B frame in image_set$_2$. The key issue with applying such structures for stereoscopic video and display is that *we only need a subset of frames from each image set at a given time for display*. Thus, overly compressing the data, as in Figure 1, will lead to both needing to retrieve a lot of data in order to decompress as well as longer latency while decompressing dependent frame sequences.

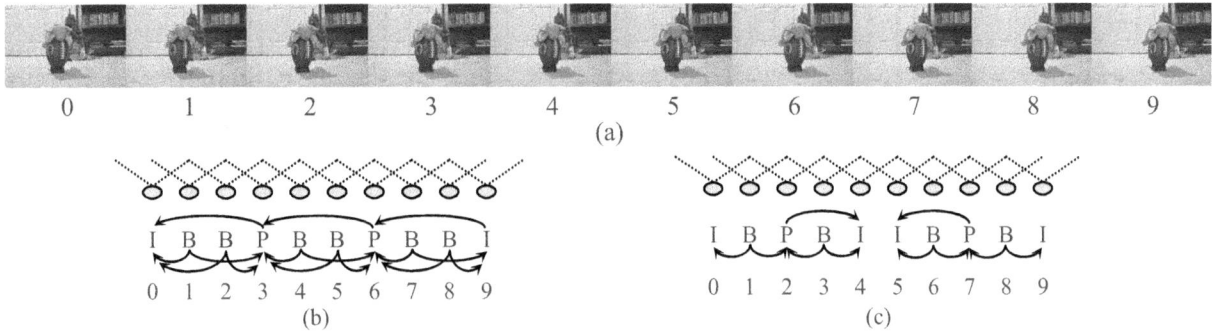

Figure 2 - Stereoscopic Imaging: (a) shows a sequence of images taken with "lens" spacing of 0.5 inches, similar to what we envision for stereoscopic cameras of the future. (b) shows an example encoding of the images using a standard mapping of the frames into an MPEG video sequence. Frame numbers are written below the frame type. (c) shows another possible encoding where the sequence for frames 0 to 4 are reversed.

Multiple camera compression has also been proposed for other scenarios. This has been applied to scenarios such a correlated compression in wireless video sensor networks [17]. Such compression has focused on using geometric relations between cameras to enhance the compression process. We believe such works are orthogonal to ours.

3. PROPOSED APPROACH

We envision a future where stereoscopic imaging will consist of an array of lens that captures an array of images. Then, depending upon the viewing distance from the screen and screen size, the display system will select or create two images from the array of images that will deliver a pleasant user experience.

3.1 A Stereoscopic Array Model

Our "standard" stereoscopic camera is an array of 10 image lenses, each 0.5" apart. Given that the standard stereoscopic camera will have the lens 2.5" apart, this configuration will give us, for each eye, two additional images to the left and two additional to the right. In Figure 2(a), we have shown a set of images representing a "multi-lens" stereoscopic array. Note, a standard stereoscopic image set taken with spacing 2.5" would correspond to the images numbered 2 and 7.

3.2 Compression for Stereoscopic Image Sets

We first start with the compression of single image sets and then extend it to video. In Figure 2(b), the arrows above and below the rows of I's, P's, and B's show example frame dependencies applying straightforward MPEG-like compression to the image set images. Thus, accessing frame number 2 requires us to decompress at least three frames: Frame 0, Frame 3, and then Frame 2. To decompress frame 7, or the right image, Frame 0, 3, 6, 9, and then 7 need to be decompressed. As an alternative, one could use the video compression algorithms in a more useful order. For example, as shown in Figure 2(c), we have broken the set of images into two sequences: (i) one that starts at frame 5 and runs through frame 9, and (ii) one that starts at frame 4 and runs through frame 0. Encoding the images in this order allows for better access. Here, in order to decompress the left frame (frame 2), frame 4 needs to be decompressed, followed by frame 2. Similarly, in order to decompress the right frame, frame 5 needs to be decompressed, followed by frame 7. The main question is which frames in each image set are the most important for display.

3.3 Content-based Key-Frame Selection

We believe that it will be important in the representation of our stereoscopic image sets that the compression algorithm takes into account some of the information within the stream in order to maximize the efficiency in retrieval. This can be either picking the most common use case scenario expected for display or some other metric. To do so requires a method to select features that are important within the left and right images, matching them up, and calculating the amount of disparity (horizontal distance) between the corresponding points. This includes both positive and negative disparity.

Among many local feature descriptors, SIFT [8] is reported to perform best by recent work [12]. We use SIFT points as features for our stereoscopic image sets. The best candidate match for each SIFT point in one image is found by identifying its nearest neighbor in the other image. As suggested by the authors, a criterion of a good SIFT match can be the ratio between the distance of the closest neighbor to that of the second closest neighbor. Since there are normally a large number of SIFT points in each frame, it is time consuming to search for the closest neighbor globally. Because images within an image set are taken at the same time the images normally will be very similar. Thus, local searching is both more efficient and accurate. We currently use a tile based method. The image is divided into uniform tiles, and the SIFT points are binned to each tile. When searching for matching SIFT points, only the points in the corresponding tile are compared. Once we find the candidate matching pairs, we eliminate the outliers using the epipolar geometry constraint of two stereo images [2].

For our approach, we pair up the left and right eye images. Thus, frame 0 is paired with frame 9 in an image set, frame 1 is paired with frame 8, and so on. We then calculate the average horizontal disparity for the set of images. One pair is chosen as the best pair for the image set and we use these for the key-frames, presumably helping to reduce the access to the image pair most likely to be used. Unfortunately, the actual choice is still an open research question, although typically 3-8% disparity is considered to be appropriate working ranges [4].

3.4 Extensions to Support Stereo Video

In order to compress multi-lens stereoscopic video data, we propose to create *stereoscopic image threads*. Each image set of data has at least one or two main frames with which to start

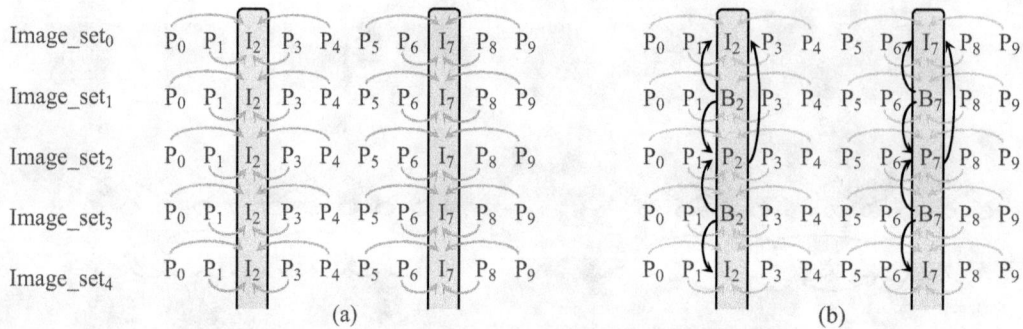

Figure 3 - Stereoscopic Threaded Compression: (a) shows a sequence of 5 stereoscopic images, applying just the image compression described in Task 1.2. (b) shows an example of threaded encoding. Here, frames 2 and 7 are anchor frames throughout. The frames in the thread are then first coded as a video sequence. Dependent frames within an image set are then determined after decompressing the anchor frames.

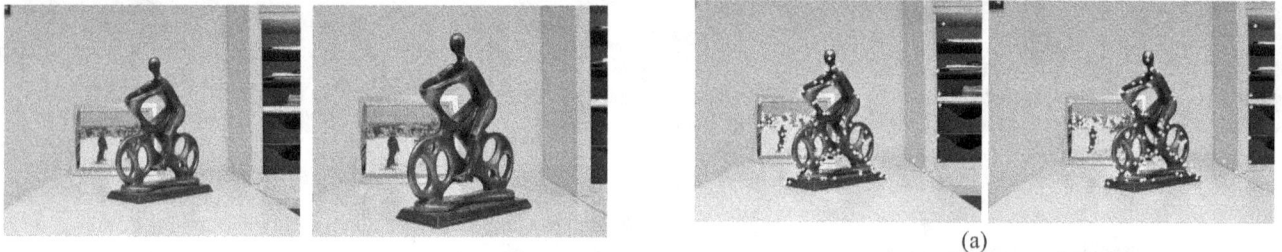

Figure 4 – Experimental Video: The left figure above shows the first image in our 6 image set stereoscopic video, while the right image shows the last frame in the video.

(a)

(b)

Figure 5 – Disparity Map Calculation: (a) shows the SIFT feature-point detection algorithm output for the left and right images for 2 and 7 from image set 0. (b) shows the disparity in the feature-point correspondence with each line showing the distance between corresponding points.

compression and decompression; we refer to these as *anchor* frames. Our approach is to create a thread that runs through all of the anchor frames and perform traditional video compression on these frames. Figure 3(a) shows an example where the image sets are independent and no inter-image set compression is employed. This is analogous to Motion-JPEG where no inter-frame compression is used. Figure 3(b) shows the threaded version. We treat each thread as a sequence of video which is first compressed separately. All dependent frames within a particular image set can then be decoded after the anchor frame has been decompressed. Thus, to decompress P_3 and P_6 of *image_set_2*, we need to (i) decompress I_2 and I_7 of *image_set_0*, (ii) decompress P_2 and P_7 of *image_set_2*, and (iii) decompress P_3 and P_6 of *image_set_2*.

It is important to note that the thread is not required to be fixed to a particular image number within each image set. If the anchor frame for a particular image set moves, we simply follow the appropriate sequence. As previously mentioned, our goal is somewhat different than what has been proposed for the MVC format used in the H.264/MPEG-4 AVC amendment. We are focused on compressing the stream to support efficient compression and retrieval for view scenario optimization.

4. EXPERIMENTATION

4.1 Experimental Setup

In order to study stereoscopic video compression, we required a sequence of many-image stereoscopic images. Because no such camera exists today, we created a 6-frame sequence using stop-gap animation. For this particular paper, we have a bike sculpture on a table and slowly zoom in on it. This was accomplished by moving the camera in 2 inch increments towards the bike

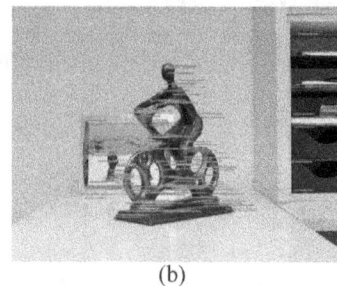

sculpture. Our model for the stereoscopic camera is 10 lenses spaced one half inch apart in a linear array. We captured the images using a Nikon D90 DSLR and a slide rail set-up. Since the individual images were not captured with a set of fixed lenses (relative to each other), there were some minor unwanted variations such as rotation, which we attempted to fix manually. The first and last images of the sequence are shown in Figure 4.

4.2 Disparity Calculation

The first set of experiments show the efficacy of using SIFT and feature point matching. Because feature point detection can be expensive, we first took the stereoscopic data we had and created multiple versions of the dataset. The full size image is 3072 x 2304. This represents a slightly cropped image from the original. We had a ruler at the bottom of the frame in order to help with alignment and accuracy. From this, we created four additional sequences of size 1536x1152, 768x576, 384x288, and 192x144.

In Figure 5(a), we have shown an example of the disparity map calculation using the SIFT algorithm for the 768x576 images.

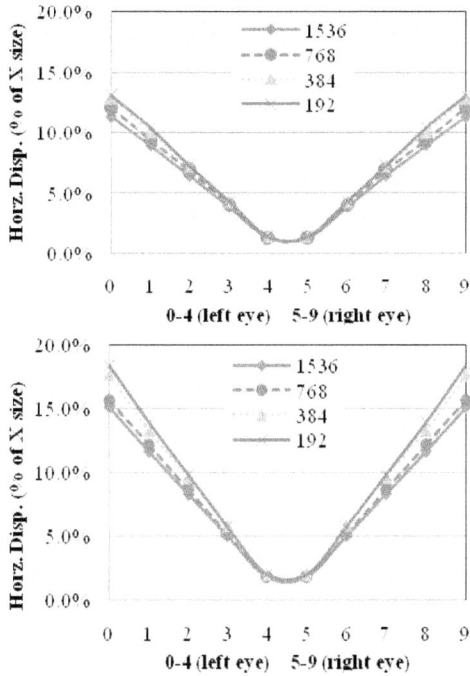

Figure 6 – Disparity: The top figure shows the average horizontal disparity for the first image set of the sequence by position (Note, the left and right eyes are paired, hence, the symmetry). The bottom figure show the average for the last image set in the sequence.

Running the feature point detection algorithm resulted in 500 and 531 keypoints for the left and right images, respectively. After correspondence matching, 235 points were matched. Figure 5(b) shows the actual disparity between the points from Figure 5(a).

In order to understand the efficacy of using feature-points in compression, we were interested in both the time and accuracy of calculation using the different sized images. Figure 6 (a) shows the average horizontal disparity calculation for the first image of the sequence, while Figure 6(b) shows the last. The x-axis denotes each of the frames within the image set. Thus, images 0-4 represent the left eye images and 5-9 represent the right eye images. Note, the images are paired (0, 9), (1, 8), (2, 7), and so on, resulting in figures that are symmetric between the left and right eye. Because the video slowly zooms in on the object, an increase in average disparity is expected (difference between (a) and (b)). While the optimal disparity requirement for a display scenario is still the focus of much research, for the images we captured selecting images 2-7 for the first image and moving towards 3-6 for the last would probably work for a desktop scenario. Thus, key frame selection would tend to start at frames 2-7 and switch over to 3-6 towards the end of the sequence. For a larger room with the viewer further away from the screen, increasing the interocular distance would be required.

In Table 1, we have listed the execution time and feature-points detected for the various resolution images we have. As shown in the table, using a smaller 768x576 image versus the 1536x1152 achieved nearly similar disparity calculations but also runs in one quarter the amount of time. While our code is relatively unoptimized, it shows the relative difference in execution speed. Furthermore, depending upon the accuracy required, the 192x144 sized images can be run at several frames per second while

	Execution Time (sec)	No. Feature Points
1536x1152	11.47	637.0
768x576	2.99	275.7
384x288	0.82	128.6
192x144	0.32	58.5

Table 1: Execution and Feature Point Experimentation – This table shows for the various image sizes, the execution time for the SIFT and feature-point correspondence routine and the average number of feature points used in the horizontal disparity calculation.

capturing the essence of the disparity using a smaller number of points. Getting back to Figure 6, we see that the main difference in the disparity calculation is the selection of the feature points. Having the focal object with more feature points will cause the disparity calculations to be more in agreement across the various size images.

4.3 Stereoscopic Compression

In this section, we present some preliminary results for compression of the stereoscopic image sets. Because artifacts in stereoscopic images may cause problems with viewing we concentrate on higher quality compression. Here, we consider the compression of three types of compression patterns:

IP1: P_0 P_1 I_2 P_3 P_4 P_5 P_6 I_7 P_8 P_9

IP2: P_0 P_1 I_2 P_3 P_4 P_5 P_6 I_7 P_8 P_9

IP3: P_0 P_1 I_2 P_3 P_4 P_5 P_6 P_7 P_8 P_9

For IP1, the left and right eyes are coded separately with a maximum decompression frame reference dependency of 1. That is, with the exception of frames 2 and 7, all frames first require an I-frame for decompression. In IP2, we create small chains in the left and right eye sides with a maximum reference frame dependency of 2. Finally, IP3 extends the compression across the right and left eye. Here, the maximum frame dependency is 3 for frames 5, 6, 8, and 9. We report the results for the first frame in our stereoscopic image sequence. The other frames have similar results. Each sequence was compressed with a fixed quantization value of 8 for all frame types.

As shown in Figure 7, the first point to examine are the differences between IP1 and IP2. We see that frames 0, 4, 5, and 9 are larger in IP1 due to larger distance between the frame and the key frame (in 2 and 7). The other frames are all the same size and quality. The difference, on average is approximately 6.2%. For IP2 and IP3, we that while achieving similar quality, the additional dependency for frame 7 to 2, improves compression by approximately 10% but adds an additional frame of latency to decompress.

5. DISCUSSION AND FUTURE WORK

There are a number of issues that have arisen as a result of our initial work into stereoscopic video compression. First, our focus is on supporting stereoscopic image capture and display.

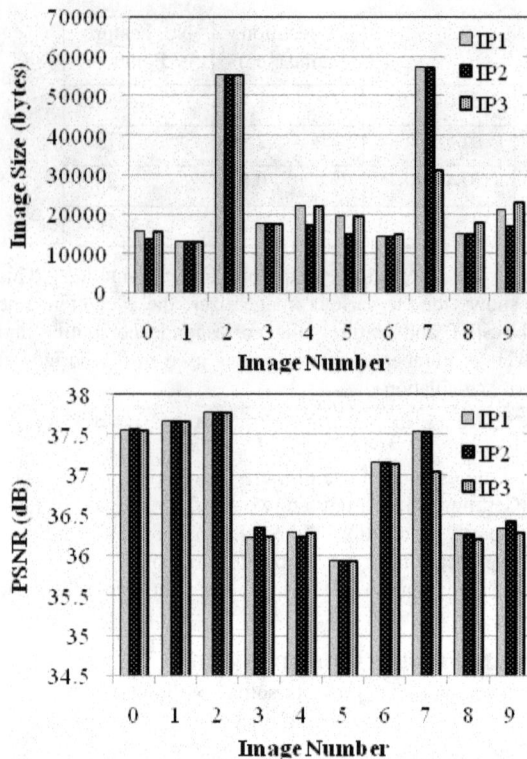

Figure 7 – Compression: The top figure shows the individual compressed image sizes for image set 0. The bottom figure shows the corresponding PSNR of each image.

Currently, professional producers have to be extremely careful with the entire environment (e.g., frame edges, depth of field, etc) when dealing with stereoscopic recording. We believe that having a multiple lens system will allow even professionals to correct environmental objects that may have been overlooked. Unfortunately, we are limited to still scenes due to the fact we are emulating a linear array of images with a single camera. Furthermore, it will be useful to determine what type of stereoscopic multi-lens video sequences might prove to be useful in testing algorithms such as the one we have proposed.

Second, we have chosen to use an average horizontal disparity measure to help guide key-frame selection. The viewing experience will typically be weighted more towards the object that they eyes need to be drawn to in the stereoscopic image. Thus, it may be useful to weight the disparity in the foreground and background differentially. Thus, segmentation algorithms may be useful in providing differential weight to foreground and background disparity. In addition, there is a potential to exceed a maximum disparity measure (e.g., a very small object with large disparity that gets washed out in the average).

For future work, we are considering the impact that frame pattern types have on compression performance, resulting image quality, and retrieval times. For our experiments, we have used a relatively small quantization value of 8. We are exploring the impact of that quantization value has on these metrics as well.

6. CONCLUSION

In this paper, we have proposed a content-based, threaded stereoscopic compression algorithm. The proposed approach leverages feature-point algorithms to help determine the placement of key-frames within image sets with the goal of creating compressed stereoscopic video that can be more easily optimized for a particular viewing scenario.

7. REFERENCES

[1] M. Guttmann, L. Wolf, D. Cohen-Or, "Semiautomatic Stereo Extraction from Video Footage", in *Proc. of the IEEE Inter. Conf. on Computer Vision*, pages 136 – 142, 2009.

[2] R. I. Hartley and A. Zisserman. *Multiple View Geometry in Computer Vision*. Cambridge University Press, 2000

[3] Y. He, J. Ostermann, M. Tanimoto, A. Smolic, "Introduction to the Special Section on Multiview Video Coding", in *IEEE Transactions on Circuits and Systems for Video Technology*, Vol. 17, No. 11, pp. 1433-S5, Nov. 2007.

[4] http://apophysisrevealed.com/apo3dblog/2009/07/192

[5] San-Uok Kum, K. Mayer-Patel, H. Fuchs, "Real-Time Compression for Dynamic 3D Environments", in *Proceedings of ACM Multimedia*, 2003.

[6] M. Lang, A. Hornung, O.Wang, S. Poulakos, A. Smolic, M. Gross, "Nonlinear Disparity Mapping for Stereoscopic 3D", *ACM Transaction on. Graphics*, 29(4), 2010.

[7] R. Lawler, "Blue-ray 3D Specifications Finalized, Your PS3 is Ready", Dec. 17, 2009, From: http://www.engadget.com/2009/12/17/blu-ray-3d-specifications-finalized-your-ps3-is-ready/

[8] D. Lowe, "Distinctive Image Features from Scale-Invariant Keypoints", *International Journal of Computer Vision*, Vol. 60, No. 2, pp 91-110, 2004.

[9] D. Marpe, T. Wiegand, G.J. Sullivan, "The H.264/MPEG4 Advanced Video Coding Standard and its Applications", *IEEE Communications*, pp. 134-143, August 2006.

[10] B. Mendiburu, 3D Movie Making: Stereoscopic Digital Cinema from Script to Screen, Focal Press, 2009.

[11] P. Merkle, A. Smolicc, K. Muller, T. Wiegand, "Efficient Prediction Structures for Multi-view Video Coding", *IEEE Transactions on Circuits and Systems for Video Technology*, Vol. 17, No. 11, November, 2007.

[12] K. Mikolajczyk, C. Schmid, "A Performance Evaluation of Local Descriptors", *IEEE Trans. on Pattern Analysis and Machine Intelligence*, Vol. 27, No. 10, pp. 1615-1630, 2005.

[13] MPEG: "Introduction to Multiview Video Coding", ISO/IEC JTC 1/SC 29/WG 11 N9580, Edited by A. Smolic, Jan. 2008.

[14] D. Sanchez, "Are 3D Movies, TV Bad For Your Eyes?", February 24, 2010, Retrieved from KGO News: http://abclocal.go.com/kgo/story?id=7278834

[15] C. Wang, A. A. Sawchuk, "Disparity Manipulation for Stereo Images and Video, in *Proc. SPIE*, Vol. 6803, pages E1– E12, 2008.

[16] Z. Yang, Y. Cui, B. Yu, J. Liang, K. Nahrstedt, S. H. Jung, R. Bajcsy, "TEEVE: The Next Generation Architecture for Tele-Immersive Environments", in *7th IEEE International Symp. on Multimedia (ISM'05)*, Irvine, CA, 2005

[17] C. Yeo, K. Ramchandran, "Robust Distributed Multiview Video Compression for Wireless Camera Networks", *IEEE Trans. on Image Proc.*, Vol. 19(4), pp. 995-1008, Apr. 2010.

Accurate and Low-Delay Seeking Within and Across Mash-Ups of Highly-Compressed Videos

Bo Gao, Jack Jansen, Pablo Cesar and Dick C. A. Bulterman
CWI: Centrum Wiskunde & Informatica
Science Park 123
1098 XG   Amsterdam, the Netherlands
{B.Gao, Jack.Jansen, P.S.Cesar, Dick.Bulterman}@cwi.nl

ABSTRACT

In typical video mash-up systems, a group of source videos are compiled off-line into a single composite object. This improves rendering performance, but limits the possibilities for dynamic composition of personalized content. This paper discusses systems and network issues for enabling client-side dynamic composition of video mash-ups. In particular, this paper describes a novel algorithm to support accurate, low-delay seamless composition of independent clips. We report on an intelligent application-steered scheme that allows system layers to prefetch and discard predicted frames before the rendering moment of indexed content. This approach unifies application-level quality-of-experience specification with system layer quality-of-service processing. To evaluate our scheme, several experiments are conducted and substantial performance improvements are observed in terms of accuracy and low delay.

Categories and Subject Descriptors

H.5.1 [**Information Systems**]: Multimedia Information Systems - *Video*; I.4.2 [**Computing Methodologies**]: Image Processing and Computer Vision - *Compression (Coding)*.

General Terms

Design, Experimentation, Algorithms, Languages.

Keywords

Dynamic video mashup, Prefetching, Low delay, Delayed binding.

1. INTRODUCTION

As networked video becomes more ubiquitous, several transformations are taking place with respect to the manner in which user-generated content is defined and managed. First, user-generated content gets created as relatively short video clips, taken by low- to medium-quality cameras (compared with professional content), often in less-than-optimal lighting, positioning or audio circumstances. Second, popular events such as concerts tend to result in many video instances of that event, taken from different angles [5]. Third, users are able to create compilation videos from these multiple sources, defining a continuous presentation: this is called a video mash-up or video remix [8][9]. We use *mash-up* to refer to a story with a consistent timeline. A *remix* may have a non-linear, looping timeline.

A video mash-up is a continuous presentation that is created from

(portions of) individual video clips. A subset of clips is selected from the total video collection for the event, the subset is temporally aligned, and relevant portions are trimmed so that a coherent story is defined. This process is sketched in Figure 1, where a video mash-up is defined that consists of three video clips. The presentation begins at the start of Video 1. At time T1 of Video 1, the playback of the video mash-up jumps to time T2 of Video 2 and then continues its rendering until time T3 of Video 2. Next, it jumps to time T4 of Video 3. This process may continue over a large collection of clips. During the presentation, the video may be accompanied by a single audio track of the event, or each video clip may retain its own audio content.

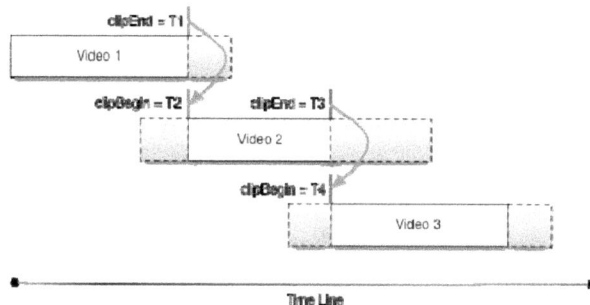

Figure 1. Cascading seeks in seamless video mash-ups.

In order to maintain a sense of continuity between clips, it is important that there is minimal presentation delay when switching between clips. Our work has indicated that this delay is bounded by no more than a delay of two frames of high-definition video (approaching 40ms). This is verified by other work on creating mash-ups [9]. When using video with a lower frame rate, a bound of one frame is typically required.

One way of ensuring that this constraint is met is to create the video mash-up by merging all of the source video clips into a single video object [9]. (This process may occur automatically or manually). The use of a single video object has advantages for content delivery: a single stream can be opened to transfer the video. Unfortunately, the use of a single container has a number of disadvantages: the video content cannot easily be adapted for different user needs or platforms and the content is static, in the sense that the collection of video fragments is predefined. From a semantic perspective, all of the original meta-information contained in the source video (if any!) is lost. This limits potential post-arrival semantic personalization of video content.

An approach that yields greater possibilities for downstream customization of the video presentation is to transfer each selected source video clip via the network and to then compose the mash-up dynamically at the client. We call this a *video mash-up with delayed content binding*. The advantage of such a strategy is that successor clips can be selected based on personalized parameters, resulting in customized presentations that are responsive to both the needs of the rendering environment and the end-user(s) experiencing the content. The main disadvantage of the delayed-binding approach is that extra processing needs to be done to ensure that the 40ms intra-clip timing constraint is met. This challenge consists of two components: ensuring that the successor video clip arrives in time for seamless playback [3], and ensuring that indexing into the successor clip occurs within the 40ms playout window. One of the main problems to be overcome is efficient seeking within highly-compressed video files.

Contribution. This paper presents an accurate and low-delay approach for seeking within highly-compressed video to ensure the continuos and seamless playback of video mash-ups with delayed content binding. In particular, our scheme supports random access to an arbitrary frame of a video clip containing sparse key frames, with a delay of less than 40ms. Furthermore, our solution is general, since it supports direct integration of different compression algorithms without any pre-transcoding needed and does not require any modification to video encoding algorithms and therefore adapts to new video encoding algorithms automatically.

The scheme presented in this paper takes advantage of a prefetching mechanism for pre-loading successive video clips in a mash-up, with extended support for fetching successive frames close to the requested frame. These predicted frames are decoded and intelligently discarded, only passing the necessary frames to play out subsequently. Our approach guides video selection and indexing from the application layer, but migrates frame decoding and discarding to more-efficient lower-level processing layers. In other words, we support application-level *quality-of-experience* specification but implement actual video manipulation in terms of lower-layer *quality-of-service* processing. In this manner, both the accuracy and the low delay of seeking within video are guaranteed. In contrast, the lack of an optimized prefetching mechanism adopted in popular video players implies that they have to either render the closest key frame as the seek position - which sacrifices accuracy - or to decode and buffer many unnecessary frames, with the cost of long delays.

The remainder of this paper is organized as follows. Section 2 presents a representative mash-up scenario which defines the motivation and the requirement of a low-delay and accurate delayed content binding system. Section 3 surveys the limitations of related work. Section 4 analyzes the issues on seek to videos. After that, the design and implementation of our seek mechanism is discussed in depth in Section 5. Section 6 introduces experiments which evaluate the performance of our algorithm. Finally, Section 7 provides summary conclusions and directions for future work.

2. SCENARIO

MyVideos is a prototype personalized video presentation service being developed as part of the FP-7 project TA2 [2]. In this scenario, parents and students contribute video fragments created during a series of high school music concerts on a wide-range of recording devices. The content is (semi-)automatically annotated and placed in a distributed repository. Using a combination of automatic and manual approaches, custom videos are generated and shared within the social networks of the community.

The traditional solutions to supporting MyVideos functionality is to compile instances of the video mash-up into separate video files, which are then stored in the repository. This approach is space inefficient; it destroys existing metadata and forestalls easy reuse of content. It also makes it difficult for the system to enforce post-collection adaptive privacy monitoring of content. In MyVideos, the delayed-binding mash-up model described in Section 1 is used. In this approach, users define content preference parameters, and videos are dynamically composed on demand.

While MyVideos investigates a number of issues related to the collection, annotation, selection, augmentation of enhancement of video mash-ups, the work reported in this paper will be restricted to considering two key requirements of MyVideos encountered within the network substrate and at the rendering engine:

- The definition of a mechanism to combine multiple source video clips (possible from different physical servers), and to direct their playback based on an end-user's narrative intention, without compromising their content.
- The definition of accurate sub-object rendering based on low-delay seeking within the successor video clips to satisfy the seamless transition among video clips.

The first requirement allows an external narrative engine (either formal or informal) to select a series of candidate clips from the distributed library of media objects. The narrative processing is outside the scope of this paper, but its presence implies that traditional one-size-fits-all mash-up generation is insufficient. The second requirement motivates the algorithm and implementation described in this paper. For a better user experience, in which the final video presentation plays as a continuous object, accurate composition and fast seeking within video content is essential.

3. RELATED WORK

As considered briefly in Section 1, the traditional method of supporting high-performance video mash-ups is to precompile a (new) video object as a derivative work of a series of source videos. In this section, we review other approaches for presenting a series of multiple videos and for seeking within a video once it is activated.

3.1 Playlist Playback

Perhaps the most obvious model for support sequenced video playback is the use of a video playlist. Video playlist playback is supported natively in most commercial and open-source media players, including *iTunes*, *Windows Media Player*, *RealPlayer*, and *VLC*. In all these players, playlists are stored as simple text files or XML documents which list in sequence the locations of the media clips. Most commercial systems make use of a simplified dialect of the W3C SMIL format, discussed below.

The advantage of the playlist structure is that it allows a collection of video objects to be defined and rendered on demand. The list may be compiled dynamically or statically. Potentially, the playlist could be used as a model for seamless playback -- that is, the playout of videos without any noticeable gap between objects. In reality, an initial study of ours indicated that, without exception, this was not supported. For all media players, obvious playback interruptions between the clips were observed lasting from hundreds milliseconds to seconds [3]. This far exceeds the 40ms inter-video requirement identified by ourselves and others.

As a side note, seamless (and even overlapping) audio playout is often supported in commercial media players, allowing a host of musical/audio transitions to take place between songs. One reason that we suspect that video cross-fades do not occur is the relative semantic and visual independence of video objects. This semantic and visual independence does not exist in delayed binding mash-ups, however: here, having visual coherence across clips is of fundamental importance.

3.2 Native SMIL Support for Prefetch

SMIL, the Synchronous Multimedia Integration Language is the W3C standard for integrating a set of independent multimedia objects into a synchronized multimedia presentation [1]. It contains *references* to media items, not media data itself, and instructions on how those media items should be combined spatially and temporally.

In SMIL documents and SMIL-compliant players, playlist operations are supported natively by the <seq> temporal composition operator, which defines a sequence of elements in which elements play one after the other. The SMIL language provides support for generic seamless playback specification via the <prefetch> element, which gives authors a mechanism to download media object before play out time. The following fragment illustrates the use of <seq> and <prefetch> to implement the flow in Figure 1:

```
<seq>
  <par>
    <video src="http://example.com/video1.mp4"
        clipEnd="9.25s"/>
    <prefetch src="http://example.com/video2.mp4"
        clipBegin="4.68s" clipEnd="476.28s"/>
  </par>
  <video src="http://example.com/video2.mp4"
      clipBegin="4.68s" clipEnd="476.28s"/>
  ...
</seq>
```

In this example, *video1* is specified as a playable object. While *video1* is playing, the player is instructed to (optionally) begin fetching *video2*. The seeked video *video2* is then ready for seamless rendering at the clipped end of *video1*. This simple example hides significant implementation problems that have to do with managing system resources and interleaving the arrival of multiple objects, especially when *clipBegin/clipEnd* is used. This is one reason that prefetch is not often supported in SMIL players.

For purposes of this paper, we focus on one particular aspect of prefetch processing. Recall from Figure 1 that it is often the case the successor video fragments do not start at the beginning of the video encoding. Prefetching alone loses its effectiveness when video clips are highly compressed. Consider an object encoded using H.264 with sparse I-frame frequency. To increase the compression ratio of video, modern codecs use the spatial redundant information among successive frames to code the frames of video. This results in the transmission of some key frames that contain the full information, and many other frames that encode the difference from their adjacent frames. The incompleteness of most frames causes a problem on random access operations. Given an arbitrary time instant, there is a high possibility that the corresponding frame is a predicted frame. In order to decode this predicted frame, the frame to which it refers has to be known in advance. Moreover, this reference frame may need to refer to its own reference frame. This process will be recursive until a full key frame is encountered.

Assuming that we want to access a frame at a specific time instant, there are two possible implementations of a low-level seek operation. One is that the timestamp of the returned frame is exactly equal to the value specified by ignoring any reference frames. However, with high possibility, visual artifacts of video will be visible for some time, until the next key frame. The other is that the closest previous key frame is returned. In this case, the artifact problem disappears at the expense of frame accuracy.

3.3 Seeking Within Compressed Videos

In order to evaluate the general seeking performance of industrial-strength media players, we tested both standalone applications and embedded plugins for the browser, including *QuickTime Player, VLC*, and the *Flash* browser plugin. For standalone video players, both local video playback and online streaming playback were measured. Since most players do not support the application-level specification of temporal fragments, we conducted seek operations by dragging the timeline slider manually. The minimum granularity for seek operation supported in both *QuickTime Player* and *VLC* is 2 seconds. For the *Flash plugin* for browsers, we measured the seek operation on YouTube by sliding the timeline slider manually and the same 2 second time granularity was observed. The description of the "start" API[1] from YouTube also verifies our finding.

Several techniques have been proposed to reduce the decoding delays on view seeking and improve the ability of switching between views [6]. A transcoding algorithm was presented to insert random access points in the pre-encoded scalable video streams [10]. Despite their effectiveness, the above approaches only improved the performance of seek operations for some specific coding schemas, such as, MVC and SVC, which limits their application fields and therefore cannot be adopted generally. Moreover, all of these methods require special modifications to either coding and or decoding algorithms, which violates compatibility and increases implementation complexity.

3.4 Seeking in HTTP Streaming

HTTP based streaming is becoming a defacto standard on the Internet for video streaming because of its wide availability on almost any device and its inherent immunity to NAT/firewall issues contrast to other media transport protocols like RTP/RTSP. In the context of HTTP streaming, Microsoft's Smooth Streaming and Apple's HTTP Live Streaming are two representative schemas. Apple solves the problem of seeking in streaming videos with non-deterministic GOP durations by partitioning the original video to a serial of 2-second segments. Smooth Streaming from Microsoft provides manifest files that map timestamps to byte-accurate offsets to support seeking. However, neither can provide frame-accurate seeking [4].

An adaptive encoding approach in the context of a zoomable video streaming systems was proposed to allow users to zoom and pan in a very high definition video. The authors of that paper mention features of H.264 AVC that would make (in combination with HTTP streaming) frame-accurate cutting easier [7].

4. PROBLEM ANALYSIS

Modern video coding technology usually encodes video using three kinds of frames: I-frames, P-frames and B-frames. This improves the compression ratio by leveraging the inherent redundant information contained in video itself.

In compressed video clips, frames are grouped into sequences: a *group of pictures* (GOP). A GOP is a sequence of frames that contain all the information that is needed to completely decode any frame within that GOP. GOP structure specifies the order in which I-frames, P-frames, and B-frames are arranged. A GOP always begins with an I-frame. Then several P-frames and possible B-frames will follow. The distance between two I-frames in the video sequence is defined as the length of the GOP. This scheme is shown in Figure 2.

---

[1] http://code.google.com/apis/youtube/player_parameters.html

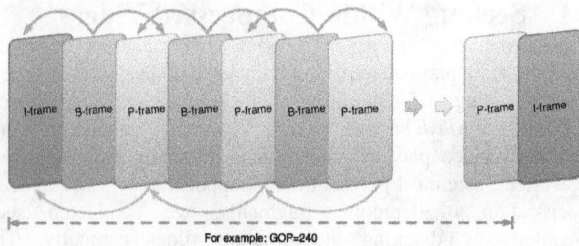

Figure 2. The structure of GOP and the dependency relation among I-frame, P-frame, and B-frame.

Based on the above discussion, reducing the frequency of I-frames, and thus extending the length of GOP, improves the compression ratio. However, seek operations ideally require an I-frame that is the only independent kind of frame due to its self-contained characteristics. If the I-frame frequency is too low, this will reduce the accuracy of the seek operation. For example, if in a 30 fps video the GOP size is 60, there will be one I-frame every two seconds. Thus, the granularity of the seek operation will be two seconds. For video playback this granularity might be tolerable, but for seamless and continuos rendering of video mash-ups this value is unacceptable. It will break the smooth transition between two adjacent videos, affecting the overall quality of the user experience.

In particular, in our use case the accuracy should not be longer than two frames, and the time delay of the seek operation should be less than forty milliseconds depending on the frame rate. Moreover, the schema of random access operation should be adaptive to the length of GOP automatically.

5. DESIGN AND IMPLEMENTATION

In this section we will introduce our accurate and low latency seek algorithm, and its reference implementation. The work reported in this paper is made available as open-source, integrated in the Ambulant Player[2]. The Ambulant Player is an open-source media playback engine that supports SMIL 3.0.

5.1 Prefetching Without Low-Level Discarding

Our initial approach was to support basic prefetching based on simple SMIL-compliant semantics. This improved the performance of the player, since the overhead of initiating a rendering object and fetching the content was eliminated. The prefetching mechanism was implemented by creating and inserting an "inactive" rendering object in the cache. This "inactive" object exists for as long as is needed. Since the object performs all the initialization actions prior to rendering time, the time spent for rendering a new video was reduced significantly.

Figure 3 details the implementation for prefetching videos in the Ambulant Player. The left side of the figure shows an example of a video mash-up composed of sequential video clips. It is described in the SMIL language. The middle part of the figure presents the basic actions executed by the player to support prefetching. Finally, the right side of the figure indicates the status of the internal cache.

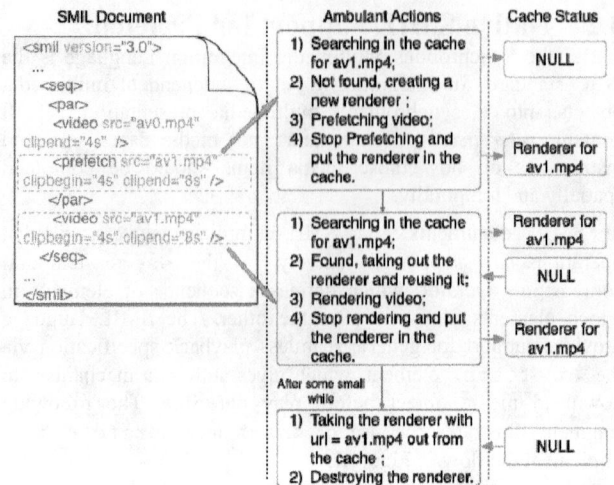

Figure 3. Prefetching mechanism in Ambulant Player.

This algorithm works well with a number of video encoding formats, but not for highly-compressed formats such as H.264. When using highly-compressed video, significant time lags - of several seconds - between adjacent video clips in the playlist were observed. The problem was caused by the seek operation. Particularly, Ambulant uses the `av_seek_frame()` function from FFmpeg [11] to retrieve the video frame corresponding to the exact time instant specified in the SMIL file. Contrary to our expectation, the timestamp values returned were *much* earlier than the requested value; we observed that it was as much as 6 seconds earlier in our examples. This means that we have to buffer and decode 180 (6x30fps) frames before the exact frame is decoded. The reason why we got these early frames is that the GOP size for these videos is around 240. Since the *seek frame* function returns the closest previous I-frame and there is only one I-frame every 8 seconds, random access becomes really random. In this specific case of a GOP size of 240, the average distance from the frame we requested will be 4 seconds (120 frames).

Given that we have to buffer and to decode the frames between the closest previous I-frame and the required P/B-frame, where should we discard these medium frames in our video processing pipeline? These frames are needed only for decoding and not for rendering. As shown in Figure 4, our baseline implementation did not check the timestamp of the frames in the prefetching phase (the area shaded in gray) and placed all frames in the buffer directly. Then, timestamp checking was done at rendering time. We must do frame discarding at the latest possible moment, to make sure the displayed video is correctly synchronized to the audio.

The late dropping procedure in Figure 4 caused the long delay before the correct frame was shown on the screen. Especially for video clips with large GOP size, the location of the frame we want typically lies in the relatively back part of the current GOP, which causes the system to be busy discarding hundreds of frames before conducting the actual frame displaying.

---

[2] http://www.ambulantplayer.org

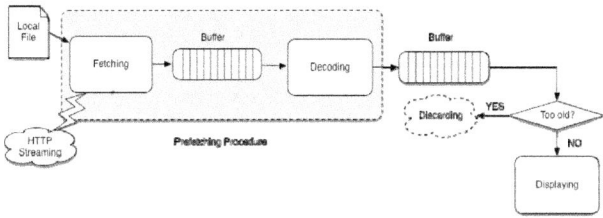

Figure 4. Prefetching without low-level discarding Ambulant.

5.2 Prefetching With Low-Level Discarding

In reality the ideal place for discarding unnecessary frames is immediately after decoding, in the prefetching stage. This is especially true if the decoding can occur directly after data arrival low in the system stack. If the discarding of the frames happens too early (before decoding), the system cannot decode P/B-frames correctly. If the frames are discarded too late (e.g., just before rendering), extra memory space is wasted and the actual rendering has to be postponed to perform the discarding operation. The ideal procedure is that we prefetch the content (fetching the I, P, B-frames in advance), decode them in sequence, and then based on the timestamp discard unnecessary frames immediately after the decoding phase. This way, only frames with a timestamp equal to or bigger than the requested time instant will be placed into the displaying buffer. More importantly, all of the above processing should happen during the prefetching stage (the area shaded in gray in Figure 5).

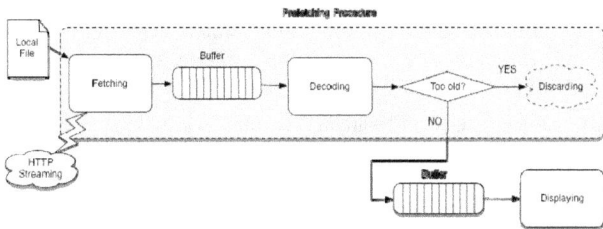

Figure 5. Prefetching with low-level discarding.

6. PERFORMANCE COMPARISON

To evaluate the algorithms, two groups of experiments were designed. Since only accurate seek operations with precision of millisecond are conducted in all experiments, we focus on the time performance of our schema. In both groups of experiments, the Ambulant Player (with and without our improved prefetching and discarding mechanism, respectively) plays a SMIL presentation that defines a video mash-up. The mash-up consists of two video clips that have been recorded by two camcorders that shot the same concert simultaneously from different angles. To ensure seamless transition between two video clips, the clipEnd value of the first video element and the clipBegin value of the second video element are assigned carefully with the intention that they should be played out as a continuous video. The time granularity of clipEnd and clipBegin is in milliseconds, which requires that the SMIL playback engine is able to perform seek to the videos with a precision of milliseconds. All experiments were carried out on a MacBook with two-core CPU and Mac OS 10.5 platform.

We measured the wall clock time interval between the showing of the last frame of the first video clip and the showing of the first frame of the second video clip to evaluate the performance. The videos in our experiments are encoded using H.264 and the frame rate of the videos is 25 fps in all the experiments. To explore the relation between time latency of seek and the GOP size, we gradually increase by 30 the size of GOP starting from 30 until

210. To test the worst performance case, the clipBegin value of the videos is carefully selected to be the timestamp of the last frame in its GOP, i.e., the 29th frame for GOP=30 or the 209th frame for GOP=210. The first group of experiments focused on the performance of seek operation to videos stored as local file. More importantly, the second group of experiments explores the effect of our design against videos over HTTP streaming. A high-speed cable connection was used to access the HTTP streaming server located in BT, UK. Both groups of experiments share a common configuration, the only exception being the source of the video clips.

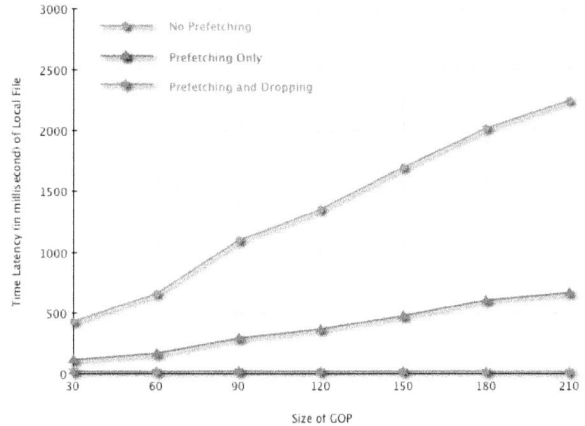

Figure 6: Time latency of seek on local file

Figure 6 shows the evolving trend of time latency for accurate seek operation against the GOP size for local files. The time latency without prefetching is significant bigger than the other two, with prefetching only and with prefetching and discarding. Moreover, both the latency of no prefetching and of prefetching only increases linearly with the growing of GOP size (for no prefetching, from 432 ms to 2249 ms, and for prefetching only, from 119 ms to 671 ms). However, the latency of seek of prefetching with discarding remains as a constant value (around 21 ms) for all GOP sizes. (Note that because of scaling issues, a detailed graph for our approach is shown in Figure 7.)

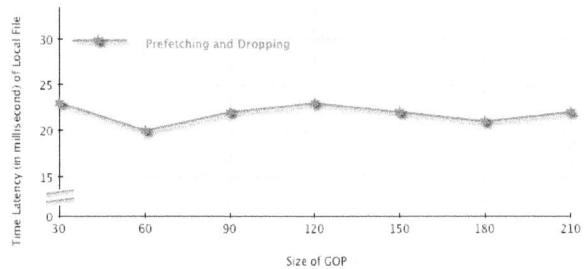

Figure 7: Time latency of seek on local file (detail).

Figure 8 depicts the time latency of random access operation for H.264 videos over HTTP streaming as a function of the GOP size. Similar results are observed with figures 6 and 7, where, our prefetching and discarding mechanism dramatically reduces the time latency compared to no prefetching and prefetching only. Furthermore, the excellent near-constant time latency feature is kept in HTTP streaming (around 25 ms). Understanding the constant feature of latency of seek operations using the prefetching and discarding mechanism is straightforward, since all discarding actions are conducted during the prefetching period, which is done before the first frame of the following video clip is scheduled to be shown on the screen.

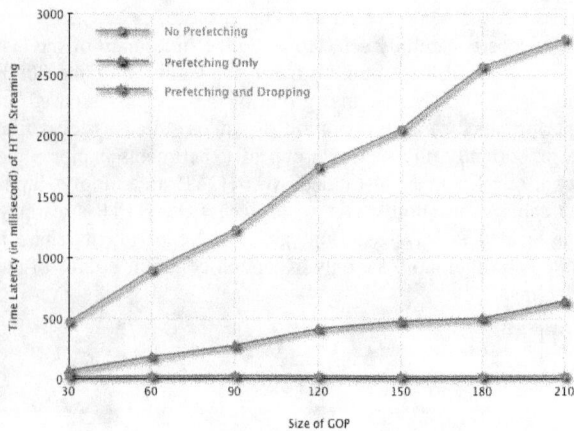

Figure 8. Time latency of seek on HTTP Streaming.

The detailed expansion for our approach is shown in Figure 9.

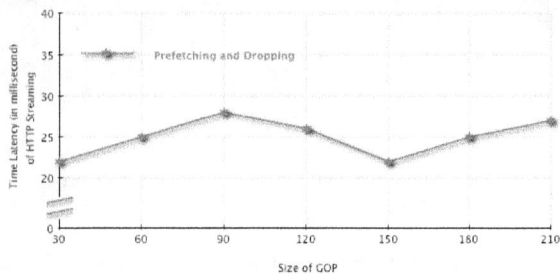

Figure 9. Time latency of seek on HTTP Streaming (detail).

Results from both experiments show that our mechanism performs well for both local files and HTTP streaming. It is worth highlighting that the good behavior of our schema over HTTP streaming has more practical significance, given the fact that online video dominates video consumption in the Web. Even slight performance variations pale when compared with the 2000ms delay in most other systems.

7. CONCLUSIONS AND FUTURE WORK

Support for efficient seeking is one of the most important features for seamless play back of delayed-binding video mash-ups. However, because of the inherent characteristics of sparse key frames included in modern codec technology, accurate seeks with low latency is inherently inefficient. In this paper, a combined prefetching and discarding mechanism is introduced to solve this problem in both terms of accuracy and low delay. With the help of prefetching, we can cache the whole GOP and then decode them and discard obsolete frames in advance, keeping only those frames which timestamp is equal to and bigger than the displaying time instant. Experiments show that our system increases the accuracy of seek from second to millisecond and decrease the latency of seek by two orders of magnitude, from more than 2000 ms to around 20 ms.

An important aspect of this work was not only the performance improvement -- which is significant and actually has allowed the delayed binding for MyVideo to operate -- but it is also the degree to which the application layer can influence efficient low-level processing. As future work, we will integrate the work presented here into the implementation user studies of the MyVideos demonstrator to evaluate the quality of experience impact of the improved seamless performance. In the longer term, we will study the applicability of our techniques to other rich media description languages. An important area of extended work will be supporting increased interaction via video linking. While linking to a new video object will always be a relatively traumatic experience for the processing architecture, we feel that intelligent, predictive linking could build on the work presented here.

8. ACKNOWLEDGEMENTS

This work was supported by the ICT FP7 IP project TA2 and the development of the open source Ambulant Player was funded by the NLnet foundation.

9. REFERENCES

[1] Bulterman, D. and Rutledge, L. 2009. *SMIL 3.0: Flexible Multimedia for Web, Mobile Devices and Daisy Talking Books*. Springer-Verlag, Heidelberg, Germany, ISBN: 978-3-540-78546-0.

[2] Cesar, P., Bulterman, D.C.A., Guimaraes, R.L., and Kegel, I. 2010. Web-Mediated Communication: in Search of Togetherness. *Proceedings of the Web Science Conference* (WebSci10).

[3] Gao, B., Jansen, J., Cesar, P., and Bulterman, D. 2010. Beyond the playlist: seamless playback of structured video clips. *IEEE Transactions on Consumer Electronics*, 56(3):1495-1501.

[4] Halvorsen, P., Johansen, D., Olstad, B., Kupka, T., and Tennøe, S. 2010. vESP: enriching enterprise document search results with aligned video summarization. *Proceedings of the international conference on Multimedia* (MM '10). ACM, New York, NY, USA, 1603-1604.

[5] Kennedy, L., and Naaman, M. 2009. Less talk, more rock: automated organization of community-contributed collections of concert videos. *Proceedings of the international conference on World Wide Web*, pp. 311-320.

[6] Liu, Y., Huang, Q., Zhao, D., and Gao, W. 2007. Low-delay View Random Access for Multi-view Video Coding. *Proceedings of the IEEE International Symposium on Circuits and Systems*, pp.997-1000.

[7] Ngo, K., Guntur, R., and Ooi, W. 2011. Adaptive encoding of zoomable video streams based on user access pattern. *Proceedings of the second annual ACM conference on Multimedia systems* (MMSys '11). ACM, New York, NY, USA, 211-222.

[8] Shaw, R., and Schmitz, P. 2006. Community annotation and remix: a research platform and pilot deployment. *Proceedings of the ACM international workshop on Human-centered multimedia*, pp. 89-98.

[9] Shrestha, P., de With, Peter., Weda, H., Barbieri, M., and Aarts, E. 2010. Automatic mashup generation from multiple-camera concert recordings. *Proceedings of the international conference on Multimedia*. ACM, New York, USA, 541-550.

[10] Wu, Z., Yu, H., and Tang, B. 2010. Video transcoding to support random access in scalable video coding. *WSEAS Trans. Sig. Proc.* 6(2): 33-46.

[11] FFmpeg. http://ffmpeg.org/

Scalable Video Transmission: Packet Loss Induced Distortion Modeling and Estimation

Shujie Liu
State University of New York at Buffalo
Buffalo, NY 14260, USA
sL252@buffalo.edu

Chang Wen Chen
State University of New York at Buffalo
Buffalo, NY 14260, USA
chencw@buffalo.edu

ABSTRACT

To provide enhanced multimedia services for heterogeneous networks and terminal devices, Scalable Video Coding (SVC) has been developed to embed different quality of video in a single bitstream. Similar to classical compressed video transmission, different packets of a video bitstream have different impacts on received video quality. Therefore, distortion modeling and estimation are necessary in designing a robust video transmission strategy under various network conditions. In the paper, we present the first scheme of packet loss induced distortion modeling and estimation in SVC transmission. The proposed scheme is applicable to numerous video communication and networking scenarios in which accurate distortion information can be utilized to enhance the performance of video transmission. One major challenge in scalable video distortion estimation is due to the adoption of more complicated prediction structure in SVC, which makes the tracking of error propagation much more difficult than the non-scalable encoded video. In this research, we tackle such challenge by systematically tracking the propagation of errors under various prediction trajectories. Supplemental information about the compressed video is embedded into data packets to substantially simplify the modeling and estimation. Moreover, with supplemental data of inter prediction information, distortion estimation can be processed without parsing video bitstream which results in much lower computation and memory cost. With negligible effects on the data size, experimental results show that the proposed scheme is able to track and estimate the distortion with very high accuracy. This first ever scalable video transmission distortion modeling and estimation scheme can be deployed at either gateways or receivers because of its low computation and memory cost.

Categories and Subject Descriptors

I.4.2 [**Image Processing and Computer Vision**]: Compression (Coding) – *approximate methods*

General Terms

Algorithms, Design, Experimentation

Keywords

Scalable video transmission, Distortion modeling, Distortion estimation, Scalable video coding, Packet loss

This research is supported by NSF Grant 0915842.

1. INTRODUCTION

With unprecedented recent advances in wired and wireless networking infrastructures, hardware technologies, and multimedia applications, video transmission over heterogeneous network links and devices is becoming more and more popular. The heterogeneity of links and devices demands that the multimedia applications be adaptive to different device capabilities, variable network access capacities and diverse quality of service requirements. For example, cell phones and PDAs usually have limited bandwidth and may access wireless network with higher bit error rate, with smaller screen and power constraints, while laptops may have better link capability and shall require higher quality of service.

To provide services to these heterogeneous networks and terminal devices, Scalable Video Coding (SVC) standard was developed and finalized by the Joint Video Team (JVT) of the ITU-T VCEG and the ISO/IEC MPEG as an extension of H.264/AVC with more degrees of scalability: temporal scalability, spatial scalability and quality scalability [1]. In order to compress the video data more efficiently, SVC allows more complicated prediction structures including both intra-layer prediction and inter-layer prediction.

During video transmission, channel impairments will introduce either bit error or packet loss on video bitstream, where bit error may lead to an undecodable packet and can be regarded as packet loss. These errors will introduce distortion on corresponding blocks, which may propagates to other video blocks and frames because of predictive coding. Because of the predictive coding structure, different packets of video bitstream will have different impacts on the received video quality and thus have different priorities.

Distortion estimation is definitely necessary for various video transmission applications in designing superior video transmission strategies under various network conditions. For example, transmitter side needs to decide optimal bit allocation between source and channel coding, while receiver side needs to decide if the lost packet needs to be retransmitted or can be recovered by Error Concealment (EC).

Furthermore, in most applications, because of the low-delay requirement and resource limitations on terminal devices, it is essential to have a distortion estimation algorithm with lower computation and memory cost.

1.1 Existing Models for Non-scalable Video

Existing approaches in distortion estimation for classical non-scalable video transmission can be classified into two categories: transmitter side distortion estimation [2] and receiver side distortion estimation [3][4][5]. At the transmitter side, the original compressed video is assumed available and only statistical channel condition, such as packet loss rate, is known. At the receiver side, original compressed video is not available while exact error patterns are usually known with lost packets detection. These approaches rely on models characterizing relations between distortion and channel parameters or on exact error pattern to estimate the distortion. They include linear model between distortion and packet loss rate [4], models based on error patterns and burst packet loss [5], and models taking into account related encoder and decoder parameters [3][6].

Furthermore, distortion estimation at intermediate nodes can be extended from receiver distortion estimation. At intermediate nodes, only video bitstream (or part of the bitstream) rather than original compressed video is available, while sometimes only statistical channel conditions are known. The distortion estimation in such scenario can be extended from receiver-based distortion estimation, with consideration of all possible error patterns and weighted average of corresponding estimated distortions.

1.2 Distortion Modeling for Scalable Video
In addition to the conventional applications as in the case of non-scalable video, distortion modeling is also essential for bitstream extraction in SVC which attempts to extract a substream under certain quality measure. Unlike channel induced distortion, the distortion in this case is due to limited rate for encoding. However, distortion modeling for scalable video in both channel induced case and rate constrained case will be much more difficult because of the more complicated prediction structure in SVC.

Several rate induced distortion (RD) models were proposed for bitstream extraction. Most of them focused on fine-grained scalability (FGS) of MPEG-4 video [7][8]. A training based distortion model was recently developed for bitstream extraction in SVC with quality scalability [9]. It used a Taylor series expansion based model to describe the error propagation between frames.

1.3 Needs of New Models for Scalable Video
Previous distortion models for non-scalable video are definitely inappropriate for scalable video because: 1) The prediction structure in SVC is much more complicated, which introduces a more complicated error propagation process; 2) Various models adopt specific limitations on application scenarios, such as the requirements for the original input video to be available and complete decoding of the received video.

Unfortunately, current rate induced distortion models for scalable video *coding* cannot be immediately adopted for loss induced distortion modeling for scalable video *transmission* due to several reasons: 1) RD model is fundamentally different from the loss distortion (LD) model: RD models represent the relations between bit rate and distortion which are usually used in video source coding, while LD models describe the relations between packet lost and distortion which are exclusively used in video transmission; 2) FGS has been removed from H.264/SVC standard which result in more complicated data dependency layers; 3) Entire original bitstream is known for bitstream extraction (coding) while this is not true for video transmission scenarios, such as receiver distortion estimation. The training based models [9] are not suitable for video transmission applications because of the time-consuming procedure.

Therefore, new distortion model for scalable video transmission needs to be developed to estimate the distortion due to channel errors. Several constraints need to be considered in designing the distortion model: 1) the model should be applicable at either receiver or intermediate nodes, where only part of compressed video is available; 2) the distortion model should have low computation and memory cost to satisfy limited resource constraints in computation and memory in certain nodes, and the transmission delay constraint in emerging applications.

1.4 Summary of Contributions
We present in this paper the first effort to model and estimate packet loss induced channel distortion for scalable video transmission. The original contribution of this research lies in: (1) elegant analysis of the error propagation under various prediction trajectories in SVC, and (2) appropriate embedding of limited supplemental information about the original compressed video into the data packet to enable the distortion estimation with partial original compressed video sequences and partial decoding of the received bitstream.

Furthermore, with additional supplemental data about inter prediction, distortion estimation can be processed without even parsing the received bitstream. This can be applied on transmission nodes which have no video bitstream parsing functionality and can only access the header information. The present model is developed based on deterministic loss pattern and could be easily extended to a broader range of applications where only statistical channel conditions are known.

Simulation results show that the scheme is able to estimate the distortion quite precisely without accessing the original bitstream. This scheme can be deployed at either receivers or gateways because of its inherent low computation and memory cost.

The remainder of this paper is organized as follows. Section 2 describes the proposed distortion model and estimation in detail. Corresponding simulation results are presented in Section 3, and Section 4 concludes the paper with a summary.

2. PROPOSED DISTORTION MODEL
In this section, the proposed distortion model is described in detail. We adopt the popular video distortion metric PSNR (Peak Signal to Noise Ratio) for our analysis, which is based on mean square error (MSE) of every frame. Other perceptual distortion model can also be adopted with simply higher computational costs. The distortion is analyzed in 2.1, with detailed analysis presented in the subsequent subsections. Finally, a conclusion on this distortion model is driven and extension of it is discussed.

2.1 System Model
For simplicity of description, Medium Grain Scalability (MGS) fragment shall not be considered in our derivation. Thus, quality scalability is similar to the spatial scalability, and the distortion estimation for these cases will be similar as well. We also assume that one frame is packetized into one packet (one packet could have multiple frames). The proposed model aims at estimating the channel error induced distortion for every frame with multiple quality layers according to MSE.

This scheme can be further extended to spatial layers easily with the consideration of upsampling process during inter-layer prediction. The frame level distortion can also be easily extended to slice level distortion, with each frame partitioned into several independent slices, which is a common technique when a frame has to be packetized into several packets.

In the following distortion estimation process, we shall focus on calculating MSE for each frame given the MSE of its reference frames. Since PSNR is calculated based on MSE, we will not distinguish between them and will use MSE as distortion measure in the following subsections for simplicity of derivations.

As indicated in (1), D(n) is the channel distortion of frame n with spatial resolution $S = N \times M$, while $\tilde{f}_n(i, j)$ and $\hat{f}_n(i, j)$ indicate the decoder output value and encoder reconstructed value for pixel (i, j), respectively.

$$D(n) = \frac{1}{S}\sum_{i=1}^{N}\sum_{j=1}^{M}[\tilde{f}_n(i,j) - \hat{f}_n(i,j)]^2 = \frac{1}{S}\sum_{i,j} d_n(i,j) \quad (1)$$

To decode a pixel (i, j) in frame n, the decoder needs to first get the prediction of current pixel from other decoded pixels, and then add residual to get the final result. For pixels coded independently from other pixels, the prediction from other pixels is always 0. Therefore, the distortion for any pixel comes from both prediction error and residual error, as shown in (2), where ref and ref′ indicate the number of pixels used to generate the prediction in encoder and decoder, respectively, $n_k(m_k)$ is the frame index for k^{th} reference pixel, (i'_k, j'_k) and (i_k, j_k) are the pixel indices used to generate the prediction, with corresponding weights α'_k, α_k, and $e^{i,j}_{res}$ is the residual error.

$$d_n(i,j) = [\sum_{k=1}^{ref'} \alpha'_k \tilde{f}_{m_k}(i'_k, j'_k) - \sum_{k=1}^{ref} \alpha_k \hat{f}_{n_k}(i_k, j_k) + e^{i,j}_{res}]^2 \quad (2)$$

Equation (2) can be used to represent distortion for most video transmission errors, as well as those non-integer pel interpolation techniques used in prediction process. It should be noticed that the number of reference pixels and the set of pixels used to generate prediction can be different for decoder and encoder because of transmission error on video bitstream and EC process utilized to generate lost frames.

To simplify the distortion model, we would like to consider two scenarios for a particular pixel respectively: 1) current pixel's data is received correctly; 2) current pixel's data is lost (or corrupted) where EC is carried out, as shown in (3).

$$d_n(i,j) = \begin{cases} d^{prop}_n(i,j), & \text{Correctly received} \\ d^{lost}_n(i,j), & \text{Lost} \end{cases} \quad (3)$$

In the following, distortions under loss and correctly received cases are addressed separately. With consideration of complexity and memory, a frame level distortion model is preferred.

2.2 Distortion for Correctly Received Case

The distortion model in this subsection is first formulated for pixels encoded with different coding modes and further simplified into frame level. Since current block's data is correctly received, distortion is only due to predictions from other blocks. Blocks encoded without predictions have no propagated error. We will focus on blocks encoded with intra or inter prediction.

2.2.1 Block Coded with Intra Prediction

There are two types of intra prediction in SVC: intra prediction modes that are the same as H.264/AVC and inter-layer intra prediction. The first one generates predictions based on encoded neighboring samples in the same frame with 8 different directions. The second one is based on collocated block in lower layer.

Correctly received block's data means that the prediction mode as well as residual information can be decoded error-free. Therefore the set of pixels used to compute prediction and corresponding weights are the same for decoder and encoder. The only possible distortion is that propagated from reference pixels, which come from the same frame or from lower layer.

The distortion for intra prediction encoded blocks can be considered negligible based on two reasons: 1) The number of intra predicted blocks are usually much fewer than the inter predicted blocks, especially for higher temporal layer frames (less than 3% for most sequences), while these frames will be lost with higher probability in Unequal Error Protection (UEP) schemes. 2) Since base layer (B layer) in SVC bitstream is more important than the enhancement layer (E layer), it is possible to provide proper UEP strategy to different quality layers. When the E layer is received correctly, we assume that the corresponding lower layer will be received correctly. For inter-layer intra prediction coded blocks, with the prediction constraint, the reference block from B layer must be intra coded and thus results in no distortion propagation.

2.2.2 Block Coded with Inter Prediction

For inter coded block, because of the predictive coding of motion vector (MV) and residual information, distortion could be introduced from three types of errors: reference frames' distortion, MV prediction error and residual prediction error. To simplify the model without loss of generality, we only consider integer-pel MV which means ref is equal to the number of reference frames. For each pixel inside this block, Eq. (2) can be simplified into:

$$d^{prop}_n(i,j) = [\sum_{k=1}^{ref} \alpha_k e_k + e^{i,j}_{res}]^2 \quad (4)$$

where $e_k = \tilde{f}_{n_k}(i'_k, j'_k) - \hat{f}_{n_k}(i_k, j_k)$

$$= \tilde{f}_{n_k}(i + mv'_{x,k}, j + mv'_{y,k}) - \hat{f}_{n_k}(i + mv_{x,k}, j + mv_{y,k}) \quad (5)$$

For a block in B layer, if corresponding data is received correctly, it means that blocks encoded before this block in the same frame are received correctly, thus MV prediction generated from neighboring blocks is the same as encoder side. The distortion is only introduced by the distortion of reference frames.

For blocks in E layer, because of the inter-layer motion and residual prediction, it is possible to have wrong motion vector or residual due to loss of B layer information. However, similar to case of intra prediction, under proper UEP scenarios, if the E layer is received correctly, the corresponding lower layer will be received correctly. Hence, we can again assume that there is no distortion introduced by motion and residual error.

Based on these detailed analyses, for inter prediction coded block with information correctly received, the distortion estimation of a pixel inside this block can be further simplified as:

$$d^{prop}_n(i,j) = [\sum_{k=1}^{ref} \alpha_k e^{n,i,j}_{prop,k}]^2 \quad (6)$$

Moreover, for an inter prediction coded block, there are only two cases: single directional prediction and bidirectional prediction. For the second one, usually the weight for is chosen as 1/2. Thus the propagated distortion per pixel can be simplified to:

$$d^{prop}_n(i,j)$$
$$= \begin{cases} \left(e^{n,i,j}_{prop,m}\right)^2, & \text{Single directional prediction} \\ \frac{1}{4}\left(e^{n,i,j}_{prop,m_1} + e^{n,i,j}_{prop,m_2}\right)^2, & \text{Bidirectional prediction} \end{cases} \quad (7)$$

where $\left(e^{n,i,j}_{prop,m_1} + e^{n,i,j}_{prop,m_2}\right)^2$

$$= e^{n,i,j}_{prop,m_1}{}^2 + e^{n,i,j}_{prop,m_2}{}^2 + 2 \cdot e^{n,i,j}_{prop,m_1} \cdot e^{n,i,j}_{prop,m_2} \quad (8)$$

113

2.2.3 Distortion Estimation at Frame Level

Based on the full scale analysis in the previous subsections, to estimate the distortion for a correctly received frame, we only need to consider blocks coded with inter prediction, where each has distortion propagated from reference frames. With the constraint in storage and computational complexity at the decoder, it is better to store frame level distortion instead of block level.

Considering the distortion on frame level, the cross term between the distortions of the two reference pictures in (7)(8) can be estimated as the frame level error correlation between two frames, which is statistically independent if the noise can be modeled as additive white Gaussian noise. In practice, they are not exactly independent and we offer the analysis as follows.

Simulations are conducted to compare the distortion propagation components for different test sequences under different packet loss conditions, while 161 frames for each sequence are encoded with GOP size 16. For each frame, the ratio of cross term to non-cross term distortion in (7)(8) is calculated based on all blocks. Figure 1 shows an example of the histogram of the ratios. It can be observed that, comparing with non-cross term distortion, the cross term between the distortions of two reference pictures can be ignored to further simplify the distortion model.

To simplify the estimation process, we can assume that the distortion is uniformly distributed in a frame. Thus the estimated distortion of current frame can be represented as (9), where n_k is the kth frame used for inter-frame prediction, α_{n_k} is calculated according to (10), with N', M' represents the number of blocks at horizontal and vertical direction in one frame respectively.

$$D(n) = \sum_{k=1}^{ref} \alpha_{n_k} \times D(n_k) \qquad (9)$$

$$\alpha_{n_k} = \frac{1}{N' \times M'} \sum_{i=1}^{N'} \sum_{j=1}^{M'} \alpha_{n_k}(i,j), \text{ where } \alpha_{n_k}(i,j) =$$

$$\begin{cases} 1 & n_k \text{ is the only reference for Block } (i,j) \\ 0.25 & n_k \text{ is one of two references for Block } (i,j) \\ 0 & n_k \text{ is not reference of Block } (i,j) \end{cases} \qquad (10)$$

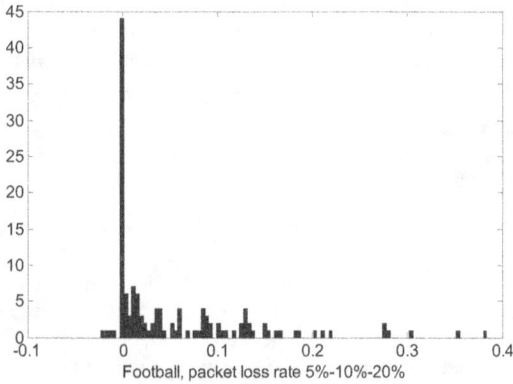

Figure. 1 Comparisons of Distortion Propagation Components (packet loss rate: B layer-E layer 1-E layer 2)

2.3 Distortion for Lost Case

If the information of a video block is not received correctly, EC schemes can be applied to estimate the pixel value. Various EC methods are available for SVC transmission. We assume simple pixel/frame copy scheme in our distortion model because 1) the error propagation for complicated EC is un-tractable with limited access of bitstream and video content; 2) more complicated EC schemes requires more powerful decoder and can lead to unrealistic delay. Suppose a lost pixel (i,j) in frame n is copied

from a decoded pixel (i', j') in frame ec_n. Thus, the concealment result should be $\hat{f}_{ec_n}(i', j')$ if all other information received correctly. As indicated in (12), the distortion includes the distortion due to EC $d_n^{ec}(i,j)$ which is independent from channel condition, and the distortion due to propagation $d_{ec_n}(i', j')$, as well as a cross term between them.

$$d_n^{lost}(i,j) = [\tilde{f}_{ec_n}(i', j') - \hat{f}_{ec_n}(i', j') + \hat{f}_{ec_n}(i', j') - \hat{f}_n(i,j)]$$

$$= d_{ec_n}(i', j') + d_n^{ec}(i,j) + 2\sqrt{d_{ec_n}(i', j') \times d_n^{ec}(i,j)} \qquad (11)$$

Therefore, the distortion for a lost frame can be represented as:

$$D(n) = D_{ec_n} + D_n^{ec} + D_{cr} \text{ with } D_{ec_n} = \frac{1}{S}\sum_{i',j'} d_{ec_n}(i', j');$$

$$D_n^{ec} = \frac{1}{S}\sum_{i,j} d_n^{ec}(i,j); D_{cr} = \frac{2}{S}\sum_{i,j}\sqrt{d_{ec_n}(i', j') \times d_n^{ec}(i,j)} \qquad (12)$$

We will analyze the three components in (11) under frame level, respectively and combine them together for a final representation.

2.3.1 Distortion Due to Error Concealment

One innovative feature of the proposed scheme is to embed supplemental information into data packets in order to achieve more accurate modeling and to keep the receiver/gateway distortion estimation simple. Such information is transmitted for each frame to indicate potential distortion due to EC, which is the MSE between concealed frame and reconstructed frame. When the concealment scheme is not predefined, this distortion can be estimated at receiver side.

2.3.2 Propagated Distortion in Error Concealment

We assume that simple frame copy is used in EC. In this case, the propagated distortion is equal to the distortion of the frame that is used in frame copy. If other EC method is used, corresponding propagated distortion can be estimated as a weighted sum of distortions from reference frames.

2.3.3 Cross Term between Two Distortions

Different from the cross term in (7), the cross term between EC distortion and propagated distortion is not negligible under certain coding scenarios. We will analyze the cross term for B layer lost and E layer lost cases respectively.

2.3.3.1 Cross Term for Concealed Base Layer

Two types of frames may be used in EC: correctly received frames and lost frames. For example, suppose there are 8 frames in display order as: *P1, P11, P12, P2, P21, P22, P23,* and *P3*, both frame P2 and P3 are lost and need to be concealed while other frames data are received correctly. Suppose EC is carried out on frame P2 by frame copy from P1. For EC of P3, the output of P2 may be used depending on the EC rule, which is generated by EC itself. When the frame used for EC is obtained by EC, this distortion sometimes has high correlation with the distortion of current frame, and introduces a large value cross term.

In the example, if frame copy is carried out for both P2 and P3, taking output of P1 and P2 as reference respectively, the distortion of P3 is the MSE between P3 and P1:

$$\frac{1}{S}\sum_{i,j}[\tilde{f}_{P3}(i,j) - \hat{f}_{P3}(i,j)]^2 = \frac{1}{S}\sum_{i,j}[\tilde{f}_{P1}(i,j) - \hat{f}_{P3}(i,j)]^2$$

$$= \frac{1}{S}\sum_{i,j}[\tilde{f}_{P1}(i,j) - \hat{f}_{P2}(i,j)]^2 + \frac{1}{S}\sum_{i,j}[\tilde{f}_{P2}(i,j) - \hat{f}_{P3}(i,j)]^2$$

$$+ \frac{1}{S}\sum_{i,j} 2 \times [\tilde{f}_{P1}(i,j) - \hat{f}_{P2}(i,j)] \times [\tilde{f}_{P2}(i,j) - \hat{f}_{P3}(i,j)] \qquad (13)$$

The last cross term has to be considered and can be estimated as:

$$\frac{1}{S}\sum_{i,j} 2 \times \left[\tilde{f}_{P1}(i,j) - \hat{f}_{P2}(i,j)\right] \times \left[\tilde{f}_{P2}(i,j) - \hat{f}_{P3}(i,j)\right]$$

$$\approx \frac{1}{S}\sum_{i,j} 2 \times [f_{P1}(i,j) - f_{P2}(i,j)] \times [f_{P2}(i,j) - f_{P3}(i,j)] \qquad (14)$$

That means that the cross term can be estimated as the frame difference correlation between the three original frames. We estimate this correlation based on the reasoning that: if we only consider the difference Δ_n between neighboring frames f_n and f_{n+1}, the correlation between Δ_n and Δ_{n+k} can be defined as:

$$\sigma_k(n) = \frac{1}{S}\sum_{i,j} 2 \times [\Delta_n(i,j) \times \Delta_{n+k}(i,j)] \qquad (15)$$

Analysis indicated that neighboring frames usually have similar $\sigma_k(n)$, and for $k > 2$ the correlation is nearly 0 and hence can be ignored. This is because of the temporal correlation in a sequence. Therefore, we can estimate this parameter from correctly received frames or pre-estimate them globally and embed this in the data packet. In current implementation, these parameters are estimated for each GOP and transmitted with the data packet.

With given global parameters $\sigma_k(n) = \sigma_k$, as in the previous example, the cross term can be estimated as:

$$\frac{2}{S}\sum_{i,j}[f_{P1}(i,j) - f_{P2}(i,j)] \times [f_{P2}(i,j) - f_{P3}(i,j)]$$

$$= \frac{2}{S}\sum_{i,j}[f_{P1}(i,j) - f_{P11}(i,j) + f_{P11}(i,j) - f_{P12}(i,j) + f_{P12}(i,j) - f_{P2}(i,j)] \times [f_{P2}(i,j) - f_{P21}(i,j) + f_{P21}(i,j) - f_{P22}(i,j) + f_{P22}(i,j) - f_{P23}(i,j) + f_{P23}(i,j) - f_{P3}(i,j)]$$

$$= \frac{2}{S}\sum_{i,j}[\Delta_{P1} + \Delta_{P11} + \Delta_{P12}] \times [\Delta_{P2} + \Delta_{P21} + \Delta_{P22} + \Delta_{P23}]$$

$$\approx \sigma_1 + 2\sigma_2 + 3\sigma_3 + 3\sigma_4 + 2\sigma_5 + \sigma_6 \qquad (16)$$

Furthermore, if the distortion estimation is based on several reference frames, the cross term can also be estimated similarly based on the globally difference correlations.

2.3.3.2 *Cross Term for Concealed Higher Layers*
If a frame in E layers is lost, frame copy can be carried out based on corresponding lower layer frame or temporal reference frames. If corresponding B layer frame is lost, temporal frame copy is used, while lower layer frame is used in frame copy if B layer is received correctly. If temporal frame copy is used, the scenario is similar to previous case and the distortion estimation model for concealed B layer is used.

If B layer is received correctly, the cross term becomes distortion propagated from lower layer and distortion due to EC. Similar to Figure 1, Figure 2 shows an example of comparison between the cross term and the non-cross term for different test sequences. Histogram of per frame ratios between cross term and non-cross term is calculated for different scenarios respectively in Figure 2. It can be observed that, different from the B layer lost case, this cross term can be ignored and thus simplify the distortion model.

2.3.4 *Distortion Estimation at Frame Level*
To estimate the distortion for a lost frame, we need to first calculate the distortion due to EC and error propagation. Then, the cross term can be estimated for certain cases, and the sum of them can be obtained as the final result.

2.4 Overall Distortion Model
To conclude the overall distortion model, for a given frame, when it is received correctly, corresponding distortion is calculated according to (9) and (10). If the corresponding packet is lost,

distortion can be estimated based on (12) according to signaled MSE between concealed frame and current frame, as well as estimated global cross term for B layer.

According to (10), the weight α_{n_k} in calculating the propagated distortion can be further signaled with data packets to avoid parsing the whole received bitstream which contains entropy coded data. The proposed model can also be easily extended to applications with only statistical channel model known.

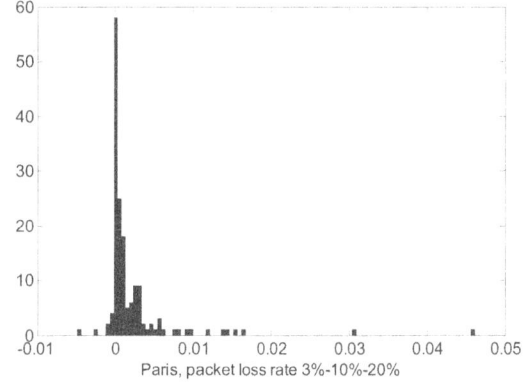

Figure. 2 Comparisons of Cross Term and Non-Cross Term (packet loss rate: B layer-E layer 1-E layer 2)

3. SIMULATIONS
3.1 Simulation Setup
The implementation of the EC and the distortion estimation is based on JSVM (Joint Scalable Video Model) version 9. Test sequences of Football, Foreman and Paris are used with resolution of 352x288, where frame rates of Football and Paris are 30fps, and that of Foreman is 25fps, each has 241 frames encoded. For each test sequence, three layers with one B layer (QP=36) and two MGS E layers (QP=32, 28 respectively) are encoded in one bitstream, with GOP size of 16.

Packet loss model reported in [10] is adopted, and each NAL unit is assumed to be packetized into a single packet, while only entire frame losses are considered. Different loss conditions for different layers are considered in the simulation. Once a lower layer frame is lost, corresponding higher layer frames are ignored.

3.2 Simulation Results
Figure 3 shows selected results of the comparison between estimated PSNR and true PSNR for every frame of two sequences under different packet loss conditions, where "PLR: x+y+z" means packet loss rates of B layer, E layer 1 and E layer 2 are x, y, z respectively. The true PSNR values are calculated between the decoded sequence and the encoder reconstructed sequence of the highest layer. The corresponding scatter plots of true vs. estimated PSNR with correlated trend line are shown in Figure 4.

Furthermore, Pearson Correlation Coefficient (PCC) is used to calculate the similarity between true PSNR and estimated PSNR. Corresponding PCC in Figure 4 are 0.995, 0.958, 0.995 and 0.984 respectively. The range of PCC is [-1, 1], where -1 and 1 indicate that X and Y have perfect linear dependence (data points of X and Y lie on a single line), 0 implies that there is no linear correlation between the variables. A value of 1 means Y will increase while X increases, and -1 means Y will decrease while X increases.

From results in Figure 3, it can be seen that the proposed scheme is able to accurately estimate and track the channel distortion frame by frame. This can be further confirmed with Figure 4 and corresponding PCCs. PCCs indicate that estimated PSNR and true PSNR can be represented very well with a linear function. Figure 5 indicates that correlation between estimated PSNR and true PSNR can be estimated with a linear function approximated by y = x. Therefore, the proposed model can track and estimate the frame level channel distortion with very high accuracy.

Furthermore, the supplemental data added into media data includes EC distortion for each frame and cross item estimation for each GOP data. Besides, percentage of blocks coded with prediction from each reference picture can also be included for each frame to avoid parsing the bitstream. If each frame only has two reference pictures, we will have on average less than 4 supplemental numbers (4 bytes each) signaled for each frame. This is negligible compared to the large size of video data.

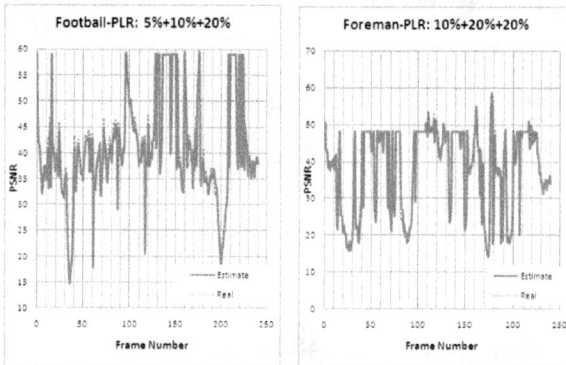

Figure. 3 Frame level estimated PSNR and true PSNR

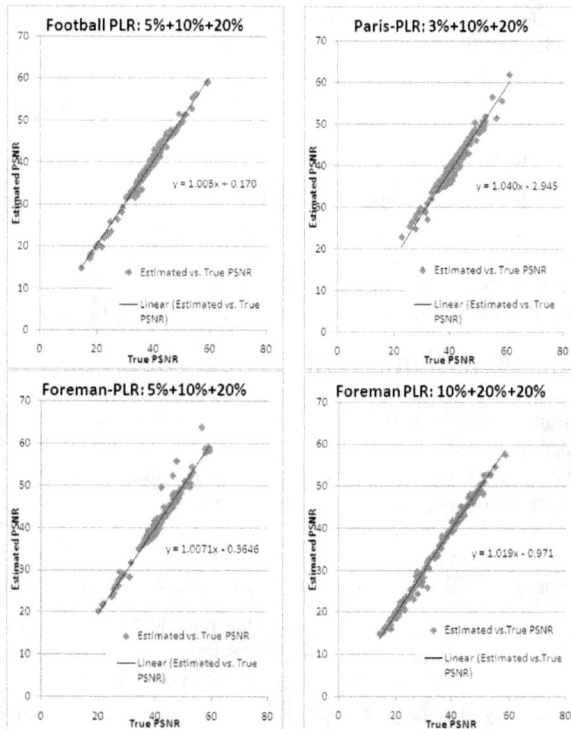

Figure. 4 Scatter plots between Estimated and True PSNR

4. CONCLUSION

In this paper, a novel packet loss induced distortion model and corresponding estimation scheme have been developed for scalable video transmission. We have demonstrated through careful tracking of error propagation in SVC and embedding negligible amount supplemental information about compressed video sequences to derive a practical distortion model with low computation and memory cost. Such model can be applied to numerous emerging video transmission applications when channel induced errors are unavoidable. This new strategy of distortion modeling and estimation produces high accuracy in tracking transmission error and will be invaluable for error correction and adaptive schemes when they need accurate distortion information. The scheme can be deployed at either gateways or receivers because of its low computation and memory cost.

For future research, we shall investigate the following possible improvement: (1) modeling of distortion distribution within each frame to achieve more accurate estimation at the block level, and (2) extension of this scheme to spatial scalability to include distortion measurement between different spatial resolutions.

5. References

[1] H. Schwarz, D. Marpe, and T. Wiegand, "Overview of the scalable video coding extension of the H.264/AVC standard," IEEE Trans. on Circuits Syst. Video Technol., vol. 17, no. 9, pp. 1103–1120, Sep. 2007.

[2] H. Yang and K. Rose, "Advances in recursive per-pixel end-to-end distortion estimation for robust video coding in H.264/AVC," IEEE Trans. Circuits Syst. Video Technol., vol. 17, no. 7, pp. 845–856, Jul. 2007.

[3] M. Naccari, M. Tagliasacchi and S. Tubaro, "No-Reference Video Quality Monitoring for H.264/AVC Coded Video", IEEE Trans. on Multimedia, Vol. 11, No. 5. Aug. 2009.

[4] K. Stuhlmuller, N. Farber, M. Link, and B. Girod, "Analysis of video transmission over lossy channels," IEEE J. Sel. Areas Commun., vol. 1, no. 6, pp. 1012–1032, Jun. 2000.

[5] Y. J. Liang, J. G. Apostolopoulos, and B. Girod, "Analysis of packet loss for compressed video: Effect of Burst Losses and Correlation between Error Frames", IEEE Trans. on Circuit Syst. Video Technol. Vol. 18, No. 7, Jul. 2008.

[6] S. Tao, J. Apostolopoulos and R. Guerin, "Real-Time Monitoring of Video Quality in IP Networks", IEEE Trans. on Networking, Vol. 16, No. 5, Oct. 2008.

[7] C.-H. Hsu and M. Hefeeda, "On the accuracy and complexity of rate-distortion models for fine-grained scalable video sequences," ACM Trans. Multimedia Comput. Commun. Appl., vol. 4, no. 2, pp.1–22, 2008.

[8] J. Sun, W. Gao, D. Zhao and W. Li, "On Rate-Distortion Modeling and Extraction of H.264/SVC Fine-Granular Scalable Video", IEEE Trans. on Circuits Syst. Video Technol., Vol. 18, No. 3, Mar. 2009.

[9] E. Manni and A. K. Katsaggelos, "Optimized Bit Extraction Using Distortion Modeling in the Scalable Extension of H.264/AVC", IEEE Trans. on Image Processing, Vol. 18, No. 9, Sep. 2009.

[10] S. Wenger, "Error Patterns for Internet Experiments," VCEG Q15-I-16r1, 2002

Energy-efficient Video Streaming from High-speed Trains

Xiaoqiang Ma, Jiangchuan Liu
Computing Science School
Simon Fraser University
xma10,jcliu@cs.sfu.ca

Hongbo Jiang
Department of EIE
Huazhong University of Science and Technology
hongbojiang2004@gmail.com

ABSTRACT

The problem of streaming packetized media has been intensively studied for a long time. In this paper, we revisit this problem in the high-speed railway context, where passengers encode and upload videos through increasingly powerful smartphones. The challenge is highlighted by the fast changing channel conditions in high-speed trains and the limited battery of cell phones. Inspired by the unique spatial-temporal characteristics of wireless signals along high-speed railways, we propose a novel energy-efficient and rate-distortion optimized approach for video streaming. Our solution effectively predicts the signal strength through its spatial-temporal periodicity in this new application scenario. It then smartly adjusts the GOF budget, schedules the video transmission to achieve graceful rate-distortion performance and yet conserves the energy consumption. Performance evaluation based on simulated railway scenarios and H.264 video traces demonstrates the effectiveness of our solution and its superiority as compared to existing solutions.

Categories and Subject Descriptors

H.5.1 [**Multimedia Information Systems**]: [Video]; C.2.1 [**Network Architecture and Design**]: [Wireless communication]

General Terms

Experimentation

Keywords

Energy-efficient Rate-Distortion optimization, High-speed trains

1. INTRODUCTION

The problem of streaming packetized media has been studied for many years [1, 2, 3]. With the rapid development of broadband wireless networks and powerful smartphones, wireless video communication (e.g., Facetime [4]) is gaining more and more popularity in people's life. In this paper, we revisit the video streaming problem in the high-speed railway context, where passengers encode and upload videos through their wireless mobile devices.

Recent decades have witnessed the fast development of high-speed railway systems in many countries, such as Japan, France, China and so on [6]. The speed of the trains can be as high as 350 km/h and thus the travel time between distant cities has been significantly shortened. Coupled with this convenience, however, is the challenge to traditional cellular techniques. For example, the handover frequency will be very high without redesigning the base station deployment, leading to increased call blocking rate and call drop rate. The channel properties will change very quickly, which prevent the fast power control in WCDMA from accurately compensating for fading [7]. The Doppler shift will also be significant, which degrades the system performance. A lot of work has been done towards overcoming the difficulties mentioned above. Uhlirz [8] outlines the concept of a GSM-based communication system for high-speed Railway (GSM-R) and proposes to make some modifications to the standard GSM system. A linear coverage is preferred to area coverage to simplify handover. Frequency compensation is used to eliminate the Doppler shift. In order to provide broadband data services, satellite-to-Wi-Fi links have been combined for Internet access on the TGV trains in France. More importantly, satellite links have limited bandwidth and long round trip times, which make them not ideal for real-time applications, such as video streaming and video conferencing [9]. The GSM Digital Remote RF Units (GRRU) private network [10] has been deployed along the Beijing-Tianjin Intercity Railway. It can provide better communication quality and use fewer handover/reselection compared with existing techniques.

While these solutions improve the channel properties, we still face another key problem that band-intensive applications are very power-consuming in terms of data transmission and thus mobile devices will run out of power in a short time. This phenomenon is especially obvious when the signal is weak, since the transceiver needs to amplify the signal [11]. When mobile users are on high-speed trains, their cell phones will work under fast-changing signal strength, mainly caused by the varying distance between cell phones and base stations. Cell phones need to implement power control on the uplink to compensate for the fading effect such that the received power level at base stations will stay fairly constant [7]. With regards to this observation, we propose a novel dynamic rate-distortion optimization approach that smartly controls the video rate, together with a transmission scheduling according to the received signal strength. Given the periodicity of channels, this strategy remarkably saves the power on data transmission and yet achieve graceful degradation of video quality.

The remainder of this paper is organized as follows, In Section 2, we introduce some related work on energy efficient approaches in wireless and cellular networks. In Section 3, we propose the system model, formulate the optimization problem and describe our solution. Simulation results on video sequences is illustrated in Section 4. Section 5 gives some discussion and we conclude this paper in Section 6.

2. RELATED WORK

Existing techniques can already guarantee high-quality voice services for users moving at high speed. Yet providing high speed data transmission for people in fast-moving vehicles is still an open issue. The FAMOUS [5] architecture is proposed to offer multimedia services to fast moving users. For the train scenario, the authors propose to combine a Radio-over-Fiber (ROF) network with movable cells. Fokum and Frost [9] present a comprehensive survey of approaches for providing broadband Internet access to trains. They present a taxonomy of architecture according to access network technologies including ROF, IEEE 802.11, satellite and so on. They then compare various implementations in both Europe and North America and summarize the lessons we can learn from.

In the research field of wireless networks, the cross-layer design approach is proposed to achieve better system performance. In [12], the authors summarize the challenges and principles of cross-layer wireless multimedia transmission and propose a new paradigm to improve multimedia streaming quality and reduce power consumption. Eric et al. [13] further explore a cross-layer design framework for real-time video streaming in Ad hoc networks. Signal strength can be viewed as the reflector of current channel properties. If we can predict the signal strength, adjustment can be made in advance. In [14], the authors propose a long range online prediction method, which is location-independent. However, they only verify their method at walking speeds, where the signal strength does not change very fast. Power control is closely coupled with signal strength. It is especially important for uplink to keep the received signal strength level at base stations within slight variation. Without power control, we will see the so-called *near-far problem* in CDMA systems [7]. A lot of previous works have been done to implement efficient and accurate power control [15]. However, power control will significantly increase the transmission energy consumption when mobile users are far from base stations. The existing work [11] proposes to transmit less data when the channel is bad .

There have been significant studies on rate-distortion optimization for video streaming. Chou and Miao [1] formulate how and when to transmit a group of interdependent data packets with delivery deadlines in a rate-distortion way. He et al. [16] further add a power dimension to the rate-distortion model to perform online resource allocation and energy optimization. Eckehard et al.[17] present an adaptive media playout technique that adjusts the playout speed according to channel conditions to improve the trade-off between buffer underflow probability and latency [17]. Our study has been inspired by these works; yet we focus on streaming from high-speed trains that creates new challenges.

3. SYSTEM MODEL

In this section, we first establish the energy model in the high-speed railway scenario. We then formulate the power-rate-distortion optimization problem and describe how to achieve energy efficiency dynamic rate control and transmission scheduling.

3.1 Energy model

Path loss model, which is important for link budget, has attracted the interest of many researchers. The basic model [18] is as follows:

$$PL(d) = PL(d_0) + 10n \log\left(\frac{d}{d_0}\right) + X_\sigma \qquad (1)$$

where $PL(d)$ is the average path loss value at distance d from a measured location to the transmitter; n is the path loss exponent, which depends on the environment; d_0 is the close-in reference distance, and $PL(d_0)$ is based on either practical measurements or on a free space path loss model at distance d_0 from the transmitter; X_σ is a zero-mean Gaussian distributed random variable (in dB) with standard deviation σ (also in dB), and is computed from measured data.

The above parameters statistically describe the path loss model. The path loss can be transformed from the measured received signal strength as [19]:

$$P_r(d) = P_t + G - PL(d) - PL_{other} \qquad (2)$$

where $P_r(d)$ and P_t (both in dBm) are the power level of received signal and transmitted signal, respectively; G is the antenna gain and PL_{other} is the attenuation caused by other factors. G and PL_{other} are constants for the same type of base stations.

Equation (1) implies that the large-scale variation of path loss only depends on the distance from the transmitter. In real life, especially in metropolitan areas with dense buildings, the small-scale fading and multipath effect will cause rapid and significant changes in signal strength over a small travel distance or time interval. However, since most high-speed railways are constructed in suburban and rural areas that can be approximately regarded as open space environment, multipath effect can be largely neglected.

As mentioned in Section 2, power control needs to be implemented on cell phones to compensate for the variation of path loss. The power needed to transmit a bit at distance d is [21]:

$$u(d) = ad^n + c_0 \qquad (3)$$

where a and c_0 are constants; n is the path loss exponent. For the sake of simplicity, in the remaining part of this paper, we only consider the former part on the right side of the above equation, ad^n, as the transmission consumption and use $c(d)$ to denote it. In practice, however, the distance can not be directly measured, so cell phones can adjust transmission power based on received signal strength. The ratio of transmission power at different places A and B is then given by:

$$\frac{p(d_A)}{p(d_B)} = 10^{\frac{P_r(d_B) - P_r(d_A)}{10}} \qquad (4)$$

where d_A and d_B are the distances from the transmitter at A and B, respectively.

To better illustrate the fast-changing received signal strength and transmission power as well as the relationship between them, we now show a series of simulated results. Our simulation is based on the path loss model in open area in [19], which is measured along the "Zhengzhou-Xi'an" high speed railway environment at the 930 MHz band:

$$P_r(d) = 6.0246 - 21.226 \log(d) \qquad (5)$$

The standard deviation of shadowing is chosen as 2.09.

In order to reduce the construction cost and keep trains running at relatively constant speed, the high speed railway is almost a straight line in a considerably long segment. This construction strategy simplifies the evaluation of path loss along the railway. We give the Beijing-Tianjing Intercity Railway as an example in Figure 1.

Figure 1: **Beijing-Tianjin Intercity Railway from Google Map [20]**

This construction strategy simplifies the evaluation of path loss along the railway. In our simulation, we use a straight line to represent a segment of 35 km railway, along which 18 base stations every 2 km have been deployed. The straight distance between each base station and the rail is 150 m. We calculate the received signal strength every 10 m, and the transmission energy at each location is represented by the ratio of it to the minimum energy consumption along the this segment of rail. We use the ratio rather than an absolute value of power consumption because the ratio is independent of the types of base stations and cell phones that are used, and thus our model can work in general cases.

From Fig. 2 we can find out that the difference of received signal strength can be as high as 20 dB and thus the maximum transmission energy is over 100 times more than the minimum. The peaks in Fig. 2 correspond to the locations with the minimum distance of 150 m to base stations.

3.2 Problem formulation

A video sequence can be encoded into frames at different rates with corresponding distortion. The encoded data are packetized into a finite set of data units. The interdependency of data units can be represented by a directed acyclic graph. Each node of the graph corresponds to a data unit,

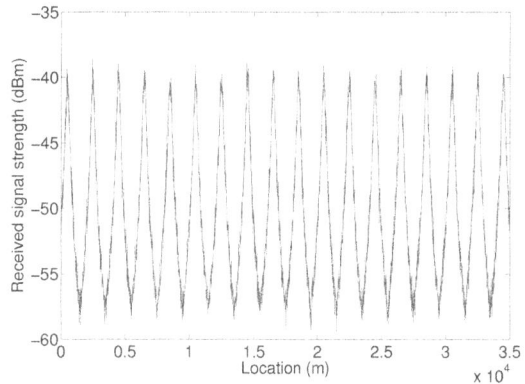

Figure 2: **Received signal strength along the railway**

and each edge directed from data unit l' to data unit l means that data unit l' must be decoded in order to decode data unit l. We use $l' \prec l$ to denote this relationship. A sample dependence graph of a group of (IBPBP) frames is shown in Fig. 3.

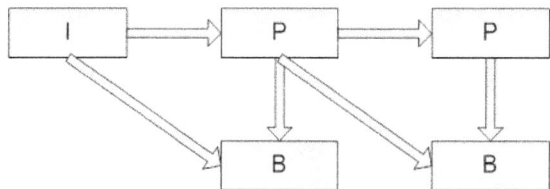

Figure 3: **Dependency between IBPBP video frames**

We use D_0 to denote the distortion if no data unit is decoded, ΔD_l the reduction of distortion if data unit l is decoded on time, and B_l the size in bits of data unit l. For each data unit, let $t_1, t_2, ..., t_N$ be N discrete transmission opportunities and let t_{DTS} be the delivery deadline. A transmission policy $\pi = (\pi(1), \pi(2), ...\pi(N)) \in \{0, 1\}^N$ is used to describe the transmission of a data unit, where $\pi(i) = 0$ means that the data unit should not be sent at opportunity i while $\pi(i) = 1$ means that the data unit should be sent at opportunity i if no acknowledgement packet was received from the feedback channel before t_i. We define an error $\epsilon(\pi)$ for policy π as the probability that the data unit cannot be successful received before its deadline t_{DTS},

$$\epsilon(\pi) = \prod_{i:\pi(i)=1} P\{FTT > t_{DTS} - t_i\} \qquad (6)$$

where FTT is the forward trip time.

The cost $\rho(\pi)$ for policy π is defined as the expected number of data unit transmissions, that is [22],

$$\rho(\pi) = \sum_{i:\pi(i)=1} \left(\prod_{j<i:\pi(i)=1} P\{RTT > t_i - t_j\} \right) \qquad (7)$$

where RTT is the round trip time.

Here we do not make any particular assumption for the probability distribution of FTT and RTT. A shifted Gamma distribution, however, is widely used [1].

The expected power consumption for transmitting data unit l is therefore,

$$C(l) = \sum_{j=1}^{\rho(\pi)} B_l c(d(t_j)) \tag{8}$$

where $d(j)$ is the distance from the train to the base station at opportunity t_j when data unit l is sent.

We then consider the problem of rate-distortion optimized transmission of a group of interdependent data units. For the sake of simplicity, we consider a group of frames with the size of L and each data unit contains exact one frame. This GOF can be encoded in M different rates and each rate corresponds to a distortion. The transmission policy for the GOF is described by a policy vector $\vec{\pi} = (\pi_1, ..., \pi_L)$, where π_l, $l \in 1, 2, ..., L$ is the transmission policy for the lth data unit of the GOF. The expected power consumption for transmitting this GOF is,

$$C(\vec{\pi}) = \sum_{l=1}^{L} \sum_{j=1}^{\rho(\pi)} B_l(k) c(d(t_j)) \tag{9}$$

where $B_l(k)$, $k \in \{1, ..., M\}$ is the size of data unit l when this GOF is encoded in rate $R(k)$.

The expected distortion for the group is,

$$D(\vec{\pi}) = D_0(k) - \sum_{l=1}^{L} \Delta D_l(k) \prod_{l' \prec l} (1 - \epsilon(\pi_{l'})) \tag{10}$$

Our objective is to jointly optimize the policy vector to minimize the expected distortion subject to a constraint on the expected power consumption. We can solve the problem by finding the policy vector $\vec{\pi}$ and the GOF rate allocation R that minimizes the expected Lagrangian, as in [1]

$$J(\vec{\pi}) = D(\vec{\pi}) + \lambda C(\vec{\pi})$$
$$= D_{0_k} +$$
$$\sum_{l=1}^{L} \left[\Delta D_l(k) \left(- \prod_{l' \prec l} (1 - \epsilon(\pi_{l'})) \right) + \lambda \sum_{j=1}^{\rho(\pi)} B_l(k) c(d(t_j)) \right] \tag{11}$$

where $(B_l(k), \Delta D_l(k)) \in \{(B_l(1), \Delta D_l(1), ..., (B_l(M), \Delta D_l(M)\}$

To minimize $J(\vec{\pi})$ for a given λ and an arbitrary pair of $(B_l(k), \Delta D_l(k)), k \in 1, ..., M$, we extends the Iterative Sensitivity Adjustment (ISA) algorithm [1]. The main idea is minimizing one variable at a time, while keeping other variable constant until convergence. For example, we can start from any initial policy vector $\vec{\pi}^{(0)}$ and determine the minimum $J(\vec{\pi})$ as follows. Select one data unit $l_n \in 1, ..., L$ to find its optimal policy vector at step n. Then for $l \neq l_n$, set $\pi_l^{(n)} = \pi_l^{(n)}$, while for $l = l_n$, let

$$\pi_l^{(n)} = \arg\min_{\pi_l} J(\pi_1^{(n)}, ..., \pi_{l-1}^{(n)}, \pi_l, \pi_{l+1}^{(n)}, ..., \pi_L^{(n)})$$
$$= \arg\min \pi_l S_l^{(n)} \epsilon(\pi_l) + \lambda \sum_{j=1}^{\rho(\pi)} B_l(k) c(d(t_j)) \tag{12}$$

where

$$S_l^{(n)}(k) = \sum_{l' \succ l} \Delta D_{l'}(k) \prod_{\substack{l'' \prec l' \\ l'' \neq l}} (1 - \epsilon(\pi_{l''}^{(n)})) \tag{13}$$

We can find the optimal policy vector for all the M rate-distortion pairs. The policy vector and the rate-distortion pair with the minimum value of $J(\vec{\pi})$ are selected to be the transmission scheduling and rate allocation for this GOF, respectively.

3.3 Signal strength prediction

The power consumption for transmitting bits at each transmission opportunity is closely related to the signal strength at that time as we mentioned before. We describe how to predict the signal strength prediction as follows.

We assume that the base stations are of the same type, and the environmental conditions have no significant change for a relatively long segment of railway, for example, tens of kilometres. Then the large-scale variation of the signal strength depends only on the distance from the cell phone to its connected base station. The cell phone first collects traces of received signal strength values at a constant frequency (In our experiment, we collected three periods of signal strengths to obtain the statistics such as the mean value and standard deviation). Since the train runs at a relatively constant speed, the period of variation T can be easily computed. Then we can have a coarse evaluation of the signal strength for the future. Suppose the current time is t_1 and the received signal strength is $P(t_1)$, and the average received signal strength at the corresponding time in the collected traces $(t - T, t - 2T...)$ is $\overline{P(t_1)}$. We can use weighted sum $(1 - \alpha) * \overline{P(t_1)} + \alpha * P(t_1)$ as the prediction of the signal strength at time instance $t_1 + T$. We have validated the accuracy of this prediction method in Section 4. We also plan to exploit new technologies, such as electronic compasses and accelerometers, to further improve the prediction accuracy and we will further discuss it in Section 5.

4. PERFORMANCE EVALUATION

In this part, we perform simulations to evaluate our algorithms and also give some analysis based on the results. We use the experimental settings mentioned in Section 3. We use Matlab R2010b as our simulation tool. We ran each experiment 10 times, and calculated the mean value.

4.1 Signal strength prediction

We first show the accuracy of our signal strength prediction algorithm. By calculating the relative errors with different choices of α, we can choose the α with smallest error in our following simulation. We use the first three periods of values as the collected traces and calculate the average value at each point. The fourth period is regarded as the current value and is used to predict the corresponding value in the fifth period. α is chosen from 0 to 1 with an interval of 0.125. The simulation results with 95% confidence level are shown in Fig. 4.

It is clearly that, with $\alpha = 0.25$, the prediction algorithm produces the smallest relative error. Hence, we choose this value in the simulation.

4.2 Streaming quality and power consumption

We next evaluate Streaming quality and power consumption compared to a baseline strategy that encodes the video sequence into the highest quality and uploads the data units at the first possible transmission opportunity for different delivery deadlines. We first show the received video quality degradation of our approach which is measured by the

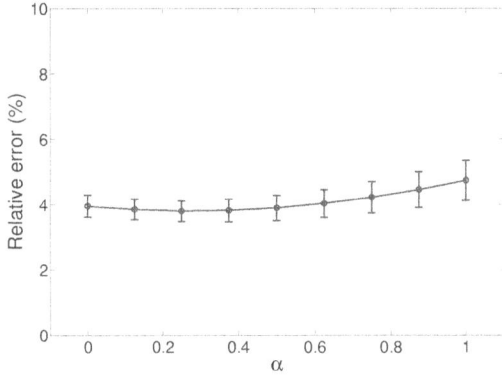

Figure 4: Relative errors of prediction with different α

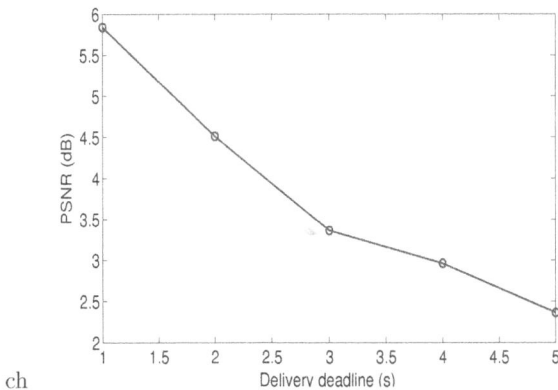

Figure 6: Power saving ratio compared with baseline approach

PSNR decrease. We then compare the two approaches in terms of power consumption on transmission.

As mentioned in Section 3.1, we calculate the received signal strength and energy radio of each location every 10 meters. We assume that both the signal strength and energy ratio will not dramatically change during the 10 meters. The time interval between two transmission opportunities is 100ms. We employ the QCIF size video sequence of *Foreman* and use JM 17.2 software of the H.264/AVC standard [23] to encode and decode it. The video sequence is encoded into 50, 100, and 150 kbps, and the corresponding PSNR are 34.8 dB, 38.58 dB, and 40.963 dB, respectively. The frame rate is 10 fps and we replicate the video sequence to 3 minutes. The structure of GOF is set of 10 frames with one I frame followed by nine P frames. We solve the optimization with the basic unit of GOF. The maximum transmission rate is 128 kbps and the mean RTT is 150ms. The transmission loss rate is set to be 10%. In the simulation, we randomly use the starting point to transmit and vary the delivery deadline from 1 to 5 seconds. With the fixed time interval of 100ms, the number of transmission opportunities varies from 10 to 50. With increased deadline, the number of transmission opportunities will also be increased. The results are shown in Fig. 5 and Fig. 6.

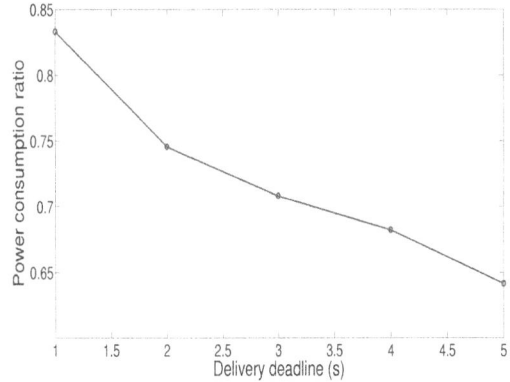

Figure 5: Received video quality degradation compared with baseline approach

We divide the transmission power consumption of our method by that of the baseline strategy to get the power saving ratio. We can see that with increased delivery deadline, both the distortion and transmission power consumption get reduced. The reason is that with more transmission opportunities, we can better exploit the signal strength prediction. Considering that the worst case complexity to solve (13) increases exponentially with the number of transmission opportunities, we suggest that delivery deadline around 3 seconds can achieve a good tradeoff between the distortion-power and the time needed to find the optimal transmission policy.

To get better results, we can encode the video sequence into more rate-distortion pairs. This method, however, would increase the computation complexity. Fortunately, we can get a approximate result by considering only a subset of rate-distortion pairs according to the signal strength prediction. To be precise, we can choose the pairs with higher rate when the signal strength is strong in the near future, and choose the pairs with lower rate when the signal strength is weak in the near future. We leave this as part of our future work.

5. DISCUSSION

In this section, we will discuss some practical issues worthy of noting.

First, the speed of trains is not absolutely constant. Instead, it can be increased and decreased, and can also have some fluctuations. The change of speed will affect the accuracy of signal strength prediction. GPS can be used to get the location information, but it consumes a lot of power to track satellites [11]. Due to the long propagation delay of satellite communication links and the high speed of trains, its error of localization can be very significant. Recently, novel localization approaches, e.g. [24], thus have to be incorporated. Electronic compasses and accelerometers, which are readily available in modern cell phones, can also be utilized to figure the location information, which is more energy-efficient and accurate than GPS. We are currently examining to use accelerometers to track the speed change of trains, which can be used to obtain more accurate channel conditions. It could be also combined with the adaptive media playout technique to adapt the video playout speed to the speed change of trains.

Second, the distance between base stations may not be

equal. To solve this problem, the mobile phone users go opposite directions can exchange the location information of base stations and the statistical information of signal strength. This can help to improve the prediction accuracy. These kinds of information can be embedded into the GPS map or saved in base stations and fetched by the passing by cell phones.

6. CONCLUSION

The rapid development of high-speed trains raises new challenges to cell phone vendors with respect to QoS management. The limited battery capacity and the increasingly popular bandwidth-intensive and power-hungry applications, such as files sharing and video streaming, attract a lot of researchers to address the power control problem to prolong the battery life. In this paper, by utilizing the construction feature of high-speed railways and the base stations as well as the motion feature of trains, we revisited the problem of rate-distortion optimized video streaming. In future work, we plan to further exploit the periodicity of the signal strength to design approximate algorithm to solve the optimization problem.

Acknowledgments

This research is supported by a Canada NSERC Discovery Grant, an NSERC DAS grant, an NSERC Strategic Project Grant, and an MITACS NCE Project Grant.

7. REFERENCES

[1] P. A. Chou, Z. Miao. Rate-distortion optimized streaming of packetized media. *IEEE Transactions on Multimedia*, 8(2):390-404, 2006.

[2] J. Chakareski, P. A. chou. Application layer error-correction coding for rate-distortion optimized streaming to wireless clients. *IEEE Transactions on Communications*, 52(10):1675-1687, 2004.

[3] H. Seferoglu, O. Gurbuz, O. Ercetin, Y. Altunbasak. Rate-distortion based real-time wireless video streaming. *Journal Image Communication*, 22(6):529-542, 2007.

[4] http://www.apple.commacfacetime

[5] F. D. Greve et al. Famous: a network architecture for delivering multimedia services to fast moving users. *Wireless Personal Communications*,: 33(3-4):281-304, 2005.

[6] http://en.wikipedia.org/wiki/High-speed_rail

[7] H. Holma, A. Toskala. WCDMA for umts: hspa evolution and lte. *Wiley*, 2007

[8] M. Uhlirz. Concept of a gsm-based communication system for high-speed trains. In *Proceeding of IEEE VTC '1994*, pages 1130-1134, 1994.

[9] D. T. Fokum, V. S. Frost. A survey on methods for broadband internet access on trains. *IEEE Communications Surveys & Tutorials*, 12(2):171-185, 2010.

[10] X. Cheng, Y. Li, X. Cao. The discussion on gsm coverage scheme of high-speed railway, In *Proceedings of IEEE ICCTA '2009*, pages 295-298, 2009.

[11] A. Schulman, V. Navda, R. Ramjee, N. Spring, P. Deshpande, C. Grunewald, K. Jain, V. Padmanabhan. Bartendr: a practical approach to energy-aware cellular data scheduling. In *Proceedings of MobiCom '2010*, pages 85-96, 2010.

[12] M. van Der Schaar, N. Sai Shankar. Cross-layer wireless multimedia transmission: challenges, principles, and new paradigms. *IEEE Wireless Communications,* 12(4):50-58, 2005.

[13] E. Setton, T. Yoo, X. Zhu, A. Goldsmith, B. Girod. Cross-layer design of ad hoc networks for real-time video streaming. *IEEE Wireless Communications Magazine*, 12(4):59-65, 2005.

[14] X. Long, B. Sikdar. A real-time algorithm for long range signal strength prediction in wireless networks, In *Proceedings of IEEE WCNC '2008*, pages 1120-1125, 2008.

[15] R. D. Yates. A framework for uplink power control in cellular radio systems. *IEEE Journal on Selected Areas in Communications*, 13(7):1341 - 1347, 2002.

[16] Z. He, W. Cheng, X. Chen. Energy Minimization of Portable Video Communication Devices Based on Power-Rate-Distortion Optimization. *IEEE Transactions on Circuits and Systems for Video Technology*, 18(5):596-608, 2008.

[17] M. K. Eckehard, E. Steinbach, B. Girod. Adaptive Playout For Real-Time Media Streaming. *ICIP '2002*, pages 45-48, 2002.

[18] T. S. Rappaport. Wireless communications. *Prentice Hall*, 1996.

[19] R. He, Z. Zhong, B. Ai. Path loss measurements and analysis for high-speed railway viaduct scene, In *Proceedings of IWCMC '2010*, pages 266-270, 2010

[20] http://maps.google.com

[21] I. Stojmenovic, X. Lin. Power-aware localized routing in wireless networks. *IEEE Transactions on Parallel and Distributed Systems*, 12(11):1122-1133, 2001.

[22] M. Röder, J. Cardinal, R, Hamzaoui. On the complexity of rate-distortion optimal streaming of packetized media. In *Proceedings of DCC '2004*, pages 192-201, 2004.

[23] http://iphome.hhi.de/suehring/tml/download/

[24] I. Constandache, R. R.Choudhury, I. Rhee. Towards mobile phone localization without war-driving. In *Proceedings of IEEE INFOCOM '2010*, pages 1-9, 2010.

Celerity: Towards Low-Delay Multi-Party Conferencing over Arbitrary Network Topologies

Xiangwen Chen
Dept. of Information
Engineering
The Chinese University of
Hong Kong

Minghua Chen
Dept. of Information
Engineering
The Chinese University of
Hong Kong

Baochun Li
Dept. of Electrical and
Computer Engineering
University of Toronto

Yao Zhao
Alcatel-Lucent

Yunnan Wu
Facebook Inc.

Jin Li
Microsoft Research at
Redmond

ABSTRACT

In this paper, we attempt to revisit the problem of multi-party conferencing from a practical perspective, and to rethink the design space involved in this problem. We believe that an emphasis on low end-to-end delays between any two parties in the conference is a must, and the source sending rate in a session should adapt to bandwidth availability and congestion. We present *Celerity*, a multi-party conferencing solution specifically designed to achieve our objectives. It is entirely Peer-to-Peer (P2P), and as such eliminating the cost of maintaining centrally administered servers. It is designed to deliver video with low end-to-end delays, at quality levels commensurate with available network resources over arbitrary network topologies where *bottlenecks can be anywhere in the network*. This is in contrast to commonly assumed P2P scenarios where bandwidth bottlenecks reside only at the edge of the network. The highlight in our design is a distributed and adaptive rate control protocol, that can discover and adapt to arbitrary topologies and network conditions quickly, converging to efficient link rate allocations allowed by the underlying network. In accordance with adaptive link rate control, source video encoding rates are also dynamically controlled to optimize video quality in arbitrary and unpredictable network conditions. We have implemented *Celerity* in a prototype system and demonstrate its superior performance in a local experimental testbed.

Categories and Subject Descriptors

C.2.4 [**COMPUTER-COMMUNICATION NETWORKS**]: Distributed System—*Distributed applications*; H.4.3 [**INFORMATION SYSTEMS APPLICATIONS**]: Communications Applications—*video conferencing*

General Terms: Algorithm, Design, Experimentation, Performance

Keywords: Peer-to-peer, Multi-party video conferencing, Low delay, Utility maximization

1. INTRODUCTION

With the availability of front-facing cameras in high-end smartphone devices (such as the Samsung Galaxy S and the iPhone 4), notebook computers, and HDTVs, *multi-party* video conferencing, which involves more than two participants in a live conferencing session, has attracted a significant amount of interest from the industry. Skype, for example, has recently launched a monthly-paid service supporting multi-party video conferencing in its latest version (Skype 5) [1]. Skype video conferencing has also been recently supported in a range of new Skype-enabled televisions, such as the Panasonic VIERA series, so that full-screen high-definition video conferencing can be enjoyed in one's living room. We argue that these new conferencing solutions have the potential to provide an immersive human-to-human communication experience among remote participants. Such an argument has been corroborated by many industry leaders: Cisco predicts that video conferencing and tele-presence traffic will increase ten-fold between 2008-2013 [2].

While traffic flows in a live multi-party conferencing session are fundamentally represented by a multi-way communication process, today's design of multi-party video conferencing systems are engineered in practice by composing communication primitives (*e.g.*, transport protocols) over uni-directional feed-forward links, with primitive feedback mechanisms such as various forms of acknowledgments in TCP variants or custom UDP-based protocols. We believe that a high-quality protocol design must harness the full potential of the multi-way communication paradigm, and must guarantee the stringent requirements of low end-to-end delays, with the highest possible source coding rates that can be supported by dynamic network conditions over arbitrary network topologies over the Internet.

From the industry perspective, known designs of commercially available multi-party conferencing solutions are either largely server-based, e.g., Microsoft Office Communicator, or are separated into multiple point-to-point sessions (this approach is called Simulcast), e.g., Apple iChat. Server-based solutions are susceptible to central resource bottlenecks, and as such scalability becomes a main concern when multiple sessions are to be supported concurrently. In the Simulcast approach, each user splits its uplink bandwidth equally among all receivers and streams to each receiver separately. Though simple to implement, Simulcast suffers from poor quality of service. Specifically, peers with low upload capacity are forced to use a low video rate that degrades the overall experience of the other peers.

In the academic literature, there are recently several studies on Peer-to-Peer (P2P) video conferencing from a utility maximization perspective [3] [4] [5] [6] [7]. Among them, Mutualcast [3] and Chen *et al.* [4] may be the most related ones to this work. They have tried to support content distribution and multi-party video conferencing in multicast sessions, by maximizing aggregate application-specific utility and the utilization of node uplink bandwidth in P2P networks. Depth-1 and depth-2 tree topologies have been constructed using tree packing, and rate control was performed in each of the tree-based one-to-many sessions. However, they only considered the limited scenario where bandwidth bottlenecks reside at the edge of the network, while in practice bandwidth bottlenecks can easily reside in the core of the network.

In this paper, we reconsider the design space in multi-party video conferencing solutions, and present *Celerity*, a new multi-party conferencing solution specifically designed to maintain low end-to-end delays while maximizing source coding rates in a session. *Celerity* is designed to operate in a pure P2P manner, and as such eliminating the cost of maintaining centrally administered servers. It is designed to deliver video at quality levels commensurate with available network resources over arbitrary network topologies, while maintaining low end-to-end delays. The highlight in our design is a distributed and adaptive rate control protocol, that can discover and adapt to arbitrary topologies and network conditions quickly, converging to efficient link rate allocations allowed by the underlying network. In accordance with adaptive link rate control, source video encoding rates are also dynamically controlled to optimize video quality in arbitrary and unpredictable network conditions. We have implemented a prototype *Celerity* system and demonstrate its superior performance in a local experimental testbed.

2. PROBLEM FORMULATION AND CELERITY OVERVIEW

2.1 Problem Formulation

Consider a network modeled as a directed graph $G = (\mathcal{N}, \mathcal{L})$, where $\mathcal{N}$ is the set of all physical nodes, including conference participating nodes and other intermediate nodes such as routers, and $\mathcal{L}$ is the set of all physical links. Each link $l \in \mathcal{L}$ has a nonnegative capacity C_l and a nonnegative propagation delay d_l.

Consider a multi-party conferencing system over G. We use $V \subseteq \mathcal{N}$ to denote the set of all conference participating nodes. Every node in V is a source and at the same time a receiver for every other nodes. Thus there are totally $M \triangleq |V|$ sessions of (audio/video) streams. Each stream is generated at a source node, say v, and needs to be delivered to all the rest nodes in $V - \{v\}$. We use E to denote the set of directed overlay links between these nodes. Note an overlay link (u, v) means u can send data to v by setting up TCP/UDP connections. For all $e \in E$ and $l \in \mathcal{L}$, we define

$$a_{l,e} = \begin{cases} 1, & \text{if overlay link } e \text{ passes physical link } l; \\ 0, & \text{otherwise.} \end{cases} \quad (1)$$

Remark: In our model, the capacity bottleneck can be anywhere in the network, not necessarily at the edge of the network. This is in contrast to a popular assumption made in previous P2P works that the uplinks/downlinks of participating nodes are the only capacity bottleneck.

A fundamental system design problem is to maximize the application-specific performance, by properly allocating the overlay link rates

to the streams subject to physical link capacity constraints:

$$\max_{c \geq 0} \sum_{m=1}^{M} U_m(R_m(c_m)) \quad (2)$$

$$\text{s.t.} \quad a_l^T(c_1 + \ldots + c_M) \leq C_l, \quad \forall l \in \mathcal{L}, \quad (3)$$

The variables in the above optimization are $c = [c_1, \ldots, c_M]^T$, where c_m is the vector of overlay link rates allocated to stream m (with one entry for each overlay link). $R_m(c_m)$ denotes the stream rate that we obtain by using resource c_m *within the given delay bound*, and is a concave function of c_m as we will show in Corollary 1 in the next section. The constraint in (3) is the physical link capacity constraint, where $a_l^T c$ describes the load on the physical link l incurred by overlay traffic c.

The objective is to maximize the aggregate system utility. $U_m(R_m)$ is an increasing and strictly concave function that maps the stream rate to an application-specific utility. For example, a commonly used video quality measure Peak Signal-to-Noise Ratio (PSNR) can be modeled by using a logarithmic function as the utility [4].

Remarks: Simulcast can be thought as solving the problem **MP** by using only the 1-hop tree to broadcast content within a session. Mutualcast can be thought as solving a special case of the problem **MP** (with node uplinks being the only capacity bottleneck) by packing only certain depth-1 and depth-2 trees within a session.

2.2 Celerity Overview

To achieve the maximum system utility, the Celerity system has two main modules: (1) *delay-bounded packet delivery* at the highest possible source rate given known rates on each of the links (i.e., how to compute and achieve $R_m(c_m)$); and (2) a *link rate control* module to determine c_m.

Video content delivery under known link constraints: This problem is similar to the classic multicast problem, and packing spanning (or Steiner) trees at the multicast source is a popular solution. However, the unique "delay-bounded" requirement in multi-party conferencing makes the problem more challenging, and we introduce a delay-bounded tree packing algorithm in this paper to address this problem (detailed in Section 3).

Link rate control: Under our setting, the formulation in (2)–(3) is a concave optimization problem. In principle, one can first infer the network constraints and then solve the problem centrally. However, directly inferring the constraints potentially requires knowing the entire network topology and is highly challenging.

In Celerity, instead of trying to learn the constraints directly, we resort to adaptive and iterative algorithms for solving an approximate version of the problem given in (2)-(3) in a distributed way (detailed in Section 4).

3. PACKING DELAY-BOUNDED TREES

Given the link rate vector c_m, achieving the maximum broadcast/multicast stream rate under a delay bound is a challenging problem. A general way to explore the broadcast/multicast rate under delay bounds is to pack delay-bounded Steiner trees. However, such problem is *NP*-hard [8]. Moreover, the number of delay-bounded Steiner trees to consider is in general exponential in the network size.

In this paper, we pack 2-hop delay-bounded trees in an overlay graph of session m, denoted by $\mathcal{D}_m$, to achieve a good stream rate under a delay bound. Note by graph theory notations, a 2-hop tree has a depth at most 2. Packing 2-hop trees is easy to implement. It also explores all overlay links between source and receiver and between receivers, thus trying to utilize resource efficiently. In fact, it is shown in [3,4] that packing 2-hop trees suffices to achieve the

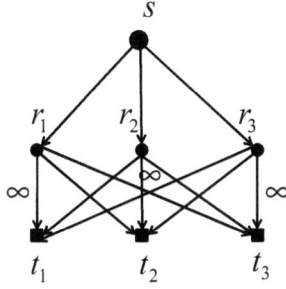

Figure 1: Illustration of the directed acyclic sub-graph over which we pack delay-bounded 2-hop trees.

maximum multicast rate for certain P2P topologies. We elaborate our tree-packing scheme in the following.

We first define the overlay graph $\mathcal{D}_m$. Graph $\mathcal{D}_m$ is a directed acyclic graph with two layers; one example of such graph is illustrated in Fig. 1. In this example, consider a session with a source s, three receivers $1, 2, 3$. For each receiver i, we draw two nodes, r_i and t_i, in the graph $\mathcal{D}_m$; t_i models the receiving functionality of node i and r_i models the relaying functionality of node i.

Suppose that the prescribed link bit rates are given by the vector c_m, with the capacity for link (i, j) being $c_{m,(i,j)}$. Then in $\mathcal{D}_m$, the link from s to r_i has capacity $c_{m,(s,i)}$, the link from r_i to t_j (with $i \neq j$) has capacity $c_{m,(i,j)}$, and the link from r_i to t_i has infinite capacity. If the propagation delay of an edge (i, j) exceeds the delay bound, we do not include it in the graph. If the propagation delay of a two-hop path $s \rightarrow i \rightarrow j$ exceeds the delay bound, we omit the edge from r_i to t_j from the graph. As a result, every path from s to any receiver t_i in the graph has a path propagation delay within the delay bound.

Over such 2-layer sub-graph $\mathcal{D}_m$, we pack 2-hop trees connecting the source and every receiver using the greedy algorithm proposed in [9], which achieves the optimal throughput in multicast. Below we simply describe the algorithm and more details can be found in [9].

Assuming all edges have unit-capacity and allowing multiple edges for each ordered node pair. The algorithm packs unit-capacity trees one by one. Each unit-capacity tree is constructed by greedily augmenting a tree edge by edge, similar to the greedy tree-packing algorithm based on Prim's algorithm. The distinction lies in the rule of selecting the edge among all potential edges. The edge whose removal leads to least reduction in the multicast capacity of the residual graph is chosen in the greedy algorithm. Our tree-packing algorithm is easy to implement.

Utilizing the special structure of the graph $\mathcal{D}_m$, we obtain performance guarantee of the algorithm as follows.

Theorem 1. *The tree-packing algorithm in [9] achieves the minimum of the min-cuts separating the source and receivers in $\mathcal{D}_m$ and is expressed as*

$$R_m(c_m) = \min_j \sum_i \min\{c_{m,(s,i)}, c_{m,(i,j)}\}. \qquad (4)$$

Furthermore, the algorithm has a running time of $O(|V||E|^3)$.

Hence, our tree-packing algorithm achieves the maximum delay-bounded multicast rate over the 2-layer subgraph $\mathcal{D}_m$. The achieved rate $R_m(c_m)$ is a concave function of c_m as summarized below.

Corollary 1. *The delay-bounded multicast rate $R_m(c_m)$ obtained by our tree-packing algorithm is equal to the minimum min-cut over $\mathcal{D}_m$, and thus is a concave function of the overlay link rates c_m.*

4. OVERLAY LINK RATE CONTROL

4.1 Packet Loss Rate Based Primal Subgradient Algorithm

The primal algorithm is derived by relaxing the constraints and adding a penalty to the objective function whenever constraints are violated. This leads to an unconstrained version of the original problem, making it easier to solve.

Consider a penalized version of the problem in (2)-(3):

$$\max_{c \geq 0} \; \mathcal{U}(c) \triangleq \sum_{m=1}^{M} U_m(R_m(c_m)) - \sum_{l \in \mathcal{L}} \int_0^{a_l^T c} p_l(y) \, dy, \qquad (5)$$

where $\int_0^{a_l^T c} p_l(y) \, dy$ is the penalty associated with violating the capacity constraint of physical link $l \in \mathcal{L}$, and we choose the price function to be

$$p_l(y) \triangleq \frac{(y - C_l)^+}{y} dy, \qquad (6)$$

where $(a)^+ = \max\{a, 0\}$. If all the constraints are satisfied, then the second term in (5) vanishes; if instead some constraints are violated, then we charge some penalty for doing so.

We seek to maximize $\mathcal{U}(c)$ as an approximation of the original constrained optimization problem. With this choice of price function, $\mathcal{U}(c)$ is a linear combination of concave functions and is thus concave. However, because $R_m(c_m)$ is the minimum min-cut of the overlay graph $\mathcal{D}_m$ with link rates being c_m, $\mathcal{U}(c)$ is not a differentiable function [10].

For the unconstrained concave optimization problem with non-differentiable objective function, we can solve it by using subgradient algorithms. To proceed with subgradient algorithm design, we need to first compute subgradients of $\mathcal{U}(c)$. The proposition below presents a useful observation.

Proposition 1. *A subgradient of $\mathcal{U}(c)$ with respect to $c_{m,e}$ for any $e \in E$ and $m = 1, \ldots M$ is given by*

$$U_m'(R_m) \frac{\partial R_m}{\partial c_{m,e}}$$

where $\frac{\partial R_m}{\partial c_{m,e}}$ represents a subgradient of $R_m(c_m)$ with respect to $c_{m,e}$.

Based on the above observation, we apply the following subgradient algorithm to solve the problem in 5: $\forall e \in E, m = 1, \ldots M$,

$$c_{m,e}^{(k+1)} = c_{m,e}^{(k)} + \alpha(k) \left[U_m'\left(R_m^{(k)}\right) \frac{\partial R_m^{(k)}}{\partial c_{m,e}} - \sum_{l \in \mathcal{L}} a_{l,e} \frac{(a_l^T c^{(k)} - C_l)^+}{a_l^T c^{(k)}} \right]_{c_{m,e}^{(k)}}^+, \qquad (7)$$

where $\alpha(k)$ is a positive step size for the k-th iteration, and function

$$[b]_a^+ = \begin{cases} \max(0, b), & a \leq 0; \\ b, & a > 0. \end{cases}$$

We have the following observations to the control law in (7):

- It is known that $\sum_{l \in \mathcal{L}} a_{l,e} \frac{(a_l^T c - C_l)^+}{a_l^T c}$ can be interpreted as the packet loss rate observed at overlay link e [11]. The intuitive explanation is as follows. The term $(a_l^T c - C_l)^+$ is the excess traffic rate offered to physical link l; thus $\frac{(a_l^T c - C_l)^+}{a_l^T c}$ models the fraction of traffic that is dropped at l. Assuming the packet loss rates are additive (which is a reasonable assumption for low packet loss rates), the total packet loss rate seen by the overlay link e is given by $\sum_{l \in \mathcal{L}} a_{l,e} \frac{(a_l^T c - C_l)^+}{a_l^T c}$.

- It turns out that the utility function, the subgradients, and packet loss rate are sufficient statistics to update $c_{m,e}$ independently of the updates of other link rates. This way, we can solve the problem in (5) without knowing the physical network topology and physical link capacities.

The subgradient method [12] maximizes a non-differentiable concave function in a way similar to gradient methods for differentiable functions — in each step, the variables are updated in the direction of a subgradient. However, such a direction may not be an ascent direction; instead, the subgradient method relies on a different property. If the variable takes a sufficiently small step along the direction of a subgradient, then the new point is closer to the set of optimal solutions.

We have the following convergence results for the algorithm in (7), which is adapted from those for standard subgradient algorithms [12].

Theorem 2. *Assume $\mathcal{U}^*$ is the optimal value of the problem in (5) and $|U'_m|$ is upper bounded by $\bar{u}$ for all $m = 1, \ldots, M$. The l_2-norm of any subgradients of $R_m(\boldsymbol{c}_m^{(k)})$ is upper bounded by $\Delta = \bar{u}^2 |V|^2 |E|^2$ for all k. Thus,*

- *if $\alpha(k) = \alpha$ is constant, then $\lim_{k \to \infty} \left[\mathcal{U}^* - \max_{i=1,\ldots,k} \mathcal{U}(\boldsymbol{c}^{(k)}) \right] \leq \Delta^2 \alpha$.*

- *if $\alpha(k) \to 0$ or $\sum_{k=1}^{\infty} \alpha^2(k) < \infty$, and $\sum_{k=1}^{\infty} \alpha(k) = \infty$, then $\lim_{k \to \infty} \left[\mathcal{U}^* - \max_{i=1,\ldots,k} \mathcal{U}(\boldsymbol{c}^{(k)}) \right] = 0$.*

In this paper, we choose a constant step size for easy implementation.

4.2 Computing Subgradient of $R_m(\boldsymbol{c}_m)$

A key to implementing the primal subgradient algorithm is to obtain subgradients of $R_m(\boldsymbol{c}_m)$. We first present some preliminaries on subgradients, as well as concepts for computing subgradients for $R_m(\boldsymbol{c}_m)$.

Definition 1. *Given a convex function f, a vector ξ is said to be a subgradient of f at $x \in \mathbf{dom}f$ if*

$$f(x') \geq f(x) + \xi^T(x' - x), \forall x' \in \mathbf{dom}f,$$

where $\mathbf{dom}f = \{x \in \mathbf{R}^n | |f(x)| < \infty\}$ represents the domain of the function f.

For a concave function f, $-f$ is a convex function. A vector ξ is said to be a subgradient of f at x if $-\xi$ is a subgradient of $-f$.

Next, we define the notion of a *critical cut*. For session m, let its source be s_m and receiver set be $V_m \subset V - \{s_m\}$. A partition of the vertex set, $V = Z \cup \bar{Z}$ with $s_m \in Z$ and $t \in \bar{Z}$ for some $t \in V_m$, determines an s_m-t-cut. Define

$$\delta(Z) \triangleq \left\{ (i, j) \in E | i \in Z, j \in \bar{Z} \right\}$$

be the set of overlay links originating from nodes in set Z and going into nodes in set $\bar{Z}$. Define the capacity of cut $(Z, \bar{Z})$ as the sum capacity of the links in $\delta(Z)$:

$$\rho(Z) \triangleq \sum_{e \in \delta(Z)} c_{m,e}.$$

Definition 2. *For session m, a cut $(Z, \bar{Z})$ is an s_m-V_m critical cut if it separates s_m and any of its receivers and $\rho(Z) = R_m(\boldsymbol{c}_m)$.*

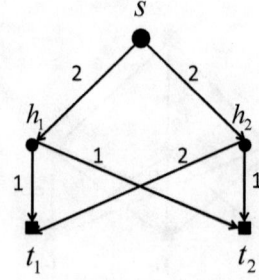

Figure 2: Critical cut example. Source s and its two receivers t_1, t_2 are connected over a directed graph. The number associated with a link represents its link capacity.

We show an example to illustrate the concept of critical cut. In Fig. 2, s is a source, and t_1, t_2 are its two receivers. The minimum of the min-cuts among the receivers is 2. For the cut $(\{s, h_1, h_2, t_1\}, \{t_2\})$, its $\delta(\{s, h_1, h_2, t_1\})$ contains links (h_1, t_2) and (h_2, t_2), each having capacity one. Thus the cut $(\{s, h_1, h_2, t_1\}, \{t_2\})$ has a capacity of 2 and it is an $s - (t_1, t_2)$ critical cut.

With necessary preliminaries, we turn to compute subgradients of $R_m(\boldsymbol{c}_m)$. Since $R_m(\boldsymbol{c}_m)$ is the minimum min-cut of s_m and its receivers over the overlay graph $\mathcal{D}_m$, it is known that one of its subgradients can be computed in the following way [10].

- Find an s_m-V_m critical cut for session m, denote it as $(Z, \bar{Z})$. Note there can be multiple s_m-V_m critical cuts in graph $\mathcal{D}_m$, and it is sufficient to find any one of them.

- A subgradient of $R_m(\boldsymbol{c}_m)$ with respect to $c_{m,e}$ is given by

$$\frac{\partial R_m(\boldsymbol{c}_m)}{\partial c_{m,e}} = \begin{cases} 1, & \text{if } e \in \delta(Z); \\ 0, & \text{otherwise.} \end{cases} \quad (8)$$

In our system, these subgradients are computed by the source of each session, after collecting the overlay-link rates from each receiver in the session. More implementation details are in Section 5.

5. PRACTICAL IMPLEMENTATION

Using the asynchronous networking paradigm supported by the asynchronous I/O library (called `asio`) in the `Boost` C++ library, we have implemented a prototype of Celerity, our proposed multi-party conferencing system, with about $17,000$ lines of code in C++.

In our Celerity prototype implementation, all peers are to perform the following functions:

- Peers in broadcast trees forward packets received from its upstream parent to its downstream children. Sufficient information about downstream children in the tree is embedded in the packet header, for a packet to become "self-routing" from the source to all leaf nodes in a tree.

- Every 200 ms, each peer adjusts the rates of its incoming links based on the link rate control algorithm, and then sends them to their corresponding upstream senders for the new rates to take effect.

- Every 300 ms, each peer sends the allocated rates of all its outgoing links for each session to the source of the session.

Upon receiving allocated rates for all the links, the *source* of each session uses the received link rates to pack a new set of delay-bounded trees, and starts transmitting session packets along these trees. When a source packs delay-bounded trees, it also calculates *one* critical cut and the source sending rate for its session based on

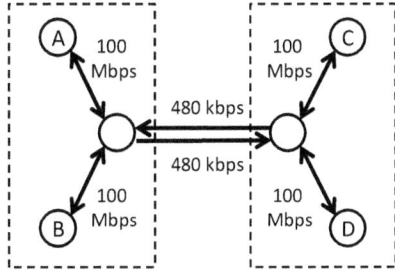

Figure 3: Dumbbell topology of the experimental testbed. Two conference participating nodes A and B are in one "office" and another twos nodes C and D are in a different "office". The two "offices" are connected by directed links, each having a capacity of 480 kbps. Link propagation delays are negligible.

the allocated link rates. In addition, the source embeds the information about the critical cut and the source sending rate in the header of outgoing packets. When these packets are received, a peer learns the source rate and whether a link belongs to the critical cut or not; it then adjusts the link rate accordingly.

The calculation of critical cuts, *i.e.*, the subgradient of $R_m(C_m)$, is the key to our implementation of the primal subgradient algorithm. There can be multiple critical cuts in one session, but it is sufficient to find any one of them. Since the source collects allocated rates of all overlay links in its own session, it can calculate the min-cut from the source to every receiver, and record the cut that achieves the min-cut. Then, the source compares capacities of these min-cuts, and the cut with the smallest capacity is a critical cut.

With respect to the *utility function* in our prototype implementation, the PSNR (peak-to-peak signal-to-noise ratio) metric is the *de facto* standard criterion to provide objective quality evaluation in video processing. We observed that the PSNR of a video stream coded at a rate z can be approximated by a logarithmic function $\beta \log(z + \delta)$, in which a higher β represents videos with a larger amount of motion [4]. δ is a small positive constant to ensure the function has a bounded derivative for $z \geq 0$. Due to this observation, we use a logarithmic utility function in our implementation.

In order to quickly bootstrap our system to close-to-optimal operating points, we implement a method called "quick start" to aggressively ramp up the rates of all sessions during a conference initialization stage, during which peers are joining the conference and nothing significant is going on. We achieve this by using larger values for β in the utility functions and a large step size in link rate adaptation during the first 30 seconds. After the initialization stage, we reset β and step sizes to proper values and allow our system converge gradually and avoid unnecessary performance fluctuation.

6. EXPERIMENTS

We evaluate our prototype Celerity system over a LAN testbed. The testbed is illustrated in Fig. 3, where four PC nodes (A, B, C, D) are connected over a LAN dumbbell topology. The dumbbell topology represents a popular scenario of multi-party conferencing between branch offices. It is also a "tough" topology – existing approaches, such as Simulcast and the scheme in [4], fail to efficiently utilize the bottleneck bandwidth and optimize system performance.

In our experiments, all four peers run our prototype system. We run a four-party conference for 300 seconds, evaluate the system performance, and show the results in Fig. 5. Since the experimental settings are symmetric for each participating peer, it is straightforward to verify the optimal source rate for each peer to be 240 kbps, and the optimal aggregate utility is around 175.

Figs. 5a-5d show the source sending rate and receivers' receiving rates of each session (one session originates from one peer to all

other 3 peers). As seen, our system demonstrates fast convergence: the sending rate of each session quickly ramps up to 95% to the optimal within 50 seconds. Fig. 5e shows that our system quickly achieves the optimal utility. The tiny gap between the converged sending rate and the optimal one is because our proposed system only aims to solve an approximate version of original problem and hence is only expected to obtain close-to-optimal solutions.

As a comparison, we also plot the theoretical maximum rates achievable by Simulcast and the scheme in [4] in Figs. 5a-5d. As seen, within 20 seconds, our system already outperforms the maximum achievable rates of Simulcast and the scheme in [4].

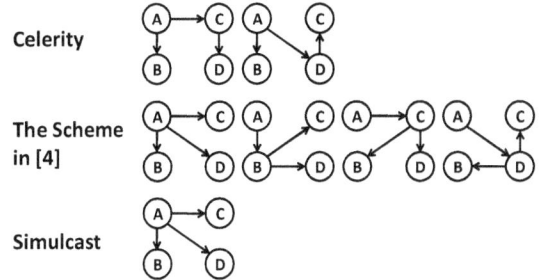

Figure 4: Session A's trees used by Celerity (upon convergence), the scheme in [4] and Simulcast in dumbbell topology.

Upon convergence, our system achieves sending rates that are nearly twice of the theoretical maximum rate achievable by Simulcast and the scheme in [4]. This significant gain is due to that our system can utilize the bottleneck resource more efficiently.

In Fig. 4, we show the trees that are used by our algorithm, the scheme in [4] and Simulcast in the dumbbell topology. As seen, for session A, every tree used by Simulcast and the scheme in [4] consumes the bottleneck link resource twice, thus to deliver one-bit of information they consume two-bit of bottleneck link capacity. For instance, the tree used by Simulcast has two branches $A \rightarrow C$ and $A \rightarrow D$ passing through the bottleneck link between the two "offices" , consuming twice of the bottleneck link resource. Consequently, the maximum achievable rates of Simulcast and the scheme in [4] are all 120 kbps. In contrast, our system upon convergence utilizes the trees that only consume bottleneck bandwidth once, thus it achieves close-to-optimal rates of about 240 kbps.

There are small gaps between the sending rate and the receiving rates in the same session. For instance, upon convergence, the lowest receiving rate is about 97% of the sending rate in session A. This is because our system relies on packet loss to adapt and converge, and the gaps are due to the packet loss that occurs at the bottleneck links. To verify, we show the end-to-end packet loss rate of session A in the bottom sub-figure in Fig. 5f. The packet loss rate is about 3% upon convergence, and explains the 3% gap between the sending rate and the lowest receiving rate of session A.

We show the end-to-end delay and packet loss rate in Fig. 5f, all for session A. The results for the other sessions are essentially the same due to their symmetric settings.

As seen in the top sub-figure in Fig. 5f, When our system converges, the average end-to-end delay from node A to the receiver in the same "office" (in this case node B) is negligible. The delays to the receivers in the other "office" (nodes C and D) are about 90 ms on average, which is contributed by the queuing delay at the bottleneck links. All delays are within the acceptable range for smooth conferencing experience.

The bottom sub-figure in Fig. 5f shows the average end-to-end packet loss rate of session A. As seen, the packet loss rate is high initially, and decreases and stabilizes to small values afterwards.

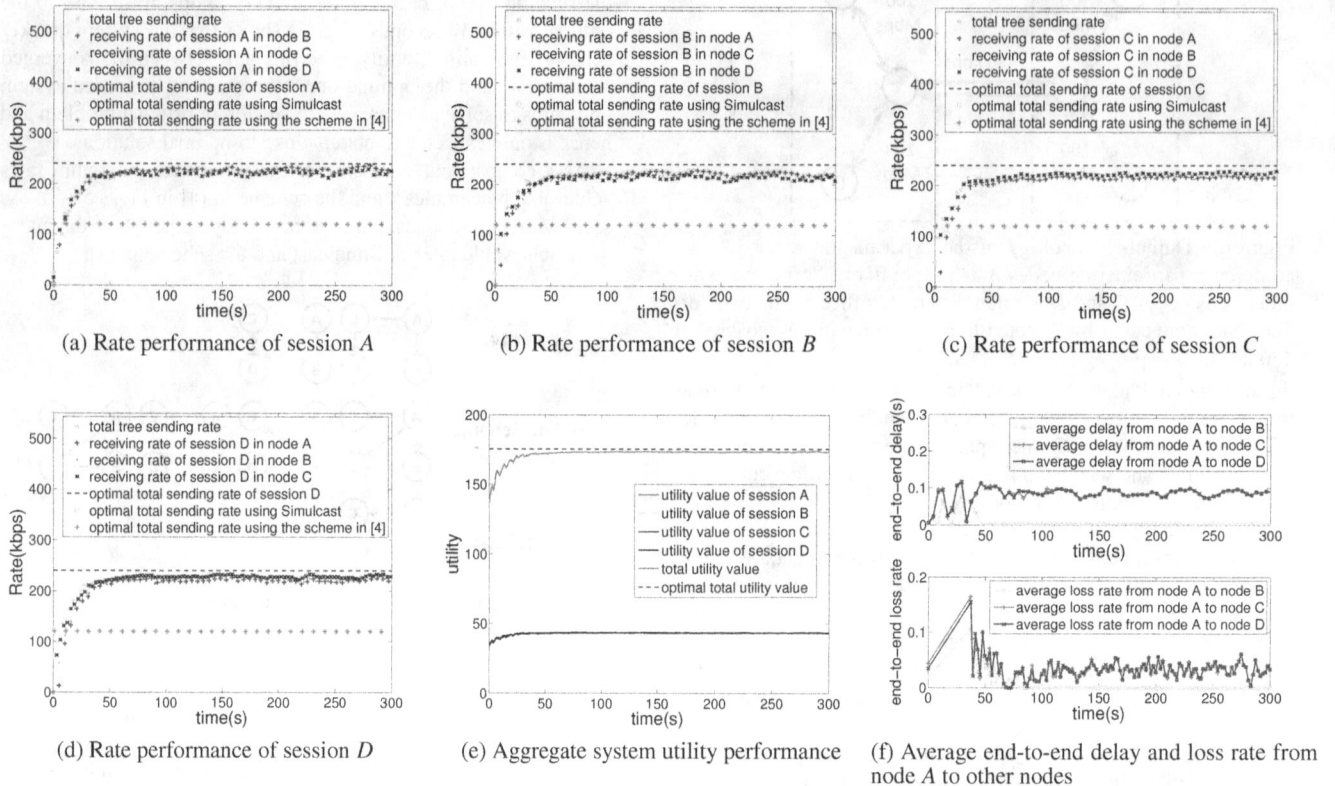

(a) Rate performance of session A

(b) Rate performance of session B

(c) Rate performance of session C

(d) Rate performance of session D

(e) Aggregate system utility performance

(f) Average end-to-end delay and loss rate from node A to other nodes

Figure 5: Performance of Celerity over a dumbbell LAN testbed. (a)-(d): Sending rates and receiving rates of individual sessions. (e): Utility value achieved compared to the optimum. (f): End-to-end delay and loss rate of session A.

The initial high loss rate is because at the beginning our system increases the sending rates aggressively to bootstrap the conference and explore the network resource limit. For instance, for session A, the source node A explores all possible paths to deliver packets to node B at the beginning, including path $A \rightarrow C \rightarrow B$ and path $A \rightarrow D \rightarrow B$. These two paths suffer from high loss rate. This aggressive behavior introduces high loss rate, but only during the conference initialization stage when usually nothing significant is transmitted. Our system quickly learns the resource bottleneck and adapts to the network topology, ending up with using the cost-effective trees to deliver data. After the initialization stage, our system adapts and converges gradually, avoiding unnecessary performance fluctuation that deteriorates user experience.

7. CONCLUDING REMARKS

With the proliferation of front-facing cameras on mobile devices, multi-party video conferencing will soon become an utility that both businesses and consumers would find useful. With *Celerity*, we attempt to bridge the long-standing gap between the bit rate of a video source and the highest possible delay-bounded broadcasting rate that can be accommodated by the Internet where *the bandwidth bottlenecks can be anywhere in the network*. This paper reports a first step towards making this vision a reality: by combining a polynomial-time tree packing algorithm on the source and rate control along each overlay link, we are able to maximize the source rates without any *a priori* knowledge of the underlying physical topology in the Internet. *Celerity* has been implemented in a prototype system, and preliminary experimental results over a "tough" dumbbell topology are very encouraging. As future work, we will

continue to fine-tune our rate control algorithm and evaluate Celerity's performance by Internet experiments. We will also consider alternatives and additions that involve random network coding.

8. REFERENCES

[1] Skype, "http://www.skype.com/intl/en-us/home."
[2] Cisco, "http://newsroom.cisco.com/dlls/2010/prod_111510c.html."
[3] J. Li, P. A. Chou, and C. Zhang, "Mutualcast: an efficient mechanism for content distribution in a P2P network," in *Proc. ACM SIGCOMM Asia Workshop*, Beijing, 2005.
[4] M. Chen, M. Ponec, S. Sengupta, J. Li, and P. A. Chou, "Utility maximization in peer-to-peer systems," in *Proc. ACM SIGMETRICS*, Annapolis, MD, 2008.
[5] İ. E. Akkuş, Ö. Özkasap, and M. Civanlar, "Peer-to-peer multipoint video conferencing with layered video," *Journal of Network and Computer Applications*, vol. 34, no. 1, pp. 137–150, 2011.
[6] M. Ponec, S. Sengupta, M. Chen, J. Li, and P. Chou, "Multi-rate peer-to-peer video conferencing: A distributed approach using scalable coding," in *IEEE International Conference on Multimedia and Expo*, New York, 2009.
[7] C. Liang, M. Zhao, and Y. Liu, "Optimal Resource Allocation in Multi-Source Multi-Swarm P2P Video Conferencing Swarms," *accepted for publication in IEEE/ACM Trans. on Networking*, 2011.
[8] L. Guo and I. Matta, "QDMR: An efficient QoS dependent multicast routing algorithm," in *Proc. IEEE Real-Time Technology and Applications Symposium*, Canada, 1999.
[9] Y. Wu, P. A. Chou, and K. Jain, "A comparison of network coding and tree packing," in *International Symposium on Information Theory*, Chicago, USA, 2004.
[10] Y. Wu, M. Chiang, and S. Kung, "Distributed utility maximization for network coding based multicasting: A critical cut approach," in *Proc. IEEE NetCod 2006*, Boston, 2006.
[11] F. Kelly, "Fairness and stability of end-to-end congestion control," *European Journal of Control*, vol. 9, no. 2-3, pp. 159–176, 2003.
[12] D. P. Bertsekas, *Nonlinear programming*. Athena Scientific Belmont, MA, 1999.

Author Index